Vedic Psychoscience

Śreyo hi jñānam abhyāsāj jñānād dhyānam viśiṣyate ।
dhyānāt karma-phala-tyāgas-tyāgāc chāntir anantaram ।।
– *Bhagavadgītā* XII.12

Knowledge is better than practice (carried on without proper insight), meditation is superior to knowledge, and renunciation of the fruit of actions is even superior to meditation, for, peace immediately follows from renunciation.

***

You exist in time, but you belong to eternity.
You are a penetration of eternity into the world of time.
You are deathless, living in a body of death.
Your consciousness knows no death, no birth.
It is only your body that is born and dies - but you are not aware of your consciousness.
– Osho, as cited in the "Speaking Tree" column,
Times of India, 11 December 2012

***

A human Being is a part of whole, called by us the Universe, a part limited in time and space. He experiences himself, his thoughts and feelings, as something separated from the rest, a kind of optical delusion of his consciousness. This delusion is a kind of prison for us, restricting us to our personal desires and to affection for a few persons nearest to us. Our task must be to free ourselves from this prison by widening our circles of compassion to embrace all living creatures and the whole of Nature in its beauty.

- Albert Einstein 1921

Vedic Psychoscience

Spiritual and Analytical Aspects in Modern Context

Radhey Shyam Kaushal

With a foreword by
S.R. Bhatt

DK PRINTWORLD
Publishers of Indian Traditions

Cataloging in Publication Data — DK
[Courtesy: D.K. Agencies (P) Ltd. <docinfo@dkagencies.com>]

Kaushal, Radhey Shyam, author.
Vedic psychoscience : spiritual and analytical aspects in modern context / Radhey Shyam Kaushal ; with a foreword by S.R. Bhatt.
pages cm
Includes bibliographical references and index.
ISBN 9788124612279 (HB)

1. Vedas and science. 2. Consciousness – Religious aspects – Hinduism. 3. Psychology – Religious aspects – Hinduism. 4. Spirituality – Hinduism. I. Title.

LCC BL1112.27.K38 2024 | DDC 294.5165 23

ISBN: 978-81-246-1227-9 (Hb)
First Published in India in 2024

Printed and published by:
D.K. Printworld (P) Ltd.
Regd. Office: Vedaśrī, F-395, Sudarshan Park
ESI Hospital Metro Station, New Delhi - 110015
Phones : (011) 4172 2626, 98713 94815
e-mail : indology@dkprintworld.com
Web : www.dkprintworld.com

To My Parents

(Late) Pt. Kshem Karan and (late) Smt. Ram Devi

and

Grandchildren

(Sanchit, Aditya, Shruti, Pragya, Shubham, Shreya and Zoey)

who made my life meaningful and joyful

The Soul: Its Characteristics and Omnipresence

I am neither ego nor reason, I am neither mind nor thought,
I cannot be heard nor cast into words, nor by smell nor sight ever caught:
In light and wind I am not found, nor yet in earth and sky –
Consciousness and joy incarnate, Bliss of the Blissful am I. (1)

I have no name, I have no life, I breathe no vital air,
No elements have moulded me, no bodily sheath is my lair:
I have no speech, no hands and feet, nor means of evolution –
Conscious and joy am I, and Bliss in dissolution. (2)

I cast aside hatred and passion, I conquered delusion and greed,
No touch of pride caressed me, so envy never did breed:
Beyond all faiths, past reach of wealth, past freedom, past desire,
Consciousness and joy am I, and Bliss is my attire. (3)

Virtue and vice, or pleasure and pain are not my heritage,
Nor sacred texts, nor offerings, nor prayer, nor pilgrimage:
I am neither food, nor eating, nor yet the eater am I –
Consciousness and joy incarnate, Bliss of the Blissful am I. (4)

I have no misgiving of death, nor chasms of race divide me,
No parent ever called me child, no bond of birth ever tied me:
I am neither disciple nor master, I have no kin no friend –
Consciousness and joy am I, and merging in Bliss is my end. (5)

Neither knowable, knowledge, nor knower am I, formless is my form,
I dwell within the senses, but they are not my home:
Ever serenely balanced, I am neither free nor bound –
Consciousness and joy am I, and Bliss is where I am found. (6)

– *The Song of Soul* sung by Ādi Śaṅkaracārya in his *Ātmaśatkam*; (cited in *Light on Yogi*, pt 1, p. 53, by B.K.S. Iyengar (rev. edn), New York: Schocken Books, 1979)

Professor S.R. Bhatt
Chairman
Indian Philosophy Congress

THE INDIAN PHILOSOPHICAL CONGRESS
(Founded in 1925 by Rabindranath Tagore and Radhakrishnan)

---

12 November 2023
Deepavali

This book penned by Dr R.S. Kaushal, an eminent scientist turned philosopher, is innovative and full of insights. It depicts the quintessence of "psychoscience" in the light of Vedic wisdom. Presented in a simple and lucid style, it presents the Vedic wisdom in a new garb of scientific knowledge which is unique and wonderful. It displays a symbiosis of spirituality and limits of behavioural sciences supplemented by yogic experiences. It is an outcome of vast reading, deep reflection and intuitive experiences. It rightly distinguishes spirituality from religion and correlates it with scientific knowledge. Therefore, it is termed as spiritual science. The subject of psychophysics is revisited in the light of Vedic wisdom and those of psychomechanics, psychochemistry and personality theory are accordingly developed. The peculiarity of this book is that it presents an interesting analysis of models of religions, and newly emerging subjects of "sociophysics", and "econophysics". This book attempts to solve the riddles of consciousness in its different phases and manifestations. It subtly distinguishes Self, Non-self and Cosmic self. In the words of Dr Kaushal, it is addressed to readers and scholars of wide categories that includes physicists, chemists, brain-scientists, etc. on the one hand and psychologists, philosophers and philosophers of science on the other. I find this book quite valuable. At places it has flashes of insight and new coinage which makes it interesting and worth reading. I congratulate the author and expect many more such works from him.

S.R. Bhatt
Former Professor and Head
Department of Philosophy
University of Delhi

Preface

WITH a view to teaching the subject of psychology philosophy in the same way as one teaches the physical science in the classroom, a humble attempt is made in this book to develop the subject of "psychoscience" in the light of Vedic wisdom. To this effect, instead of focusing on the glorification aspect of Vedic wisdom the initiatives are taken here, perhaps for the first time, to give deeper foundations to various aspects of this grand wisdom in the spirit of modern science. For this purpose, we use analogies from modern science and thereby demonstrate the eternity and universality of certain aspects of Vedic concepts. In fact, the subject matter discussed here is not the last word on the topics highlighted but offers the guideline to several new dimensions of study. It also encourages the younger generation, particularly those who have scientific attitude, to fill up the blanks at several places and to explore further the theoretical developments and applications on these lines, particularly in the fields of personality development and behavioural science.

According to Vedic science, an experience of absolute reality in Nature consists of three basic aspects, viz. its "perception" at the level of gross body (consisting of biological body and senses of knowledge and action), a "rational thinking" about it at the level of micro body (consisting of mind, intellect and ego or self-sense) and a "realization" at the level of causal (astral) body (consisting of soul or the innermost existence that acts as a source of consciousness). It is the consciousness emanating from soul that illuminates gross and micro bodies of a living Being and makes them functional; otherwise the latter are said to be dead. Coincidentally, these three aspects of grasping absolute reality in Nature are in accord with the three-world concept advocated by Karl Popper and John Eccles (1981). The three worlds considered are: world-1, which really exists; world-2, which can be perceived and world-3, which can be modelled by (objective) scientists. Ideally speaking, the world-1 is purely a matter of realization and solely independent of space and time, and the world-2, involving the individual-based processes of rational thinking and perception or the "internalization of the exterior", can be explored in terms of the space, time and the consciousness, or the variants of the latter (like meditation, attention and concentration). The quantifiable and measurable world-3 is the game purely of space–time-mediated models and associated interactions, of course, for the conscious observer whose consciousness is ignored at every stage of modelling, i.e. in the "externalization of the interior" kind of process.

Vedic science focuses on the entire gamut of human experiences, actions and behaviour of an individual through certain fundamental processes taking place inside the human being at the levels of his gross, micro and causal existences and in the background of his conscious Self. Essences of life (EOLs), viz. biological body (B), senses of knowledge and action (SE), mind (M), intellect (I), ego (E) and soul (SO) play an important role in the performance of these actions by a human Being (b) (or by a conscious/functional Self) in the field of worldly objects and stimuli (WO). As per Vedic wisdom, this field of WO essentially consists of five cosmic elements (*pañca-mahābhūtas*), viz. earth, water, air, fire and ether, or their composition and variants. In recent times, a quantitative study of these concepts, of course, as tenets of a Sovereign (subjective) Science of the Self, has become essential for more than one reason, particularly for devouring these Vedic concepts by a scientific mind. An understanding of this science perhaps will inculcate human values better in one's personality.

An attempt in this direction has already been made by the author in his earlier publications: *The Science of Philosophy: Theory of Fundamental Pressures in Human Behavior and Experiences* (2011) (hereafter referred to as *SOP*) and *Psychophysics of Personality Development: A Vedic View* (*Art and Science of Integrating Body, Mind and Soul*, 2018) (hereafter referred to as *PPD*). In these works, we have attempted to look for a unifying framework to understand the Nature's working in entirety with reference to a conscious (functional) human Being. In particular, the human Being, as a composite of above intangible EOLs, is described through a philosophical atom-like model (in brief termed as "patomic" model). Like the atomic model of matter, this patomic model, through the dynamics of EOLs, does offer a reasonable explanation not only of human actions, behaviours and experiences but also of his interactions with other humans, non-humans and physical world. In spite of the fact that this picture has made certain aspects of these studies about human Being rather easy, the role of the innermost existence, i.e. of soul, is somehow not explored to a desired extent. Here, we plan to explore and analyse the role of SO or of its derivative "consciousness" in human actions in analytical terms. As a matter of fact, it is the state of mind corresponding to its dwelling in the causal, micro and/or gross existences of a human Being that determines the quality of his actions and the personality in general. Further, in accordance with this dwelling of mind, the intellect of the person passes through spiritual, moral or ethical and physical living zones in a society as per *sākṣī*, *vicāra* and *kartā bhāva* of Vedic science. A chronological development of the patomic model is as follows: (i) Designing (Article, 1990); (ii) Elaboration (Book, 1994); (iii) Honouring (PhD Thesis, 1998a); (iv) Magnification (Book, 2011); (v) Simplification (Book, 2015, 2018b); and (vi) Prospects as a new discipline (Book, 2024, i.e. the present book).

The fundamental processes, as discussed in *SOP*, revolve around the above three existences of a human Being and contribute to his character building and thereby to the vertical component of his personality. On the other hand, when these processes revolve around societal and natural existences of a person (cf. *PPD*, chapters 14-15, appendix A), then this defines the horizontal component of his personality. In fact, the complete personality of a person is an amalgamation of these two components and the same, in turn, will generate an element of spirituality in one's lifestyle by way of establishing cosmic connections of his attitudes, actions and behaviours (cf. Chapter 2). In other words, the best of human actions performed in the domains of all the five existences towards the maintenance of world/cosmic order defines the quality of his spiritual life (cf. *PPD*; appendix A). It is this theme which will be elaborated in this package and again in a modern scientific spirit.

For this purpose, we shall continue to exploit the patomic model of human Being to explain the fundamental processes and interactions responsible for his spiritual evolution and in some sense this will offer justification to call spirituality as a Sovereign (subjective) Science. This science, when practised by an individual, eventually leads him in feeling eternal joy (a state of *mokṣa* or salvation) at the end point beyond the domains of pleasure and peace – a prerogative of the *yogī* category of persons who always dwell in the realm of conscious-self by establishing connections with the Self and the cosmos as well. Note that the common man, while dwelling mostly in the domain of gross body, is satisfied with sensual pleasures. The philosopher and scientist category of persons (cf. *PPD*, chapter 1), on the other hand, are satisfied with both peace and pleasure by dwelling in the realms of micro and gross bodies. On the scales of personality development, note that the zone of spirituality is somewhat higher than the zones of psyche and physical existences of a person and also of a religion. Any person (independent of caste, colour, creed and country) can be a spiritual person even if he lacks in religiosity, education and scientific temperament. On the other hand, a philosopher or a scientist category person need not be a spiritual one. In summary, the spirituality just adds to the degree of perfection in a person as far as his personality development is concerned.

In fact, the viability and universality of physical theories in terms of the underlying concepts, fundamental laws and the derived mathematical constructs thereby are so intriguing and appealing that an academic inquisitive mind does not feel satisfied unless his favourite subject is decorated with these ornaments of natural sciences. In this respect, the subject of psychology was already decorated by Gustav Theodore Fechner of Leipzig about 150 years ago but mostly by using the physics-based instruments and the data analysis techniques. This gave birth to the subject of psychophysics, which, in present times, is considered almost dead as far as the research activities in this subject are concerned. In its new incarnation, the author has however revived (cf. *PPD*) the development of this subject by way of bringing in modern physical theories, models and conceptual frameworks in an analogous manner. Attempts are also made here to develop the subjects of psychomechanics, psychochemistry, etc. in the same vein.

It may be mentioned that the subject of psychoscience, through the dynamics of inner EOLs (viz. M, I and E) and through the actions of outer EOLs (viz. B and SE) in the field of WO, while connects with the spirituality at the one end, it does connect with the behavioural science, on the other. It basically deals with the problems in physics–philosophy interface or with those in the space–time-mediated physics but in the realm of consciousness. The subject of psychoscience so developed would definitely prove an asset in understanding an individual or a collection of individuals better at the most fundamental level. From this point of view, this subject will be a prerequisite for the purposes of unifying the studies of newly emerging disciplines like sociophysics and econophysics, or of other disciplines in humanities and social sciences.

No doubt, the mother Nature "expresses Herself better" when it is understood through the language of mathematics, but unfortunately most of her expressions in the present case are the matter of realization only and that too by a conscious observer. Even in objective sciences, only a few of these expressions of Nature are quantifiable in mathematical terms and can be understood through this language. Truly speaking, the study of spirituality involves subjectivity or realization of the highest degree. Still a rationale behind some of its aspects can be thought over and pursued. Any discussion in this zone, in fact, leads to confusion rather than clarity. Attempts will be made in this book to rationalize at least the path to this zone and not the details of the murky depth due to the limitations of the author. In the same way as the physical world offers a laboratory for testing the concepts of physical science, both physical and mental worlds do offer the laboratories for testing the concepts of spiritual science, oftentimes at the cost of rationality but definitely with an element of universality and the eternity in the experiences through which a conscious experiencer undergoes.

The book is divided into three parts. Part 1 accounts for the link of psychoscience with causal existence, which basically deals with the art of enlightenment of an individual, Part 2 deals with the foundation of the subject of psychoscience in its new incarnation and Part 3 briefly covers the behavioural and application aspects of psychoscience. The book is written truly in an objective, non-sermon-delivering style. It is addressed to readers and scholars of wide categories, including physicists, chemists, brain-scientists, etc. on the one hand and psychologists, philosophers and philosophers of science on the other, but with some scientific temper. At times, convenient mathematical methods are also employed to justify the universality and eternity of inherent truths. To this effect, some sections/ chapters in the text can easily be skipped by the reader but without any loss of continuity of ideas. With due apology to our female readers, all throughout the book the English pronouns corresponding to masculine gender are used for the human Being and the Supreme, of course, without any prejudice on the part of the author. Moreover, except for a little difference in the gross body domain, these are the same EOLs and their dynamics which prevail equally in both man and woman at the philosophical level.

Kṛṣṇa Janmāṣṭamī
6 September 2023

Radhey Shyam Kaushal

Contents

Part 1
Spiritual Hold on Psychoscience

Part 3
Behavioural Links of Psychoscience

Acknowledgements

IT is the Vedic wisdom that I have been listening to and experiencing since my schooldays from various religious forums in India. I also had opportunity to interact with some leaders and the followers as well of other religions during my visits abroad, primerily for my academic pursuits in physics and several times as a tourist or a visitor. The present book is an outcome of my lifelong experiences with spiritual journey on the one hand and with my passion for research in theoretical physics on the other. In fact, an Invisible Power always inspired me to do this task. Naturally, it is not possible to acknowledge all those who have invisibly contributed to this endeavour. A few following names and personalities, however, cannot be deleted from the RAM of my "mental" computer. These personalities have been instrumental, not only in supplying a moral boost but also their valuable help in physical terms, by way of discussions, conversations, communications, critical readings of some draft chapters, assistance in preparing the manuscript, etc.:

- (Late) Professor Bindhya Basani Prasad (Guru Ji), for inspiring and introducing me to Hindi commentary of the *Śrīmad Bhagvadgītā* by Acharya Vinoba Bhave, at the age of 18.
- Professor Dayanand Parashar: My friend, colleague, collaborator, co-author in a book and in several research papers, for all sorts of possible help from the beginning to the end.
- Professor S.R. Bhatt: My PhD (Philosophy) Supervisor, for moral boost and many useful conversations and appreciation

of my work in words and letters, and also obliging me with a foreword to this book.

- Delegates of various WAVES conferences including (Late) Professor Bhudeo Sharma and Professor (Mrs) Shashi Tiwari, for many useful discussions and encouragement.
- Mr Aman K. Rajoria, Professor (Mrs) Mukta Sharma, Mr Govind Kaushal, for a meaningful collaboration in some articles related to contents.
- Dr Medha Garg, Dr Vijay Garg and Dr Himanshu Sharma, for discussions on Ayurveda, naturopathy and horoscope science.
- Professor Awadhesh Prasad, Dr Chand K. Bharadwaj, Dr Girish Upadhyaya, Ms. Shraddha Kaushal, for many useful discussions and help in preparing the manuscript.
- Shri A.C. Sogani, for useful discussions and critical reading of some draft chapters.
- Professor Ashutosh Bharadwaj, Professor J.B. Gupta, Professor Anil K. Kavathekar, for moral encouragement. Shri J.N. Bathla and Shri V.S. Agrarwal, for many useful discussions during morning walks.
- Mr Sanchit Garg, Mr Aditya Gaur, for their help in preparing the manuscript.
- Mrs Shashi Kaushal (wife), for everything in life, particularly for showing her patience not only in tough times but at all stages of my involvements.
- Mr J.S. Patwal, for taking pain in typing the manuscript, oftentimes during extra hours.
- Shri Susheel Mittal of D.K. Printworld (P) Ltd., for giving the present shape of the book.

R.S.K.

Abbreviations, Notations and Symbols

AAD	action-at-a-distance
AADT	action-at-a-distance-time
AAT	action-at-a-time
b	Being (or *jīva* or life principle)
B	biological body
B	non-Self body (a composite of gross and micro existences)
$\mathcal{C}$	causal body (existence)
(CCW)	consciousness carrier wave
E	ego or self-sense
EBGs	elements of basic goodness
EBI	experience-based invariant
EFLs	essentials for life
EOLs	essences of life
EP	epi-physical (matter/particle)
EQ	emotional quotient
$\mathcal{F}$	"field" (mathematical)
FOA	fruits of action
FOU	faculty of understanding
$\mathcal{G}$	gross body (existence)
G	A part of gross body (B + SE)
GMW	God-made world
HVs	human virtues

I	intellect, faculty of decision
IF	intuitive feelers
IQ	intelligence quotient
ISO	“inside out”
IT	intuitive thinkers
$\mathcal{M}$	microbody, mindset function
M	mind, faculty of emotion/feeling
MMW	Man-made world
$\mathcal{N}$	natural-existence
OMU	objective, motivation and utility
OSO	“outside out”
P	personality vector (matrix)
P	physical (matter/particle)
PCM	personality creation mechanism
PMs	*pañca-mahābhūtas* (five cosmic elements)
POSO	polluted form of SO (“self”)
PPD	*psychophysics of personality development*
PUSO	pure form of SO (“Self”)
r	*rajas*
RAM	random access memory
ROM	read only memory
S	*saṅkalpa* matrix
s	*sattva*
S	societal existence
SE	senses of perception and action
SEA	senses of action (motor organs)
SEK	senses of knowledge
SEP	special epi-physical (matter/particle)
SF	sensation feelers

SMBG	*Śrīmad Bhagavad-Gītā*
SNP	systematic of negative pursuits
SO	soul, the innermost existence
SOA	seed of action
SOP	*science of philosophy*
SPP	systematic of positive pursuits
SQ	spiritual quotient
ST	sensation thinkers
STW	spatio-temporal world
t	*tamas*
$\mathcal{V}$	linear vector space
V	*Virāṭ*
μ	meditation variable/parameter
σ	circumstances
τ/*t*	*tanmātra*
Φ_{cc}	(all-pervading) cosmic consciousness field
WO	worldly objects or outer world of objects

1

Introduction

1.1 "Self", "Non-Self" and "Cosmic Self" in the Cosmos

THE word "Self" is synonymous with consciousness, and the purest form of consciousness that dwells in an individual living Being is called "Self", spirit or soul. The word "self", on the other hand, will be used in this book in the context of the polluted version of the "Self" which is responsible for giving an experience of "I-ism", "mine" or "me". Naturally, the stuff in the body of a living Being without "Self" is termed as "non-Self". These Self and non-Self in the body appear in a localized sense; otherwise, they are supposed to be spread all over in the cosmos in the form of animate and inanimate stuff. It is a different thing that non-self exists in or originates from the Self. Note that the Self while present in an individual, also spreads all over in the cosmos and this fact cannot be denied by any standard whatsoever in view of several human experiences and realizations, and this implies the cosmic character of consciousness. This aspect of the Self, in fact, defines the "Cosmic Self". Not only the Vedic wisdom but also the wisdom of other cultures of the world also has been emphasizing such connections between the localized Self in an individual and the Cosmic Self. Now the question arises as to how these connections work in maintaining the world or cosmic order in Nature. Although the answer to this question has been a subject of study in different philosophies, an anxious aspirant would like to know its answer in modern scientific terms, if possible.

When a person looks into the bewildering and subtle working of Nature (not only at the levels of world and cosmic orders but also at the level of individual), he is really amazed and thereby constrained to postulate a Supreme Controller of things. This Supreme Controller, when considered responsible for the existence (Generator), survival (Organizer) and decay (Destruction) of the entire stuff in the cosmos, it is termed as "GOD" in the English language; otherwise the existence and feeling of such an entity has been perceived by seers of almost all the cultures of the world.

In philosophical sense, an important characteristic that is attributed to all the three, viz. "Self", "Non-Self" and "Cosmic Self", is consciousness and this accordingly links them with conscious, unconscious and supra-conscious features of the stuff in the cosmos. An enlightened individual, no doubt, will require detailed and deeper meanings of these terms; for a layman the term consciousness, however, can be defined as:

Living or a functional Being – his dead body = consciousness.

Such a symbolic relationship, in fact, defines the animate and inanimate categories of objects in the cosmic stuff, leaving behind consciousness only as an agent or a catalyst in the entire working of Nature. With regard to the studies of the Self, non-Self and the Cosmic Self, note the following elaboration:

Study of non-Self	⇒	The science of the inanimate (Natural Sciences)
Study of (conscious) Self	⇒	The science of the Self (psychology and psychoscience) that includes biosciences as the Self (soul) is assumed to be seated in a biological body and manifests through the actions performed by body and senses
Study of Cosmic Self	⇒	The spiritual science or the science of the "Cosmic Essence" or of the Supreme (Self or Being) that controls the cosmic order as a whole in a holistic manner,

including the existence, survival and decay of the Self and non-Self and also their functional roles, if any, in the underlying processes.

Thus, the study of spiritual science requires the wisdom of all sciences in the background and that too with a deeper insight.

According to B.M. Puri Maharaj (Website Sadhu Sang Reply on 6 July 2017 to Serge Patlavskiy), the understanding of consciousness can be questioned through following possible statements:

i. "Is consciousness an epiphenomenon of physical processes in the brain?"

ii. "Consciousness possesses Supreme, Prime, Divine or Cosmic fundamentality".

iii. "Consciousness (as a special case of activity of information factor) has equal fundamentality with other factors, such as material factor and energetic factor".

iv. "We have conscious psychological aspect, viz. the unconscious mental aspect and conscious mental aspect, equally fundamental and so on."

Not only a search for the answer(s) of such queries is the aim of this book but efforts will also be made to find as to how such an understanding of the fundamental puzzle of life would enlighten the modern scientific mind. Following examples will further enlighten the reader about this puzzle:

Example 1.1.1: *Conscious Self and non-conscious Self (i.e. Self and non-Self)*: According to Indian mythology, once the Cosmic Couple (Lord Viṣṇu (LV) – a symbol of consciousness (spiritualism) and Goddess Lakṣmī (GL) – a symbol of wealth (materialism)) had an argument as to what is more powerful – spiritualism or materialism? To justify their arguments, they came down on earth from heaven. They saw the dead body of a person was carried by four persons on their shoulders for its last ritual – the cremation. A group of persons, while murmuring some *mantra*, was following the dead body. Seeing this, GL tried to show her power by downpouring the gold coins from the sky. In such an environment, not only the group of persons, following the dead body but also the four persons carrying the dead body, ran after to collect the gold coins. On this event, GL was happy and taunted LV, "Sir, see, after all I have won over your spiritualism". Then LV retorted, "True, you have won, however note that only those who had conscious Self (alive) have come to collect the coins but not the one who was non-conscious (i.e. the dead one). Hearing this, GL, for a while was puzzled over her victory.

Example 1.1.2: The power house of consciousness (Supreme Controller or *Puruṣa*) transfers a fraction of consciousness in unmanifest form to make the Nature (*Prakṛti*) functional and the same manifests in the cosmos in the same way as a potter gives different shapes and sizes (manifest) to the same clay spread all over by applying his intellect and supplying necessary forces in the unmanifest form.

Besides that both Cosmic Self and localized Self exist and survive, each of them does manifest through its functional form. The localized Self in a body while transcends from the Cosmic Self via certain processes and so they are interconnected, they both play their distinct roles in functional forms, of course, with respect to the same non-Self. The underlying processes, in fact, are very intrigue, subtle, self-organized and self-consistent, and they appear at different space, time and mental scales. The Cosmic Self or the localized Self in its pure form is hardly attached to the occurrence of these processes. In fact, both work like a "chemical agent" in their respective domains. At the first stage, these processes give birth to the functional forms and at the next stage to their functionality with regard to the same non-Self. In spite of all this, the localized functional Self maintains an effort to understand these processes by way of using its limited but expandable machinery; but note that as how a "finite" can understand the "infinite". This is an eternal question discussed deeply and in great detail in Vedic literature. As mentioned, the functional Self is a polluted version of the pure Self and it is also called *jīva* in Vedic contexts. This pollution is the result of interaction of pure (cosmic and/or localized) Self with the non-Self. In fact, now time has come when one needs to understand this eternal philosophy of Vedas in a modern scientific spirit. The following example will further give insight into this philosophy.

(Note that the message conveyed through an example may not be a reality but it definitely suggests a roadmap leading to the reality.)

Example 1.1.3: *Working of a mobile phone and a human body:* Note that in a cellphone there is a battery to keep the SIM card and other parts of the handset functional. This also keeps the handset ready to receive the signals coming from outside space mostly in the form of electromagnetic waves. While the battery present in the handset makes it functional, it also assists it in giving various output in the form of music, audio, video, information, memory, etc. The important point to be noted here is that it is the same electric, magnetic or electromagnetic field that exists inside and also makes the system sensitive to receive the similar signals from outside, of course, only after rightly matching of the frequencies. This matching aspect varies from handset to handset in terms of the type SIM cards used. Similar is the case with the working of Cosmic Self (outside electromagnetic signal), localized Self (SIM card through battery) and human (biological) body (handset without SIM card). Note that these Cosmic Self, localized Self and non-Self, in Vedānta philosophy, are respectively designated as *Puruṣa*, *jīva* and *Prakr̥ti.*

1.2 Religion, Science and Spirituality as Products of Rational Thinking

It may be noted that a creamy layer of intellectuals in every society has been trying to understand the existence, survival and decay related to the trio of Self, non-Self and cosmic Self since time immemorial. In this regard, the wisdom gathered about the Self and cosmic Self has given birth to the subject of religion and deals with certain explanations not only of life and style thereof, but also of inner-world-based (subjective) experiences and that too in a variety of contexts. On the other hand, the wisdom gathered about the non-Self (by a conscious observer who also has an element of religiosity since he is also a part of society) has given birth to science that deals with the study mostly of outer-world-based (objective) experiences which are actually quantifiable and measureable and the methodology followed therein is also logical. Note that the same set of senses and essences of life (EOLs) has been instrumental in gathering information and dissemination of both the types of wisdom. Also, both these subjects grew hand-in-hand during the evolution of human race. The development of science somehow remained on the back-foot until recently. It is only during the last few centuries that the growth in science has been exponential, particularly in the West; otherwise, in the East the religions, relying on the subjective science of the Self and cosmic Self, have been growing far and wide in both scope and scale.

1.2.1 SPIRITUAL SCIENCE: A SEARCH FOR GLOBAL AND SCIENTIFIC RELIGION

Ideally speaking, in both religion and science, attempts have been there in the pursuit of the same ultimate truth or absolute reality in Nature in spite of the different approaches followed for this purpose. Each of these paths, no doubt, leads to the same goal but with different motives and thus each one explores only the partial truth. With a view to knowing the complete ultimate truth (which, in fact, in the end remains only the matter of realization) in Nature, a subject like "spiritual science" need to be explored and the same is expected to embrace the extract of wisdom pertaining to both religion and science. Note that every religion has three components and same is the case with the methodology followed in a scientific pursuit, viz. knowledge (*jñāna*), methodology (*upāsanā*) and practice (*karma*) (see Kaushal 2003; Chapter 7 herein). The "knowledge" components (leaving aside the "methodology" and "practice" components) involved in both religion and science are expected to provide a basis for spiritual science. (In the context of Indian philosophy, note that the subject of "spiritual science" or "the science of spirit or soul" is studied as *ātma-vidyā* or *adhyātma*). As will be clear from discussions in Part 1 of this book, spirituality deals with the wisdom of eternity (*sanātana*) that perhaps originated with the human race as per Vedic seers.

Obviously, in spite of the fact that a component to this spiritual wisdom comes from the space–time-mediated scientific methodology and truth, yet this wisdom has to be space–time independent (or invariant) as far as the changes in the world and/or cosmic order at different scales are concerned. Further, note that this wisdom, when fine-tuned, at the end-point, it first culminates into the knowledge of the Self and then into that of cosmic Self with a realization of their intimate (cosmic) connections. The universal laws so derived on this basis are verifiable not only in the laboratory of sciences in manifest form but also in the laboratory of experiences in unmanifest form. Vedic scriptures are full of such wisdom and in this regard the Vedic seers repeatedly emphasize on its realization aspect at the subtle level rather than on its quantification aspect at the gross space–time level.

With regard to the methodology followed in attaining this wisdom, note that religion goes with the concept of "externalization of the interior", whereas science deals with the concept of "internalization of the exterior". Alternatively, in the former case it is the "top-down" or "mind over matter" (i.e. it is the "mind" and hence the consciousness that creates "matter" – a view of certain Vedic scholars) approach. (In fact, the "top-down" approach, based on the inclusion of pre-assigned store of knowledge, is followed by a religious aspirant.) On the other hand, in the latter case, it is the "bottom-up" or "matter over mind" (i.e. it is the matter that creates mind and hence consciousness – a view of modern neuroscientists) approach. (In fact, the "bottom-up" approach in which the rules of operation are not stored in advance but are subject to continual modifications is followed by a scientific aspirant.) We shall return to some of these discussions in forthcoming chapters.

As a metaphor, note that the science through scientists offers a high resolving power "human-instrument" that analyses and resolves the finer and finer details of the world and its order better. In this regard, as far as the limitations of science and scientific laws are concerned, they can be understood through a well-known three-world concept of absolute reality in Nature, viz.

the world-1 (W_1) that really exists and remains only a matter of realization, the world-2 (W_2), that can be perceived by our senses of knowledge and action, and the world-3 (W_3) that can be modelled. The science, in fact, accounts only for the world W_3, whereas the understanding of the worlds W_2 and W_1 come under the domain of religion, in spite that the world W_2 does deal with W_1 through certain overlapping phenomena. As a matter of fact, the spirituality or the wisdom leading to spirituality, in general, is expected to account for the entire gamut of human experiences pertaining to all the three worlds W_1, W_2, W_3 and that too in a coherent manner. With regard to the description of these worlds, W_3 is space–time knitted and attention or concentration (i.e. an outward focusing of consciousness) dominated, W_2 is conscious-thinking knitted and meditation (i.e. an inward focusing of consciousness) dominated and W_1 is experience knitted and realization dominated. Realization is something that goes deep inside the Being and merges with the inner-most existence, i.e. soul. It never returns in form but reflects through actions performed at various levels of human existences, viz. gross, micro, societal and natural. Obviously, it is beyond the feelings belonging to the domain of event-based space–time (Kaushal 2019).

1.2.2 "SPIRITUAL BUT NOT RELIGIOUS" (SBNR) IDEOLOGY: A MOVE TOWARDS A GLOBAL RELIGION

As history reveals, there have always been differences among the creamy layer of intellectuals in a society with regard to the setting of a role model of religion. The demand of individual-originated religions is now on decline in this age of science and technology. Why should it not be? After all, human values were very much there prior to the birth of that individual prophet. The prophet only revived the values and not created them or at the most presented her/himself as a role model of ideal/true follower of these values in all the odd situations and circumstances. No doubt, the ideal follower of these values may be respected and worshipped, but more than this is to worship (or follow) the values themselves which, in certain limit, characterize the Supreme. An inculcation and following up of these values in one's life in totality, if becomes possible, then it will make the person spiritual. A systematic arrangement of wisdom relevant to this aspect of life, in fact, forms the part of "spiritual science".

In this regard, when one analyses a case, it has been found that the wisdom of the East derived mostly from Vedic literature in one form or the other, has given better insight than that of the West in author's opinion. In fact, when one focuses on such a global way of thinking, the question of the East and the West should not arise. Note that the set of basic human values required to prepare a character in this case is universal – independent not only of space and time but also of religions and religious scriptures. In this context, the work of Ron Hubbard – an attempt to assimilate the spiritual wisdom of the East with the modern science of the West is worth mentioning. The philosophy of Hubbard is essentially based on the three existences of a human Being, viz. causal, micro and gross, as described in Upaniṣads and *SMBG*. To this effect, a new cult through the Church of Scientology is emerging and advocating a new theory of peace and stress management through a subject of Dianetics, i.e. a theory of peace and stress resolution (for details see, www.dianetics.org). We shall highlight some of these human values in the next section. No doubt, several individual-originated religions have started importing and incorporating these values in their way of thinking either directly or indirectly but the fact is that a new cult with a slogan "I am spiritual but not religious (SBNR)" has been emerging in the West. It appears that for the values and their depth, this cult has to look forward to the wisdom of the East including other searches. In this context, it is worthwhile to discuss here the results of a recent survey (Goldberg 2014) made by researchers of different organizations and institutions in the US on the need of a religion for modern society. Studies are summarized in Table 1.1.

Table 1.1: A Summary of Research Studies on American Population with Regard to Their Religiosity and Belief System (Goldberg 2014). The Questionnaire Prepared for this Purpose Includes the Following Aspects and Entries with Corresponding Results of the Survey

Object of Study (religious feature adjudged)	*Question/Explanation*	*Conclusion drawn from the study (percentage in favour)*
1. Spiritual independence (recent survey)	"Do you think of spirituality more in a personal and individual sense or more in terms of organized religion and church doctrine?"	"Personal and individual" (~75%)
2. Direct experience-(survey, 2005)	"Why do you practise religion?"	"To forge a personal relationship with God" (~39%)
3. Tolerance (Survey, 2008)	"Exclusivism is in decline; pluralism is in ascendancy."	"Many religions can lead to eternal life" (~70%)
4. Fluidity (survey by a Princeton-based sociologist)	A shift has been identified from a "dwelling spirituality" (in which a spiritual habitat defines one's relationship to God) to a "seeking spirituality" (in which, one seeks God in many different venues).	The shift is noticeable
5. Nonliberalism (survey by Wuthnow)	The number of people who believe "the Bible is the literal word of God" has (declined).	"Dropped remarkably since the 1960s"
6. A different kind of God	When asked whether they believe in God or not.	The answer was "Yes" (>90%) but they see God as an Abstract

In the context of US population, note from Table 1.1 that (i) the belief in religious scriptures is on the decline, (ii) religion is personal; people do believe in God but not in a form rather in an abstract (unmanifest) form, and (iii) people want to become SBNR. That is why people are embracing SBNR ideology with individualized spirituality that includes picking and choosing knowledge-components from a wide range of alternative religions. They view spirituality as a development process in which each person's path must constantly be adjusted to suit his temperament, circumstances and ever-evolving needs. In this endeavour, they have an eye on India's rich spiritual traditions as described in Vedānta philosophy. No doubt, this philosophy has already emerged out of logical thinking and practical experiences by the seers of the past but its availability in a modern scientific spirit, if becomes possible, will be a great asset, particularly for a modern scientific mind.

1.3 Humanity, Human Consciousness and Spirituality

It may be mentioned that the progress of humanity and the progress of human consciousness are two quite different dimensions. The human values, which in some sense are synonym of human consciousness, are eternal, whereas the humanity sounds like a historical evolution of human race. Also, it is the human consciousness in its functional form that maintains the eternity of human values which in certain limit characterize the localized source of consciousness, i.e. soul present in the human body. When seers and aspirants, in search of ultimate truth, look for a connection among souls present in different Beings, they consistently realize that individual localized souls are not only linked with cosmic source of consciousness (Supreme) but they all are part of that entity. This kind of realization of cosmic connections through one's experiences at all of human existences, viz. physical (gross), mental (micro) and astral (causal), constitute the subject of spirituality. This defines only one dimension of human values and the other dimension that contributes to these values comes from the coexistence aspect of a Being with other Beings and also with Nature. In other words, in order to have a better grasp of the absolute truth through human consciousness or values, the experiences gained through coexistences, viz. societal and natural (see Kaushal 2015; chapter 14), do also form the part of spiritual life. A systematic study of such a gamut of human experiences leading to an understanding of the ultimate truth through cosmic connections, in fact, defines the "spiritual science". Naturally, it has to be an amalgamation of natural and social sciences, psychoscience and the science of the functional Self.

According to Osho (Interactions: Osho 2017) history can never be in tune with the evolution of human mind or never be in contact with the formless, rather, it can only talk about the form. Moreover, it can never transcend time, rather, it can know only about those events that can occur in time. In other words, human mind or consciousness is not only formless and beyond time but it is the creator of time and at times it also settles the score with time in certain phenomena (cf. Chapter 7). In fact, there are certain features in the character building or in the personality development at the individual level (Kaushal 2015) or in the knowledge component of a religion at the societal level that remain invariant with the changes in time or even during the evolution of the formless-mind alias consciousness. Vedānta philosophy emphasizes on such features more than any other philosophies associated with individual-originated religions of the world. This, in some sense, justifies the term "*Sanātana Dharma*" attached with the Vedic philosophy in general. In this context, following remarks are in order:

i. In spirituality, efforts are individual or personal, but results could be organizational or institutional.

ii. Religion is a world of forms whereas spirituality is beyond forms – formless or even beyond time and space.

iii. Religious evolution is not collective but individual, however, yet universal. On the other hand, religious revolution is collective.

iv. It is the knowledge-component of a religion that inspires the individual to connect himself with the cosmic Self and has roots in the spirituality. Deeper are the roots in the spirituality, longer lived is the religion in the outer world, viz. "*Sanātana Dharma*", in the Vedic way of life.

v. In some sense, the absolute truths as revealed from the study of the worlds W_3 (objective science) and W_2 (subjective science or religion) remain partial unless the truth of the world W_1 (the art of assimilation of both subjective and objective sciences or of spirituality) is perceived (cf. Section 1.2.1).

It is the interplay of three existences of a human Being, viz. gross, micro and causal, that distinguishes between any two individuals or reflects in their personalities through the level of development of their faculty of understanding (Kaushal 2015). Further, it is not difficult to find common parameters, may be at a crude level, to analyse the behaviour and working of an individual through these existences. In Table 1.2, we try to identify these common parameters in all the three existences associated with the vertical component of one's personality (Kaushal 2015). As to how these parameters describe the functional form of these existences and accordingly the behaviour of an individual at different levels is demonstrated in Table 1.2, possibly under the six heads. Table 1.2, in fact, displays that while the causal existence accommodates and controls micro and gross existences, the micro existence accommodates and controls gross existence. Coincidently, these considerations respectively are in accordance with the concepts of *cidākāśa*, *cittākāśa* and *bhūtākāśa* as advanced by Ādi Śaṅkarācārya about absolute reality. Note that the world of micro-body controls the working of gross body and the worlds of both of these existences are controlled by the causal body. Further, the spiritual thinking, while working mainly through astral body, also controls and dominates over the three domains of working of an individual. It also takes care of his societal and natural existences in a self-consistent manner (see Kaushal 2015; Chapter 14 and Appendix A).

1.4 Consciousness and Physical World: Identifying the Domains of Psychoscience and Spiritual Science

Consciousness prevails among and within both animate and inanimate objects in a variety of ways and at different scales and

Table 1.2: Search for Some Common Parameters to Study the Functionality of Three Existences

Existence (main constituents, i.e. EOLs)	*Main common features of study with regard to maintenance of world/cosmic order (six possible heads)*	*Discipline of study*
1. Physical or gross- (*sthūla* or *bhūtākāśa*): (Biological body, senses of knowledge and action)	- Behavioural science - Physiotherapy and other methods for treatment - Zone of physical and mental exchanges - Role of consciousness in human actions through expression, concentration and meditation - Human values appear through ethics, norms of society; the change with space–time. - Tendency to achieve physical comfort and pleasure	Sociology, social science and anthropology Humanities (philosophy and psychology), behavioural science
2. Mental or micro (*śūkṣma or- cittākāśa*): (mind, intellect, ego)	- Psychology and psychoscience - Psychotherapy - Zone of feeling and intellectual exchanges - Role of consciousness through meditation and realization - Human values appear through morality and character; there is an element of universality but slow change with space–time - Tendency to draw both pleasure and peace	Spiritual science (via religiosity)
3. Astral or causal (*kāraṇa or cidākāśa*): (soul).	- Spiritual science - Spirituo-therapy by spiritual masters - Zone of spiritual experiences - Role of consciousness through realization only - Human values appear through divine qualities, which are universal; no question of change with space–time - Tendency to draw all three – pleasure, peace and joy (eternal)	

again in both unmanifest and manifest forms. This happens in the same way as the electric current plays the role in a variety of household appliances and gadgets. Some gadgets may contain cell or battery (a source of electricity) inside them to act and react with the external electromagnetic signal (as in a remote or mobile phone, for example), but at a finer level, they deal with digital circuits and also a SIM card.

Note that each object in the universe, whether animate or inanimate, is made up of something (subtle and subtler constituents) and also it makes something (gross and grosser composites). It is the nature and hierarchy of binding forces at the subtle-constituent or gross-composition level that is responsible for the existences, survival and nature of the product objects in the history of time. These binding forces in Nature (whether space–time-mediated ones for the case of physical world and inanimate objects or the non space–time-mediated ones for the case of mental world and animate objects), in fact, are the manifestations of consciousness. More precisely, again for the existence and working of the so-called inanimate objects, the well-defined force laws (as revealed in physical sciences) are the acts of an "intelligent design" – an expert player with consciousness. As a matter of fact, it is the consciousness that not only creates space and time but also experiences the world of inanimate and the same emanates either from/through a mini source (present in a living Being) or from the cosmic source of consciousness like an all-pervading finest possible cosmic consciousness field. In this way, the consciousness enters in the description of Nature at the most fundamental level, whereas, the rest remains the question of mechanisms pertaining to biological evolution in the case of animates and space–time evolution in the case of inanimates. Recall the *pudgal* (*pud* + *gal* or "making" + "breaking") theory of Jainism in this context.

A meaningful description of inanimate objects at present proceeds in terms of four fundamental interactions of physics, viz. strong, electromagnetic, weak and gravitational, which, in general, are explored in terms of action-at-a-distance (AAD) type forces. For the description of animate or living objects, the use of physical laws formulated on the basis of these forces somehow show limitations. In fact, for the description of living objects one also needs to account for action-at-a-time (AAT) type (for memory aspect) and action-at-a-distance-time (AADT) type (for spiritual aspects) forces in addition to the AAD type. As a matter of fact, there does exist an "intelligent design" that runs the Nature as a whole which at lower strata consists apparently of both animate and inanimate objects, and works through such a variety of forces and that too in most precise terms but best known only to Him. The human Being, who is also the part of the system and perhaps a perfect creation of that design, can only make an effort to understand a bit of this grand design, of course, with his limited faculty of understanding. (No doubt, this faculty for a common man is limited, but for some persons its potency can be enhanced beyond bounds by mental processes like meditation and thereby enabling them to establish connections with the cosmos.) The features of universality and space–time invariance of physical laws, while supporting the concept of intelligent design, an element of eternity involving in certain behavioural facts (Kaushal 2015) and also in the associated spiritual wisdom, on the other hand, shows the solidarity with this concept of "intelligent design". In fact, the nature of intelligent design (Supreme Intelligence) is to create and maintain order, and thus from this perspective the universe comes out obeying certain set of supreme ordering principles that are functional at every level of creation – an interwoven and nested hierarchy. In order to have a feel for these features in the context of physical laws, the following examples come in handy:

Example 1.4.1: *Universal constants and conservation laws:*

i. The fact that there exist some universal constants like velocity of light, Planck constant, electronic charge and mass, etc. is well known.

ii. Recall the fact that some dynamical variables like linear and angular momentum, energy, parity, charge, etc. in a physical process though remain conserve (or are the constants of motion) but under some idealized conditions.

iii. Note that for a certain class of systems, even the functions of dynamical variables do not change with time (dynamical invariants) that lead to the concept of integrability of the system.

Example 1.4.2: *Universality of inverse square and other power laws:*

i. Note that similar mathematical constructs are found to work consistently for a variety of micro, macro, mega and giga systems to a fair degree of accuracy (structural invariance) (Kaushal 2003);

ii. when one solves the inverse n^{th} -power law problem in the central field case in mechanics, it turns out that the orbits are closed (or the system attains the stability) only for $n = 2$, i.e. for an inverse square law in radial coordinate; otherwise even for a infinitesimal departure from this value of n, the system becomes unstable, i.e. orbits are not closed; and

iii. similar to the case (ii), recall the example of a non-linear system, like Henon-Heiles system in two dimension. Here too the system remains integrable only for some fixed values of the coefficient in the corresponding Hamiltonian (Kaushal 1998).

These are a few cases listed here, otherwise deep studies in natural and biosciences clearly hint for many such eternal features of the underlying laws and systems. On the other hand, note that in the same tone there exists eternal (time-independent or *sanātana*) wisdom in Vedic literature pertaining to the behavioural and spiritual sciences (Kaushal 2015). These considerations force one to believe in the Intelligent Design or Super Regulator of the world and cosmic orders.

When the question comes of interactions between and among objects, three cases are possible, viz. (i) between inanimate objects, (ii) between inanimate and animate objects, and (iii) between animate objects. Even among animates (cf. case (iii)) one should consider the cases of human and non-human categories separately, mainly because human Being provides the example of a perfect creation (cf. patomic model in Chapter 6) of God and non-human offers the example of fractured patomic model (Kaushal 2011). With the concept of intelligent design in the background, note that the case (i) falls solely in the domain of physical science (cf. world W_3 of Section 1.2.1), whereas the case (ii), where an animate (human) perceives the inanimate, comes in the domain of psychoscience (cf. world W_2 of Section 1.2.1); case (iii) while works partly through psychoscience towards the realization of complete truth, it however solely comes in the domain of "spiritual science" with a wisdom (= knowledge + experience) of the both worlds W_1 and W_2.

At this stage, it is worthwhile to define three types of matter in the universe, viz. physical (P-matter) – the matter that is detectable by the physical instrument alone; epi-physical (EP-matter) – the physical matter that is illuminated by consciousness, particularly the one illuminated by a mini source like soul, and special epi-physical (SEP-matter) – the EP-matter that contains the source of consciousness in it, like a working biological body. Although whole stuff in the universe is the manifestation of the all-pervading cosmic consciousness field, but for specific studies pertaining to EP- and SEP-matter, we shall consider the role of localized mini sources of consciousness present in the vicinity as the illuminating agency.

It may be mentioned that modern science does not have answer to every "how" and "why" pertaining to the manifest (physical world), then what to say of the answer pertaining to the unmanifest (consciousness or its variants). Human senses and thinking have limitations for this purpose and so is the case with the man-made scientific instruments – physical or otherwise. As far as their studies are concerned, both the manifest and the ways by which it become manifest appear to be very complex. For the simple manifest of physical world while cause and effect principle works in a limited space–time zone, for a complex manifest, however, a hierarchy of such principles is found to work at different scales and at different times for different parts of the system. In this way, the study of unmanifest for complex systems becomes even more difficult.

1.5 The Subject of Spiritual Science and Its Possible Contents

In preceding sections, we have tried to identify the subject of spirituality in the continuously flowing stream of human actions and experiences, particularly in the domains of his different existences. In a nutshell, the lessons obtained from this survey can be listed as follows:

i. Spiritual experiences belong to a domain that is over and above the domains of religion and science. In fact, spirituality accommodates both religion and science.

ii. One can be spiritual but need not be a religious or a scientist – clearly, a support to the SBNR movement in the US.

iii. Spirituality deals with the realization of complete (ultimate) truth in Nature by way of realizing a phenomenon in its totality and not only at the levels of all the three, viz. local, global and cosmic scales, but also in a domain beyond space and time.

iv. Note that a religion, particularly its knowledge component, guides one only to a partial truth of subjective nature, whereas the science provides him with another partial truth of objective nature. The spirituality accepts only their assimilation and sublimation within. Thus, spirituality accommodates the practices of both religion and science that enables one to realize a super cosmic order in the universe.

v. It is the psychoscience (or psychophysics, in particular) that connects to both the spirituality at one end and the behavioural science at the other.

vi. While containing the roots of both religion and science in it, the Vedic wisdom, as we shall see, is rich enough of spiritual wisdom and practices as well.

A logical understanding of spiritual practices and experiences, in fact, requires a subject of "spiritual science" which definitely is going to be a "science of sciences" or a combination of both soft (behavioural) and hard (natural) sciences. It may be mentioned here that the tools developed in psychoscience are going to be equally viable and effective for the studies in spiritual science, since any quantification in the later, if at all becomes possible, it would manifest through the domain of psychoscience or behavioural science. In what follows, we briefly highlight some possible contents which need to be explored in this context.

1.5.1 SPIRITUAL WISDOM AS A SCIENCE OF SELF, NON-SELF AND COSMIC SELF

When a person learns the art of living with the knowledge and starts distinguishing among the roles of Self, non-Self and cosmic Self in the world order and human actions, then one can say that the person has become spiritual. Further note that in this case the person either is a God-gifted one with this art or else he has achieved this art as an aspirant. It is the second category of person for whom the subject of spiritual science needs an exploration and development. Naturally, for this purpose, a prerequisite is that the person concerned has to be conscious enough about his actions. What a surprise? How can a conscious (alive) person himself be further conscious? Meaning is that an alive person has to develop the extra dimension of understanding, the so-called "enigma of consciousness". The starting step in this direction is to follow a practice of "meditation". During this process one basically tries to channelize his consciousness or focuses his attention inwardly on a "self-thought" goal. When this process is carried out on an external object or stimuli through senses of knowledge and action (SE), then this very process is called "concentration". Vedic literature and various other cults and religions suggest a variety of ways to become expert in this art.

As the intensity of meditation increases by way of drawing "c-energy" (or "cenergy" or "consciousness energy") from its source present already inside as an entity, called soul, then, at the next step, the person concerned acts as a "human instrument" with an increased resolving power towards the understanding of the world and its order in general. As a result, the level of development of his faculty of understanding (FOU), consisting of mind (M) – the faculty of emotion, intellect (I) – the faculty of decision and ego (E) (or self-sense) – the faculty of memory, increases. This improves his personality (Kaushal 2016a) and subsequently his family and social life in the outer world. After a bit of guidance from experienced elders the person concerned also develops the art of realizing the connections of the individual Self to the cosmic Self at the level of inner world. This, in fact, at a later stage, after a continued practice, germinates the seed of spirituality first within and then without in one's behaviour.

1.5.2 SPIRITUALITY AS AN ADVANCED STATE OF MINDSET

A functional entity created out of the trio of inner essences of life, viz. mind, intellect and ego, constitute the mindset or in general the mindset function $\mathcal{M}$ (Kaushal 2015). Further, this function in general, as will be discussed later, is a function of both types of variables responsible for the working of inner and outer EOLs. During the meditation, note that each of the constituents of $\mathcal{M}$ gets dress-up with consciousness or charged with cenergy and thus gives rise to an enlightened $\mathcal{M}$ which in turn leads to a higher level of development of one's FOUs (cf. Chapter 4). In mathematical terms, one can say that the function $\mathcal{M}$ undergoes a kind of evolution with consciousness and attains a stage where the level of development of one's FOUs is well within the spiritual zone. When an individual passes through this zone, then it all reflects in his personality and behaviour in the outer world.

On the basis of level of development of one's FOUs, one can define four possible types of persons in this world, viz.:

i. common man category: whose FOU (including both inner and outer EOLs) works only for his survival in this world;

ii. philosopher category: (an intuition-dominated personality) who is basically an introvert and develops his FOUs accordingly to go to any extent in the exploration of the inner world,

iii. scientist category: who is mostly an extrovert and develops his FOUs accordingly to go to any extent in the exploration of the outer world and believes in quantification and measurement, and

iv. *yogī* category: who has command over the working of both inner and outer worlds, and is capable enough to think and work beyond space and time.

1.5.3 SPIRITUAL SCIENCE AS THE "SCIENCE OF SCIENCES" OF WHICH YOGĪ-CATEGORY PERSONS ARE EXPERTS

Note that the categories (ii) and (iii) of persons defined above in Section 1.5.2, in fact, are the two sides of the same coin, i.e. of the intellectual personality. The category (ii) is, while linked and akin to religion, the category (iii) is linked with and akin to science. The category (iv) personality not only accommodates categories (ii) and (iii) but also thinks of the well-beings of category (i). In this way, if one compares the categories of persons in this world, then they basically are the offshoots of three existences of a human Being highlighted in Table 1.2. In particular, the *yogī*-category persons always and everywhere try to remain in astral or causal existence, the intellectual ones in the mental or micro existence and the common men in the physical or gross existence. In the same vein, one can extend the analogy or accept the next stage reality as to call the wisdom of astral domain as the *adhyātma vidyā* of Vedic living or the "science of sciences" of modern scientific wisdom that helps in revealing the ultimate truth in Nature.

1.5.4 SPIRITUALITY: THE BEST OF HUMAN EXISTENCES

As discussed above, a human Being is born with three existences causal, micro and gross. His evolution with consciousness, in fact, defines the character part (or the vertical component) of his personality. The fact is that the birth of a person takes place in a certain society and also in a certain natural environment. The societal (and subsequently the culture and the nation) and natural environments, in fact, also offer an important base for the development of one's the so-called "horizontal" component of personality. In this way, in addition to causal, micro and gross existences, the societal and natural existences of a person also affect his working and behaviour. Note that a person with these five existences in general is exposed to the world or cosmos to interact with.

In accordance with three degrees of a qualitative adjective in English grammar (or with three *guṇas* of Vedānta philosophy), each of the five existences, viz. causal ($\mathcal{C}$), micro ($\mathcal{M}$), gross ($\mathcal{G}$), societal (S) and natural ($\mathcal{N}$) come in three flavours, i.e. best, better and good (*sattva, rajas, tamas*). We all know that the world always recognizes the superlative degree "best" (and so is the case with *satoguṇa* in Vedānta) all over as far as the maintenance of world or cosmic order or the values in a society is concerned. In the same vein, it is not difficult to realize that the "best" only, as established for the functional domain of each of the five existences of a person, will contribute to his spiritual life (Rajoria et al. 2018). Though it is not easy to attain such a "super best" state by an individual but such a state has been achieved in the past by some selective individual prophets and accordingly standards are set for comparison of personalities (cf. Appendix A of Kaushal 2015) towards the maintenance of the world and cosmic orders.

With a view to making the best of the three existences of a conscious human Being (namely gross, micro and causal), note that three types of arts are suggested and they are still in practice. These beautiful arts are: *yoga,* corresponding to gross body; "meditation", corresponding to micro body or mental world; and "realization", corresponding to causal body. It may be mentioned that *yoga* is already popular worldwide, meditation is gaining the market of peace, obviously then it is the realization that might transform the world into a "spiritual world" with a global scientific religion or spiritual science.

1.6 Is a Spiritual Life God-Gifted or the Achieved One?

Recall that the human Being, considered as a perfect creation of God, has certain extra degree of freedom as compared to non-humans or other Beings. According to the three-component *kārmika* theory of Vedic science, there are three causes in the root of providing the results of any action performed by a person, viz. *prārabdha* – due to latencies of past actions or actions as destined by Nature (including those performed in the past/previous births), *sañcita* – due to actions accumulated in this birth itself and *kriyamāna* – due to actions as going on in the present. Note that the role of the last two components is easily understandable, but that of *prārabdha*, it still remains a mystery. The details of this *kārmic* theory while we postpone to forthcoming chapters, here we look for the answer to the question as to whether the spiritual life, defined as the best of all five existences of a person, is a God-gifted one or can it be achieved in this birth itself? The answer is both, or in practice all three possibilities are there since spiritual life is the result of continuous conscious efforts made not only in this birth but also in previous births as per *SMBG* (cf. verses VI.40-45). Thus, for some, it is totally God-gifted; for some, it is the combination of both God-gifted and efforts-based and, for others, it is totally effort-based. Again, it may be noted that in all the cases, a person is free and capable to enjoy the fruits of spiritual life in terms of pleasure, peace, joy and eternal joy, depending on his attitude towards life.

1.7 Scope of the Book and Arrangement of Chapters

From the above survey, it becomes clear that spirituality is a subject, based totally on the realization of the world and its order by an individual. This realization takes place at the level of innermost existence in a person, i.e. soul, not only of physical objects and processes in the cosmos but also of mental objects and processes. In fact, beside the physical objects, the realization could be of any concept, event, sequences of concepts and events or any phenomenon either in parts or as a whole. Truly speaking, spirituality deals with the wisdom of all sorts of wisdoms which a human mind can think of, or create it for his best natural survival. Even the creator(s) of this Supreme Wisdom is (are) expected to be dwelling ever in a world beyond the space and time, i.e. he must be a *yogī* of the highest category.

The present book is an exploration of the wisdom conveyed to his disciple, psychic patient, Arjuna, in *SMBG* by the Lord, the greatest ever known psychologist of the time. Attempts have been to transcribe this wisdom in modern scientific spirit using concepts and theories of physics and tools of mathematical sciences. In order to have an overall grasp of the contents, an elementary course on science and mathematics at undergraduate level, is a prerequisite; otherwise some sections/chapters can be skipped easily to have a feel for spiritual and/or behavioural aspects in the contents. As a matter of fact, it was the necessity on the part of the author to use these methods, mainly to comply with the objectives of the book, i.e. to bring the deep-rooted philosophy of *SMBG* in the mainstream of modern science. Moreover, when one talks of the eternity, universality and sustainability of the facts described in *SMBG*, they can be understood better when expressed in the language of physics and mathematics, like the development of any other soft discipline (cf. Chapter 12) in recent times.

The three parts of the book, of course not sharply divided, are chosen in the spirit of three human-existences, viz. Part 1 (Chapters 2-5) corresponds to causal- or astral-existence, dealing with spiritual aspects; Part 2 (Chapters 6-10) corresponds to micro-existence, dealing with main psychoscience in its new incarnation and Part 3 (Chapters 11-13) corresponds to gross-body existence, dealing with behavioural and analytical aspects of this psychoscience.

In the next chapter we carry out a brief survey of recent studies on the phenomenon of consciousness in bottom-up approach (i.e. from materialism to spirituality). Chapters 3-5 are devoted to find an answer of the question as to why a person has to be spiritual. To this effect, in Chapter 3, a meaning of what one calls as "cosmic essence" is sought in some Vedic verses and also in the verses of *SMBG*, by way of tracing new interpretations of the verses in a modern scientific spirit. The concepts of an all-pervading cosmic consciousness field (Φ_{cc}) and also of a method, like the method of "second quantization" of a field in physics, are investigated in this context. By considering the presence of eight epi-fields (corresponding to five cosmic elements plus three inner EOLs) in Φ_{cc} in a seed-like form, in accordance with the *aṣṭāṅga prakṛti* of Vedānta philosophy, a theory of procreation is discussed in Chapter 4. Further, several viable and plausible implications of these concepts are discussed here in analogy with physical theories. While all these studies support the spiritual links of psychoscience, further examples of such links are sought in various other Vedic scriptures, like in *SMBG* and in some Upaniṣads in Chapter 5. For this purpose, several ways of classifying the human virtues, qualities and characteristics, as per in *SMBG*, are analysed.

The psychophysics discussed in Chapter 6 through a philosophical atom-like patomic model of a human being forms the basis of all discussions in the book. In Chapter 7, we develop the subject of psychomechanics by treating the meditation variable μ at par with the time variable t. To this effect, a computable definition of μ, the concepts of a "mindset function" at par with the Lagrange function in classical mechanics – as a measure of "cenergy (consciousness energy) function", an "effort integral" at par with the action integral in mechanics, etc. are introduced here, perhaps for the first time, and a pair of psycho-dynamical equations of motion is derived. The century-old problem of handheld (Chevreul) pendulum, which has become a common tool to study several phenomena in occult sciences, is investigated in Chapter 8. Here, while a laser-beam experiment is suggested to measure the effect of divination, if any, complex phase space approach is adopted to study the handheld pendulum, mainly with a view to keep the track of psychic processes through the imaginary part. Further, in Chapter 9, we continue to study some exotic phenomena of occult sciences by way of developing the theories of attention-dominated matter, waves, energies and processes. In particular, the role of the proposed concept of mind waves is investigated and it turns out to be a useful tool in these studies. The subject of psychochemistry is developed in Chapter 10 within the framework of patomic model. In particular, a theory of human interactions and relations is investigated in terms of exchanges of different types of *tanmātras* between and among human Beings.

On the application front, in Chapter 11, we demonstrate, as to how the patomic model of Chapter 6 opens the new dimensions and depths of study of the personality theory of Carl Jung with reference to the search of spiritual content in a personality. The role of the developed psychoscience in unifying the newly emerging disciplines of sociophysics and econophysics is discussed in Chapter 12. In analogy with the concepts of conservation laws and dynamical invariants in physical theories, attempts are made in Chapter 13 to find certain criteria for a religion to be global, eternal and sustainable. Finally, we summarize our studies and highlight some future prospects of the present scheme of study in Chapter 14. Some ideas, derivations and discussions in the text are further supplemented by five Appendices in the end.

High Skill Exercises and Projects

1.1 Write Notes on the underlying philosophies behind each of the following categories:

   i. "three world" concept: W_1, W_2 and W_3;

   ii. "three types of matter in the Universe": P – matter, EP – matter and SEP – matter;

iii. "four types of forces": contact, AAD, AAT and AADT;

iv. "three types of cause and effect-based human actions": *prārabdha*, *sañcita* and *kriyamāna*;

v. "four categories of persons in a society": common man, philosopher, scientist and *yogī*;

vi. "four types of physical forces": strong, weak, electromagnetic and gravitational.

1.2 Write an essay on the subject of "spiritual science" accommodating various aspects and types of contents highlighted in Section 1.5.

Part 1
Spiritual Hold on Psychoscience

2

Consciousness and Related Studies

Bottom-Up Approaches

As mentioned in Section 1.1, it is the functional self with all its accessories that attempts to understand the world or the cosmic order in general, naturally using the common characteristics of both cosmic and localized Self and that is the consciousness – a subtlest and all-pervading entity. An individual (functional self), while conforming to these orders, becomes amazed by the working of intelligent design that also works behind the functional (cosmic) Self. Depending on his attitude towards the world/cosmic order, the functional self adopts either or both of the two ways for this purpose, viz. from manifest to unmanifest (materialistic or bottom-up approach) or from unmanifest to manifest (spiritual or top-down approach). While the top-down approach based on Vedic wisdom will be followed throughout the book, particularly in this chapter we make a survey of bottom-up approaches, adopted to understand the phenomenon of consciousness in recent times.

2.1 The Phenomenon of Consciousness

The survey in Chapter 1 hints that consciousness is an essential part of the intelligent design that works behind the existence, survival and destruction of the cosmos and its order. Further, the consciousness – a subtlest possible (most tenuous or rarefied) entity manifests through both animate and inanimate stuff. In inanimate, while it manifests through the nature of force laws (like their universality) that govern the existence and working of sub-structures or of Nature as a whole at different space–time scales; in case of animate, it, however, forms the basis, for example, for their growth, evolution and reproduction. In some animates, like human and non-human Beings including the plant kingdom note that the consciousness adds some extra degrees of freedom but in varying proportions with regard to their existence and survival, which otherwise are curtailed in case of inanimate. Such is the intricate nestling of consciousness and only a few scholars come forward to realize and understand this kind of unifying role of consciousness.

Recall that the phenomenon of consciousness is as universal as the phenomenon of gravitation in physics or even more. In fact, it is much more fundamental and subtle than the gravitation in the sense that the latter is confined to inanimate matter or to matter-fields which not only are space–time-mediated but also are the outcome of rational thinking of conscious minds. Note that it is the consciousness of certain degree that again makes the mind and the faculty of thinking functional; otherwise the mind and the intellect of a dead body are of no use as far as the reaction to the external stimuli is concerned. As a matter of fact, while the *yogī* category of persons enjoy living in this eternal and omnipresent consciousness and the common man is rather least aware of this nestling of consciousness, the scientist- and philosopher-category of persons, on the other hand, do bother most to understand this phenomenon. For this purpose, the latter categories use their own methodologies, expertise and styles to pick a drop out of the ocean and often come out with their disagreeable arguments. The fact is that this eternal, all-pervading entity acts only as a catalyst in the whole game of world and cosmic orders.

Note a striking similarity between the all-pervading cosmic consciousness field and the Higgs field of physics. Through certain mechanism, Higgs field gives mass to the matter-particle which in turn becomes a source of gravitation field and then at a later stage it offers a plausible basis for the Mach's principle. This is how the infinitude converts into finitude or the vice versa. Although it remains yet to understand as to how the gravitation generates "weak", "electric" or "strong" charges (analogous to mass) on a matter particle to give rise respectively to weak, electromagnetic and strong interactions of different strengths and ranges, the fact is that the latter three interactions show analogous behaviour at a certain value of the energy-dependent coupling constant (grand unification). Exactly the same is the picture with cosmic consciousness field Φ_{cc} (postulated or realized by the seers of Vedic wisdom, see Chapters 3 and 4) and the fields of *pañca-mahābhūtas* including those of inner EOLs, viz. mind, intellect and ego (i.e. *aṣṭāṅga prakṛti* (cf. *SMBG* VII.4)). (Details will be discussed in Chapter 4.) The field Φ_{cc}, through certain mechanism(s), gives rise to "consciousness-charge" (c-charge) in varying proportions to different species of animate and inanimate entities in the cosmos, so that some of them (animate) become the source of consciousness in themselves and some (inanimate) are driven by the consciousness of others. This discretized c-charge when energized appropriately by "c-energy" through certain psychophysical mechanism(s) like meditation, then it again becomes capable of merging into the continuum of Φ_{cc} but only at an appropriate stage of spiritual evolution.

In its discrete form, this consciousness, particularly after plantation in an individual entity, passes through two types of situations; either it remains static (passive) and becomes the source of universal force laws towards the existence and survival of the so-called inanimate entities (non-Beings) or else it takes a dynamic form (active) and evolves with appropriately defined or created space–time for itself towards the existence and survival of the so-called animate entities (Beings). In the latter case, in some species, the consciousness while plays a limited role, in others like human Beings it plays a very vital role due to the presence of some extra degrees of freedom in the species. Thus, peculiar and also amazing are the ways of plantation of seed of consciousness in species and more peculiar than this are the ways of its evolution and manifestation in an animate with space–time. In biological terms, the c-energy not only energizes the inner organs of an individual but also makes both inner and outer organs functional. Note that in some species the existence of psychophysiological or intangible entities like mind, in addition to the biophysiological organs, cannot be denied. It is the c-energized version of (inner) psychophysiological entities that controls the working of outer organs in a judicious and creative spirit.

Going back to the Vedic wisdom, a beautiful description of the phenomenon of consciousness can be traced in the Sanskrit word *satcidānanda* (= *sat* + *cit* + *ānanda*), i.e. a composite of three words *sat*, *cit* and *ānanda*. Note that like Φ_{cc} there is another eternal entity – *sat* (a non-functional form of Nature). The *sat*, in the presence of Φ_{cc}, becomes *sadcit* (functional form of Nature). The resultant product is adjudged and characterized by certain characteristics – *ānanda* or through three *guṇas* – *sattva* (quality of goodness), *rajas* (principle of activity) and *tamas* (principle of inertia). (These *guṇas*, in fact, are the very fabric of creation and are believed to permeate through all living and non-living, tangible and intangible objects and also are in accordance with three degrees of adjective – superlative, comparative and positive, e.g. the best, better and good.) Thus, it is the same eternal entity *sat* that manifests in a variety of ways with *ānanda* and in the presence of *cit*. Truly speaking, *sat* is the P (physical)-matter, *satcit* is the EP (epi-physical)-matter and the embodiment of all the three *sat*, *cit* and *ānanda* is the SEP (special epi-physical) matter, in the universe, as discussed earlier (cf. Section 1.4). The following example will further corroborate this rather involved concept. Coincidently, these three types of stuff in the universe are also synonym of *bhūtākāśa*, *cittākāśa* and *cidākāśa* concepts (cf. Table 1.2) of Vedānta philosophy (Ādi Śaṅkara 1966).

Example 2.1.1: *Potter, clay and clay-products*: It is the same clay (*sat*) prevailing all over, but when it passes through the hands of a potter (*cit*) the pots (*satcit*) of different shapes, sizes and qualities are produced. In order to characterize the products in terms of their beauty (*ānanda*), note that, one talks of the degrees (*guṇas*) of the latter.

As far as the role of modern science in understanding the phenomenon of consciousness is concerned, truly speaking for the most of scientists, it remains a black box. As a matter of fact, a good percentage of scientists do not want to tread into this domain in spite of the fact that at times they themselves encounter with it either at the personal level or in their research problems. They tactfully avoid any of its account in their theoretical studies by way of introducing certain assumptions or by postulating certain tricks in mathematical terms like linearity, centrality and harmonicity at the modelling stage, while their role in reality cannot be denied at least in some cases (Kaushal 2011, 2015). One possible reason for this, in author's opinion, is the following: No doubt the modern science is the gift of the West and it has collectively given the best to the world, but when the question of the depth of the individual philosophy of a scientist or of a person in general arises, it is not as deep as offered by great seers of Vedic wisdom. In some sense, a scientist is able to explain science, but ... "Is science able to explain scientist?" is a billion dollar question – a slogan advanced by Sri Chaitanya Saraswat Institute, Bengaluru (an organization focused on consciousness studies). In spite of all this, in recent years, some efforts have been there to understand this complex phenomenon of consciousness independently or jointly by physicists, bioscientists, neuroscientists and others, of course, in a piecemeal manner but not in a holistic sense.

It may be reminded again that modern scientists still follow the bottom-up approach in this regard, i.e. from materialism to spiritualism, whereas Vedic way of thinking is based on top-down approach, i.e. from spiritualism to materialism. In fact, it is the subject of psychoscience that will offer a smooth linkage between these two extreme views. In the next section, we try to establish some analogies with physical theories and see if the same can guide us to understand the consciousness-manifesting phenomena better. In Section 2.3, we discuss the mind–matter interaction, where matter is considered as a stimulant. Besides, the philosophical aspect, the studies of consciousness are desirable in modern times in several other contexts and the same is briefly highlighted in Section 2.4. In Sections 2.5 and 2.6, we revisit famous mind–brain problem and briefly review some recent works in brain science. In view of the available studies, it is argued that this is the area of neuroscience where the top-down and bottom-up approaches to understand the phenomenon of consciousness can converge. Finally, concluding remarks are made in Section 2.7.

2.2 Lessons from Physical Theories I

2.2.1 INTELLIGENT DESIGN: CREATOR AND CREATION

Spirituality deals with absolute reality which in effect consists of contributions from both science and religion. Absolute reality manifests through two distinct but complementary ways as far as the working of Nature is concerned, viz. as an energy source (the Creator of energy) and as an appliance that works with or in the presence of that energy (i.e. the creation). An effort to understand either or both in fact leaves the aspirant or truth-seeker in bewilderment. Note that in *Example 2.1.1* the potter is the source (or energy supplier) and the clay or its various given shapes are the appliances in whose construction and working reflects the intelligence (c-energy) of the potter. Thus, an understanding of the role of intelligent design in Nature's working poses queries on two fronts – first regarding the existence, survival and decay (if at all they are there!) of the grand Creator and next regarding the existence, survival and decay of the grand creation(s). It is the interplay between the two components of the same consciousness (one from the cosmic source and the other from its microcosm (i.e. the Being)) that makes the creation functional. While we all carry with us and enjoy the manifest creation in a variety of ways, hardly any one of us, rarest of the rare, is the true seeker of that unmanifest Grand or rather Unique Creator. Some analogies from physics will further help in understanding such intricate working of Nature. In this context, one should however keep in mind that there is a wonderful coherence between the space–time-mediated energy source and the appliance so designed in terms of the corresponding space–time-based "cause and effect" principles. The situation is however different for the present non-space–time-mediated source(s) and the corresponding appliances (systems) thereon.

***Example 2.2.1**: The working of an appliance conforms the nature of energy emanating from the source*: In physics studies, note that an appliance is designed in accordance with the nature of available energy source and the same works effectively when connected directly or indirectly with that source. It is a different thing that at times the available energy is converted to its other forms, mainly for the use of the same appliance. (Recall the cases of heat energy source and thermal systems; electric energy source and electrical systems; mechanical energy source and mechanical systems; etc.) The same is the case with the cosmic source of consciousness (c-energy) and the designed biological bodies of various living species or Beings.

The designed biological bodies, which are capable of evolving with space and time, become functional only in the presence of c-energy. In this process, the "intelligent design" goes one step ahead by way of planting a mini-source of c-energy inside the biological body itself that also makes other EOLs, like SE, M, I and E (in case of a human Being) functional. It is a different question as to how this mini-source is planted in the body or where it goes after the decay of the biological body B.

Thus, there are three possible aspects of studying the phenomenon of consciousness: first, to understand its source; second, to understand as to how the c-energy flows and works through the appliances (species); and third, perhaps of less importance, is to know as to how the c-energy manifests in actions performed by an appliance. Truly speaking, truth seekers or aspirants in a society have been concentrating on some or on all the three aspects since time immemorial, depending upon the development of their FOUs. It has been noticed that most of the philosophies of world cultures are focused on the search of source and its role in actions in a subjective manner. It is only in the recent years that a move has been initiated by scientists to study this phenomenon of consciousness in an objective and rational manner and that too through its manifestation in actions, whether these actions take place at mental or physical level (see, for example, Penrose 1994; Stapp 2009).

Example 2.2.2: *How the consciousness crops up in actions*: (see, for example, "K-effect" in Section 8.5.1 and also Appendix F in Kaushal 2011).

2.2.2 COLLISION THEORY

In tune with modern physics methods, note that when we want to explore the structure, nature or interactions inside or with the surroundings of an inanimate entity, then experiments are done with an appropriate collision probe and with a suitable detector for the detection of the after effect. The data so collected is then analysed by conscious minds having a rational thinking and a preconceived theoretical framework/model for this purpose. This is how the existence of four fundamental physical forces for inanimate objects is established in physics. Note that the consciousness in this case plays its role mainly at the level of measurement and analysis with a view to verify, correlate, predict and utilize the data of the experiment. Further, when similar experiments are done in psychology departments but on living objects, by the living objects and sometimes by using the living objects as probes, then the situation becomes quite different. The word "living" here is a synonym of consciousness and the same manifests at the variety of stages in psychology experiments as compared to that in physics experiments. This makes the consciousness studies difficult even at the individual level, though bio- or neuro-scientists try to explore it through brain studies (cf. Section 2.5), but with space–time-mediated physics devices like electromagnetic signals and related apparatus – a bottom-up approach (Angel et al. 2001; Fell et al. 2003).

2.2.3 ATOMIC, NUCLEAR AND NUCLEON STRUCTURE STUDIES AND MODELS

Recall that while the electromagnetic force in physics is fairly well established earlier, the same is not the case with strong and weak forces even today. The understanding of the latter is not yet up to the mark. For similar reasons, while the studies in atomic physics have proven an asset to mankind, those in nuclear physics (or for that matter in particle or quark physics), however, still remain a subject of exploration even after about hundred years of discovery of the nucleus. Similar is the case with quark physics. Despite the fact that the study of nature of strong and weak forces is still a hot topic of research, a variety of models based on electromagnetic probes for the nucleus as well as for the nucleon is successfully used. The positively charged (in Coulomb sense) nucleus at the centre of the atom is found to have a variety of other type of "charges" at the substructure level or, for that matter, a positively charged proton inside the nucleus is found to have a variety of other type of "charges" at the quark level. Attempts have also been made to explore inner details of fractionally charged (in Coulomb sense) quarks present inside the nucleon.

In fact, the presence of multiplicity of charges (beside the Coulomb one) in increasing order for the successive substructures one after the other, creates the problem of finding an appropriate probe for the purpose in the respective experiments. In this context, while the pure electromagnetic probes like electron or photon could provide meaningful results on atoms and also on nuclei to some extent any probe used at further substructure level will provide only the partial information about the target. Thus, as far as the understanding of Nature in general is concerned, the picture at the substructure level in physics experiments is in no way different from that in psychology experiments in which all the three – the probe, the target and the detector are animate objects – like human Being. A living human Being, in spite of being a perfect creation of God, is a complex system in itself as his working is based on a hierarchy of cause and effect principles of different orders and at different scales in the gross, micro and causal domains of his existences.

In summary, the studies of consciousness in the above spirit through physics or psychology experiments will provide only the partial truth about consciousness in the same way as the four blind persons trying to realize the existence of an elephant just by touching him and drawing the conclusions about his shape and size. No doubt, a holistic approach to study this phenomenon is desirable and the same, as will be discussed in the next chapter, is provided by Vedic seers. Before embarking on that, here we carry a brief survey of the approaches followed by modern scientists in different contexts.

2.3 Role of Consciousness in Mind–Matter Interactions: Matter as a Stimulant

Consciousness of a person plays an important role when the person interacts with the external world of inanimate (cf. chapter 8 of Kaushal 2011). As a matter of fact, there are two possibilities as per Vedic science. In one case, the conscious "mind" (consisting of the trio of inner EOLs mind, intellect and ego) can directly interact with the matter (in general consisting of five cosmic elements) through five *tanmātras* corresponding to five senses of knowledge. In the second case, the external matter acts only as a stimulant and subsequently the inner trio of EOLs starts working. While we postpone the details of the first situation to Chapter 10, here we briefly remark on the second situation, however, with the concept of mind as perceived by Western thinkers. In this case, although a person does not interact directly with matter, but inspired or attracted by its derived attributes – wealth, beauty, position and fame – are a few such attributes of the external world that stimulate the mind of an interacting person. In fact, in Western schools of thought, the "mind" is considered as synonym of consciousness and as a gross body, it is treated as a different matter from the physical one and thus scientists talk of "category error" (Penrose

1994) in the observations performed on the two types of matter. While apparently unaware of Vedic wisdom, they talk of conscious, unconscious and subconscious minds in the context of physical theories (Mlodinow 2012; Stapp 2009) or of "system 1" and "system 2" or of two "selves" associated with a personality in the context of economic sciences (Kahneman 2011).

Whether one talks of conscious (functional or aware), subconscious (existing without one's awareness), supraconscious (awareness dominated to its limit) or unconscious (unaware) mind (Acharya 1995), in any case the role of consciousness in mental processes cannot be denied by any standard, mainly because a dead person can never respond to an external stimulant. No doubt, it is difficult to objectify these different stages of consciousness but one can easily achieve and realize these stages by enhancing the intensity of meditation in steps. As far as the quantification of this intensity is concerned, one can define (cf. Eqn (7.20)) a meditation variable (μ) and try to identify its ranges corresponding to these different stages. Not only this, there have been attempts in the past to find a connection between the psychological intensity and the physical magnitude of a particular feature associated with a stimulant. Swiss scientist Daniel Bernoulli, about 300 years ago, thought over this problem and investigated, for example, the utility (a concept of mental domain) as a function of quantity of wealth one possesses (a concept of physical world). Many such phenomena can be traced in daily life. Like utility there are several other abstract concepts such as choice, value, probability of occurrence, etc. which need to be investigated with reference to an external stimulant.

Later, German psychologists Gustav Fechner (1860) and Ernst Heinrich Weber attempted to quantify such a relationship of psychological intensity and physical magnitude of a feature through a logarithmic function – the so-called Weber–Fechner law, and thus the subject of psychophysics was developed (for details, see Nowak and Vallachar 1998). This law basically describes the perception of change in a given stimulus. (For further details and generalization of this law, see Section 7.4.2 and Appendix E.) In what follows, we briefly remark on the recent works of Kahneman and Mlodinow.

a. *The role of consciousness in "Thinking, Fast and Slow"*: With reference to the phenomenon of consciousness, Kahneman (2011) conveys a wonderful message to the world through his (hypothetical) psychodrama whose characters are "system 1" and "system 2" or the "two selves" in a personality. He applies these concepts rather successfully to handle problems of economic sciences. Interestingly, the role of these characters in the drama is very much similar to the one discussed in the *Śvetāśvatara Upaniṣad* (cf. chap. 4, verses 6-7) through a metaphor of two bird-friends sitting on the same tree. The spirit behind these verses can be summarized as (Kaushal 2018, Appendix B) always and everywhere mutually cooperative two bird-friends (having the same generic name) with beautiful wings (which add to their intricate dynamics) live by the same tree. One of them enjoys the tasty fruits of the tree and the other remains a mere spectator and enjoys only watching the former eating fruits and their growth on the tree. Clearly, both birds while living in the realm of the same consciousness field (i.e. on the same tree), the one enjoying the tasty fruits corresponds to the "thinking fast" processes whereas the other who watches the eating bird corresponds to the "thinking slow" processes in philosophical terms. We postpone further details to Section 12.4 (or, see Appendix B of Kaushal 2018).

b. *"Unconscious mind" shapes one's behaviour and experiences* as per Mlodinow: While searching the roots of conscious thoughts, Mlodinow (2012) holds that our the so-called "unconscious mind" is responsible for shaping our behaviour and experiences in daily life. But the fact is that the mind is an intangible entity and does not remain functional in a dead body. Naturally, it draws energy from some (!) source of consciousness to remain functional in a living person. Only such a (conscious) mind can have memory and/or ratiocinative faculties to use the same in shaping one's behaviour and experiences. This clearly shows that the concept of "mind" in the theory of Mlodinow, is misunderstood. What he calls as "unconscious mind" is basically an "unaware mind" or the mind that is not loaded with precise information but it is conscious. For this reason, it perhaps undergoes for misperception, misunderstanding and misremembering with regard to one's behaviour and experiences. As a matter of fact, a sufficiently "dressed mind" with consciousness (cf. Section 4.3) that comprises of faculties of emotions, reasoning and memory will never undergo such personality traits. Further note that the information is also contained in this subtle entity mostly in a latent form. The "system 2" (effortful system) of Kahneman fulfils such terms. In summary, the "unconscious mind" of Mlodinow corresponds to the "system 2" of Kahneman, which is not only conscious but also comprises of subtle components of various faculties responsible for mental processes. In fact, this latter entity plays a role when one tries to explore finer details of a conscious thought, of course with somewhat more intense meditation (for further details, see Kaushal 2023a).

Another confusing phrase analysed by Mlodinow is the symbolic relation, viz. "senses plus mind equals reality". Here, no doubt, the word mind is used in a broad sense as discussed in the Western philosophy and the senses can include the brain (matter) but still the concept of reality is vague, not cited in precise terms. It is not clear whether the reality in question is subjective (which is a matter of realization and experiencing) or objective (which is quantifiable as well as derivable from measurement) or a combination of both (the one that belongs to psychic world). In fact, all such details become transparent by using the Vedic wisdom with regard to the phenomenon of consciousness.

2.4 Consciousness Studies in Modern Times

This is a fact that consciousness or its role manifests in several phenomena which are under the lens of modern science, particularly the ones in which a living Being is either directly involved in the measurement process or the concerned experiment is done on living objects. The worst part of these studies is that a modern (objective) scientist does not want to tread into the highly subjective and yet unexplored realm of consciousness. It may be mentioned that in view of the advancing technologies and progressive rational thinking by scientists in modern times, such studies cannot be postponed indefinitely. In fact, several top scientists, particularly physicists, biologists and neurologists have already started working on this subject in collaboration with psychologists and philosophers – who, in fact, follow a bottom-up approach, i.e. a route from materialism to spiritualism. As mentioned before, for any kind of a meaningful understanding of consciousness, it is the philosophy of the East, particularly the Vedic wisdom that will guide and pave the way for these studies and that too in a "top-down" manner, i.e. a route from spiritualism to materialism.

With regard to consciousness studies there is a common feeling that "one is trying to understand something that already makes him capable to understand". True! But the fact is that the inquisitive nature of a person has always been pressing him to analyse such consciousness-manifesting phenomenon as perceived at the level of senses and realized later at the level of mind and soul, in the same way as an objective scientist analyses a phenomenon of physical world but purely in terms of space–time-mediated processes and interactions. No doubt, the consciousness phenomenon can arise equally at the level of both classical and quantum physics, but the pity is that the limitations of physical laws in this regard have been discussed only in the quantum domain.

As a matter of fact the phenomenon of consciousness arises when the conscious (living) objects are involved in the process under study either as a participant, an observer or as a detector. Even in this case, the role of consciousness is tactfully minimized or eliminated, by using an (inanimate) instrument for detection, or else in the case of a conscious observer, the latter is considered as a spectator while formulating the theory or modelling the process. This is mainly to treat the system as a closed one – a prerequisite for the effectiveness of physical laws. (Note that the conscious systems as such are not closed. The processes, involving the conscious objects directly or indirectly, are also not closed and thus are not bound to obey physical laws.) Even in this case the following situations arise:

A. Consider the case when a physical process involving the inanimate objects occurs and a conscious observer carries out the measurement. In this case, at macro-scale (classical domain) one is justified in neglecting the role of consciousness but at micro level (i.e. in quantum domain), this role has been the subject of study in modern times.

B. In recent years, another rather hot topic of study of consciousness has emerged and it is the case of mind–brain interaction as pursued by neuroscientists and psychologists. As to how the material brain works in perceiving the conscious human intents like emotions, decisions and memory by a new kind of matter, called "mind" has been the subject of study of several theoretical physicists (Mlodinow 2012; Penrose 1994; Stapp 2009).

C. An individual, while sitting in meditation and undergoing self-realization or observation, is a conscious system in itself but with a polluted version of soul or a functional Being that works through the EOLs body, senses, mind, intellect and ego.

D. When two individuals interact and each of them tries to share experiences at different levels of gross, micro and causal existences.

E. The following two situations arise in case D above when the third conscious observer watches the interactions of the first two interacting conscious participants: (i) as an active third participant; and (ii) as a silent spectator.

F. When a collection of conscious objects, in general, interact among themselves, then the following two cases arise: (i) when the objects interact at the level of an individual EOL; and (ii) when they interact at the level of several EOLs or, in general, at the level of their gross, micro and/or causal existences.

While we plan to study cases C-E under the head of psychochemistry in Chapter 10 in a top-down manner, here we briefly survey some recent studies on cases A and B pursued in a bottom-up manner.

2.5 Consciousness Studies in Modern Science: Mind–Brain Problem

As a particular case of mind–matter interaction, the study of mind–brain interaction (where "brain" is a particular type of matter) has become a puzzling problem for modern scientists. Keeping in mind the works of psychologist W. James on the conception of "mind", John Eccles on the theory of relationships between "mind" and matter through a kind of "soul" (where "soul" is considered as a "knower" and "controller" of what is going on in the brain), Stapp (2009) has presented an exhaustive review of contemporary works on the phenomenon of consciousness. This beautiful survey of Stapp also includes his own work on the subject and comparative studies of works of other philosopher-scientists of modern times, like Einstein, David Bohm, Gilbert Ryle, M. Lockwood, D.C. Benett, Roger Penrose and several others. When the question comes to a consistent and full-fledged theory of consciousness, particularly with reference to an individual whose existence cannot be isolated from the cosmos, all these theories show limitations and offer only a piecemeal answer to the question. Without going into details of these works (based mostly on bottom-up approach) here, in what follows, we make some pertinent observations on these works in the present context:

i. While the "mind", as perceived by W. James, is responsible for conscious thoughts and processes, these thoughts basically are the complex ones and they need to be analysed further in terms of some "component thoughts". The component thoughts are experienced together in a particular way that makes the experienced whole as an essentially new entity (a case of highly non-linear superposition). An analogy between "mind processes" and "brain processes" is further emphasized by James that justifies the working of the brain with reference to a particular thought. In these studies, while the concept of "mind" remains dubious, its functionalities like thinking, feeling, recognition and understanding as outcome of consciousness are however restored.

ii. The work of Gilbert Ryle hints at a kind of category error in the studies of mind and brain. According to this view "mind" refers to a way a body (brain) can behave, for example intelligently, not to something that belongs to the same category as body. This kind of dualistic model is further pursued in the work of Penrose (1994) when he is looking for the missing concept of consciousness between mind and brain with a view to having a smooth transition between the two categories.

iii. Most of these works on consciousness and conscious thought, including that of Stapp, however, focus on developing a quantum mechanical description of the brain and its functioning. John Eccles approach is however different in several respects; in that in the relationship of mind and brain the concept of a kind of "soul" is considered, which, in turn, acts as a "knower" and "controller" of what is going on in the brain. Clearly, this concept of "soul" is not the same as considered in Vedānta philosophy (cf. Chapter 6). Also, the characteristics of this entity as "knower" and "controller", though in some sense, sound as the faculties of "memory" and "reasoning" in a human Being but are not used in the Vedānta spirit.

iv. To understand the role of missing concept of consciousness in the mind–brain interaction, Penrose discusses the role of microtubules. These entities considered present as substructures within brain neurons, play a dominant role in biochemical reactions taking place inside the brain.

v. A model of the quantum–classical and mind–brain connections is investigated by Stapp (2009). In fact, attempts have been made to explain the gamma synchronous frequency of about 40 Hz that is observed in brain studies with regard to gamma EEG Band (Fell et al. 2003). In order to have a consistent quantum mechanical description, Stapp (2009), in this context, discusses a theoretical model for brain dynamics in which the coordinate–momentum coupling is introduced from outside. For details, we refer to Section 8.4.

2.6 Do Bottom-Up and Top-Down Approaches to Consciousness Studies in Brain Science Converge to the Same Reality?

It appears that the brain science offers a common platform where the two approaches, viz. the bottom-up (i.e. from "matter" to "mind", from materialism to spirituality, or from tangible to intangible) and the top-down (i.e. from "mind" to "matter", from spirituality to materialism, or from intangible to tangible) ones, can converge to describe the same absolute (!) reality in Nature. From the discussions in preceding sections, it becomes clear that the understanding of the phenomenon of consciousness or of the "mind" seems inadequate in modern scientific terms. This, however, becomes possible if one resorts to use a self-contained and scientifically viable package of Vedic wisdom on consciousness. Such a package will be discussed in Chapter 6 and will be used all through the book. With a view to have some glimpses of this linkage between the two categories of stuff, viz. "mind" and "matter" (in the spirit of category error), here, in what follows, we discuss two situations which, not only offer a feel for these considerations but also the answer to the question posed in the title in the affirmative. Note that one situation is just speculative and based on some analogous results in physics whereas, the second situation is somewhat realistic and noticed from some recent studies in brain science.

A. *The question of "category error" and "mind"-"brain" connection*: In physics, we come across several situations when one connects the energies of different categories. For example, (i) we connect mechanical work done (W) with heat energy (H) through the so-called "Joule's constant" (J), viz. $W = JH$; (ii) we connect magnetic moment (μ) of an elementary particle with its spin (S) (or a mechanical quantity like angular momentum) through the so-called gyro magnetic ratio (g) (or, the Lande's g-factor), viz. $\mu = g\ S$ (recall the concept of magnetic shell for the case of orbital angular momentum); and (iii) the famous mass (m) – energy (E) relation in special theory of relativity through the square of the velocity of light (c), viz. $E = mc^2$, which is verifiable in nuclear and elementary particle reactions.

Here, whether these are W and H, or μ and S, or E and m, each member in the pair belongs to different category stuff (or matter) in the respective relation and thus offer cases of "category error" of Ryle and Penrose.

Note that this list of analogies from physics can be extended to psychology and one can add the famous Weber–Fechner law to this list. This law, when written in the form $a_{ex} = \ln a_{ev}$, connects perceived (experience-based psychological intensity) a_{ex} and the actually measured (event-based physical magnitude) a_{ev} versions of a quantity a through a logarithmic-law of correspondence. a_{ex} lies in the domain of consciousness (mind), whereas a_{ev} lies in the domain of physical world (brain). As far as the question of category error in this case is concerned, a logarithmic function connects the two categories unlike a proportionality constant in physics examples.

B. *Neuroscience hints at a plausible mind-brain connection:* Neuroscience studies suggest that every emotion and conscious thought of an individual reflects in the distinct patterns formed in the brain space as a result of firing of electric impulses by brain neurons from different directions. In fact, this firing of neurons takes place in synchronization and to this effect five electro-encephalogram (EEG) bands with certain synchronous frequency ranges, viz. delta (1-3 Hz), theta (4-7 Hz), alpha (8-12 Hz), beta (13-38 Hz) and gamma (39-42 Hz), have been identified. Not only this, it is found that the five bands also characterize the five categories of personality traits, if present in the concerned personality. In this respect, the window of gamma synchronous frequency at about 40 Hz, in particular, is found to offer a threshold for consciousness-initiated brain processes. On the other hand, the personality features related to this band turn out to be similar to a *satoguṇa*-dominated personality as per Vedic wisdom. This kind of striking resemblance in the behavioural domain in the two situations forces one to think of a deep connection between the mental and the neuron-initiated brain processes. For further details, we refer to discussions in Section 9.3.

2.7 Concluding Discussion

The present book is planned to invoke Vedic wisdom in the top-down (i.e. from spirituality to materialism) manner. This particular chapter is devoted to review some recent works on consciousness studies pursued, in the bottom-up (i.e. from materialism to spirituality) manner. To this effect, after listing some analogies of concepts and phenomena from physical theories, a brief survey of century-old problem of mind–body interaction in the Western schools of thinking is carried out. This problem, particularly after recent advancements in brain sciences, has, however, been reduced to the case of mind–brain interaction. In these studies the entity "mind" is considered as a synonym of consciousness. As far as the use of this concept in understanding consciousness is concerned, only a limited success seems to be achieved in spite of tackling the problem concerned from several directions.

It may be mentioned that in recent times the expertise of different disciplines has come together to understand and model the phenomenon of consciousness. It appears that there is no unanimous view about the understanding of consciousness or no unique (or nearly unique) way to describe this phenomenon in totality that occurs at individual, collective and at cosmic levels. While philosophers have yet to arrive at a unified picture, psychologists, on the other hand, have their own way to analyse the data in behavioural and cognitive sciences. Most of the natural scientists outrightly reject the role of consciousness in their theories, some are afraid of treading into this domain, mainly because their philosophy does not give definite clue about the origin and sustenance of this intriguing phenomenon. While brain scientists in terms of neurons and their substructures (microtubules) are able to provide some clue about consciousness, social and economic scientists have their own way to handle the problem. For example, the studies like as to how the social psychology – a manifestation of collective consciousness – gets affected by natural calamities on the one hand, or as to how the fluctuations of share market index affects the psychology of shareholders in society, has become the topic of particular interest in recent years on the other. While physicists seem to discard the role of consciousness in the classical domain, however, are keen to account for it in quantum domain, mainly to justify the probabilistic interpretation of quantum wave function, or its collapse in quantum measurement. In fact, they have a tendency to think that the role of consciousness is important only for microscopic systems.

In brief, we emphasize that whether it is a physical phenomenon (like in quantum measurement or collapse of wave function) or a non-physical one (like processes in human behaviour and experiences), the role of consciousness is bound to be present as long as the human Being is involved in the process. To account for this, a full-fledged theory of consciousness is desirable and, for this, Vedic wisdom offers a case of reasonable, rational and consistent picture for human behaviour and experiences. We plan to pursue this picture in future chapters.

High Skill Exercises and Projects

2.1 "Whether it is 'cosmic consciousness' or the 'localized one (soul)', in either case it acts as a catalyst in all cosmic and/ or worldly processes." Elaborate and justify the meaning of this phrase in the light of verses III.27 and III.28 of *SMBG*.

2.2 Comment on the compatibility of the nature of energy emanating from a source and the nature of the appliance designed for its consumption in physics context. Explain as to how the same concept is applicable for c-energy in a functional human Being vis-à-vis cosmic consciousness energy.

2.3 Explain as to how the focused consciousness works effectively in certain human actions and processes, and thus does wonders in the behavioural domain (cf. Example 2.2.2).

2.4 Following the seminal work of Kahneman on "Thinking, Fast and Slow" write an essay on the psychodrama of "system 1" and "system 2" of Kahneman in the context of economic sciences.

2.5 The concept of "category error" highlighted in Section 2.6 requires further elaboration. Enlarge and explain the list of examples from other disciplines in general and science in particular.

2.6 Following the work of Penrose, explain as to how the concept of microtubules can account for the consciousness aspect of a thought/experience in brain science.

3

Being Spiritual: Thirst of Soul

3.1 Looking for the Elements of Basic Goodness in an Individual

It is the mindset in general, or the EOL ego or self-sense in particular, of an individual that makes the difference between the purest (primordial) and the existing forms of the EOL soul in the sense that the Being b now takes over different levels of description in the patomic model (cf. *fig*. 6.1). Moreover, it is the conscious evolution (Kaushal 2011) of FOUs of an individual that matters in preparing him to know the inherent reality in the world order. Otherwise, an "atheist" is hidden in a believer or a *śaitāna* in a common man in the same way as "GOD IS NO WHERE" (during the pleasure) is contained in "GOD IS NOW HERE" (during the pain). It is just a matter of looking at the things as an observer.

After a survey of different belief systems and their tenets all over and over a period of time, modern researches have shown that there exist certain common elements among all faiths with regard to the evolution of an ideal (!) human race, at least at their foundation stage. These are the followers and the subsequent generations of a prophet that pollute the ideology of the given faith mainly to maintain their separate identity from others often by not updating the tenets as per their changed daily lifestyle. At this stage, the variation, even in a single postulate of the belief system, is enough to create a new model and hence there exists a plurality of faiths. Consequently, this affects the way of life of the respective followers at the mundane level. In fact, the tencts of a faith are meant to inculcate "humanism" or a set of human values first in an individual and later in a society of such individuals. While these tenets always remain in the background, they are not often updated for subsequent generations. The latter generations, in fact, are becoming increasingly wiser year after year as the studies in evolutionary biology reveal.

In order that the tenets of a faith should remain eternal and universal, not only their quality at subtle level matters but also the level of development of FOU of their originator matters. Note that besides the quality of tenets in their subsequent follow-up, next come the roles of external parameters defined by the changing society and circumstances. (The word "ideal" above should be considered as a limiting case of the best of all basic qualities pertaining to goodness inside an individual.) This limit definitely exists at all times and in every culture even though for a few individuals or a few societies. Vedic science through "*Sanātana Dharma*" offers one such ideal way of life at least at the foundation or philosophical level. As and when this ideal path of *Sanātana Dharma*" has been polluted at the level of practitioners, a prophet is believed to be born to revive the same in totality or in parts.

An undeniable fact is that there is an element of basic goodness (EBG) in everyone – a seed of spirituality and the same grows like anything in the prophet of a faith model or belief system. The prophet first experiences in himself some or all these EBGs and then tries to tune or awaken them in common masses. Despite everyone already having these EBGs inside him, they are somehow suppressed for a number of reasons attributed to his own actions performed at the level of micro- and gross-bodies. Thus, only a few persons actually get tuned to that particular faith. Another undeniable fact is that the faith model, originating from an individual prophet, has space–time boundary as it explores and propagates only a countable and a particular set of hidden EBGs out of a lot present already in a person. This, in turn, appeals only to limited ones and thereby defines their "faith model"; otherwise the best of all EBGs characterizes the same innermost existence, i.e. soul of a human Being. Often the name of the faith model is coined after the explorer prophet. In spite of the efforts of the followers to universalize such a faith model, it still remains space–time dependent. Followers survive only with sharply defined boundaries and ideologies. What will actually happen when a number of anonymous prophets contribute to this kind of exploration of EBGs hidden inside an individual and that too over a long period of time with varying experiences? Obviously, the resulting faith model would cover a bigger set of EBGs and will hardly depend on the boundaries of space–time or limited to a few individuals or societies. Its revival, of course, becomes a necessity from time to time in accordance with the changed environment of a person or of a society but without questioning the "backbone" of the model. Such is the faith model of *Sanātana Dharma* contained in Vedic wisdom. It is neither the imposed faith nor is the model in a strict sense but a "way of life". With regard to the quality of tenets in *Sanātana Dharma* note the following analogy:

Example 3.1.1: With regard to any household appliance, note that the manufacturing company supplies a manual and the same is followed by all users (irrespective of their social status) so that the appliance works properly. The same is the case with the manual provided by the Great Seers of *Sanātana Dharma* in the form of the scriptures and the evergreen tenets written therein for running the life rather ideally.

Next, we discuss as to how the pure form of SO gets polluted to give rise to the innermost composite existence, the so-called Being b – a "polluted version" of SO. In Sections 3.3 and 3.4 we look for the common sources of origin of both animate and inanimate in the Universe within the frameworks of modern science and of Vedic science, respectively. In Section 3.5, we argue as to how the concepts of Vedic science take over those of modern science as of today and thus assist a person to become spiritual. A justification to the common saying that "human Being is a true miniature of cosmos" is sought in this section. In Section 3.6, certain laws in human behaviour and experiences are emphasized which, if followed by an individual, make the person spiritual.

3.2 Pure and Polluted Versions of SO

The EOL SO never participates in an action performed by a human Being (Kaushal 2015) neither at the micro (mental) nor at the macro (gross or physical) body level. It only provides a background of consciousness which in turn illuminates the remaining EOLs to make them functional. As such, the droplet SO of the ocean of Φ_{cc} field is the purest representative inside a Being; it, however, gets polluted once it becomes functional through EOLs B, SE, M, I and E. This is mainly because each EOL, when in action, draws power from the source SO and in return leaves behind some imprints (which, of course, are stored temporarily for the case of a *yogī* and permanently for a common category of persons) in SO as the outcome of actions performed by the Being. While the quantity of these imprints in SO varies from person to person, a fraction of them is also carried over by the Being from one lifespan to another in most of the cases. In fact, carried-over imprints in the new lifespan further reflect in the actions of the Being as *prārabdha*. This phenomenon, although known to occur with human Beings, but it is hardly noticed with other living Beings perhaps due to their expressing capacity and other limitations. It appears that God has co-opted human Being as co-creator by way of giving him highly developed M, I and E. This, in fact, makes him different from other species in the world, whose mind and instincts function only for the basic needs and survival.

No doubt, the concept of good and bad deeds is relative, but as such, it is defined with reference to a particular faith model. As far as the above-mentioned EBGs are concerned, they are above all such pairs of opposites. Note that at the level of SO the seed of all these EBGs continue to remain despite all odds that may occur at lower hierarchy. When the so-called "good" deed at the lower level is performed, it gives an element of satisfaction at the innermost level. On the other hand, when the so-called "bad" deed is performed, it also pinches at that level. It is only the EOL, E, in conjunction with I and M that interprets the "bad" as a "good" or the vice versa for an elusive satisfaction of a lower category. This normally happens when the "bad" deed occurs for the first time; otherwise, the lower hierarchy later becomes habitual for supplying convenient interpretations which result in illusive satisfactions for a limited period of time. In absolute sense, these EBGs are the qualities of SO or indirectly that of the Φ_{cc} field. Note that this quota never diminishes in an individual.

Now the question arises as to how the purest form of SO (PUSO) characterized by the EBGs becomes a polluted form of SO (POSO) when it is inside B and also in action through other EOLs. The answer to this question can be sought again in several stages in accordance with three main causes responsible for the nature of the outcome of a deed performed by a person and described in Vedic science as *prārabdha*, *sañcita* and *kriyamāna* (cf. table 3.1, entry 2 of Kaushal 2011). Then first cause, *prārabdha*, is linked with the deeds of previous birth(s) of a person whereas the latter two are linked with the deeds in a given birth. Here, we shall concentrate on the details of the first one only and look for an underlying mechanism that converts the PUSO to POSO at the very primordial stage. Although modern science has yet to accept the rebirth theory of Vedic science, the former still does not have a convincing unified theory for the origin of both Beings and non-Beings at the primordial level. We shall return to some of these details in later sections.

3.3 Search for a Common Source of Origin of Both Beings and Non-Beings in Modern Science

Obviously, the answer to the above query is going to be negative. Particularly, the answer is also negative when the searches are also made in logical terms in various philosophies of the world order and cultures except for those in Jainism and Vedic science. While Jainism, in the opinion of the author, shows limitations in this regard as the postulate of five cosmic elements in it is somewhat unrealistic, Vedic science, on the other hand, provides convincing answer to a scientific mind if the complexities of the underlying philosophy are interpreted in the light of modern science, particularly that of modern physics. We shall pursue this in the next section. Here, however, we make a brief survey of the recent scientific works available on this aspect of common source of origin of Beings and non-Beings. While scientists in general (except for some remarks from the philosophers of science) have not yet started pondering over the answer to such questions right now, evolutionary biologists and astro-particle physicists, in some sense, are approaching the answer rather independently. Astrologers, on the other hand, seem to unnecessarily intersect these parallel studies. As a result, mainly out of confusion, there is emergence of two major classes of people – "theists" and "atheists" – on this same planet earth. At the same time, the laws of modern science particularly those of physics, within which the theories are formulated and experiments are expected to conform to them, they have begun to show limitations (see Section 1.6; Appendices B and C of Kaushal 2011; Weisskopf 1977) even after the bewildering advancements in computational and mathematical tools.

In philosophical terms, while the human Being is a perfect creation of God (in terms of possession of intangible EOLs), according to evolutionary biologists, it is not yet the end-product of this creation. According to Darwin's theory, not only the physical (biological body B) body getting improved in terms of its features but also the working of inner EOLs and functioning of organs like brain and heart (in terms of an improved IQ and EQ health quotients of an average person) can be noticed improving in generations after generations. During the male–female interaction, particularly at the time of conception, there are some biological, chemical and biochemical reactions that lead to the creation of an improved human Being. Further, there exist varieties of ways in which this interaction between the male and female takes place for the animal, plant and bacterial kingdoms. In some cases both male and female counterparts are not required, even a single organism is sufficient to have reproduction. The characteristics of species are also preserved during these creations/reactions. Peculiar are the ways of the Supreme Being to run the world and its order!

According to modern science, once the seed is germinated in the case of human Being, the so-called perfect creation, then the rest remains the game of biological, chemical and biochemical reactions in addition to the physical environment available inside the womb for further evolution of the germinated seed. In fact, scientific theories do not account for anything beyond these processes; for example, for the effect of mindsets of the participating male and female or for their level of evolution or for the circumstances in which the couple is placed. In terms of genetics, the genes of male and female are supposed to carry some of these features but in what way and to what extent, that has not been understood so far. In the womb of a mother, the germinated seed, embryo, evolves and grows in a big way for about nine months. During this period the growth and development of the foetus in terms of physical and biological features, passes through all the stages that a vertebrate species has passed through over a period of billions of years to attain the present shape and size of a human. What a startling similarity Nature offers for an evolutionary biologists! After about nine months when the baby comes out of the womb, its external features are often found to resemble with those of parents or of grandparents in a big way. When one compares the entire set of body-, mind- and soul-based actions of the baby with that of its earlier generations, it is found that in every generation the nature of performance of these actions is not necessarily the same; it differs in several respects and in a substantive way. The genetic engineering or the science of genome is, however, not yet able to explain many of these facts. It is also found that this difference between successive generations is much more for humans than for non-humans. In any case, several uncontrollable parameters are encountered on the way when the analysis of data is carried out in theoretical terms.

With some modifications, similar is the scientific understanding of the origin of other living Beings including the plant and bacterial kingdoms. With regard to the origin of non-beings, the available scientific theories are completely different. This is mainly because of the fact that the physical laws successfully work only for inanimate objects. It has been noticed that as and when the system or the phenomenon under study involves the consciousness or the free will, the well-tested physical laws (as of today) show limitations. Thus the source of origin of non-Beings, i.e. of inanimate matter is considered different from the Beings. According to astrophysicists space and time came into existence only after the Big Bang and it is only later that there was formation of galaxies, stars, solar systems, planets, etc. out of the clusters of elementary particles like quarks, gluons and leptons in addition to some other gauge bosons. First, mesons and nucleons, then nuclei, atoms, molecules and so on, and finally the present picture of universe came into existence. As cooling took place in space, and time passed on after the Big Bang, these structures emerged one after the other.

At this stage, there arises a puzzling question: Inanimate matter itself cannot visualize or realize the creation of space and time; only a conscious Being can have a feel of it. Who noticed the creation of space and time when Big Bang occurred? It is the Being and in particular the human Being, who later became part of the system that was present at the time of Big Bang; may be in the form of a field that is subtler than all known physical fields. Therefore, the consciousness in its cosmic form as a fundamental primordial field or its derivatives in a localized or limited form (like a seed or primordial version of Beings or human Beings) must have been present at the time of Big Bang; the same, in fact, must have noticed not only the events like the Big Bang but also the subsequent evolutes of space and time. Such a puzzling question forces one to think of the existence of a common source of origin of both Beings and non-Beings at the primordial stage; otherwise, the physical theories cannot be more than just the extrapolation of ideas derived mainly from the scanty and ever-changing astrophysical data about this grand creation of God – the Universe.

Like the growth and evolution of embryo in the womb of a mother, there is yet another interesting scientific observation in the laboratory of relativistic heavy ion collisions (RHIC). In RHIC experiments, when ions of heavy atoms like O^{16}, Au^{69} and Pb^{208} collide with each other at ultra-relativistic energies, there is a formation of new "matter" (fire ball) in a highly localized region and for a very short time, the so-called "quark gluon plasma". This new matter, in fact, is found to possess all the features which the matter had produced at the time of Big Bang and later during the fractions of its first few seconds of the Big Bang occurrence. The RHIC experiments support the theory of Big Bang in the same way as the growth and evolution of the embryo in the womb of a mother supports the Darwinian theory of evolution of humans.

Another science with somewhat weaker foundations and poor predictions, that has been growing since the beginning of human race, is the "science of astrology", i.e. the study of influence of stars and planets on the life and behaviour mostly of human Beings. From this point of view, there are three categories of persons all over the globe: One, who do not believe in this science; second, who deniably believe but do not act accordingly and the third who believe and act accordingly as well. The interesting aspect of this science is that its knowledge has been increasingly influencing minds of newer generations in spite of their having a scientific thinking and living in a modern world of science. In some sense, this science of astrology seems to form a bridge between the above two disjoint sets of theoretically and experimentally established scientific truths in bioscience and astro-particle physics. Modern science, however, does not provide any clue for such a linkage whatsoever between them except for the facts that:

i. these are the different wavelength ranges of electromagnetic (EM) radiation coming from different stars and galactic systems beside the gravitational lensing that helps in detecting their existence and other features,

ii. there are electric, magnetic or electromagnetic signals of varying intensity or impulses given to stimulate the brain and subsequently used to study the behaviour of an affected person (for details, see Chapter 9); and

iii. the physical environment available for the evolution of embryo inside the jelly is not the same as the one that exists outside the womb of the mother at the time of birth, mainly because of the presence of another type(!) of consciousness (energy) inside.

Other questions that naturally come to one's mind are:

a. As to why the same laws of physics should work for the matter (in solid, liquid and gaseous states) in the three regions, viz. inside the jelly, outside the jelly but inside the womb and outside the womb, if one wants to understand the phenomenon in theoretical terms,
b. as to how the outer cosmic radiation (including the EM one) is going to affect the growth of different biological organs (chiefly the heart and brain) of the newly-born baby, or else,
c. as to how the mindsets of the mating male and female at the time of conception affect the mental/spiritual growth of the baby at the subtle level.

Though a partial answer to some such questions is already sought by the author (Kaushal 2011) but further details need to be investigated in future sections.

3.4 Search for a Common Source of Origin of Both Beings and Non-Beings in Vedic Science

3.4.1 PRIMORDIAL FIELD AND THE ASSOCIATED MATTER IN VEDIC SCIENCE

In modern times, there are several cults and belief systems in India which do not encourage the practice of the so-called orthodox rituals of *karma-kāṇḍa* (practice component of *Sanātana Dharma*) and also try to comment on their source. They rather believe directly in the prescriptions of Vedas and the Vedic science therein. One such cult is "Arya Samāja", prevailing mostly in the north, and founded by Swami Dayanand Sarasvati about 150 years ago. The philosophy of this cult, derived basically and directly from Vedas, is given in his famous writing – *Satyārtha Prakāśa*. In this book, somehow the reference to the later epics like the *Rāmāyaṇa* and *Mahābhārata*, written after the Vedic period, is minimal.

It may be mentioned that the Vedic *ṛcā* (verses) spoken by and addressed to some anonymous entities, carry absolute truth about the Nature and its creator. In fact, they are more abstract in linguistic terms as compared to other later epics in Sanskrit literature. The aspect of multiple meanings of words, phrases and also of verses as such is well known. At times, the level of understanding of the interpreter of these *ṛcā* with regard to the world order has also been questioned in extracting the meaning(s) of these *ṛcā*. In what follows, we cite some verses of Vedas from this book (cf. eighth *samullāsa*) (Sarasvati 1984) and look for their plausible meanings in the present context:

iyaṁ visṛaṣṭiryata ābabhūva yadi vā dadhe yadi vā na ।
yo asyādhyakṣaḥ parame vyomantso aṅga veda yadi vā na veda ॥ (3.1)
– *Ṛ*V X.129.7

(Oh Man!) know only him and not any other who is creator, sustainer and destroyer, and also responsible for enlightening this multifaceted, all-pervading Creation (*sṛṣṭi* derived from the word *srajana*) in which the entire Universe (or Universes) also constantly undergoes creation, sustenance and destruction.

tama āsīttamasā gūdhamagre 'praketaṁ salilaṁ servmā idam ।
tucchyenābhvapihitaṁ yadāsīttapasastanmahinājāyataikam ॥ (3.2)
– *Ṛ*V X.129.3

Prior to Creation, this entire Universe in its subtle but ether-like form was completely dark, neglected, not even knowable during darkness and was locally embedded in the Creation.

hiraṇyagarbhaḥ samavarttatāgre bhūtasya jātaḥ patireka āsīt ।
sa dādhāra pṛthivīṁ dyāmutemāṁ kasmai devāya haviṣā vidhema ॥
(*ṚV* X.121.1) (3.3)

Oh man! that Creator, who is and would still remain the basis of all glitters like sun, who is the only (unparallel) Master of this Universe, was also present prior to its creation (*prakṛti*). You should not forget him who has given birth to all – ranging from the Earth to the Sun.

And the another one from *Ṛgveda* X.90.2 says:

puruṣa evedaṁ sarvaṁ yadbhūtaṁ yacca bhavyam ।
utāmṛtatvasyeśāno yadannenātirohati ॥ (3.4)

(Oh man!), one who is present in all in totality, imperishable, Master of all Beings and who is beyond the concept of animate and inanimate, is the Creator of the past, present and future of this time-bound Universe.

The verse (3.1) actually defines the Supreme (the Creator of the grand creation, termed as *sṛṣṭi* – a cosmic consciousness field, now onward denoted by Φ_{cc}) in terms of several of its characteristics and emphasizes the creation, sustenance and destruction of the Universe(s) in this grand creation. Before its manifestation, the Universe existed in this grand creation but was covered with darkness or was not noticeable in the absence of consciousness (a characteristic of Φ_{cc}). The Universe in its micro (or seed-like) form while covered with darkness (note that the "darkness" discussed here is with respect to the (cosmic or local) consciousness, unlike the "darkness" discussed in physics which is with respect to the light or in general with respect to the electromagnetic field), was highly localized (or confined). It is only after that that it was illuminated with consciousness, the causal form of the Universe became dynamic manifest form as elaborated in verse (3.2). According to verse (3.3), the cosmic consciousness field, Φ_{cc}, was present even prior to this manifestation. The Universe not only contained *pañca-mahābhūtas* (PMs) in primordial form but also evolved out of a sequential chain in terms of their fineness. Clearly, the *sṛṣṭi* or Φ_{cc} is all in all as far as the creation and the subsequent realization of the Universe(s) via both animate and inanimate substances in it are concerned as per verse (3.4). Now it is a question of developing and understanding the underlying mechanism that has led to the creation of substances out of Φ_{cc}. Other adjectives added to Φ_{cc} in Vedic literature (cf. *SMBG* verses XII.3-4) are expressed as it is unthinkable, all-pervading, imperishable, ineffable, eternal, immobile, unmanifest and immutable. We shall take the spirit of these adjectives in the further development of the subject.

3.4.2 THE SOVEREIGN SCIENCE OF ŚRĪMAD BHAGAVADGĪTĀ

The knowledge of manifest and unmanifest or that of *saguṇa* and *nirguṇa* aspects of divinity is termed as the "Sovereign Science" or the "Sovereign Secret" by the Lord in *SMBG* IX.2. This extremely holy knowledge is directly enjoyable, easy to practise and imperishable. While this secret knowledge inspires and leads a person to spirituality, it is attained by a person with a faith in the Supreme. The science of creation of Beings and non-Beings in this Universe out of Him (i.e. Φ_{cc}) is termed as "His" *māyā* in *SMBG* and described by the Lord in the following verses:

mayā tatamidaṁ sarvaṁ jagadavyaktamūrtinā ।
matsthāni sarvabhūtāni na cāhaṁ teṣvavasthitaḥ ॥ (3.5)

– *SMBG* IX.4

The whole of this Universe is permeated by Me as unmanifest divinity, like ice by water and all Beings dwell on the idea within Me. But, really speaking, I am not present in them.

na ca matsthāni bhūtāni paśya me yogmaiśvaram ।
bhūtabhṛnna ca bhūtastho mamātmā bhūtabhāvanaḥ ॥ (3.6)

– *SMBG* IX.5

Nay, all those Beings abide not in Me; but behold the wonderful power of My Divine Yoga; though the Sustainer and Creator of Beings, Myself in reality dwell not in those Beings.

It is important to note the following five points here in this process of Grand Creation (*sṛṣṭi*):

i. The Lord is Creator,

ii. He is sustainer,

iii. He is present but has no role as such in the creation; everything goes in a self-consistent manner like a catalyst, and

iv. also the creation as such is not present in Him but works well in His presence.

   The example often cited here is that of ice and water which coexist as separate entities; on the other hand, these are the two forms of the same single entity but at times (for a common man) it becomes difficult to visualize/realize them as separate. It is the *māyā* (the ignorance or the limited capacity of understanding the world order associated with an individual Being or with a group of individuals; while the majority remains in dark, these groups of individuals are often in unison with a modelled mindset) that allows one to visualize ice and water as the two separate entities. And

v. the features of Him described in these four points are independent of the creation of Beings or non-Beings via *māyā*.

The question that arises here is how such an entity with these features and details (called Supreme/God) can exist and side by side becomes all-pervading and permeable through all.

A plausible answer to the above question can be extrapolated from the above survey as follows: While God and *sṛṣṭi* are inseparable or they are synonym of each other, one can as well think of such an entity and postulate it without any loss of generality in accordance with the Vedic verses (3.1)-(3.4). In fact, it is the most subtle, fundamental and finest possible field (subtler than the known gravitational- or Higgs-like physical fields) that conforms to all the adjectives listed at the end of Section 3.4.1 and termed here as "cosmic consciousness field" (Φ_{cc}) defining *sṛṣṭi* or the

Grand Creation of the Supreme Creator. It manifests through all Beings via their existence (structure) and actions, and through all non-Beings via their necessary dynamism for the motion in this Universe and that too in the presence of Φ_{cc}. The Universe(s) exists in Φ_{cc} in a subtler, seed- or quantum-like form at micro level. In the same way, as the gravity is embedded in the space, the space (or for that matter all the *PMs* of Vedic science including ether) is embedded in the cosmic consciousness field. While this Φ_{cc} defines (creates) space and time at cosmic scale (via the events like the Big Bang), the same Φ_{cc} at micro level creates space, time and geometry with reference to an individual (human) Being through POSO. Such is the omnipresent, all-pervading and all-covering, the most fundamental field Φ_{cc}.

Next, a few verses in the same chapter of *SMBG* further support these features of Φ_{cc} and also highlight the underlying mechanism responsible for these creations and also for the cause thereof, viz.:

yathā ākāśasthito nityaṁ vāyuḥ sarvatrago mahān ।
tathā sarvāṇi bhūtāni matsthānītyupadhāraya ॥ (3.7)

– *SMBG* IX.6

Just as the extensive and all-pervading air (which is born of ether) always remains in ether, likewise know that all Beings (sprung as they are from My thought) abide in Me.

Further,

prakr̥tiṁ svāmavaṣṭabhya visr̥jāmi punaḥ punaḥ ।
bhūtagrāmamimaṁ kr̥tsnamavaśaṁ prakr̥tervasāt ॥ (3.8)

– *SMBG* IX.8

Laying hold of My Nature, I bring forth, again and again (according to their respective *karma* (action)) this whole multitude of Beings subject to the influence of their own nature.

It is the nature of Beings that is responsible for the entire set of actions performed not only in the domains of causal, micro and gross existences of a person, but also in its societal and Natural existences (cf. Appendix A of Kaushal 2015). These actions do not bind the Lord (God) in general or the PUSO in particular as such; He also remains indifferent and unmatched to them. In another verse, the Lord emphasizes the role of Himself vis-à-vis that of Nature (*prakṛti* or *māyā* – an object of study in all objective sciences) in the performance of this entire set of actions towards the maintenance of both world and cosmic orders and with reference to both Beings and non-Beings, viz.:

mayādhyakṣeṇa prakṛtiḥ sūyate sacarācaram ।
hetunānena kaunteya jagadviparivartate ॥ (3.9)

– *SMBG* IX.10

Again, with Me as the supervisor, Nature brings forth the whole creation, consisting of both animate (Beings) and inanimate (non-Beings); it is due to this cause the wheel of *saṁsāra* is going round, i.e. the world-order is maintained.

These rather localized and limited creations and annihilations (in the ocean of Φ_{cc}) of both animate and inanimate (objects) continue in a self-consistent manner in accordance with "*guṇa guṇesu vartanta* ..." (cf. *SMBG* III.28) and with certain laws relevant to the existence, survival and destruction of both Being and non-Being contents of the Universe. For these creations and annihilations, the Lord also defines the timespan in a symbolic language through the verse:

sarvabhūtāni kaunteya prakṛtiṁ yānti māmikām ।
kalpakṣaye punastāni kalpādau visṛjāmyaham ॥ (3.10)

– *SMBG* IX.7

Arjuna, at the end of every *kalpa* (Brahmā's day) all Beings enter in My *prakṛti* (the Prime Cause) and at the beginning of every *kalpa*, I bring them forth again.

Several interesting points can be noted from this verse:

i. This verse in conjunction with another verse (*SMBG* VIII.17) defines the age of the Universe as 100 days (including nights) of Brahmā. The age of the Universe in solar days so calculated (Kaushal 2006) from Vedic science agrees with that obtained from modern scientific studies as 13.6 billion solar years.

ii. These are only the Beings who enter into or emerge from *prakṛti* (*māyā*) (desolution and evolution in the domain of cause and effect) and not the non-Beings. In fact, the non-Beings are the second-stage creations of consciousness whether at a small scale (like worldly objects for the human Being) or at the cosmic scale (like cosmic elements (*pañca-mahābhūtas*) for the Virāṭ Puruṣa). As a matter of fact, the cause of dynamism that works behind the structure or the motion of a non-Being, in some sense, is the manifestation of cosmic consciousness (Grand Creation) in which it is embedded.

Another point relevant to the present context and emphasized in *SMBG* is the manifestation of the same quantum of consciousness, i.e. soul, in each and all Beings (*SMBG* IX.29). The God Himself is expected to act as the seed (source) of all of them and this is possible only through the Φ_{cc}. The latter aspect is clear from the verse:

yaccāpi sarvabhūtānāṁ bījaṁ tadahamarjuna ।
na tadasti vinā yatsyānmayā bhūtaṁ carācaram ॥ (3.11)

– *SMBG* X.39

Arjuna, I am even that, which is the seed of all Beings. There is no creature, moving or unmoving, which can exist without Me.

As to how the modern scientific mind would absorb these facts about the common origin of both Beings and non-Beings out of the same stuff (Grand Creation or Φ_{cc}) is a big question. We shall look for a plausible answer to this question in the next chapter and develop a consistent theory to this effect using the language of quantum field theory and other concepts of modern physics. Next, we list a few grand correspondences between the mini (human Beings) and the cosmic (*Virāṭ Puruṣa*) existences out of the same Grand Creation Φ_{cc}.

3.5 Human Being as a Miniature (Microcosm) of Cosmos

In Vedic science, the human Being is considered as perfect creation of the Supreme. With this spirit we have analysed its working and the experiences so gathered earlier (Kaushal 2011) within the framework of an atom-like model and also of non-human Beings as a particular case of this general study. Recall that there is a well-known concept in Vedic science, viz. *yathā piṇḍe tathā brahmāṇḍe* (whatever is in the human body, the same is there in the cosmos or the vice versa). The only question remains as to how the *Virāṭ Puruṣa* of cosmos becomes the localized human Being. To this effect, we shall explore the underlying mechanism in the next chapter. It is, however, worthwhile to highlight here certain correspondences between the EOLs of a human Being – a miniature of cosmos – and the concepts introduced above with reference to a *Virāṭ Puruṣa* (Cosmic Man) – a personified version of Φ_{cc} at cosmic scales (cf. Table 3.1).

As far as the structure of the human Being in terms of EOLs is concerned, the arrangement of the latter is considered in a

Table 3.1: Some Analogies between the Mini Version (Human Being) and the Cosmic Version (*Virāṭ Puruṣa*) of the "Grand Creation" (Φ_{cc}) from the Point of View of Field Theory in Physics

Human Being (b)	*Virāṭ Puruṣa* (V)
1. Soul (SO)	Cosmic consciousness field (Φ_{cc})
2. Ego (E)	Cosmic Desire of Creator (Φ_{CE})
3. Intellect (I)	Field of cosmic intelligence (Φ_{CI})
4. Mind (M)	Field of cosmic mind (Φ_{CM})
5. (i) Biological body (B) and the senses of knowledge and action (SE) (matter inside the body in the form of solid, liquid, gas, plasma and ether form);	(i) Field of cosmic elements (Φ_{CEL}) or *pañca-mahābhūtas* (PMs) along with their perception/reception features with reference to gross and micro bodies of b; and
(ii) b is finite with infinite potency, but without its complete use	(ii) V is infinite with infinite potency, but with its perfect use
6. The *jīva* or Being (b)	The *Virāṭ Puruṣa* (V)
7. Worldly objects (WO) or the stimuli therein	Manifest cosmic creation and world order

particular fashion (cf. *fig.* 6.1). If some EOLs in this patomic model are absent, then such species are described by the so-called "fractured" patomic model (Kaushal 2011). Other living Beings in this world are particular cases of this patomic picture. The inanimate objects, on the other hand, are the creations of consciousness either of the *Virāṭ Puruṣa* (cosmic consciousness, realizable via Φ_{cc}) or of the Being (localized consciousness, realizable through SO). The spatio-temporal world is also the creation of this consciousness and the same is viewed differently by human and non-human Beings as each of them has differently developed FOUs. In the process of realization of spatio-temporal world by Beings, the extent to which the details of these inanimate objects can be perceived by an individual or by a group of individuals depends on the degree of development of their FOUs which, in turn, is linked with the *kārmic* theory. However, the universality of the force laws governing the structure and motion of inanimate objects in the universe is reminiscent of the role of *Virāṭ Puruṣa* in their existence and survival.

Note that the present picture of *Virāṭ Puruṣa* is actually the one discussed in Vedic literature. However, other cultures of the world do have similar pictures at gross and mental levels. The styles of performing prayers in different cultures are clear indications of a personified *Virāṭ Puruṣa*. Islamic style of prayer in the morning also hints to this and *SMBG* (cf. Chapter 11) has also clearly indicated to this fact. In recent years the revelation of Christ in Cosmic form (cf. Gomes 2012) has also been discussed. In summary, when a common man is exposed to all or either of the five cosmic elements in Nature, he gets a feel of *Virāṭ Puruṣa* through Φ_{cc} and undergoes a kind of eternal joy, at least momentarily if not permanently, because he feels himself part of the cosmos and in fact he actually is. In some sense this experience is linked with the cosmic existence of a person. The universality of cosmic connections of a person is also clear from the rituals performed in different cultures. For example, recall the ways of disposing of a dead body after the death of a person in different cultures, e.g. the dead body is buried in the ground (cosmic element, Earth) in some cultures like Islam; it is thrown into a flowing water (cosmic element, Water) as in some cults of "Sufi" saints; in some it is exposed in air (cosmic element, Air) to be eaten by birds and vultures; in some it is burnt in the open (cosmic element, Fire) as in Vedic culture and in some it is left on fast unto death (cosmic element, *ākāśa* or Ether) as in *santhārā* process of dying in Jainism. Thus, all the five cosmic elements play a role in the life of human race.

***Example* 3.5.1:** *Two personalities are in race: One is the Master and the other is the disciple: Virāṭ Puruṣa* and the human Beings are like the Master and the disciple. Indeed the latter is the creation of the former; otherwise, it had no existence at all. On the other hand, the former wants the latter to become like Him. For this purpose, He has supplied all possible accessories, whatsoever He had, to the latter. Somehow, the disciple does not use the entire set of accessories supplied by the Master because of his ignorance or self-created boundaries, i.e. his limited free will and self-sense. At times, the Master shows hard time to the disciple to judge his ability of overcoming the self-sense or of using the free will rightly. In this endeavour, the disciple often fails and does not succeed in proving his self like his Master. This continues more or less in a non-stop manner on earthly scales under His constant watch, but there is every possibility that in the end, after long and sustained efforts, perhaps in several cycles of birth and death, the disciple will become like his Master by eliminating all his negativities and deficiencies.

3.6 Universality of Force Laws that Governs the Structure of and the Dynamism in Both Animate and Inanimate Objects

At gross level, there are distinct force laws which govern uniformly but separately the motion and structure of both animate and inanimate objects. In fact, at micro level, there might exist a unified, abstract and generalized version of these laws. Further, the universality of these laws for all species in case of animate and for all varieties of matter in case of inanimate, if established, then it is a direct hint for a common source of origin of both animate and inanimate out of the same Φ_{cc}. For example, the consciousnees through the force of love (cf. Section 8.1; Section 10.6 of Kaushal

2015) – an attribute of the source of consciousness, i.e. soul, is a prerequisite for the existence and coexistence of animates in the same way as the force of gravity is a prerequisite for the existence and coexistence of inanimate. In fact, the latter (in which the entities are bound by spatio-temporal features) are the much later creations in the sequence of evolution, perhaps only after animates came into existence or they became manifest out of Φ_{cc}.

While the conscious objects have self-conscience of varying degree (ranging from zero to infinity among the entire set of species or, for that matter, in each individual of a particular species in itself), the gravity force, on the other hand, does not have independent existence. It is rather a creation of consciousness either at the level of *Virāṭ Puruṣa* or at the level of its miniature Being. Note that the dynamism of an inanimate object with respect to another inanimate object is meaningless (like the objects on the chessboard) but it becomes important with respect to another animate or several animate objects (like the living objects playing the chess). Thus, the gravity or for that matter any other space–time-mediated physical force becomes the creation of consciousness but at the cost of some characteristic features of the object; at the same time it becomes the most fundamental cause in physical theories for the existence of the inanimate. It may be mentioned that both animate and inanimate objects are governed by some well-defined yet distinct laws as far as the role of the originator Φ_{cc} in their creation is concerned. Similar is the case with the structure of both animate and inanimate objects. The detailed structures of both animate and inanimate exist at increasingly subtle levels as a result of some well-defined laws; after all, they both originate from the same Φ_{cc}, of course, at different stages of their evolution.

3.7 Concluding Discussion

Attempts are made in this chapter to find answer of the question as to why a person has to be spiritual. To this effect, a search is made to find a common source of origin of both animate and inanimate stuff in the universe and within the framework of both, modern science and Vedic wisdom. The search initiated in this chapter will continue in the next chapter till a plausible and logical answer to the question in scientific terms is sought.

When one tries to find the "elements of basic goodness" in a person, it turns out that a human Being is more spiritual than being a human (i.e. the causal existence basically dominates the micro and gross existences) as far as his actions towards the world/ cosmic order are concerned. It is the strong attraction or the deep involvement of a Being b in WO (cf. Chapter 6, patomic model) that converts the purest version of SO into a polluted one via various (both outer and inner) EOLs, which again work under the influence of three modes (*guṇas*) of Nature. In spite of all this, the thirst or journey of soul continues in the search of *mokṣa* (liberation), preferably following a spiritual path. In fact, the liberation basically is the merging of finite SO into the infinite Φ_{cc} over a period of time, which in most cases, if necessity arises, may span to several births and only a few Beings succeed in this endeavour. All this becomes possible if one understands the common source of origin of both animate and inanimate and its functioning to this effect. No doubt, the modern science, based on modelling game, has offered quantifiable and measurable truth in this regard but that objective truth remains only a partial truth. The studies are not holistic in the sense that the subjective or realizable aspect of absolute reality is not accommodated in the modelling game. For this purpose one has to look into philosophy and in which every aspect is not quantifiable, a great deal of it is left for realization and that too by an enlightened individual.

"b–V correspondence" and realization of "cosmic connections": We have noticed from Table 3.1 that there exists an elegant correspondence (termed as "b–V correspondence") between the human Being b and the *Virāṭ Puruṣa* V of *SMBG*. Interestingly, this correspondence can be noticed at every level of description, i.e. from WO to SO level. It is the extent of realization of such "cosmic connections" by an individual that works behind various mechanisms known for this

purpose. The realization process in this work is translated into the "dressing" of EOLs or of *PM*s with consciousness and quantified through the increasing values of the meditation variable μ. In the next chapter, we shall see as to how the infinite order of dressing of a *PM* or of an EOL with consciousness develops the tendency to merge into Φ_{cc}, suggesting a meaning to *mokṣa* (liberation). In fact, the merging of b into V or Φ_{cc} through different levels of description implies different ways of worshipping the Supreme.

While the Vedic scriptures clearly emphasize on the existence and its role towards the maintenance of cosmic order (cf. Section 3.4), this Φ_{cc}, in different cultures of the world, is known by different names. As a matter of fact, this Φ_{cc} always remains in the background in the existence and working of all (animate) Beings and in the existence of inanimate, in the spirit of the meaning of the phrase of Vedic science, viz. *satcidānanda* – an embodiment of existence, knowledge and bliss (cf. Section 2.1). In Table 3.2, we present some conceptual trios of Vedic science that support the meaning of this

Table 3.2: Understanding the Consciousness at Different Levels of Human Existences in the Sense of Increasing Gross Features, Mainly in Terms of Some Trios of Vedic Science

Human Existence and Its Role in WO	*Three Worlds*	*Three Type of Matter: A Vedic View*	*Three Components of a Religion or of a Scientific Study*	*Remarks on Consciousness Studies (Subtlety of Consciousness Field; Ādi Śaṅkara)*
1. Causal ($\mathcal{C}$) (realization)	W_1	SEP (special-epiphysical)	*Jñāna* (J) (Theory); shaped by three *guṇas*	Studies of *cidākāśa* (absolute reality; pure consciousness; cosmic connections; matter of realization and its intensity)
2. Micro ($\mathcal{M}$) (meditation)	W_2	EP (epiphysical)	*Upāsanā* (U) (methodology): shaped by three *guṇas*	Studies of *cittākāsa* (reality pertaining to perception; space-time-consciousness mediated; matter of meditation and its intensity)
3. Gross ($\mathcal{G}$) (perception)	W_3	P (physical)	*Karma* (K) (Experiment); shaped by three *gunās*	Studies of *bhūtākāśa* (reality based on quantification and measurement; analogies and modelling; space-time mediated; matter of perception and its intensity)

phrase and assign a place value to "cosmic connections" in this context. In fact, Table 3.2 displays a philosophical roadmap to study the subject of psychoscience, mainly through three existences of a person in the field of worldly objects and stimuli, viz. through causal (astral), micro and gross existences.

High Skill Exercises and Projects

3.1 "These are the 'elements of basic goodness' present in an individual or in the tenets of a religion, that are responsible for the maintenance of both the world and cosmic orders." Explain and justify this statement with examples from various cults.

3.2 Explain as to how the purest form of SO becomes polluted when it is embedded in and fully functional through the EOL B.

3.3 In the light of discussions in Sections 3.3 and 3.4, and keeping in mind both Vedic wisdom and modern science, write an essay on the possibility of a common source origin of both – "Beings and non-Beings" in the Universe.

3.4 Make an attempt to justify the correspondences shown in Table 3.1 between the microcosm (b) and the *Virāṭ Puruṣa* (V) in the light of Indian Sufi philosophy expressed through Hindi couplets

pānī kā hai bud-budā aisā mānasa kī jāta ।
dekhat hi chipa jāta hai jyoṅ tārā parabhāt ॥

Human life is like a bubble in the ocean, which disappears in the same way and as a star in the morning.

jala meiṅ kumbha, kumbha meiṅ jala hai bāhara bhītara pānī ।
phūṭā kumbha jala jalahi samāno yaha tatha katho jñānī ॥

Human Being is like a pot filled with water and placed in the ocean of consciousness; as the pot breaks, its water disappears in the ocean.

3.5 Elaborate on the "b-V correspondence" as discussed in Table 3.1 and thereby comment on as to how one is inspired to have a feel for cosmic connections.

4

Vedic Concepts Take Over Modern Science

A Theory of Procreation

As we have seen in Section 3.3, the modern science as of today does not provide hint to any common source of origin of both animate and inanimate objects in this Universe. However, in the disjoint fields of evolutionary biology and astroparticle physics separately we have seen the evolutions of animate and inanimate objects, keeping aside the question of a common source (the answer to which in modern science seems to remain only a far cry). Moreover, the scientists of atheist category are afraid of treading into the phenomena involving consciousness for this purpose and those of theist category, somehow, are not fully aware of the intricacies and details of consciousness either in an individual or in the cosmos. The Vedic science, as we have seen in the previous chapter, seems to provide some plausible answers to such questions with reference to the conscious Self and its cosmic version. In this chapter, we shall strengthen the concept of "b–V correspondence" and "cosmic connections" highlighted in Section 3.7. With regard to the details of the underlying mechanism, although the philosophy of the same is quite transparent in the Vedic verses, the question remains as to how to put it in a quantifiable form, particularly in the context of modern science. Such an effort, comprehensible to a scientific mind, is made in this chapter. The Vedic science in this endeavour has perhaps gone much ahead of the modern science. To this effect, we prepare a ground for the theory of procreation by starting with a discussion on dressing rules of an object with consciousness.

4.1 Epi-physical Matter and the Evolution of Physical Matter with Consciousness

Three categories of matter in the Universe have been discussed earlier (Kaushal 2011, 2015). First, the physical (P-) matter, which exists even in the absence of consciousness; second, the epi-physical (EP-) matter, which basically is the P-matter but becomes cognizable after it gets illuminated by consciousness (irrespective of whether the source of consciousness is cosmic or a localized soul). As the intensity of this illuminating energy increases, the P-matter starts revealing its increasingly finer details in terms of its structure, properties and finally its cosmic connections that exist in a domain beyond space time. This happens in the same way as a physical instrument with an increasing resolving power reveals finer and finer details of the object at different space–time (energy) scales. The third category is the special epi-physical (SEP-) matter, in which the source of consciousness in EP-matter is also present, e.g. a functional body of a living Being. In fact, for a functional Being, this non-stop supply of consciousness to illuminate the P-matter is termed here as the dressing (or the evolution) of P-matter with consciousness.

In mathematical terms, during dressing this non-stop supply of consciousness energy (termed as "cenergy") to P-matter could be in either a discrete or continuous form. By and large in this book we shall consider discrete evolution through some symbolic recurrent relations (called "dressing rules"). Continuous evolution, however, can be accounted by the use of difference or differential equations. An example to this effect is discussed in Appendix A with reference to the study of some mental processes. In what follows, we shall frame certain dressing rules in the light of Vedic wisdom, separately for *pañca-mahābhūtas* in which a Being is left for survival and for EOLs which make the human Being functional. An important and inherent hypothesis (based on the observations of great seers of highest realization), used in this chapter, is that "an infinitely dressed version of P-matter with consciousness has the tendency to merge into the source of consciousness or it develops the quality of identification with the source".

4.2 Pañcīkaraṇa Rule of Vedic Science and Its Possible Generalizations

4.2.1 PAÑCĪKARAṆA RULE OF VEDIC SCIENCE AND ASSOCIATED TANMĀTRAS

The *pañcīkaraṇa* rule in Indian philosophy, through the concept of *tanmātras*, offers (Kaushal 2011) a wonderful theory of interaction between an individual and the physical world including the explanations of various bioclinical and biomedical phenomena in Āyurveda and of fundamental processes taking place in human behaviour and experiences. According to the Vedānta philosophy, whole physical world is made up of five cosmic (subtle) elements (*pañca-mahābhūtas* (*PMs*)), viz. earth (E_a), water (W), air (A), fire (F) and ether (E_t) and the *pañci-karaṇa* rule makes an individual to perceive these *PMs*. As a matter of fact, these *PMs*, in the language of modern science, can be considered as five states of matter, viz. the earth for all solids, the water for all liquids, the air for all gases, the fire for all plasma states and the ether state of matter in which all the remaining four elements are contained, and the existence of the same is yet to be confirmed in the relativity theory (e.g. Michelson–Morley type) experiments in physics.

According to this rule (Ādi Śaṅkara 1962; Shukla 1992) a perceived (also called *pañcīkṛta*) *mahābhūta*, say, for example, the perceived earth, is the sum total of 50 per cent of physical (*apañcīkṛta*) earth and of 12.5 per cent of each of the remaining four *mahābhūtas*. The same is the case with other perceived *mahābhūtas*. Symbolically, one can thus write the five perceived *mahābhūtas* by an individual as

$$\tilde{E}_a^{(1)} = (1/2)E_a + (1/8)W + (1/8)A + (1/8)F + (1/8)E_t \quad (4.1a)$$

$$\tilde{W}^{(1)} = (1/2)W + (1/8)A + (1/8)F + (1/8)E_t + (1/8)E_a \quad (4.1b)$$

$$\tilde{A}^{(1)} = (1/2)A + (1/8)F + (1/8)E_t + (1/8)E_a + (1/8)W \quad (4.1c)$$

$$\tilde{F}^{(1)} = (1/2)F + (1/8)E_t + (1/8)E_a + (1/8)W + (1/8)A \quad (4.1d)$$

$$\tilde{E}_t^{(1)} = (1/2)E_t + (1/8)E_a + (1/8)W + (1/8)A + (1/8)F. \quad (4.1e)$$

As a matter of fact, during the process of perception of a *mahābhūta* it is the consciousness of a Being which dresses up the *mahābhūta* and thus makes the same perceivable from its nascent (physical) version. The superscript "(1)" on various quantities on the left hand side of Eq. (4.1) indicates that this dressing of a *mahābhūta* with consciousness has taken place in the lowest (first) order and thereby making it perceivable and confirms its existence. In mathematical terms, this process of dressing of an object with consciousness can continue in increasingly higher orders and, accordingly, the perceiver enriches his faculty of understanding (FOU) with more and more knowledge about the perceived object. The five *tanmātras* postulated in Vedic science, viz. τ_{ea}, τ_w, τ_a, τ_f and τ_{et} correspond to five quanta of interaction of five senses of knowledge of an individual with five cosmic elements in the order, earth–smell–nose, water–taste–tongue, air–touch–skin, fire–light–eyes and ether–word–ears. For example, the interaction of the human Being *b* with the nascent version of earth, E_a, can be expressed symbolically as: $b + E_a = b' + (\tau_{ea} + E_a) = b' + \tilde{E}_a$, where $\tilde{E}_a$ is the dressed version of E_a and the same now becomes an EP-matter, and b' is the enlightened version of the human Being b. Similarly, one can understand the role of other *tanmātras*.

4.2.2 HIGHER-ORDER DRESSINGS OF PMs

At the first level of generalization, we consider the repeated dressing (or evolution) of an object with consciousness that reveals increasingly finer details about it. In mathematical terms, an object can evolve (or dress) with consciousness in two distinct ways: viz. in the spirit of Eq. (4.1) and through a differential equation in which the meditation variable appears as an independent variable (cf. Appendix A). Clearly, here we are following the case of discrete evolution through Eq. (4.1) and write the second-order dressing, for example, of the *mahābhūta* E_a as

$$\tilde{E}_a^{(2)} = (1/2)\tilde{E}_a^{(1)} + (1/8)\,\tilde{W}^{(1)} + (1/8)\tilde{A}^{(1)} + (1/8)\tilde{F}^{(1)}\ (1/8)\tilde{E}_t^{(1)}$$

$$= \frac{20}{64}E_a + \frac{11}{64}W + \frac{11}{64}A + \frac{11}{64}F + \frac{11}{64}E_t, \tag{4.2}$$

where the results of Eq. (4.1) are used. In the same vein, the third- and fourth-order dressed versions of E_a in terms of nascent *PMs* are given by

$$\tilde{E}_a^{(3)} = \frac{124}{512}E_a + \frac{97}{512}W + \frac{97}{512}A + \frac{97}{512}F + \frac{97}{512}E_t \tag{4.3}$$

$$\tilde{E}_a^{(4)} = \frac{884}{4096}E_a + \frac{803}{4096}W + \frac{803}{4096}A + \frac{803}{4096}F + \frac{803}{4096}E_t. \tag{4.4}$$

and the similar expressions exist for $\tilde{W}^{(3)}$, $\tilde{W}^{(4)}$, $\tilde{A}^{(3)}$, $\tilde{A}^{(4)}$, $\tilde{F}^{(3)}$, $\tilde{F}^{(4)}$ and $\tilde{E}_t^{(3)}$, $\tilde{E}_t^{(4)}$.

For further details about dressing rules, we refer to our earlier work (Kaushal 2011, 2015). Here, however, we only give expressions for the nth-order dressing of *PMs* in terms of their $(n-1)^{\text{th}}$-order dressing with a view to have a feel for the computational details, viz.:

$$\tilde{E}_a^{(n)} = (1/2)\tilde{E}_a^{(n-1)} + (1/8)\tilde{W}^{(n-1)} + (1/8)\tilde{A}^{(n-1)} + (1/8)\tilde{F}^{(n-1)} + (1/8)\tilde{E}_t^{(n-1} \tag{4.5a}$$

$$\tilde{W}^{(n)} = (1/2)\tilde{W}^{(n-1)} + (1/8)\tilde{A}^{(n-1)} + (1/8)\tilde{F}^{(n-1)} + (1/8)\tilde{E}_t^{(n-1)} + (1/8)\,\tilde{E}_a^{(n-1)} \tag{4.5b}$$

$$\tilde{A}^{(n)} = (1/2)\tilde{A}^{(n-1)} + (1/8)\tilde{F}^{(n-1)} + (1/8) + \tilde{E}_t^{(n-1)} + (1/8) + \tilde{E}_a^{(n-1)} + (1/8) + \tilde{W}^{(n-1)} \tag{4.5c}$$

$$\tilde{F}^{(n)} = (1/2)\tilde{F}^{(n-1)} + (1/8)E_t^{(n-1)} + (1/8)\tilde{E}_a^{(n-1)} + (1/8)\tilde{W}^{(n-1)} + (1/8)\tilde{A}^{(n-1)} \tag{4.5d}$$

$$\tilde{E}_t^{(n)} = (1/2)\tilde{E}_t^{(n-1)} + (1/8)\tilde{E}_a^{(n-1)} + (1/8)\tilde{W}^{(n-1)} + (1/8)\tilde{A}^{(n-1)} + (1/8)\tilde{F}^{(n-1)} \tag{4.5e}$$

with

$$\tilde{E}_a^{(n)} + \tilde{W}^{(n)} + \tilde{A}^{(n)} + \tilde{F}^{(n)} + \tilde{E}_t^{(n)} = E_a + W + A + F + E_t, \tag{4.6}$$

by construction. If we denote the set of nth-order dressed *PM*s as $\tilde{P}M^{(n)} = \{\tilde{E}_a^{(n)}, \tilde{W}^{(n)}, \tilde{A}^{(n)}, \tilde{F}^{(n)}, \tilde{E}_t^{(n)}\}$, then the variation of the dressing fraction δ with the order of dressing for a nascent *mahābhūta* and for each dressed *mahābhūta* is shown in Table 4.1. Here the numbers are presented in the same order as the elements appearing in the set $\tilde{P}M^{(n)}$. The behaviour of δ as a function of *n* is also displayed in *fig.* 4.1 for both dominating (solid curve) and non-dominating (dashed curve) terms in this generalized version of *pañcīkaraṇa* rule.

As an extension or the next level generalization of the *pañcī-karaṇa* rule (4.1) of Vedic science, we pursue it with reference to five EOLs, viz. two outer EOLs B and SE, and three inner EOLs M, I and E. Note that these two types of EOLs work at different scales of consciousness through meditation variable μ.

Table 4.1: Relative Contribution of the Nascent E_a W, A, F and E_t in the Construction of Their Dressed Versions in Different Orders

Dressed Mahā-bhūta	*δ Correspon-ding to $\tilde{PM}^{(n)}$*	*δ Correspon-ding to $\tilde{PM}^{(n)}$*	*δ Correspon-ding to $\tilde{PM}^{(n)}$*	*δ Correspon-ding to $\tilde{PM}^{(n)}$*
E_a	(0.50.0.125, 0.125, 0.125, 0.125)	(0.313, 0.172, 0.172, 0.172, 0.172)	(0.242, 0.189, 0.189, 0.189)	(0.216, 0.196, 0.196, 0.196, 0.196)
W	(0.125, 0.50, 0.125, 0.125, 0.125)	(0.172, 0.313, 0.172, 0.172, 0.172)	(0.189, 0.242, 0.189, 0.189, 0.189)	(0.196, 0.216, 0.196, 0.196, 0.196)
A	(0.125, 0.125, 0.50, 0.125, 0.125)	(0.172, 0.172, 0.313, 0.172, 0.172)	(0.189, 0.189, 0.242, 0.189, 0.189)	(0.196, 0.196, 0.216, 0.196, 0.196)
F	(0.125, 0.125, 0.125, 0.50, 0.125)	(0.172, 0.172, 0.172, 0.313) 0.172)	(0.189, 0.189, 0.189, 0.242, 0.189)	(0.196, 0.196, 0.196, 0.216, 0.196)
E_t	(0.125, 0.125, 0.125, 0.125, 0.50)	(0.172, 0.172, 0.172,, 0.172, 0.313)	(0.189, 0.189, 0.189, 0.189, 0.242)	(0.196, 0.196, 0.196, 0.196, 0.216)

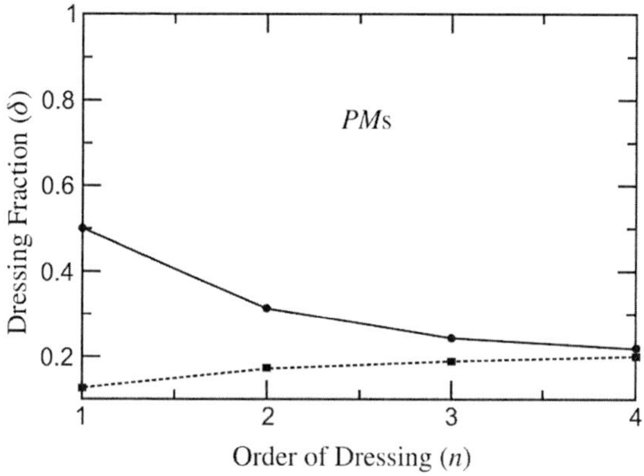

fig. 4.1: Behaviour of the dressing fraction (δ) as a function of the order of dressing (*n*) for *pañca-mahābhūtas*. Note that δ decreases for the dominating *mahābhūta* (solid curve) and increases for the non-dominating *mahābhūta* (dashed curve) with *n*

4.3 Dvikaraṇa and Trikaraṇa Rules of Dressing for EOLs with Consciousness

Similar to the *pañcīkaraṇa* rule (4.1), another *pañcīkaraṇa* rule for the EOLs B, SE, M, I and E has been discussed earlier (see Kaushal 2011, eq. (8.1)). Note that while the dressing of these five EOLs with consciousness goes uniformly for all in the lowest order, in the second and higher orders, however, the dressing affects these EOLs differently and at different scales. As a result, this *pañcīkaraṇa* rule splits into a *tri-karaṇa* rule for $\tilde{M}^{(1)}$, $\tilde{I}^{(1)}$ and $\tilde{E}^{(1)}$, and a *dvi-karaṇa* rule for $\tilde{B}^{(1)}$, and $\tilde{SE}^{(1)}$. However, the dressings of B and SE beyond 2nd order are not required in real life since the biological processes take over after that. Therefore, we concentrate here on the *trikaraṇa* rule and, accordingly we write the second-order dressings of M, I and, E as,

$$\tilde{M}^{(2)} = (1/2)\tilde{M}^{(1)} + (1/4)\tilde{I}^{(1)} + (1/4)\tilde{E}^{(1)}, \tag{4.7a}$$

$$\tilde{I}^{(2)} = (1/2)\tilde{I}^{(1)} + (1/4)\tilde{E}^{(1)} + (1/4)\tilde{M}^{(1)}, \tag{4.7b}$$

$$\tilde{E}^{(2)} = (1/2)\tilde{E}^{(1)} + (1/4)\tilde{M}^{(1)} + (1/4)\tilde{I}^{(1)}, \tag{4.7c}$$

and similarly for the nth-order dressing as

$$\tilde{M}^{(n)} = (1/2)\ \tilde{M}^{(n-1)} + (1/4)\tilde{I}^{(n-1)} + (1/4)\tilde{E}^{(n-1)} \tag{4.8a}$$

$$\tilde{I}^{(n)} = (1/2)\ \tilde{I}^{(n-1)} + (1/4)\tilde{E}^{(n-1)} + (1/4)\tilde{M}^{(n-1)} \tag{4.8b}$$

$$\tilde{E}^{(n)} = (1/2)\ \tilde{E}^{(n-1)} + (1/4)\tilde{M}^{(n-1)} + (1/4)\tilde{I}^{(n-1)}, \tag{4.8c}$$

with

$$\tilde{M}^{(n)} + \tilde{I}^{(n)} + \tilde{E}^{(n)} = \tilde{M}^{(1)} + \tilde{I}^{(1)} + \tilde{E}^{(1)}. \tag{4.9}$$

For the above *tri-karaṇa* rule, an analysis similar to that of the *pañcīkaraṇa* rule of Section 4.2 has been carried out and again up to the fourth-order. The numerical results so obtained are listed in Table 4.2 for $\tilde{M}^{(n)} = \{\tilde{M}^{(n)}, \tilde{I}^{(n)}, \tilde{E}^{(n)}\}$ and for n = 1, 2, 3, 4 and the corresponding behaviour of the dressing fraction δ as a function of n is displayed in *fig.* 4.2 for both the dominating (solid curve) and non-dominating (dashed curve) EOLs.

Table 4.2: Relative Contribution of the nascent M, I and E in the Construction of Their Dressed Version in Different Orders

Dressed Inner EOL	*δ Corresponding to* $\tilde{M}^{(1)}$	*δ Corresponding to* $\tilde{M}^{(2)}$	*δ Corresponding to* $\tilde{M}^{(3)}$	*δ Corresponding to* $\tilde{M}^{(4)}$
M	(0.50, 0.125, 0.125)	(0.312, 0.219, 0.219)	(0.266, 0.242, 0.242)	(0.254, 0.248, 0.248)
I	(0.125, 0.50, 0.125)	(0.219, 0.312, 0.219)	(0.242, 0.266, 0.242)	(0.248, 0.254, 0.248)
E	(0.125, 0.125, 0.50)	(0.219, 0.219, 0.312)	(0.242, 0.242, 0.266)	(0.248, 0.248, 0.254)

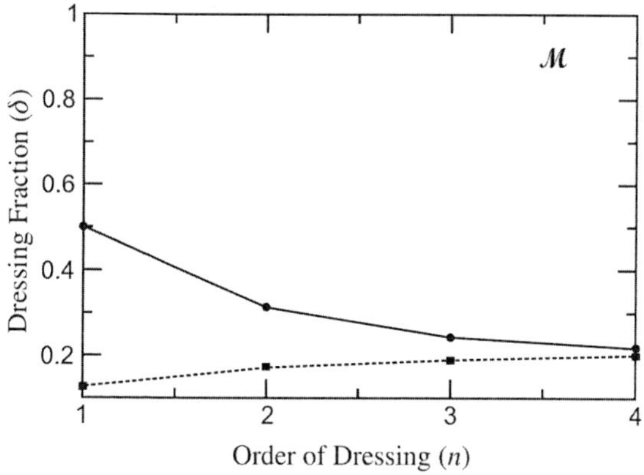

fig. 4.2: Behaviour of the dressing fraction (δ) as a function of the order of dressing (*n*) for inner EOLs. Note that δ decreases for the dominating EOL (solid curve) and increases for the non-dominating EOLs (dashed curve) with *n*

4.4 Analysis of Results and the Effect of Infinite Dressing

4.4.1 EFFECT OF DRESSING IN THE LIMIT WHEN $n \to \infty$ AND TRANSCENDING OF COSMIC CONNECTIONS

Note that at initial stages of the dressing (small *n*) of a *mahābhūta* with consciousness only the existence of the latter in terms of its colour, shape, size and geometry appears. At the next stage, when *n* increases further the consciousness successively explores in the object its nature and subsequently its structure, substructure, history, etc. It is at these later stages when the pure consciousness emanating from SO, in conjunction either with M, I or E separately or with their pairs or with all the three of them together assist in the exploration of the external object to a maximum possible extent and thereby starts noticing in it some kind of cosmic connections and thereby identifies it with Φ_{cc}. As a matter of fact, the level of understanding of an individual goes on increasing or his faculty of understanding becomes increasingly sharper with increasing *n* or by intensifying his meditation.

It can be seen from Table 4.1 that the dressing fraction δ decreases for the dominating *mahābhūta* and increases for the non-dominating *mahābhūta* with *n*. All this happens in such a way that in the limit when $n \to \infty$, δ for both dominating and non-dominating *mahābhūtas* tends to attain the same value (cf. *fig.* 4.1), meaning thereby that all *PMs* (whether dominating or not) become identical in the limiting case in their infinitely dressed versions. In some sense, each of them attains all or maximum attributes of the source of consciousness SO. Thus, whether one worships earth, water, air, fire or ether or any of their composites, it leads to the same Supreme state.

4.4.2 JÑĀNA, KARMA AND BHAKTI YOGĪS OF SMBG

Next we analyse the results of dressing of inner EOLs (cf. Table 4.2 and *fig.* 4.2). In this case, the lowest order dressing makes both, the inner EOLs M, I and E, and the outer EOLs B and SE, functional jointly. Their successive dressings with consciousness later makes them more and more efficient in different proportions as far as the inner and outer EOLs are concerned (Kaushal 2011) since they work at different scales of consciousness. In this case also, the varying trend of δ with the order of dressing *n* is the same as for the *PMs*, i.e. it decreases for the dominating inner EOL and increases for non-dominating inner EOL. Here, however, the dressing fraction δ attains the same value for both dominating and non-dominating EOLs faster with *n* as compared to the case for *PMs*. In other words, the dressing of an inner EOL somehow becomes more intense than that for an external *mahābhūta*.

In the limit when $n \to \infty$ note that all the three inner EOLs attain the same value of the dressing fraction, though a little higher than that for *PMs*. In the language of *SMBG*, whether one proceeds through the path of devotion (i.e. by way of dressing the mind $\tilde{M}^{(n\to\infty)}$), through the path of reasoning (i.e. by way of dressing the intellect $\tilde{I}^{(n\to\infty)}$) or through the path of knowledge (i.e. by way of dressing the ego $\tilde{E}^{(n\to\infty)}$); in either case one becomes capable of achieving the same Supreme state or accordingly becomes *bhakti*, *karma* or *jñāna yogī* respectively. As a matter of fact, the observations

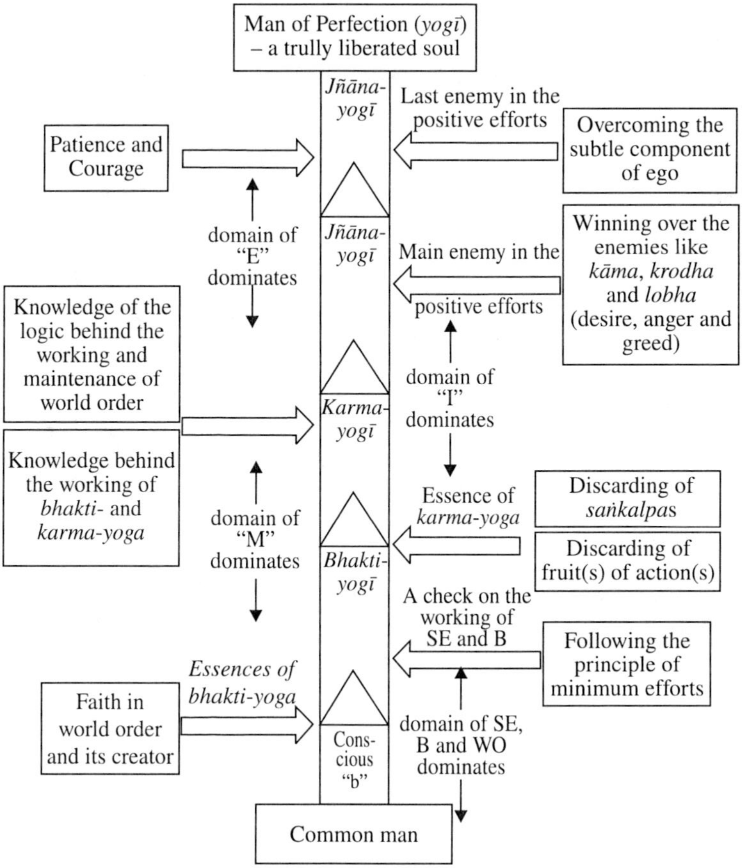

fig. 4.3: Vedānta philosophy and the theory of action. Hierarchy of stages which a conscious common man has to pass through to become a man of perfection. To some extent, the contents of the specified blocks on the left and right respectively are the dominant qualities of the philosopher and scientist categories of persons. Note the different domains of EOLs, where they have their respective domination from *fig.* 4.2 clearly emphasize on the *kārmic* theory of *SMBG*. In view of these results it is easy to understand as to how a common man, through the ladder of meditation and continued efforts, can attain the state of a *yogī* or of a man of perfection by following the blueprint displayed in *fig.* 4.3 (cf. Kaushal 2011, chapter 4). For small *n*, one remains in the domain of *bhakti-yoga*, for medium *n* in the domain of *karma-yoga* and for higher values of *n* in the domain of *jñāna-yoga*. Note that in this whole journey the inputs at various stages and several stopovers as shown in the figure are desirable.

Whether it is the case of a *PM* or of an EOL, the infinitely dressed version of each has the tendency to merge into Φ_{cc}. In fact, when the dressing corresponding to $n = \infty$ takes place each dressed *PM* or EOL attains its cosmic character (cf. *Virāṭ Puruṣa* of Table 3.2) and exists in this seed-like form in Φ_{cc}. This seed-like version, at a later stage in certain phenomena (like in the growth of foetus in the womb of a mother) can also undress of or devolve with consciousness in the same way as it has been evolved with consciousness.

4.5 Some Preliminaries of Modern Physics: Lessons from Physical Theories II

4.5.1 QUANTUM FIELD THEORY: DISCRETENESS AND CONTINUUM

Space–time-mediated four fundamental interactions in physics, viz. strong, electromagnetic, weak and gravitational, have been studied rather elegantly through their "field" character. These interactions are characterized by their range and strength. While strong and weak interactions are of finite range and active mostly in the nuclear domain, electromagnetic and gravitational are of infinite range and are spread all over the Universe. With regard to their strength, at a finer level it depends on the energy scale used. Further, it has become possible to bring down the first three interactions to the same strength at the energies of the order of 10^{15} GeV and for this purpose the grand unified theories have been developed. On the other hand, the finest possible gravitational interaction is accommodated in the theory just by bringing a modification in the geometry or in the space–time structure of Nature in philosophical terms up to the distance of the order of 10^{-33} cm. Whether it is the question of studying the behaviour of coupling strength or spatio-temporal distance (towards the modification of geometry), in either case two entities (physical particles in case of strong, electromagnetic and weak interactions or the geometrical points in the gravitational case) are considered. With these concepts, no doubt, the theoretical predictions beautifully conform to the experiments but the fact is that the theoretical analysis is always focused around the relative aspects between the entities. For absolute studies, however, the concept of "field", in which the number of particles (or the degrees of freedom) or of geometrical points becomes infinite, has been introduced.

Basically, the physical field is considered as a continuum, all-pervading medium, consisting of the above infinite number of entities and described by the so-called "field variable" $\varphi(x, t)$ – a measure of displacement of particle at position x and time t. Not only this, the "method of second quantization" (the first being the quantization of dynamic variables as considered in the standard quantum mechanics) turns out to be an important mathematical tool to study the continuum of the field once again as an infinite system of discrete (granular) entities. Each of these discrete entities so obtained (called field quantum), in fact, carries all the basic properties of the associated field. For this purpose, there are different types of quantization schemes that have been used in the past (see, for example, Itzykson and Zuber 1986; Kaku 1993). However, we shall work in the spirit of the most convenient one that is the canonical quantization in which the quantized entity turns out to be a harmonic oscillator. In this case, one writes the field variable as the combination of two terms – corresponding to particle–antiparticle (or "particle-hole") description of the system in view of the Dirac concept of negative energy. This in turn introduces the concept of creation–annihilation operators in the description.

In brief, such concepts of quantum field theory of physics will be freely used in an analogous manner to analyse the deep-rooted concepts of Vedic science with reference to the Grand Creation at the primordial level of the so-called "GOD" (which can appropriately be considered as an abbreviation of His qualities like "generator", "organizer" and "destroyer") – a universally accepted concept in all cultures of the world.

4.5.2 SECOND QUANTIZATION AND VEDIC WISDOM

Here we continue with the interpretation of Vedic verses that started in Section 3.4. As per interpretation of these verses by Swami Dayanand Sarasvati (cf. verses (3.1)–(3.4) and also of the verses (3.5)-(3.11) of *SMBG*, one clearly infers for a common source of origin of both Beings and non-Beings in this Universe and also for the underlying mechanism that describes such creations out of the Grand Creation (*sr̥ṣṭi*). In *SMBG*, yet there is another verse that gives a direct hint to the process of "second quantization" used in quantum field theory. In some sense, it is a mathematical trick used successfully while going from a continuum description to a discrete one of the same stuff (all-pervading field). This verse states:

avibhaktaṁ ca bhūteṣu vibhaktamiva ca sthitam ।
bhūtabhartr̥ ca tajjñyeyaṁ grasiṣṇu prabhaviṣṇu ca ॥ (4.10)
– *SMBG* XIII.16

In other words, "though indivisible (like the ether field), it stands as if divided among Beings. That knowable substance is the sustainer of Beings (as Viṣṇu), destroyer (as Rudra) and creator (as Brahmā)." Thus, the continuous (indivisible) cosmic consciousness field, Φ_{cc}, has been considered as if it is also manifesting through different (discrete) individual Beings in the same way as the discreteness of the continuum field in physics takes place via second quantization (a process that converts continuum into a granular form). If one extends the analogy further, then the creation, annihilation and number operators of physics field can respectively be considered here as Brahmā, Rudra and Viṣṇu of Vedic perception (!) and embodiment regarding the cosmic order.

4.6 Theory of Procreation

4.6.1 COSMIC CONSCIOUSNESS FIELD AND SPATIO-TEMPORAL WORLD: SOME BASIC POSTULATES

With a view to developing a unified theory of creation of Beings and non-Beings (cf. Sections 3.3 and 3.4), here we are inclined to make the following plausible assumptions in the spirit of field theory of physics:

i. It is the finest possible cosmic consciousness field, Φ_{cc}, with the adjectives like unthinkable, all-pervading, imperishable, ineffable, eternal, immobile, unmanifest and immutable that exists now and also existed at the primordial stage. The words like "God" of the West and *Virāṭ Puruṣa* of Vedic science are the personified versions of this finest subtle substance with the above characteristics.

ii. The field Φ_{cc} consists of many sectors responsible for the creation of varieties not only of Universes but also of animate and inanimate objects. The spatio-temporal world (STW) of objective scientists is a highly particularized sector in this infinite Φ_{cc}. The newly discovered spatio-temporal Higgs field of modern science is one particular composite sector of Φ_{cc}.

iii. Like the other Universes, our own Universe is also an outcome of some cosmic desire. Basically, it is the creation of, creation in and creation by Φ_{cc} and Φ_{cc} alone, of course, via a well-defined (but not well-understood (!)) mechanism.

iv. Other important sectors that exist in Φ_{cc} with similar properties and large overlapping regions are the fields of Cosmic Ego (Φ_{cE}), Cosmic Mind (Φ_{cM}), Cosmic Intelligence (Φ_{cI}) and Cosmic Elements (Φ_{cEL} of Section 3.5) (*pañca-mahābhūtas*). As these fields exist in the background of Φ_{cc}, in some sense they are embedded in it. In brief, they are called "epi-fields". The sector STW (and so is the Higgs field of modern physics) is a particular part of Φ_{cEL} of which the physical fields like gravitation and electromagnetic are the constituents at their primordial or grand unified stage.

v. The Φ_{cc} in itself is pure but the presence of other sectors pollutes it in a big way. The sector of Cosmic Ego (leading to Cosmic Desire) at times inspires Φ_{cc}, to create the sequence of sectors Φ_{cI}, Φ_{cM}, Φ_{cEL} and hence a STW as well in some of their manifest forms. In fact, the latter are always present in Φ_{cc} in primordial forms but in their different stages of dressings with consciousness (cf. next section).

vi. The quanta or seeds of Φ_{cE}, Φ_{cI}, Φ_{cM} sectors respectively are $\tilde{E}^{(\infty)}, \tilde{I}^{(\infty)}, \tilde{M}^{(\infty)}$, i.e. they are infinitely dressed versions of E, I, M, as discussed earlier (cf. Section 4.4).

vii. In the same way, as we have infinitely dressed versions of E, I and M, as the quanta of Φ_{cE}, Φ_{cI}, Φ_{cM} sectors, the quantum of Φ_{cEL} in its seed-like form is also there. The latter in Φ_{cE} consists of highly dressed versions of its constituents, namely of E_t, F, A, W, E_a as $\tilde{E}_t^{(\infty)}, \tilde{F}^{(\infty)}, \tilde{A}^{(\infty)}, \tilde{W}^{(\infty)}$ and $\tilde{E}_a^{(\infty)}$ produced via a Cosmic *pañcīkaraṇa* rule (Kaushal 2011).

viii. The undressing of $\tilde{\mathcal{M}}^{(\infty)} = \left\{\tilde{M}^{(\infty)}, \tilde{I}^{(\infty)}, \tilde{E}^{(\infty)}\right\}$ in conjunction with that of $\tilde{\Phi}_{cEL}^{(\infty)} \equiv \left\{\tilde{E}_a^{(\infty)}, \tilde{W}^{(\infty)}, \tilde{A}^{(\infty)}, \tilde{F}^{(\infty)}, \tilde{E}_t^{(\infty)}\right\}$ at different stages gives rise to varieties of animate and inanimate objects. In this process, an element of Φ_{cc} is always crept in to create in them the dynamism and structure in the STW. For animate objects, while the dynamism is interwoven in the structure itself, in inanimate ones, it manifests in the presence of animate(s).

ix. The undressing or unwrapping of $\tilde{\Phi}_{cEL}^{(\infty)}$ or any of its constituents gives rise to the existing spatio-temporal worlds at an appropriate stage of devolutions, when experienced or noticed by the unwrapped or partially wrapped quanta of Φ_{cc} or by its polluted versions at another arbitrary stage.

x. Time with different reference points starts as and when an event (grand events like the Big Bang or small events like creation of a Being) takes place in Φ_{cc} as a result of certain mechanism, like the spontaneous symmetry breaking or nucleation mechanism for Beings (animates) or due to the perception of inanimate objects by Beings at a later stage. It is the perception mechanism that converts the P-matter into EP-matter whose detailed study later gives a feeling of the grace of the Supreme in one way or the other.

xi. Relatively less finer fields like the constituents of, $\tilde{\mathcal{M}}^{(\infty)}$, and $\tilde{\Phi}_{cEL}^{(\infty)}$, though embedded in Φ_{cc}, these constituents (viz. $\tilde{M}^{(n)}$, $\tilde{I}^{(n)}$ and $\tilde{E}^{(n)}$ for $\tilde{\mathcal{M}}^{(n)}$ and $\tilde{E}_a^{(m)}$,$\tilde{W}^{(m)}$,$\tilde{A}^{(m)}$,$\tilde{F}^{(m)}$,$\tilde{E}_t^{(m)}$ for $\tilde{\Phi}_{CEL}^{(m)}$), in their undressed versions at arbitrary stage, say at n and m orders of dressing, also coexist in Φ_{cc}, prior to the germination of the seeds of a Being or non-Being. It is the matching of n and m existing already in Φ_{cc} for the partially dressed objects and that of parent(s) at the time of conception, which is responsible for the extent to which the EOLs M, I, E and the constituents of Φ_{cEL} are transmigrated in the newly-created Being.

xii. The object $\tilde{\Phi}_{cEL}^{(\infty)}$, while is the result of cosmic desire $\tilde{\Phi}_{CE}^{(\infty)}$ at a cosmic scale, its limited exploration by the limited instrument, viz. those of a Being, is the result of the EOL, E, present in the Being. It is like the exploration of ocean by a drop or of an infinite object by an instrument of finite capacity. The appearance of space–time-mediated Nature or its laws based on the space–time-mediated interactions, however, is the result of evolution only at a very late stage and that too with reference to the finite Being; otherwise with reference to Φ_{cc} the outcome of such evolutions already existed in primordial forms.

Note that the first seven postulates in the above are basic and the remaining last five in some sense are the derived ones. In view of these, it now becomes easier to understand the human Being as a miniature of cosmos as per Vedic science (cf. Table 3.2). Next, we deliberate on the dressing (rules) of epi-fields with cosmic consciousness.

4.6.2 FURTHER COMMENTS ON THE FIELD THEORETIC MODEL AND THE DRESSING OF EPI-FIELDS WITH COSMIC CONSCIOUSNESS

With regard to the above field theoretic picture and the dressing of epi-fields with cosmic consciousness, the following remarks are in order:

1. The field Φ_{cc} acts as a pure source of consciousness in its nascent or unmanifest form, its manifestation in various sectors is only through epi-fields. Space–time, however, enters in its manifest forms.
2. The epi-fields Φ_{CE}, Φ_{CI}, Φ_{CM} and Φ_{CEL} in their partially dressed (or undressed) form in general are the functions of space (q), time (t) and the meditation (consciousness) variable μ, but their primordial versions, viz. $\tilde{\Phi}^{(\infty)}_{CE}$, $\tilde{\Phi}^{(\infty)}_{CI}$, $\tilde{\Phi}^{(\infty)}_{CM}$, $\tilde{\Phi}^{(\infty)}_{CEL}$, which basically represent their infinitely dressed versions with cosmic consciousness are independent of these variables. Further, we denote $\Phi_{CEL} = \{E_a, W, A, F, E_t\}$ for the nascent version of *PMs* and $F_{CJ}\,(q, t, \mu)$ (for J = E, I, M, EL) for the epi-fields, in general. As a matter of fact, as the order of dressing of an epi-field with cosmic consciousness tends to infinity, its dependence on space–time accordingly decreases and becomes zero for the infinitely dressed versions. On the other hand, in the totally undressed case, the epi-fields attain their nascent versions but in a limited domain and attain strong space–time dependence. The epi-fields become perceptible with certain lowest orders of dressing with cosmic consciousness.
3. Such a field, consisting of Φ_{cc} and epi-fields in their primordial versions, viz. $\tilde{\Phi}^{(\infty)}_{CE}$, $\tilde{\Phi}^{(\infty)}_{cI}$, $\tilde{\Phi}^{(\infty)}_{CM}$, $\tilde{E}_a^{(\infty)}$, $\tilde{W}^{(\infty)}$, $\tilde{A}^{(\infty)}$, $\tilde{F}^{(\infty)}$, $\tilde{E}_t^{(\infty)}$, when quantized to give a quantum like Being b, in general, the latter will carry the features of all these primordial fields including that of Φ_{cc} in the background.

4. At any stage of dressing, we have seen that

$$\tilde{E}_a^{(n)} + \tilde{W}^{(n)} + \tilde{A}^{(n)} + \tilde{F}^{(n)} + \tilde{E}_t^{(n)}$$
$$= \tilde{E}_a^{(n-1)} + \tilde{W}^{(n-1)} + \tilde{A}^{(n-1)} \tilde{F}^{(n-1)} + \tilde{E}_t^{(n-1)}$$
$$= E_a + W + A + F + E_t \qquad (4.6)$$

and similarly for the trio of M, I and E, we have

$$\tilde{M}^{(n)} + \tilde{I}^{(n)} + \tilde{E}^{(n)} = \tilde{M}^{(n-1)} + \tilde{I}^{(n-1)} + \tilde{E}^{(n-1)} = M + I + E. \qquad (4.9)$$

by constructions. Results (4.6) and (4.9) imply that while the consciousness dresses the entities separately, its net effect on a particular set of entities is absent or not noticeable. It acts only as a catalyst. In other words, this particular system works in a self-consistent manner, i.e. without involving the external agency (consciousness) directly in its working, but definitely in the presence of the external agency. This supports the spirit of *guṇā guneṣu vartanta ....* – an intricate concept of *SMBG* III.28.

5. Modern physical theories deal with the concepts of many universes and higher dimensions. These concepts can easily be understood in the present scheme of study. For example, as n increases from 0 to ∞, there is a possibility of having infinitely many categories of universes as a result of partitions of elements of the set $\tilde{F}_{EL}^{(n)}(q,t,\mu) = \{\tilde{E}_a^{(n)}, \tilde{W}^{(n)}, \tilde{A}^{(n)}, \tilde{F}^{(n)}, \tilde{E}_t^{(n)}\}(q, t, \mu) \equiv \tilde{U}^{(n)}(q, t, \mu)$, possibly with different orders of dressing for each constituent. While they are functions of q, t and μ, the nature of these universes depends on the dominance of some constituent(s) present in these partitions. In fact, the *pañcīkaraṇa* rule is the discrete way of evolution or de-evolution of an entity with consciousness, or for converting a P-matter entity into an EP-matter entity and finally into a SEP-matter entity (Kaushal 2011).

6. While the meditation variable μ is directly linked with the order of dressing n, the nascent versions (at the end-point of undressing or at the initial point of dressing) of *PMs* exist in

four space–time dimensions of Einstein; otherwise at every stage of dressing with consciousness (i.e. by using a physical instrument with an increasingly improved resolving power or by an individual with his increasingly developed FOUs) the extra dimensions of the nascent entity start appearing and this goes up to infinity until the entity merges with Φ_{cc}. At this stage the entity becomes infinite dimensional – a feature of a field in the physical sense.

7. Note that the functioning of inner EOLs, whether in their nascent or dressed form, does not depend on space–time explicitly, like that of the constituents of $\tilde{F}_{EL}^{(n)}$, but only on μ. For a conscious person, this μ, while originating from the micro version of Φ_{cc}, i.e. from SO, nonetheless has limitation and the same, in turn, limits the development of his FOUs.

Although it depends on the quality of the perceiver in terms of the development of his FOUs, there is no reason why the order of dressing of $\mathcal{M}$, in general, should be the same as that of the order of undressing of Φ_{cEL}. In order to discover the constituents of $\tilde{U}^{(n)}(q, t, \mu)$, the order of dressing of $\tilde{F}_{\mathcal{M}}^{(m)}$ of a scientist, i.e. m should be the same as the order of undressing n of the primordial form. Only then a scientist will perceive the entity in a true sense. This is how the knowledge transcends to an individual from the cosmic agencies like the primordial versions of epi-fields. Perhaps, this was the way in which the knowledge of Vedas transcended initially to early seers. An explanation of both evolution and de-evolution of Beings in Φ_{cc} can also be analysed in the same spirit.

4.7 Application Aspects of the Theory of Procreation

4.7.1 AN INTERESTING CLUE TO UNDERSTAND THE PROCESS OF PROCREATION

Within this framework, several salient points regarding the origin of life at the time of conception are easily understandable.

i. In fact, the mindsets of the parents at this time will bring in the roles of q, t and μ. Depending upon the state of their respective mindsets, the parents will accordingly transcend these features available already in the cosmos in primordial forms by way of undressing them. The rest remains a biological evolution more or less in accordance with Darwin.

ii. The same cosmic consciousness now manifests in two forms – the cosmic one with a "hole" $\bar{b}$ (Kaushal 2015) in it and the quantized (or localized) one through the created Being b. (The "hole-particle" formalism is an effective tool to study the nuclear structure properties within the framework of the so-called field-theoretic methods; see, for example, Brown (1964).) Note that corresponding to this b, the hole ($\bar{b}$) is unique but only at the time of quantization or conception, otherwise both b and $\bar{b}$ keep on changing with the order of undressing of primordial versions and that of dressing of microcosm versions with consciousness respectively. An entity is now perceived by the two – by *Virāṭ Puruṣa* of *SMBG* at the cosmic scale as a result of undressing of the primordial forms and by b at the microcosm level as a result of dressing of his EOLs with consciousness.

iii. While both b and $\bar{b} \equiv \Phi_{cc} - b$ always remain in the networking and the interplay, each of them tries to merge in Φ_{cc}.

iv. The "hole" (the structure created in Φ_{cc} as a result of second quantization)-particle (the Being b, that has now come in the womb of the mother) dynamics continues not only for one but for several lifespans. In fact, each of them gets chance to undergo changes with respect to the roles of consciousness at the level of both its cosmic and localized versions in conjunction with appropriately undressed epi-fields or appropriately dressed EOLs. At times, these cosmic and micro versions work like a teacher and a disciple in consonance.

4.7.2 DESTINY (PRĀRABDHA) OF A HUMAN BEING AND THE "HOLE-PARTICLE" PICTURE OF CREATION

Note that epi-fields with their infinitely dressed versions are embedded in Φ_{cc}. For all other orders of dressing (or undressing) with consciousness they, however, float around in Φ_{cc}, including their nascent versions. On the other hand, every human Being, *b*, also carries at least partially dressed versions of his inner EOLs. At the time of conception, this is the matching of the three dressed versions of apparently different entities in their subtle form that influences the nature of creation of a baby in the womb. Besides the given physical environment, the orders of dressing of mindsets of both mother and father and that of the floating epi-fields around matters. Of course, all this happens in the background of Φ_{cc} or of its micro version SO of each of the parents. In fact, at the time of conception it is a kind of "Big Bang" or "second quantization" that takes place in Φ_{cc} and the Being *b* (synonym of "particle" in physical theory) is created leaving behind a unique and identical "gap" ($\bar{b}$) (synonym of "hole" in physical theory) in the sea of Φ_{cc}, at this particular point of space–time. These "hole-particle" interactions starting now, continue till the death of the Being (i.e. when *b* finally merges with Φ_{cc}) and the same constitute the main cause of the so-called *prārabdha*-category of actions of *b* as described in Vedic science.

Note that both hole and particle ($\bar{b}$ and *b*) undergo continuous changes during the lifespan of *b* as a result of separate dynamics taking place at the cosmic level on the one hand and at the microcosm level of inner EOLs of *b*, on the other. Thus, in the *kārmic* theory of Vedic science, the *sañcita* and *kriyamāna* types of actions of a Being are the attributes of local (microcosm level) dynamics of EOLs, whereas the *prārabdha* category is the result of cosmic dynamics taking place between *b* and $\bar{b}$ or among various epi-fields. In fact, the networking of holes and particles corresponding to all Beings in Nature distinctly continues throughout their respective lifespans. Further, this distinctness arises due to the different orders of dressing (or undressing) with consciousness at different levels.

4.7.3 MASTER–DISCIPLE TYPE RELATIONSHIP AND THEY ARE IN RACE

Once the Being b (consisting of EOLs SO, E, I, M, B, SE in the field of WO, which consists of *PMs* ≡ $\{E_a, W, A, F, E_t\}$), is created out of the sea of epi-fields (which are embedded in Φ_{cc}), then the gap left behind, $\bar{b} = \Phi_{cc} - b$, remains in a peculiar type of relationship with b. In some sense, it is of disciple (b) and Master ($\Phi_{cc} - b \approx \Phi_{cc}$) type relation. In fact, these are the respective pictures of the human Being and the *Virāṭ Puruṣa* described in Vedic science and hinting at their cosmic connections. While the latter is the Creator of the former, He wants the former to be like Him. For this purpose, He has supplied all possible accessories, whatever He had, to the former. As mentioned in Example 3.5.1, the disciple somehow does not use the entire set of accessories supplied by the Master because of his limited free will and self-sense. At times, the Master shows hard time to the disciple to judge his ability of overcoming the self-sense or of using the free will rightly. In this endeavour, the disciple often fails and does not succeed in proving his-self like his Master. This continues now and then on earthly scale under the constant watch of the Master, but there is every possibility that in the end, after prolonged efforts, perhaps in several cycles of birth and death, the disciple will become like his Master by eliminating all his negativities.

4.7.4 WHY THE ANTI-MATTER OF PHYSICAL THEORIES DOES NOT EXIST

The hole particle picture, proposed by P.A.M. Dirac for spin-half fields, is better applied to nuclear structure studies rather than to the problems in quantum field theory. For physicists, no doubt, the fields are systems with infinite degrees of freedom but are still localized in space and time or with reference to their all-pervading property – a property that can be attributed to Φ_{cc}. While antiparticles (and hence the antimatter) do exist in the localized region and for a limited timespan, their existence at the cosmic scale is not yet established. In the present context of cosmic consciousness field, it is not difficult to understand the non-existence of $\bar{b} = \Phi_{CC} - b$. Clearly, in the limit when the order of dressing tends to infinity, $b \equiv \mathcal{C}\mathrm{U}\mathcal{M}\mathrm{U}\mathcal{G}$, develops tendency to merge with Φ_{cc}, independent of the nature of $\bar{b}$. Moreover, in comparison with infinite Φ_{cc}, the microcosm $\bar{b}$ is merely a negligible entity. Further, $\bar{b}$ in comparison to b, does not evolve with consciousness to the same extent. In physical theories, however, the particle and anti-particle retain their entities and their annihilation is considered only in a localized region of space–time.

4.7.5 COSMIC CONSCIOUSNESS FIELD VIS-À-VIS HIGGS FIELD OF PHYSICS

An interesting feature about Φ_{cc} and associated epi-fields can be derived from the phenomenon of spontaneous symmetry breaking in physics. As a matter of fact, the field Φ_{cc} with two types of embedded epi-fields, viz. $\tilde{F}_{\mathcal{M}}^{(m)}(\mu) \equiv \{\tilde{M}^{(m)}, \tilde{I}^{(m)}, \tilde{E}^{(m)}\}(\mu)$ and $\tilde{F}_{CEL}^{(n)}(q, t, \mu) \equiv \{\tilde{E}_a^{(n)}, \tilde{W}^{(n)}, \tilde{A}^{(n)}, \tilde{F}^{(n)}, \tilde{E}_t^{(n)}\}(q, t, \mu) \equiv \tilde{U}^{(n)}(q, t, \mu)$, are symmetrically spread all over in the Universe. While the first category of epi-field is the direct attribute of consciousness (as they are the functions of μ alone), the second category is linked with space, time and meditation variable (material world). Naturally, the space–time dependence would acquire mass and the same generates in the process of evolving, whereas the first category goes without mass. Coincidently, these two situations match with two types of Bosons (field quanta) investigated in the so-called "Higgs mechanism" in physical theories (Itzykson and Zuber 1986; Kaku 1993).

Now in the calmly distributed Φ_{cc}, there occurs spontaneous symmetry breaking through a Higgs-like mechanism (see, e.g. (Itzykson and Zuber 1986; Kaku 1993)) dealing with the concept of degenerate vacua. Accordingly, two types of epi-fields come into existence – one has field quantum without mass and the other with mass. Further studies in this direction will open new vistas about the common source of origin of both animate and inanimate.

4.7.6 APPLICATIONS IN THE FIELDS OF ASTROLOGY, ĀYURVEDA AND NATUROPATHY

In what follows, we discuss certain clues, which the theory of procreation discussed in this chapter, can offer with regard to the subjects of astrology, Āyurveda and naturopathy, used for the treatment of diseases, mental or otherwise.

Astrology (*horoscope science*): It is known worldwide that just by using the place, date and the time of birth of a person as input, experts can predict a lot about the nature, habits, behaviour and the future events of that person. This describes the science of "astrology" or the "horoscope science". No doubt, the predictions of this science, in spite of a logical computation with some well-defined postulates, remain poor, but the number of believers in these predictions is reasonably good. This science, in fact, accounts in its own way for the position and movement of planets and stars by considering the place, date and time of birth of the person as initial inputs and the same indeed is decided by the delivery of the baby after it is born.

To some extent, one can understand the cause of poor predictions of this science as follows: At the time of delivery note that the baby undergoes a kind of change of surrounding environment, in spite of that its gross (biological) body still consists of five cosmic elements but now with their nascent versions. The micro body of the baby also starts developing now with space–time. As a matter of fact, the environment inside the mother's womb was not only different but consisted of epi-physical matter due to the consciousness of mother. On the other hand, whatever little it may be but the radiations coming from various planets and stars start affecting the growth of both gross and microbodies of the baby. One possible modification to these considerations in the light of procreation theory is that one can shift the implementation of initial conditions, i.e. instead of accounting for them at the delivery time, one need to start accounting for them from the conception time and that too in terms of the quality of mindsets of both father and mother. As a matter of fact, it is the evolution of their respective mindsets (in terms of order of dressing) that will accordingly transcend the dressed epi-fields in seed-like form out of the sea of Φ_{cc} (for more details, see Kaushal 2023a). Although it is a tedious task, if taken care of, then it will improve the quality of astrological predictions.

Āyurveda and Naturopathy: The medical system of Āyurveda basically works on maintaining a balance of three intangible entities, viz. *vāta*, *pitta* and *kapha*, in the body. In a healthy body, certain proportion of each of them, depending on an individual, maintains the equilibrium. Once this equilibrium in the body gets disturbed (either by the nature of food intake or by other habits), then a disease creeps in to the body and the cure of the latter lies in supplying an Āyurvedic medicine from outside to maintain the balance of the trio of these entities.

Like the role of *vāta*, *pitta* and *kapha* in the Āyurvedic system, five cosmic elements (*PM*s), viz. earth, water, air, fire and ether, form the basis of treating a disease in naturopathy. According to experts, they not only constitute the body but they do maintain equilibrium in a healthy body (Kaushal 2011a). Recall that these *PM*s in their nascent form are tangible, whereas their dressed versions are intangible. Here comes the role of consciousness of the doctor who is treating the disease. Further, note that at subtle level the trio of *vāta*, *pitta* and *kapha* can be considered as a certain combination of the dressed version(s) of *PM*s. This establishes the connection between Āyuveda and naturopathy systems of treatment of diseases. Further discussions will be continued in Chapter 9 in terms of a newly-introduced concept of mind waves.

Now the question arises as to how the theory of procreation discussed in this chapter can be useful in these systems of treatment of diseases. A hint to this effect is already given in case of astrology. In case of Āyurveda or naturopathy, it is the use of dressed versions of the epi-fields with the consciousness of the doctor in $\tilde{F}_{CEL}^{(n)}(q,t,\mu) \equiv \{\tilde{E}_a^{(n)}, \tilde{W}^{(n)}, \tilde{A}^{(n)}, \tilde{F}^{(n)}, \tilde{E}_t^{(n)}\}(q,t,\mu) \equiv \tilde{U}^{(n)}(q,t,\mu)$ that will expedite the process of treatment of a disease. In other words, these are the consecrated or sanctified (*abhimantrita* or attention dominated as elaborated in Chapter 9) versions of *PMs* or of their combinations in the form of *vāta*, *pitta* and *kapha* which will expedite the process of treatment.

4.8 Concluding Discussion

Keeping the knowledge of Vedic science in mind and using the tools of quantum field theory, a search for the common source of origin of both animate and inanimate started in Chapter 3 is now concluded in this chapter. While attempts are made here to understand the origin, sustenance and destruction of both animate and inanimate entities in the cosmos, the applications of the proposed theory of procreation are hinted in a variety of diverse fields of research. The theory clearly supports the concepts of "b–V correspondence" and of "cosmic connections" (cf. Table 3.1) – a prerequisite for a person to become spiritual.

To make an object perceptible and realizable by an individual, the rules of dressing it with consciousness are proposed. This consciousness can accordingly pertain to that of microcosm individual or to that of *Virāṭ Puruṣa*. As per Vedic wisdom, the latter, argued as the Creator (God) of the Grand Creation (*sṛṣṭi*), is identified here with the cosmic consciousness field Φ_{CC}. The associated epi-fields are postulated in it. The second quantization of the latter forms the basis of origin of Beings, in general, and the human Beings, in particular. The "explanatory aim" of these studies is very much fulfilled by generalizing the dressing rules (Kaushal 2011) for inner EOLs (*tri-karaṇa* rule) and for *PMs* (*pañcīkaraṇa* rule) with consciousness for a variety of situations. An important outcome of these generalizations is that in the limit when the order of dressing of any of these entities tends to infinity both dominating and non-dominating entities in the symbolic relations for dressing rules tend to merge in Φ_{cc} (cf. *figs.* 4.1 and 4.2), meaning thereby, that in whatever way a practitioner approaches God, he attains Him. While the present formalism offers explanation of several questions posed in different contexts (cf. Section 4.7), it also suggests improvements at the foundation level in the sciences of astrology, Āyurveda and naturopathy in terms of their viability in society.

The word GOD, as an abbreviation of "generator", "organizer", "destroyer" and the synonym of Φ_{cc}, is justified and defined as the cause of dynamism in the cosmos via cosmic desire. In fact, at the microcosm level, it is also the cause of dynamism that leads to actions of animate and cause of binding forces that describes the structure and motion of inanimate entities for a scientist towards their existence, survival and sustenance. Some conclusions can also be drawn here with reference to two striking coincidences in modern scientific observations – one pertains to the creation of animate and the other to the creation of inanimate entities in the cosmos in terms of creation of fire-ball in RHIC experiments (cf. Section 3.3). In the womb of the mother, the germinated seed, embryo, evolves and grows in a big way for a period of about nine months. During this period the growth and development of the foetus in terms of physical and biological features, passes through all the stages that a vertebrate species has passed through a period spanning over billions of years or so in order to attain the present shape and size of humans. In another case, when two heavy ions with relativistic (high) energies collide in the laboratory, they produce, possibly in a localized region and for a small enough duration, the same stuff (called quark-gluon plasma) as was produced during the first few fractions of a second after the Big Bang which occurred during the origin of early Universe. Both these phenomena, no doubt, occur in the present space–time domain, however, take the mind or the faculty of understanding of a scientist back to billion years back. In philosophical terms, while all this is a modelling game (see Kaushal 2011; Appendices B and C), a possible absolute truth hidden behind could be that they are the undressed versions of the primordial epi-fields in Φ_{cc} present earlier, now and also in future. It is a matter of realizing them now at the FOU level by an individual scientist.

Further studies on the phenomenon of consciousness will be continued in Chapter 9 under the heading of attention dominated matter, waves, energies and processes. In particular, attempts will be made to trace a common basis in Φ_{cc} of several somewhat less known but interconnected disciplines, like Āyurveda, naturopathy, teletherapy, astrology and some exotic phenomena in occult sciences in terms of a newly-proposed concept of mind waves.

High Skill Exercises and Projects

4.1 Explain as to how the symbolic relations (4.1) (or for that matter (4.7)) describe the enhanced state of left-hand quantity in the space of focussed consciousness (meditation).

4.2 Explain and analyse the behaviour of dressing fractions with increasing orders of dressing in *fig*. 4.1 (for PMs) and *fig*. 4.2 (for inner EOLs). From these figures explain as to how the attainment of *mokṣa* could be faster for a *jnāna* yogi (by the evolving $\mathcal{M}$) than for a *Bhakti* yogi (by way of worshipping an idol or PMs), if practised properly.

4.3 Write an essay on the use of quantum field theoretical model of physics for understanding the creation of both animate and inanimate objects out of the same cosmic consciousness field Φ_{cc}.

4.4 Note that eight epi-fields Φ_{cE}, Φ_{cI}, Φ_{cM}, Φ_{cJ} (with J = E_a, W, A, F and E_t) in Φ_{cc} are in accordance with "*asthānga prakruti*" of SMBG (cf. Verse 7.4). In the light of discussions in Sect. 4.6, explain as to how they are responsible for the creation of both animate and inanimate by way of creating (event-based) spacetime for their partially dressed versions in collusion with cosmic consciousness and with reference to manifest worlds and Universes.

4.5 Write an essay on the application aspects of the theory of procreation propounded in this chapter with reference to (i) Astrology, (ii) Ayurveda, (iii) Touch and tele-therapies (cf. Chapter 9).

4.6 Comment on the multifaceted applications of the theory of procreation proposed in this chapter. Hence elaborate the meaning of the phrase, namely "in whatever way a practitioner approaches God, he attains Him".

4.7 Write a note on the hole-particle picture of creation of Beings in Φ_{cc}. Explain how the "*prārabdha*"-type actions by the human Being b are controlled by the dynamics of the hole $\bar{b}$ in Φ_{cc}.

5

Spiritual Links of Psychoscience

Further Examples from Vedic Literature

FROM the discussions in preceding chapters, it becomes clear that

i. the methodology adopted in modern science with reference to quantification and measurement is inadequate and insufficient as far as the study of the phenomenon of consciousness is concerned;

ii. human Being is basically a spiritual Being and a thirst of its soul to become spiritual to this effect is natural, particularly towards the maintenance of the world and cosmic orders;

iii. Vedic wisdom clearly reveals a deep-rooted and intricately interwoven connection between an individual Being and the cosmic consciousness field (Φ_{cc});

iv. in order to understand these subtleties, a quantum field theoretic model of modern physics seems to offer a plausible framework;

v. according to this framework, an individual as a "second quantized" (discretized) version of Φ_{cc}, while carries all the features of the latter, however, it always remains a part of Φ_{cc} (like a *kaḍhī-pakoḍā* relation); and

vi. there is no doubt about the fact that the astral (causal) existence of a person has a control over the workings of both his micro and gross existences.

It may be emphasized that the psychoscience, while describing the dynamics of micro existence, however, it has links with both astral and gross existences at the two ends (cf. Table 3.2). Further, this science while transcends guidance from causal existence at a slow pace, it however transmits the same to the gross existence at a fast pace and later to the behavioural domain but in an elaborated manner. In this chapter, we continue to cite some more examples from Vedic literature to support the linkage of psychoscience with the spiritual thinking of a person. For this purpose, we once again elaborate on top-down and bottom-up approaches to absolute reality via the common route of micro existence. Then, in Section 5.2, we emphasize on the presence of two important barriers which come on the way during the spiritual journey. Some more examples of spiritual hold on psychoscience are discussed from *SMBG* and from other Vedic scriptures respectively in Sections 5.3 and 5.4. Finally, concluding remarks are made in Section 5.5.

5.1 Bottom-up and Top-down Approaches to Absolute Reality: The Role of Psychoscience

In order to understand the value and place value of psychoscience in the spectrum of eternal and universal Vedic wisdom, we shall be guided by the contents of Table 3.2. As shown in this table, the psychoscience describes the working of the world W_2 or of the micro-existence of a person in which all three variables, viz. space, time and consciousness, play roles in the underlying processes sometimes on an equal footing, whereas the variables space and time suffice for the description of the world W_3 and the only consciousness variable is needed for the world W_1. Whether it is the route from $W_1 \rightarrow W_3$ or from SEP $\rightarrow$ P, i.e. "externalization of the interior" (top-down approach) or from $W_3 \rightarrow W_1$ or from P $\rightarrow$ SEP, i.e. "internalization of the exterior" (bottom-up approach), in either case, the psychoscience has the place value in the middle and accounts for the behaviour and experiences of a person at the level of his micro-existence. Thus, it is linked with the spirituality at the one end and with the behavioural and objective sciences at the other.

Coincidently, the concept of three worlds W_1, W_2 and W_3 respectively agrees with the Vedic concept (see, for example, Ādi Śaṅkara 1966) of *cidākāśa* (void filled with consciousness and in which both *cittākāśa* and *bhūtākāśa* are embedded), *cittākāśa* (void responsible for the working of the trio of mind, intellect and ego and in which *bhūtākāśa* is embedded) and *bhūtākāśa* (void in which *pañca-mahābhūtas* including the body and senses of an individual are embedded and also responsible for their working, i.e. the physical world). In mathematical language, one can say that $W_1 \supseteq W_2 \supseteq W_3$ in the sense of fineness. Absolute reality in Nature consists of both, subjective part, i.e. the one realized by a philosopher or a Vedic seer in the process of "externalization of the interior" and objective part, i.e. the one perceived by an objective scientist in the process of "internalization of the exterior". In fact, a combination of both these parts does not make a whole unless the realities of the micro-existence as explored through psychoscience are incorporated in this whole. Moreover, such a role of psychoscience is desirable for the following reasons:

i. Any transition from W_1 to W_3 (top-down) or from W_3 to W_1 (bottom-up) has to be smooth, particularly through the links at W_3 to W_2 threshold and at W_2 to W_1 threshold. These two thresholds are discussed in detail in Vedic literature as the two barriers, viz. mind and ego, in the journey upward or downward. We shall return to some of these discussions in the next section.

ii. Thinking domains of the expertise of worlds W_1 and W_3 often are disjoint sets, i.e. there is no overlap between them. Though they both believe in the whole truth and each assumes the outcome of their efforts as a complete truth but in reality it is not so, each achieves only a partial truth through his methodology from the point of view of description of both the world and cosmic orders. This is mainly because the expert of W_1 cannot express his realization and experiences by any of the known objective methods of expression. On the other hand, the expert of W_3 believes in the quantification and precise (!) measurement and the same is not possible in W_1. As a matter of fact, the methodologies adopted by each type of expertise not only have limitations but are inadequate and insufficient as far as the search of absolute truth by them, from the point of view of a common man, is concerned. Here enters the role of psychoscience as a kind of "middle man" doing some sort of patchwork between the worlds W_1 and W_3.

5.2 Psychoscience and Micro-Existence of a Person

5.2.1 ANTAḤKARAṆA CATUṢṬAYA OF VEDIC SCIENCE

A systematic understanding of the dynamics or the style of working of the inner EOLs M, I and E in the outer world constitutes the so-called "psychoscience". While we have attempted to develop this subject in this book as an interplay of M, I and E in conjunction with EOLs, B, SE and *PM*s, Vedic science, however, emphasizes (Ādi Śaṅkara 1966) on four inner EOLs termed as *antaḥkaraṇa catuṣṭaya*, viz. mind, intellect, *citta* and ego. As it is the job of micro-existence, $\mathcal{M}$, to carry out rational and logical thinking, i.e. *cintana*, the fourth inner EOL *citta* is also included in this *antaḥ-karaṇa catuṣṭaya* of Vedic wisdom. However, in the present scheme of study this role of *citta* is taken care of by the dressed versions (with consciousness as a result of certain amount of meditation) of I and E; thus, the *citta* is not included as the part of inner EOLs. The proposed *trikaraṇa* rule for the dressing of inner EOLs, as discussed in Chapter 4, accounts for such a role of *citta*, of course, by some necessary orders of dressing with consciousness via meditation. As an alternative to this method, in some contexts, we also consider a separate grouping of gross and subtle components of inner EOLs, and thus partition (cf. *fig.* 12.2) of the micro-existence $\mathcal{M}$ itself into gross ($\mathcal{M}_g$) and subtle ($\mathcal{M}_s$) parts. It is the $\mathcal{M}_s$ part of $\mathcal{M}$ that is held responsible for the *cintana* of Vedic science. Further, note that M_s is close to the threshold E and works at a slow pace whereas $\mathcal{M}_g$ is close to the threshold M and comes into action rather fast with reference to an external stimulant.

Another departure from Vedic science, which has been pursued in this work, is the ordering of *PM*s in terms of their fineness. In this case, the well-known sequence followed in Vedic science is E_a, W, F, A, E_t, whereas in the present work the sequence followed is E_a, W, A, F, E_t, i.e. the roles of A and F are interchanged. In other words, Vedic science assumes the element fire F as less finer than the element air A, whereas in our case it is the other way round. In modern scientific terms, the reason is simple. In fact, the five cosmic elements also represent the five states of matter, viz. the earth E_a stands for all solids, water W for all liquids, air A for all gases, fire F for all plasma states and ether E_t for all voids. Naturally, air A is an attribute of molecular motion, whereas fire F is an attribute of ionic (plasma) motion and the latter motion is definitely subtler than the molecular motion and hence the element F is considered finer than the element A in the present work. Vedic science counts A as finer than F perhaps due to its vital role in the maintenance of an individual and also of cosmos.

It may be mentioned that dressing rules, viz. *tri-karaṇa* rule for inner EOLs and *pañcīkaraṇa* rule for *PM*s as discussed in the previous chapter, naturally give rise to a variety of mind, intellect and ego, and similarly varieties of earth, water, air, fire and ether as discussed in Vedic and Jaina philosophies. In the present context, this however is the outcome of the designed mathematical constructions followed through dressing rules.

5.2.2 ROLES OF MIND AND EGO (SELF-SENSE) AS TWO BARRIERS IN THE SPIRITUAL JOURNEY

As argued in Chapter 3, a person basically is a spiritual Being and the spirituality should constantly flow from the source of consciousness, SO, to the sink of consciousness, WO, i.e. in a top-down manner. This is mainly because the domination of consciousness in the working of all the three causal, micro and gross existences of a person which brings him closer to the cosmic thinking and motivates him to realize cosmic connections. This, in turn, helps in an ideal maintenance of both world and cosmic orders. In other words, the domination of consciousness in every action will tantamount to the best of spiritualism in causal domain, best of psychoscience or intellectualism in the micro domain and the best of actions in the gross-body domain or in the outer world towards the maintenance again of both the world and cosmic orders.

As a matter of fact, whether it is the best of spiritualism or the best of performing actions in the outer world, in either case, the credit goes to the best of individual's psyche or his intellectualism. By definition, such intellectualism is the doctrine that knowledge is wholly or mainly derived from pure reason and the guidance to this effect comes only during the domination of consciousness. In principle, such a constant flow of consciousness from SO to WO or to outer world should take place in a natural way. This actually happens at subtle level but at the gross level, in practical terms, something goes wrong with the quality of actions performed with reference to physical survival of a Being through its gross existence (mainly due to cravings for the "essentials for life"). In this case, at times, situation demands (may be temporarily) a reasoning, that does not favour the maintenance of world and cosmic orders. As a result, the origin of negative thoughts takes place in the domain of micro existence. In the language of Vedic wisdom, in this situation the *bhāvas* (intents) at the level of all three *sākṣī* ($\mathcal{C}$-domain), *vicāra* ($\mathcal{M}$-domain) and *ācāra* ($\mathcal{G}$-domain) get polluted, may be for a short while.

In philosophical terms, if one considers the human Being as a temple in terms of the arrangement of his EOLs, WO, B, SE, M, I and E with the inner most idol as SO, then the art and science of working of an individual in the outer world, according to Vedic wisdom, can be visualized as follows: The three existences $\mathcal{G}$, $\mathcal{M}$ and $\mathcal{C}$ with $\mathcal{G}$ = {WO, B, SE}, $\mathcal{M}$ = {M, I, E} and $\mathcal{C}$ = {SO}, constitute three corridors with increasing fineness in the meditation space or with the increasing intensity of mediation. While the details are postponed to the next chapter, still note that the EOLs, M and E of micro-existence represent two thresholds or windows in the corridor of $\mathcal{M}$, where the door of the former opens towards $\mathcal{G}$ and that of the latter towards $\mathcal{M}$. Also, the window M is effective for relatively less meditation and window E for relatively more intense meditation. When a person with materialistic thinking wishes to enter the temple, i.e. towards SO, he has to cross these two barriers, first at M (by way of controlling it from senses and sense-objects) and then at E (by way of suppressing it or overpowering certain negativities present in $\mathcal{M}$) to reach the idol SO (or the spiritual zone).

Elements of Basic Goodness (or badness) and the Two Barriers in the Journey through Human Consciousness

For every action of an individual in the outer world, there exist roots in the psychic zone and possibly for some in the spiritual (causal) zone at subtle level. As a matter of fact, depending upon whether an action performed in the outer world goes in favour or against the maintenance of world and cosmic orders, we accordingly define the goodness or badness of an action so performed. These features of the performed action are the outcome of a corresponding human quality that nurses in the psychic zone and at times in the spiritual zone. To this effect, a large number of human characteristics and personality traits have been identified as good or bad and thus accordingly lead to the classification not only of actions but also of individuals and societies over a period of human history. In this way, behind the performance of any action in the physical world there is an element of basic goodness or badness that is rooted in psychic zone. There are still some such but rare elements whose roots are extended to still subtler zone of spirituality.

The filtering of elements of basic goodness (or badness) is done at two stages or at two thresholds M and E. For the elements to have roots in psychic zone the filtering at M-level (by way of controlling it) is sufficient, whereas for the elements to have roots in the subconscious or spiritual zone the filtering at both M (by way of its controlling) and E (by way of its minimizing or suppressing) levels is necessary. In fact, these features of human qualities, if present in an individual, not only reflect through his mindset but also form a part of his character and subsequently that of his personality.

Who and What Decides the Nature (Good or Bad) of the Action Performed by a Human Being

Basically, it is the outcome of an action vis-à-vis its utility towards the maintenance of both world and cosmic orders that decides good or bad actions of a Being. To this effect, note that for non-human Beings there is not much freedom, however for humans, who have extra power of reasoning, there is variety of choices towards the performance of an action. Further, for different category of persons there are different criteria and parameters to decide the quality. In brief, we list some such observations for human Beings in Table 5.1.

In what follows, we continue to analyse these elements of basic goodness (or badness) vis-à-vis their filtering aspects through M and E, particularly in the light of *SMBG* and other Vedic scriptures.

Table 5.1: Who and What Decides the Quality (Good or Bad) of an Action for a Human Being?

Type of Person	*What Decides*	*Criterion Plus Other Parameters*
1. *Yogī* category, who resides in spiritual zone	Style and outcome of an action	Relevance towards maintenance of both world and cosmic orders (MWCO) + self-realization
2. Intellectual (philosopher and/or scientist) category, who reside in psychic zone	- do -	Relevance towards MWCO + self-observation + role models of the past and present
3. Common man category, who resides in the real world of his body and senses for survival	- do -	Relevance towards MWCO + self-observation + role models of the past and present + scriptural injunctions and evidences

5.3 Grand Psychoscience in SMBG

In the context of great Indian epic *Mahābhārata*, when Arjuna, the intelligent disciple-friend of Lord Kṛṣṇa, was overcome by infatuation and went into depression in the battlefield of Kurukṣetra, particularly after looking at the armies ready to fight on both sides of the field and consisting of his near and dear relations, Lord Kṛṣṇa at this point of time came forward with a wisdom for his psychological transformation. This eternal and universal wisdom imparted by the Lord (only Supreme Being) to Arjuna is termed as the *Bhagavadgītā* ("song divine") and is spread over in eighteen chapters and in about 700 verses. This grand wisdom conveyed to the world through Arjuna, mostly consists of psychology of a person with its connections to the spirituality on the one end and to the behavioural science in practical life on the other end. As it is not easy for a teacher to convince an intelligent disciple like Arjuna, the Lord describes several models and pathways to reach and achieve the same ultimate reality and finally convinces him to fight and win the battle. Here, we attempt to highlight, some aspects of this grand psychoscience with a view to demonstrate the links of this science with spirituality.

It may be emphasized that *SMBG* describes the finest and deepest possible philosophy of life of an individual irrespective of his caste, colour, creed or country. Basically, it is a capsule version of the Vedic wisdom that is distributed all over among various Vedic scriptures. At times, this wisdom is considered as evidence of divine truth to justify the quality (good or bad) of a concept and the actions performed thereafter. In order to look for a divine base of various human qualities, here we classify and analyse a variety of them mainly to demonstrate their links with the spiritual zone. Before we proceed to such an analysis, it should be made clear that the subtle component of $\mathcal{M}$, i.e. $\mathcal{M}_s$ is E-dominated and has a great overlap with spiritual zone, whereas the gross component of $\mathcal{M}$, i.e. $\mathcal{M}_g$ is M-dominated and has a great overlap with the behavioural zone in the outer world (cf. *fig.* 5.1). The causal or spiritual zone by and large, while accounts for cosmic existence and connections of a person, at the same time it is independent of the lower strata. A small part of it, however, has an overlap with the subtle component $\mathcal{M}_s$ of $\mathcal{M}$. Similarly, the gross-body zone identified with material existence, while has its own connections with the physical or material world as a part of it through B and SE, also has an overlap with the gross component $\mathcal{M}_g$ of $\mathcal{M}$ as shown in *fig*. 5.1. In author's opinion, while the human intent love is synonym of consciousness and as such is a part of the spiritual zone, most of other human qualities are however limited only up to $\mathcal{M}_S$ zone. Thus, a human quality, depending on its nature, can have two, three, or multiple-components and can be projected in one or in several zones at

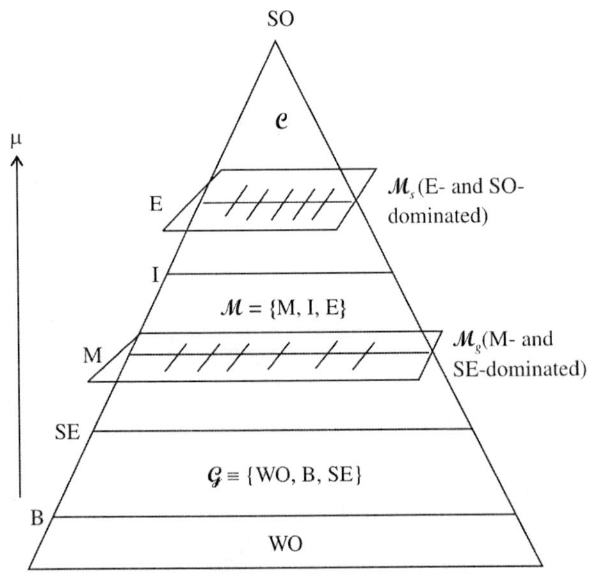

fig. 5.1: Identifying the place values of gross ($\mathcal{M}_g$) and subtle ($\mathcal{M}_s$) components of the micro-existence $\mathcal{M}$ in the arrangements of EOLs with respect to increasing meditation (μ). Here, M and E (with shaded regions $\mathcal{M}_g$ and $\mathcal{M}_s$) display two barriers at the two ends of $\mathcal{M}$-domain during the spiritual journey of a person the same time but in different versions. Indeed, these zones are $\mathcal{G}$ (gross), $\mathcal{M}_g$ (gross component of $\mathcal{M}$), $\mathcal{M}$ (normal), $\mathcal{M}_s$ (subtle component of $\mathcal{M}$) and $\mathcal{C}$ as shown in *fig.* 5.1.

5.3.1 A CLASSIFICATION OF HUMAN QUALITIES IN SMBG

Depending upon one's level of development of his faculty of understanding, one basic desire a person always has for his best survival in this world is to achieve pleasure, peace, joy and/or eternal joy. These objectives respectively belong to the domains of his $\mathcal{G}$ ($\mathcal{M}_g$), $\mathcal{M}$, $\mathcal{M}_s$ and $\mathcal{C}$ modes of existence. For example, an attainment of worldly objects including the fruits of action performed thereof, not only provides bodily and sensual pleasure but a kind of their spatio-temporal satisfaction at mental level that provides peace. Further, a kind of stable satisfaction attained again at mental level provides joy, mainly by dissociating oneself from the fruits of action so performed. Once a person develops the science and art of his living to the extent that he is capable of disclaiming the doership of actions by way of establishing the cosmic connections, not only of his self but also of his performed actions, the person qualifies himself for the eternal joy and at this stage the person can feel as a liberated one.

A Hierarchy in Various Modes of Human Existence

A huge spectrum of human qualities and characteristics, which also form the part of personality, is described by the Lord in *SMBG* at several places and in different contexts. For example, some qualities as symptoms of a man of perfection (or wisdom) or of stable mind are discussed in chapter 2 of *SMBG* (cf. verses II.54-II.72). On the other hand, two major classes of qualities associated respectively with divine and demoniac personalities are discussed in chapter 16 of *SMBG* (cf. verses XVI.2-XVI.4) and listed here in *fig.* 5.2. In fact, some human qualities, which also form the part of a personality, are further shown to come in different flavours in actual practice in accordance with three Nature-born *guṇas* (cf. chapters 17-18 of *SMBG*). With a view to make the classification of qualities more exhaustive and general, the $\mathcal{M}_S$-rooted qualities are further divided into three categories: divine, human and demoniac. Here, the human category is no doubt a newly added one to the divine and demoniac endowments of *SMBG* (cf. chapter 16), but this beautifully accommodates the *triguṇa*-based concept of classification (cf. Section 5.3.2).

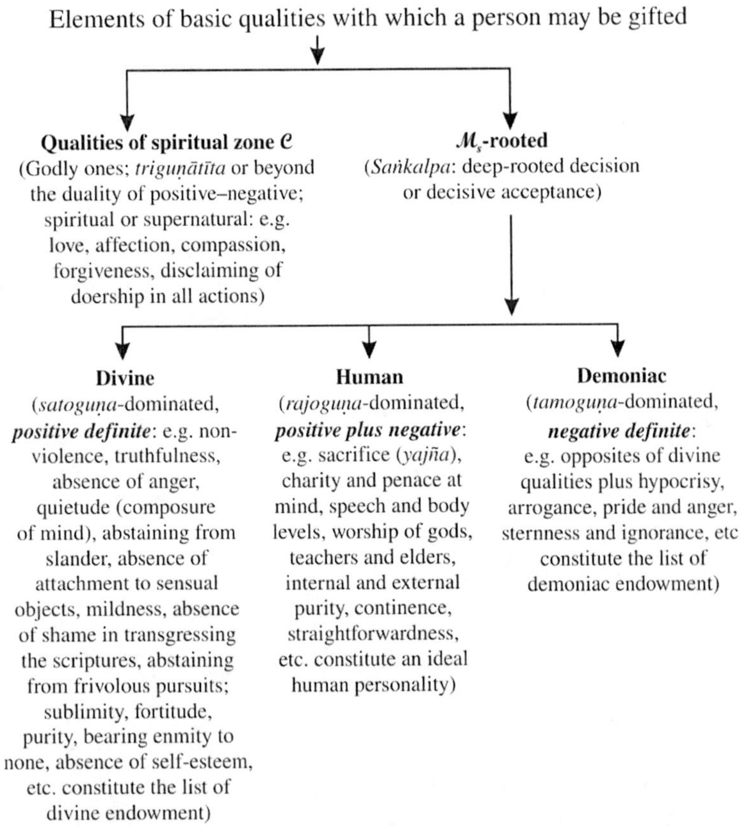

fig. 5.2: A possible classification of elements of basic qualities and characteristics with which a person may be gifted in his two innermost modes of existence, viz. $\mathcal{C}$ and $\mathcal{M}_S$

In preceding chapters, we have discussed various aspects of spiritual wisdom in terms of three – causal, micro and gross – existences or the modes of existence of a person. However, from the point of view of finding deeper meanings and roles of some of these qualities in the behavioural domain, we now include the just discussed subtle and gross components of $\mathcal{M}$, viz. $\mathcal{M}_s$ and $\mathcal{M}_g$, in the list. Thus, the hierarchy of the modes of existence which need to be considered for the analysis of qualities is $\mathcal{G}$, $\mathcal{M}_g$, $\mathcal{M}$, $\mathcal{M}_s$, $\mathcal{C}$ in the order of increasing meditation (μ) (cf. *fig.* 5.1). Note that $\mathcal{M}_g$ and $\mathcal{M}_s$, now take specific places as they offer two barriers (line-marked regions shown shading given in *fig.* 5.1) in the spiritual journey. With regard to these barriers, in fact, there are some clear hints in *SMBG* in chapter 2. In particular, note the following verses:

prajahāti yadā kāmānsarvānpārtha manogatān ।
ātmanyevātmanā tuṣṭaḥ sthitaprajñastadocyate ।। – II.55 (5.1)

Arjuna, when one thoroughly abandons all cravings of the mind, and is satisfied in the Self through (the joy of) the Self, he is then called stable of mind.

tāni sarvāṇi saṁyamya yukta āsīta matparaḥ ।
vaśe hi yasyeindriāṇi tasya prajñā pratiṣṭhitā ।। – II.61 (5.2)

Therefore, having controlled all the senses and concentrating his mind, he should sit for meditation, devoting himself (heart and soul) to "Me". For, he, whose senses are under his control, is known to have a stable mind.

rāgadveṣaviyuktaistu viṣayānindriyaiścaran ।
ātmavaśyaīrvidheyātmā prasādamadhigacchati ।। – II.64 (5.3)

But the self-controlled practitioner, while enjoying the various sense-objects through his senses, which are disciplined and free from likes and dislikes, attains placidity of mind.

prasāde servaduḥkhānāṁ hānirasyopajāyate ।
prasannacetaso hyāsu buddhiḥ paryavatiṣṭhate ।। – II.65 (5.4)

> With the attainment of such a placidity of mind, all his sorrows come to an end; and the intellect of such a person of tranquil mind, soon withdrawing itself from all sides, becomes firmly established in God.

First of all, it should be noted that the English words are not the correct translations of the corresponding Sanskrit words. In fact, the latter have somewhat deeper and distinct meanings than those of former. Verses (5.1) and (5.4) while clearly suggest the existence of subtle component $\mathcal{M}_s$ of $\mathcal{M}$, verses (5.2) and (5.3) support the existence of gross component $\mathcal{M}_g$ of $\mathcal{M}$. There is a direct hint for $\mathcal{M}_s$ from verse (5.1) as the first "Self" stands for (soul) and the second one for $\mathcal{M}_s$. Further, according to verse (5.2) it is necessary to control the senses and also $\mathcal{M}_g$ in order to attain better meditation and later devoting the same to self ($\mathcal{M}_s$) and then to the Lord (Self, $\mathcal{C}$). Similar is the case with verse (5.3) in which, with regard to the placidity of mind, the Lord emphasizes on enjoying the sense-objects (a subject of $\mathcal{G}$-domain, whereas the enjoyment is a subject of $\mathcal{M}_g$-domain, since the role of the intellect, I, is also involved) in such a way that the likes and dislikes (again a subject of $\mathcal{M}_g$) developed for them do not leave any impact first on $\mathcal{M}_s$ and later on $\mathcal{C}$. As per verse (5.4), even for a person with stable mind, M, there remains a tranquillity in $\mathcal{M}_g$ due to the nature of emotions like "sorrow" (as a result of events in $\mathcal{G}$), but they all end-up at the level of $\mathcal{M}_s$ and thereby leaving the "Self" unaffected.

In fact, there are several other verses in *SMBG* which directly or indirectly hint to the domains of $\mathcal{M}_g$ and $\mathcal{M}_s$. For example, verse II.50 in *SMBG* delivers the message of training one's intellect in such a way that it remains neutral in giving decisions about the so-called "goodness" or "badness" of an action, performed in the outer world (i.e. a "skill in action" kind of role). Here, actions end up at $\mathcal{M}_g$-level, whereas training comes naturally from $\mathcal{M}_s$-level. This *yoga* of equanimity, i.e. joining of one mode of existence with another after balancing and withdrawing the intellect from its basic decision-making quality, is not an easy task, but more practical in results.

5.3.2 A BROAD CLASSIFICATION OF HUMAN QUALITIES: THE ROLE OF GUṆAS

Coming back to *fig.* 5.2, recall that three Nature-born *guṇas*, viz. *sattva*, *rajas* and *tamas*, in some sense also support the classification of personalities respectively as divine, human and demoniac. They indeed characterize the nature and objectives of the performed actions with reference to the maintenance of world and cosmic orders and thereby results into three types of outcome, viz. positive definite, combination of both positive and negative, and negative definite. Such inherent prescriptions can be traced in *SMBG*, particularly when the Lord lists these qualities under the two extreme heads, viz. the divine and the demoniac endowments, in the following verses:

> *ahiṁsā satyamkrodhstyāgaḥ śāntirapaiśunam* ।
> *dayā bhūteṣvaloluptvaṁ mārdavaṁ hvīracāpalam* ॥ – XVI.2 (5.5)

> Non-violence in thought, word and deed, truthfulness and geniality of speech, absence of anger even on provocation, disclaiming doership in respect of actions, quietude or composition of mind, abstaining from slander, compassion towards all creatures, absence of attachment to the objects even during their contact with the senses, mildness, a sense of shame in transgressing the scriptures or social conventions, and abstaining from frivolous pursuits.

Further,

> *tejaḥ kṣamā dhṛtiḥ śaucamadroho nātimānitā* ।
> *bhavanti saṁpadaṁ daivīmabhijātasya bhārata* ॥ – XVI.3 (5.6)

> Sublimity, forgiveness, fortitude, external purity, bearing enmity to none and absence of self-esteem – these are, Oh Arjuna! the marks of him who is born with the divine endowments.

Contrary to them,

> *dambho darpo abhimānaśca krodhaḥ pāruṣyameva ca* ।
> *ajñānaṁ cābhijātasya pārtha sampadamāsurīm* ॥ – XVI.4 (5.7)

> Hypocrisy, arrogance, pride and anger, sternness and ignorance too, Arjuna, these are the marks of him, who is born with demoniac properties.

It can be noted from *fig.* 5.2 that the spiritual zone of $\mathcal{C}$ while remains unaffected from the working of the lower strata (in the same way as the catalyst in a chemical reaction), it is the component $\mathcal{M}_s$ that now works through three *guṇas*. Even for this case, $\mathcal{C}$ remains *triguṇātīta* or beyond the goodness or badness aspects of a quality with reference to a personality or a human society in general. A large number of qualities are listed under the "divine" head and a equal number under the "demoniac" head in this figure, but the fact is that still a large number of personalities fall under the "human" head. It appears that like the three Nature-born *guṇas*, the three personality traits, viz. divine, human and demoniac, are equally fundamental as far as the study of personality dimensions is concerned. Further, note that the divine endowment is conducive to liberation (*mokṣa*), whereas the demoniac one leads to bondage, of course, in conjunction with $\mathcal{C}$.

In *fig.* 5.2, the qualities are listed as per verses (5.5)-(5.7). They are classified according to their *satoguṇī*, *rajoguṇī* and *tamoguṇī* flavours, which in a weak sense also conform to divine, human and demoniac type of classification of qualities. Again, note that one can as well group the three-flavour qualities appearing in some verses of chapters 17-18 in *SMBG*, as follows:

Human intents and qualities: *śraddhā* (innate faith), *tapa* (penance), *dhṛti* (perseverance), *tyāga* (renunciation), *tyāgī* (man of renunciation);

Material stimulant: *āhāra* (food), *dāna* (gift or charity), *yajña* (sacrifice), *sukha* (pleasure/joy);

Non-material stimulant: *jñāna* (knowledge), *karma* (action), *kartā* (doer of action);

Essences of life: *buddhi* (intellect).

All these cases are discussed in detail by the Lord. Based on the domination of a particular flavour out of the three (viz. *sāttvika*, *rājasika* and *tāmasika*), there also exists a corresponding classification of actions performed by a person in *SMBG* as divine, human and demoniac. For other aspects of study of these human virtues, qualities and intents in terms of flavours we refer to the method outlined in Appendix D.

5.3.3 SOME "GOLDEN RULES" IN SMBG TOWARDS THE UPLIFTMENT OR DOWNFALL OF A PERSONALITY

A "golden rule" in personality development can be defined as a cluster of human virtues, qualities, characteristics and intents whose systematic and sequential arrangement (in terms of values and/or place values), if pursued and followed in daily life, then it becomes a cause for an overall upliftment or downfall of one's personality. In fact, the frequent occurrence of such golden rules in Vedic philosophy and wisdom defines the *Sanātana Dharma* and makes the latter as eternal and universal (cf. Chapter 13). In *SMBG*, there are several situations and places where the Lord narrates such "golden rules" (in analogies with physical theories, they can also be termed as "laws of Nature" in psychoscience). Two situations worth citing here are as follows:

i. In chapter 2 (cf. verse II.61), the Lord advises Arjuna to concentrate on higher objects including on His own glories after withdrawing senses from their respective sense-objects and also controlling his mind. If Arjuna does not succeed in doing so, then the Lord emphasizes on a wonderful sequence leading to a downfall, viz.:

   dhyāyato viṣayānpuṁsaḥ saṅgasteṣūpajāyate ।
   saṅgātsañjāyate kāmaḥ kāmātkrodho 'bhijāyate ॥ – II.62 (5.8)

   The man dwelling in sense-objects develops attachment for them, from attachment springs up desire, and from desire (unfulfilled) ensues anger.

krodhād bhavati sammohaḥ sammohātsmṛti vibhramaḥ ।
smṛtibhraṁśād buddhināśo buddhināśātpraṇaśyati ।। – II.63 (5.9)

From anger arises delusion, from delusion, confusion of memory, from confusion of memory, loss of reason and from loss of reason one goes to complete ruin.

What a wonderful and practical sequence of emotions and other human intents is demonstrated in these verses which one normally forced to follow in the event of provocation or fight; otherwise, if understood properly, this sequence becomes a stepping stone in the direction of one's upliftment and in attaining peace. Next example we cite here concerns the individual's philosophy of life or his spiritual upliftment.

ii. A verse in chapter 12 that brings out still deeper philosophy and quoted on the cover page of the book is as follows:

śreyo hi jñānamabhyāsājjñānāddhyānam viśiṣyate ।
dhyānātkarmaphalatyāgastyāgācchāntiranantaram ।।
– XII.12 (5.10)

Knowledge is better than practice without discernment, meditation on God (or on higher objects) is superior to knowledge and the renunciation of the fruits of action is even superior to meditation; for, peace immediately follows renunciation.

Once permanent peace, if attained by a practitioner, then it becomes a stepping stone in the path of spiritual journey.

We try to depict this sequence of human actions and qualities listed in verse (5.10) in *fig*. 5.3, which in actual practice describes the steps to be followed to attain the ultimate peace, and thereby joy and later eternal joy. It is worthwhile to elaborate here the underlying concept through a metaphor. In fact, after attaining permanent peace, it is the oil of joy that gathers in the bowl which later burns to give the flame of eternal joy and the light of this flame becomes instrumental in establishing cosmic connections of the practitioner. Among other examples of "golden rule" in Vedic wisdom one is the famous *aṣṭāṅga-yoga* of Patañjali. In this case, not only the eight components, viz. *yama, niyama, āsana, prāṇāyāma, pratyāhāra, dhāraṇā, dhyāna* and *samādhi,* follow a sequence, which needs to be followed by a practitioner to achieve the highest in the world. In fact, the sub-components of each of these components are also found to follow a sequence as per Āyurvedic wisdom and the science of Yoga.

5.4 Spiritual Links of Psychoscience in Other Ancient Indian Scriptures

While *aṣṭāṅga-yoga* of Patañjali presents a rich example of golden rules, it however offers a clear case of spiritual links of psychoscience. Particularly, the last three components, viz. *dhāraṇā,*

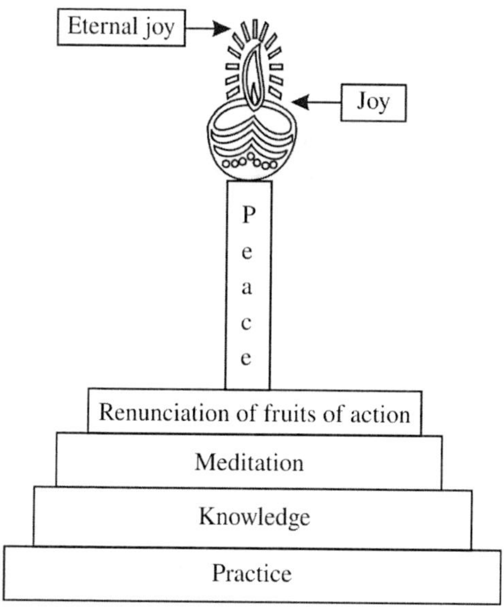

fig. 5.3: The figure highlights the steps of a grand golden rule as discussed in *SMBG* (verse XII.12) to tread into the spiritual zone. Note that a bulk and volume of the practical aspect of wisdom goes on decreasing in steps in the process of attaining peace, joy and later eternal joy *dhyāna* and *samādhi*, are the main steps to be followed to tread into the spiritual zone and finally to attain the state of liberation from worldly bondage via one's psyche including the steps of *pratyāhāra* and *prāṇāyāma*.

Indian system of medicine, i.e. Āyurveda, is a holistic system of treatment of diseases in the sense that the methodology adopted in it not only cures diseases and helps in maintaining one's physical health but also heals his psyche. Both material and non-material treatments given therein are so chosen that they ultimately drag one's mind to the realm of spiritual zone. In fact, the underlying science behind the naturopathy (which is also a branch of Āyurveda) directly connects one to cosmos through the use of *pañca-mahābhūtas* in the treatment. In Āyurveda, it is the *vāta-doṣa* as a particular combination of *PMs* (cf. Chapter 9) that connects mind with soul on the one hand and mind with body on the other hand as per the *Caraka Saṁhitā* (Gaur 1990), when the latter says:

yato mārutastato manaḥ pravartate । (5.9)

Wherever *māruta* (a synonym of cosmic element air or *vāta*) resides, the mind dwells in there.

And

niyantā praṇetā ca manasaḥ । (5.10)

It is the *vāta* that controls and inspires the mind.

Through another verse, it says:

śarīram hi gate tasmine śūnyāgāramacetanam ।
pañca bhūtāvaśeṣatvātā pañcatvam gatamucyate ॥ (5.11)

After the departure of soul from this body, the latter becomes inanimate and devoid of the "Master" in spite of prevalence of all the five elements, but in *apañcīkṛta* (nascent or undressed with consciousness, i.e. unperceived) form.

There are innumerable places in the great Indian Epics, *Rāmāyaṇa* and *Mahābhārata*, where the characters, during their conversations and discussions, cover almost the entire wisdom possible in the universe and cosmos at the most fundamental level, may be in a fragmented form. Needless to emphasize that the *Adhyātma Rāmāyaṇa* version of the first epic and the *Śrīmad Bhagavadgītā* as the offshoot of the second are clear examples of the present situation. Thus, it is not difficult to trace the spiritual links of the psychological discussions carried out in different contexts.

Some Examples of Spiritual Links of Psychoscience in Upaniṣads

In the *Vivekacūḍāmaṇi* (Ādi Śaṅkara 1966) there are several verses which clearly show the spiritual link of *liṅga śarīra* (micro-body) first with *citātmā* (subtle component $\mathcal{M}_s$) and later with *cidākāśa* (causal body $\mathcal{C}$). As an example, we cite one case here, viz. verse 102:

sarvavyāpuṭikaraṇam liṅgamidam syāccidātmanaḥ puṁsaḥ ।
vāsyādikamiva takṣṇastenaivātmā bhavatijasaṅgo 'yam ।। (5.12)

This, in brief, means that "this *linga śarīra* is responsible for all actions and representations of *cidātmā* and therefore the latter is inseparable from the former, in the same way as the identity of a carpenter cannot be established without his *vasūlā* (a particular type of hammer used by a carpenter and the same acts as his identity)", or of a musician without his musical instrument concerned.

Like in *SMBG*, the spiritual links of micro-body can also be traced in various Upaniṣads in different contexts. Here, as examples, we cite one case from each the *Kaṭhopaniṣad* and *Aitareyopaniṣad* (Goyandaka 1994) respectively as:

indriyebhyaḥ parā hyarthā arthebhyaśca paraṁ manaḥ ।
manasastu parā buddhirabuddherātmā mahānparaḥ ।।
– *Kaṭhopaniṣad* 1.3.10 (5.13)

Sense-objects like sound, etc. are more powerful than senses, mind is more powerful than sense-objects, intellect is even more powerful than mind and most superior and powerful than intellect is *ātmā* (soul).

As a matter of fact, it is this wisdom of the *Kaṭhopaniṣad* that is also narrated by the Lord in *SMBG* (cf. verse III.42). In fact, the essence of verses (5.13) and (*SMBG*: III.42) is conceptualized in the next chapter in the form of the atomic model of matter and used as a basis for all discussions in subsequent chapters to study Vedic psychoscience in a modern scientific spirit.

Next we cite another place in *Aitareyopaniṣad* 3.1.2, which emphasizes on the spiritual links of psychoscience. Similarly, in *Taittirīyopaniṣad* 2.4, Upaniṣad seer clearly emphasizes on the spiritual hold on different aspects of psychoscience. For further details, we refer to the literature concerned.

5.5 Concluding Discussion

From the discussions in Chapters 3 and 4, it becomes clear that the localized soul in an individual is a part of "eternal cosmic essence", i.e. of cosmic consciousness field. In the present chapter, however, it is demonstrated that this localized soul, in order to make its existence meaningful, does not exist in isolation but exists with all its supplementary, viz. micro, gross, societal and natural existences. These existences, including $\mathcal{M}$g and $\mathcal{M}$s, maintain certain hierarchy. Side by side, they are linked together in a subtle manner and the same reflects in the day-to-day actions of a person. In fact, it is the micro existence (a domain of psychoscience) that has very strong links and works in collaboration with all remaining existences, in spite that the causal existence has a very stronghold on it. This fact is illustrated in this chapter through a variety of examples from ancient Indian scriptures and by highlighting the existence of two important barriers in the path of spiritual journey.

For this purpose, besides exploring the capsule-wisdom of *SMBG* which offers a case of fine psychological theories, several examples are cited here from other ancient Indian scriptures. Several "golden rules" related to human behaviour and experiences are traced to this effect and the same are found to work in a down-to-earth manner in the daily life of a common man. As far as the search for spiritual links of the psychoscience are concerned, besides *SMBG*, they are also traced in the philosophy of Āyurveda, *aṣṭāṅga-yoga* of Patañjali and also in various Upaniṣads. It is worthwhile to highlight following examples of such links in different existences: For a person who is suffering from certain type of pain (a state of mind), the tears (a gross-body process) often come out automatically. This demonstrates a link between $\mathcal{M}$ and $\mathcal{G}$. Similarly, a person who is in a sorrow state of affairs does not feel like eating anything even if he is hungry – a link perhaps among all the three $\mathcal{M}$, $\mathcal{G}$ and $\mathcal{C}$.

Lastly, it may be of interest to view the discussions in this chapter in the language of "category error" of modern scientists (cf. Section 2.6). While scientists are talking of two types of matter, viz. (physical) matter and "mind" stuff, which we later corroborate by some examples from physics in terms of different types of (physical) energies, here, however, it seems that one has to talk now of category errors among three types of matter, viz. soul (spiritual), "mind" (psychic) and matter (physical). Further, while such studies are desirable now on the physics front, one can as well think of correlating three categories of energies, viz. mechanical (W), heat (H) and magnetic (μ), via a relation, like $W = \alpha H = \beta\mu$, where α and β could be some constants of proportionality or may be some functions (law of correspondence, as in Weber–Fechner law), and W, H and μ are analogue of physical, mental and soul energies. Of course, this latter class of "category error" is much more subtle in philosophical terms than the one thought over by modern scientists.

High Skill Exercises and Projects

5.1 Justify the place value of psychoscience between spiritualism and materialism in the spiritual journey of a person. Discuss and analyse the role of two barriers (viz. mind and ego) in this journey, particularly in the process of attaining salvation (*mokṣa*).

5.2 Explain and elaborate as to how the three nature-born qualities or modes of *Prakṛti*, viz. *sattva*, *rajas* and *tamas* remain in the background in classifying three types of flavours in each category, viz. (i) *saṅkalpas*, (ii) human qualities, (iii) human intents like *śraddhā*, *tapa*, *dhṛti*, *tyāga*, *tyāgī*, (iv) material stimuli like *dāna*, *yajña*, *sukha*, (v) non-material stimuli like *jñāna*, *karma*, *kartā*, and (vi) essences of life like *buddhi*. [Hint: *SMBG* chapters 17 and 18]

5.3 Discuss, the so-called "golden rule" in the context of health care and/or personality development. Explain with examples the utility and viability of such rules in the upliftment or downfall of a personality.

5.4 While the "*aṣṭāṅga-yoga* of Patañjali offers an example of 'super golden rule' through its eight components, it also offers the examples of 'golden rules' associated with each of its components, viz. *yama*, *niyama*, *āsana*, *prāṇāyāma*, *pratyāhāra*, *dhāraṇā*, *dhyāna* and *samādhi*". Explain and justify this statement.

5.5 *Steaming and Streaming of Consciousness*: Recall the principle of steam engine and the principle of "Joule–Thomson effect" in the context of cooling in physics. In the former case, it is the heat energy through the focused version of water steam that helps in dragging heavy load like a railway engine and train. Similarly, in the second case of Joule–Thomson effect when high-pressure gas is allowed to pass through a narrow orifice, cooling is produced. Compare these concepts with the philosophy hidden in the drawing of *fig*. 5.3. In the lower steps depicted in this figure, viz. during practice, knowledge and meditation steps, the human Being is first Being dragged by a "burning desire" for liberation. At each step, the intensity of meditation increases. Then, as soon as the practitioner starts discarding the fruits of action, the peace follows (streams out) immediately. When peace persists constantly joy gathers and in the end, the persistency of perpetual joy is nothing but a state of eternal joy (liberation or *mokṣa*). Write a Note on elaborating these analogies further.

Part 2
Psychoscience in Its New Incarnation

6

Psychophysics and the Patomic Model of Human Being

6.1 Introduction

In the history of physical sciences, there was a time when mathematics was considered as the "queen" of natural sciences since every branch of physics, chemistry and even of biology wanted to marry it. Over a period of time, however, the scenario has changed. The laws of mathematics are not only in use in the realms of almost all soft disciplines including humanities and social sciences but now physics too seems to take the earlier place of mathematics in the sense that several soft disciplines are standing in the queue to marry physics. Why should it not be? After all the nature of physics laws, their universality, and over and above them all, the methodologies used therein through modelling games are a few salient features of physics which impress the experts of other fields to marry it. This sponsors the fact that if mathematics offers the language in which Nature expresses Herself better, then physics does carry the theme to be conveyed (expressed) through that language.

As early as in 1860, Gustav Theodore Fechner of Leipzig introduced (Adler 1960; Fechner 1860) the subject of psychophysics which, according to him, is an exact science of functional relations or the relations of dependency between body and mind, or more generally, between physical and psychic worlds. Thus, in historical perspective, psychophysics is the branch of psychology that deals with the relations between physical stimuli and sensory response. Unfortunately, in the Western way of thinking, while the sensory world is well understood through the subject of physics (for example, the sense eye takes over the subject of optics, the sense ear takes over the subject of sound, the sense skin takes over the subject of heat through touch, etc.), the psychic or mental world is not explored to the same extent. As a result, the development of the subject matter of psychophysics somehow has not been kept in tune with other philosophies of the mental world or of mental processes and also with the progress made over the years in physical theories and brain sciences as well. While neuroscience has already started investigating the processes of learning, feeling and thinking in terms of neuron dynamics, the Indian philosophy, on the other hand, does offer (Kaushal 1990, 1994, 1998a, 2011) an elegant framework to study and analyse the entire gamut of human experiences in the finest possible manner and in terms of the so-called essences of life (EOLs). In fact, the same stimulant of the physical world can leave different imprints on the minds of different persons depending upon the level of development of their faculties of understandings (FOUs). As a result, the role of FOUs of an individual in the perception process needs to be understood prior to relying on any conclusion drawn from the observations on the stimulant. In what flows we briefly discuss a well-studied framework of Vedic science for this purpose.

In the next section, we briefly review the Vedic framework of patomic model of human Being with reference to its designing and the reduced version. In Section 6.3, we discuss an interesting outcome of the (*tri-karaṇa*) dressing rules of Section 4.2 to explore the degeneracy of M, I and E states in patomic picture, which, in turn, will be attributed to the multiplicity of *manas, buddhi* and *smr̥ti* of Vedic and Jaina sciences. The details of application of patomic model while are left for the rest of the book, in Section 6.4 we briefly highlight some, mainly with reference to the interactions of a human Being with other Beings and environment. Finally, we comment on the use of physical theories and concepts in understanding the psychological problems in Section 6.5.

6.2 Patomic Model and Human Being

6.2.1 SOME UNDENIABLE FACTS ABOUT THE HUMAN BEING AS PER VEDIC WISDOM

Essences of Life (EOLs) and Their Arrangement

We all have biological body (B) consisting of inner and outer organs in it; we do have ten senses of knowledge and action (SE) (five senses of knowledge or of perception are eyes, ears, nose, tongue and skin, sensitive respectively to light, sound, smell, taste and touch, and five senses of actions or motor organs are hands, feet, speech, anus and copulatory organ). They, in conjunction with the stimuli from the worldly object (WO), constitute the set of outer EOLs. The other set of inner EOLs consists of mind (M), intellect (I) and ego (or self-sense) (E) which respectively are responsible for defining the faculties of "emotion", "decision" and "memory" inside the human Being. Notably they all are like inanimate objects but work and become functional (*SMBG* VII.4) only in the presence of another non-physical element called "consciousness" that originates from, what is termed as "soul" (SO) - the innermost existence present in a Being and cannot be denied (since a dead body, in spite of having all these EOLs cannot act and become functional in the absence of SO alone). A human Being (b) (also called as *jīva* (life principle)) is a composite entity of all these inner and outer EOLs who, while having a strong base in SO, does work consistently in the field of WO.

With regard to the arrangement of these EOLs in a human Being (cf. *fig*. 6.1), we again use the essence of verse III.42 of *SMBG*, which, in philosophical terms, clearly suggests an atom-like picture at the mental level. For this purpose, a patomic (philosophical atom-type) model of human Being has been proposed earlier (Kaushal

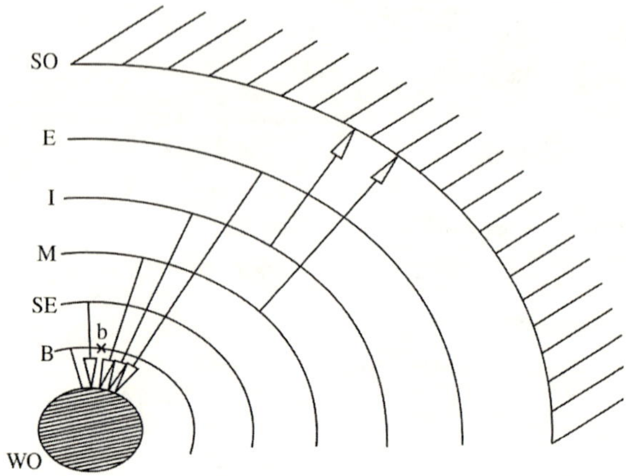

fig. 6.1: Philosophical atom-like model of human Being

1990, 1994, 1998a, 2011) by the author in which the nucleus WO is in the centre and the discrete (energy) states B, SE, M, I and E are placed around it in accordance with their increasing fineness and the strength of meditation. (Meditation is a process in which one uses the focused and/or directed consciousness or the so-called attention to peep into his own inner Self.) Much beyond the state E, it is all continuum of SO. As mentioned above, this type of arrangement is also in tune with the philosophy of *SMBG*.

In fact, the author, about thirty-three years ago (Kaushal 1990), was inspired to have such a picture (cf. *fig*. 6.1) of human Being in mind from the following verses of *SMBG*:

bhūmirāpo 'nalo vāyuḥ khaṁ mano buddhireva ca ।
ahaṁkāra itīyaṁ me bhinnā prakr̥tirasṭadhā ॥

SMBG – VII.4 (6.0a)

apareyamitastvanyāṁ prakr̥tiṁ viddhi me parām ।
jivabhūtāṁ mahābāho yayedaṁ dhārayate jagat ॥

SMBG – VII.5 (6.0b)

> In addition to five *mahābhūtas* – earth, water, fire, air and ether – the mind, the intellect and also the ego constitute the eightfold insentient (inanimate) mode of My Nature; the other than this, by which the whole Universe is sustained, know it as My higher or sentient (animate) Nature in the form of *jīva* (life principle), Oh Arjuna.

The sentient mode is the domain of soul in whose presence the entire insentient mode becomes operative (or exists). Further,

indriyāṇi parāṇyāhurindriyebhyaḥ param manaḥ ।
manasastu parā buddhiryo buddheaḥ paratastu saḥ ॥
SMBG – III.42 (6.0c)

> The senses are said to be greater than the body; but greater than the senses is the mind. Greater than the mind is the intellect; and what is greater than the intellect is He (the Self or soul).

This verse of *SMBG* beautifully introduces the essences of life and their relative ordering as far as their role in the day-to-day actions of a human Being is concerned. In fact, it is the ego (the self-sense, *saṁskāras, vāsanās* or the memory aspect) that does prevail even beyond the intellect.

Note that this gradation of various states, in which an electron-like object b can stay and accordingly perform upward and downward transitions, is on the scale of meditation (see Chapter 7) and not with respect to the physical space–time. As a matter of fact, the position of EOLs B, SE, M, I, E offers some kind of islands in the space of increasing intensity of meditation from WO to SO. Further, while the upward transitions of b are rare, the downward transitions are natural and more frequent.

Even on the meditation scale the increasing spacing between successive states corresponds to a rigid binding/rigid rotator in quantum mechanics between the Being b and the worldly objects WO. In order to have a feel for the increasing spacing between successive levels in the above patomic model we analyse here a quantum rigid rotator model for b–WO binding. In analogy with the quantized energy levels of (quantum) rigid rotator, viz.,

$$E_q = L(L+1)\hbar^2/(2\, I_m), \qquad (L = 0, 1, 2, - .....), \qquad (6.1)$$

where L is orbital angular momentum quantum number and I_m is the moment of inertia and $h = 2\pi\hbar$ is Planck constant, we can write energy levels for a philosophical quantized rigid rotator as

$$E_{ph} = J(J + 1)\, g^2/(2\, \mathcal{J}), \qquad (J = J_{min}, J_{min} + 1, ..., J_{max}), \qquad (6.2)$$

where $g = 2\pi g$ is a Planck-like constant in the meditation domain in the same way as h is a constant in the space–time world. Here J_{min} and J_{max} for a common man remain arbitrary as each of us has born with certain amount of rigid binding between b and WO, depending on the level of development of one's faculty of understanding. Here, the moment of inertia like quantity, $\mathcal{J}$, characterizes the individual's efficiency and efforts that he makes towards his functional nature.

Further, note that such an arrangement of EOLs in a human Being that includes the role of SO in it is subject to expose to a finest possible cosmic consciousness field in the Universe, in the same way as a functional mobile handset (which contains a battery in it) is exposed to the electromagnetic signal spread all over in the space. Interestingly, such a philosophical picture of a human Being in terms of some minimum number of intangible EOLs has not only helped in understanding human experiences and actions at the most fundamental level (Kaushal 2011) but has also suggested several new dimensions of study in the personality theory of Jung (cf. Chapter 11), particularly with reference to the spiritual content (Kaushal 2016a; Rajoria et al. 2018) in it.

6.2.2 REDUCED VERSION OF PATOMIC MODEL AND THE GROUPING OF EOLs

While trying to analyse the human behaviour in terms of the dynamics of EOLs, no doubt, the role of each EOL needs to be accounted for at a deeper level but some gross features of behaviour and personality traits can be understood (see Rajoria et al. 2018 and chapter 9 of Kaushal 2015) easily just by grouping the outer EOLs as gross body ($\mathcal{G}$) as $\mathcal{G} \equiv$ {WO, B, SE}, inner EOLs as "micro" body ($\mathcal{M}$)

as $\mathcal{M} \equiv \{M, I, E\}$ and the only EOL SO as "causal" or astral body ($\mathcal{C}$) as $\mathcal{C} \equiv \{SO\}$ as per Vedic science. In this way, the (perfect human) Being b basically is a union of $\mathcal{G}$, $\mathcal{M}$ and $\mathcal{C}$, viz. $b = \mathcal{G} \cup \mathcal{M} \cup \mathcal{C}$ or it is a set of all EOLs, i.e. $b \equiv \{WO, B, SE, M, I, E, SO\}$. Further, note that the absence of any one or more EOLs in b constitutes the classes of physically or mentally challenged persons or of nonhuman Beings (cf. "fractured" patomic model, see Kaushal 2011). Such a grouping of EOLs, in fact, has been helpful in explaining a variety of aspects of human actions, human and nonhuman interactions, etc. at least in the lowest order.

Faculty of Understanding and the Level of Its Development in an Individual

In analogy with a generalized version of *pañcīkaraṇa* rule of Vedic science known for the perception of five cosmic elements (*PMs*), viz. earth, water, air, fire and ether, recall that a *tri-karaṇa* rule for inner EOLs M, I and E, and a *dvi-karaṇa* rule for the outer EOLs B and SE are proposed (cf. Chapter 4). These rules define the dressing of an object with consciousness in different orders through some sort of symbolic recurrence relations and thereby suggest a mechanism to differentiate clearly between dressed (perceived) and undressed (unperceived or nascent) versions of entities. In other words, these dressing rules demonstrate as how the EP-matter is generated from P-matter in a self-consistent manner. These rules, demonstrating the discrete evolution of an EOL with consciousness (meditation), have further helped in understanding the perception process in a more logical manner (Kaushal 2015). Here, however, we emphasize only on the *tri-karaṇa* rule for the dressing of inner EOLs from their nascent version M, I and E. As a matter of fact, the faculty of understanding of an individual is a composite (set) of differently dressed versions of his inner EOLs with his own consciousness, viz. $\tilde{F}^{(l,m,n)} = \{\tilde{M}^{(l)}, \tilde{I}^{(m)}, \tilde{E}^{(n)}\}$ where $\tilde{M}^{(l)}, \tilde{I}^{(m)}$ and $\tilde{E}^{(n)}$ are the ℓth, m^{th} and n^{th} order-dressed versions of $M (\equiv \tilde{M}^{(0)}), I (\equiv \tilde{I}^{(0)})$ and $E (\equiv \tilde{E}^{(0)})$ respectively and according to the *tri-karaṇa* rule they are given by the symbolic recurrence relations (cf. eqs (4.7)-(4.9)). Here $\ell, m, n = 1, 2, 3, \ldots, \infty$. In nutshell, as a result of dressing of all the three of mind, intellect and ego of an individual with his consciousness, each EOL enriches itself with its respective intrinsic characteristics, particularly when it is constantly exposed to the consciousness through the process of meditation.

In view of relations (4.8), the three limiting cases corresponding to $\ell, m, n \to \infty$, while separately define three ideal personalities, viz. the most emotional, the most intelligent, the most learned respectively for a common man; however, one can as well define an index r as a set of integers l, m and n, viz. $r = \{\ell, m, n\}$ which characterizes the level of development of one's FOU. Further, note that the order of dressing of an EOL in general is a measure of intensity of meditation attained by an individual. Such an interplay of inner EOLs has already offered explanations of variety of aspects of human behaviour and experiences (Kaushal 2011, 2015). We refrain ourselves from going into these details here. These dressing rules become an asset when defining the intensity of meditation (consciousness) (Chapter 7) or looking for the coordinate–momentum coupling at the most fundamental level (Kaushal 2016b).

6.3 An Interesting Outcome of Dressing Rules: Origin of Sub-(Energy)-States in Patomic Model

In quantum mechanics, the discrete values of orbital quantum number give rise to sub-energy-levels in the atom. Here, we have traced other alternative for this kind of discretization, i.e. in terms of discrete dressing rules expressed through relations (4.8). Although a continuous evolution of mindset function (a function of attributes of M, I, E) with consciousness is also considered elsewhere (cf. Appendix A), but we concentrate here only on discrete dressing (or evolution) of inner EOLs with consciousness. This, in fact, leads to infinitely many discrete sub-levels of each of M, I and E, which are not equally spaced. This kind of extension of patomic model makes it more viable towards the studies of human/non-human behaviour. This also suggests a possible explanation for distinct levels of development of FOUs for different individuals in this framework. Interestingly in the present mathematical setting, the spacing between successive sub-levels for each M, I and E decrease by a factor of four at each order of dressing. While similar results can be computed easily for the EOLs I and E, here we demonstrate this fact only for the EOL M for some low-order dressings for simplicity.

Though the contribution of B and SE is necessary in the lowest order dressing (cf. Kaushal 2011, chapter 8) but we ignore it here and confine to pure *tri-karaṇa* rule for the trio of M, I and E. According to this rule, the functional version of the EOL M is the result of a combination of 50 per cent of the nascent mind M and the 25 per cent of each of intellect I and ego E. If we denote n^{th}-order dressing of M as $\tilde{M}^{(n)}$, then for $n = 0$, $\tilde{M}^{(o)} = M$, $\tilde{I}^{(o)} = I$ and $\tilde{E}^{(o)} = E$, symbolically, then the functional mind $\tilde{M}^{(1)}$ in the lowest (first)-order dressing is given by

$$\tilde{M}^{(1)} = \frac{1}{2}\tilde{M}^{(0)} + \frac{1}{4}\tilde{I}^{(n)} + \frac{1}{4}\tilde{E}^{(0)} = \frac{1}{2}M + \frac{1}{4}I + \frac{1}{4}E, \tag{6.3}$$

and similar relations for $\tilde{I}^{(1)}$ and $\tilde{E}^{(1)}$ with the replacements M $\rightarrow$ I $\rightarrow$ E $\rightarrow$ M, in the resultant relations. Note that $\tilde{M}^{(1)}$, $\tilde{I}^{(1)}$ and $\tilde{E}^{(1)}$ are the functional forms of M, I and E in the lowest order of meditation. They become increasingly sharp as they are dressed with consciousness in higher orders using the relation like (6.3) recursively. Here, M, I and E are the inert or nascent versions like the unperceived *pañca-mahābhūtas* of Vedic science (cf. Section 4.2).

Next we list the second, third and fourth order results of dressing of M, viz. $\tilde{M}^{(2)}$, $\tilde{M}^{(3)}$, $\tilde{M}^{(4)}$, as follows:

$$\begin{aligned}\tilde{M}^{(2)} &= \frac{1}{2}\tilde{M}^{(1)} + \frac{1}{4}\tilde{I}^{(1)} + \frac{1}{4}\tilde{E}^{(1)} \\ &= \frac{1}{2}\left(\frac{1}{2}M + \frac{1}{4}I + \frac{1}{4}E\right) + \frac{1}{4}\left(\frac{1}{2}I + \frac{1}{4}E + \frac{1}{4}M\right) \\ &+ \frac{1}{4}\left(\frac{1}{2}E + \frac{1}{4}M + \frac{1}{4}I\right) \\ &= \frac{3}{8}M + \frac{5}{16}I + \frac{5}{16}E \end{aligned} \tag{6.4}$$

and similar results for $\tilde{I}^{(2)}$ and $\tilde{E}^{(2)}$ with M → I → E → M. Similarly, one can derive results for

$\tilde{M}^{(3)}$ and $\tilde{M}^{(4)}$ as

$$\tilde{M}^{(3)} = \frac{1}{2}\tilde{M}^{(2)} + \frac{1}{4}\tilde{I}^{(2)} + \frac{1}{4}\tilde{E}^{(2)}$$

$$\text{or} \quad \tilde{M}^{(3)} = \frac{11}{32}M + \frac{21}{64}I + \frac{21}{64}E; \tag{6.5}$$

$$\tilde{M}^{(4)} = \frac{1}{2}\tilde{M}^{(3)} + \frac{1}{4}\tilde{I}^{(3)} + \frac{1}{4}\tilde{E}^{(3)}$$

$$\text{or} \quad \tilde{M}^{(4)} = \frac{43}{128}M + \frac{85}{256}\tilde{I} + \frac{85}{256}E. \tag{6.6}$$

From results (6.3)–(6.6) it is not difficult to note that

$$\tilde{M}^{(4)} - \tilde{M}^{(3)} = \frac{1}{4}\left(\tilde{M}^{(3)} - \tilde{M}^{(2)}\right) = \left(\frac{1}{4}\right)^2\left(\tilde{M}^{(2)} - \tilde{M}^{(1)}\right)$$

$$= \left(\frac{1}{4}\right)^3\left(\tilde{M}^{(1)} - \tilde{M}^{(0)}\right),$$

or, in general,

$$\tilde{M}^{(n)} - \tilde{M}^{(n-1)} = \frac{1}{4}\left(\tilde{M}^{(n-1)} - \tilde{M}^{(n-2)}\right) = \dots\dots\dots = \left(\frac{1}{4}\right)^{(n-1)}\left(\tilde{M}^{(1)} - \tilde{M}^{(0)}\right),$$

and similar expressions for

$$\left(\tilde{I}^{(n)} - \tilde{I}^{(n-1)}\right) \text{ and } \left(\tilde{E}^{(n)} - \tilde{E}^{(n-1)}\right). \tag{6.7}$$

From these analyses, following additional observations about patomic model are in order:

i. On the meditation scale, while the spacing between successive states B, SE, M, I, E and the continuum SO increases on the basis of common experience, the spacing between successive sub-levels of inner EOLs M, I and E decreases at a very fast pace, i.e. by a factor of 4 at each order of dressing. It is an interesting point to check whether the continuum achieved in the two cases, i.e. in the original case (through eq. (6.2)) and in the limit when $n \to \infty$ in $\tilde{M}^{(n)}$, $\tilde{I}^{(n)}$ and $\tilde{E}^{(n)}$(cf. eq. (6.7)) are the same or different. Obviously, for a good practitioner these limits are expected to be there in the same cosmic consciousness field (cf. Chapter 3), but they culminate at different end-points (seed) in it.

ii. Dressing with consciousness does not affect the outer (tangible) EOLs B and SE: According to *dvi-karaṇa* rule, first-order dressings of B and SE are given by

$$\tilde{B}^{(1)} = \frac{1}{2}B + \frac{1}{2}SE, \qquad \tilde{SE}^{(1)} = \frac{1}{2}SE + \frac{1}{2}B.$$

Also

$$\tilde{B}^{(2)} = \frac{1}{2}\tilde{B}^{(1)} + \frac{1}{2}\tilde{SE}^{(1)} = \frac{1}{2}B + \frac{1}{2}SE;$$

$$\tilde{SE}^{(2)} = \frac{1}{2}\tilde{SE}^{(1)} + \frac{1}{2}\tilde{B}^{(1)} = \frac{1}{2}SE + \frac{1}{2}B,$$

Implying,

$$\tilde{B}^{(2)} - \tilde{B}^{(1)} = \tilde{SE}^{(2)} - \tilde{SE}^{(1)} = 0,$$

i.e. B and SE are differently (permanently) inert with reference to consciousness.

iii. Now we have a new picture of patomic model (cf. *fig.* 6.2) in which the Being b has many rather infinitely more choices (that include states and substates) to stay in different space–time situations besides meditation intensity.

iv. "Conscious" mind(s) $\tilde{M}^{(n)}$ is (are) created on "unconscious" mind $\tilde{M}^{(0)}$; so are the "conscious" intellect $\tilde{I}^{(m)}$ and ego $\tilde{E}^{(r)}$. In fact, the states corresponding to $n \neq 0$ here are the states of enlightenment for an individual.

v. It is not difficult to realize that the concepts like *citta* and *saṅkalpa* (or for that matter other synonyms for intellect and ego of Vedic science) are the by-products of this new scheme of study. For example, *citta* belongs to the domain of $\tilde{M}^{(\ell)} \times \tilde{I}^{(m)}$ or *saṅkalpa* belongs to the domain of $\tilde{I}^{(n)} \times \tilde{E}^{(r)}$.

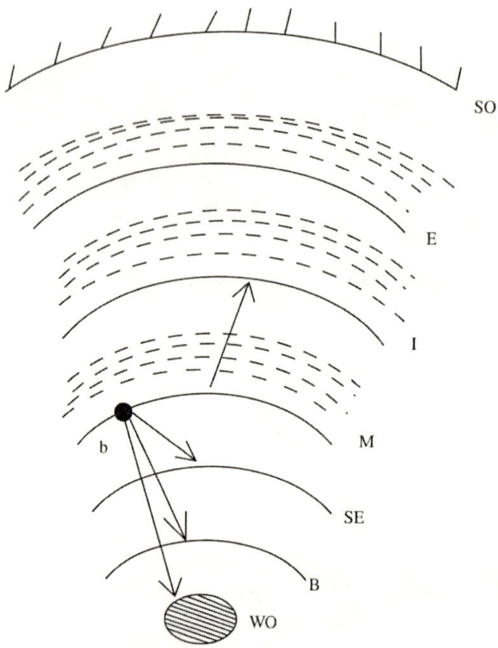

fig. 6.2: A modified version of patomic model

Even varieties of different states (including subconscious or supraconscious states) of mind, different types of intellects or memories discussed in Vedic, Jaina and other philosophies of the world can be accommodated in this scheme of study. As a matter of fact, it is the first enlightened state of mind, intellect or memory that takes time to attain; otherwise subsequent enlightened states of these EOLs become just a matter of little effort to attain by a good practitioner in view of the relations like (6.7) for all three, M, I and E.

vi. As a matter of fact, in between the states B and M, there exist yet three more intangible substates, called *tridoṣas* of Āyurveda. These *doṣas*, viz. *vāta* (υ), *pitta* (π) and *kapha* (κ), in fact, are the combination of *PMs* E_a, W, A, F and E_t in varying proportion (see, Section 9.4.2(c)). For example, in *kapha*, E_a and W dominate; in *pitta* F and W dominate and in *vāta*, A and

E_t dominate. With regard to their subtlety, κ lies in between B and SE, π and υ lie in between SE and M in *fig.* 6.2. As per Āyurveda, an equilibrium among these *doṣas* play a dominant role in the maintenance of good health, not only of biological body including inner organs but also of psyche in terms of M, I and E. Further, note that their dressed versions also play roles in teletherapy, distant healing, etc. (for details, see Chapter 9).

6.4 Human Behaviour and Environment

(a) *Human actions and their patterns (behavioural dynamics)***:** As far as the analysis and understanding of human actions is concerned, the same has been carried out in psychology in modern times mostly by using statistical methods and the so-derived empirical models. A formal and absolute approach to understand the subject matter and the collected data in terms of certain minimal at the input level is somehow missing. The proposed patomic model of human Being which has roots in Vedic science (cf. Sections 6.1 and 6.2), in some sense can prove to be a powerful alternative for such experts. For this purpose one can start analysing actions in terms either of ways, namely, using the reduced version of the model but for studies at a crude level or using the individual EOL for studies at a finer level. As far as the "kārmic theory" of Vedic science is concerned, there is enough scope for studying further deep features of human actions in terms of three Nature-born *guṇas* (modes of *Prakr̥ti*). As a matter of fact a systematic study of the dynamics of these EOLs in an individual defines a broad spectrum of human virtues (cf. Appendix D), a pattern of which, reflects in the so-called his personality or the behaviour at a later stage (cf. Chapter 11).

When such a picture of human Being (i.e. patomic model) interacts with the outer world – consisting of both inanimate and animate objects (stimuli) – a new dynamics (which basically differs from the one that appears for physical atoms, mainly because now the role of free will and consciousness of participating persons appears in the system) emerges. Attempts will be made to understand such psychochemistry, of course, by way of having certain lessons from existing physics theories (cf. Chapters 10 and 11). In fact, a study of these interactions becomes an asset with reference to the personality development and character building by an individual.

(b) *Two, three and many human Being interactions (collective behaviour and sociology)*: Keeping in mind the roles of willpower and consciousness of an individual, a theoretical understanding of fundamental processes involving two, three and many human Being interactions is developed in analogy with physical concepts and many–body theories in physics (Kaushal 2015). As far as the role of patomic model of human Being in these studies is concerned, the same appears in a somewhat different way from that of atomic model of matter. In the latter case, while valence electrons play a dominant role in many atom systems, here, however, the Being b participates in the interactions in two distinct ways, viz. in an "inside out" or in an "outside out" manner, depending upon the process under study. In some sense, the level of development of one's FOU also matters in this regard. (For details see, Chapter 10 and Kaushal 2015.)

6.5 Using Physical Theories to Understand Psychic Phenomena and Processes: Concluding Remarks

(a) *Psychophysics in new incarnation and psychoscience from psychophysics*: For the purposes of understanding the fundamental processes that take place inside the human Being in relation to his behaviour and experiences, in the same way as one studies the physical processes in physics, the richness and depth of Vedic wisdom in this regard is demonstrated in the above sections. The framework developed here is not only viable for applications in human- and humanity-related problems, but this also gives birth to several new interdisciplinary subjects like psychomechanics, psychochemistry and psychobiology (cf. Chapters 7-9), in addition to psychophysics. When other disciplines of natural science are accommodated in this scheme of study, then it is worthwhile to call this new subject as psychoscience. This type of methodology, based on the top-down approach, when used in psychology, is definitely going to provide better and, in fact, precise solution of problems as compared to those obtained using the prevailing statistical methods based on the bottom-up approach. Such conclusions, as will be clear from the forthcoming chapters, are applicable in the context of both individual-based and their collective version (sociology)-based studies. Note that this type of psychophysics is completely different from the one conceived by Fechner in 1860 and elaborated later by others. No doubt, the present book itself is an example of the viability of these new methods, still more works on application front are desirable.

(b) *Comments on perception process*: The dressing rules, whose glimpses given in Chapter 4, basically are the recurrence-type relations originated out of the extension and generalization of *pañcīkaraṇa* rule of Vedic science for five cosmic elements. These rules, in fact, have not only greatly facilitated the understanding of the perception process at the most fundamental level - a long-standing problem of panpsychism in psychology (Seager 1995), but also defined an index to characterize the level of development of faculty of understanding of a person.

(c) *An effort towards quantification of consciousness*: This new psychophysics is not only dealing with the interplay of various mental processes but always keeps an eye on the role of consciousness in them through the use of meditation variable μ. Once the quantification of meditation becomes possible, of course under some simplifying assumptions, the subject of psychomechanics can be developed on the lines of classical mechanics (see, next chapter). In these endeavours, physical theories and concepts will be frequently used in an analogous manner towards the formulation of several new psychic phenomena in terms of the dynamics of EOLs, i.e. a step towards the quantification of consciousness or to understand the subjective science of the Self better.

(d) *The Being b and the epi-physical matter*: The epi-physical (EP)-matter is defined as the physical (P)-matter plus consciousness. Now the question is as to how the Being b, as the polluted version of SO, is formed (cf. Section 3.2). In fact, the consciousness first transcended from Φ_{cc} to SO at the time of conception and then from SO it transcends in two distinct ways:

i. in one case, it illuminates both inner and outer EOLs, viz. B, SE, M, I, and E to make them functional simultaneously, and
ii. in second case, it emanates first from M and later from B, SE, I and E in a directed manner (the so-called "attention") to make the outer world perceptible.

A collective and also a capsule version of the illuminated B, SE, M, I and E in the first case and again in the background of SO, is called the Being, b. In this case, the Being is termed as special epi-physical (SEP)-matter or the "Type I" EP-matter. The EP-matter of case (ii), we term as the "Type II" EP-matter. In the later, this b becomes functional in the outer world in conjunction with attention. Further, it is the dominating order of dressing of any one of the EOLs B, SE, M, I and E (at times including WO) with consciousness, that not only helps in forming the attitude of b towards the world-order but also forces b to stay in the corresponding EOL including in WO.

Thus, we have two distinct classes of EP-matter – in one case (Type I) the working EOLs (both inner and outer, including the brain and other biological organs) are the examples of EP-matter and in the second case (Type II) the matter outside the human body, i.e. P-matter but illuminated with SO or with its characteristics consciousness, is the EP-matter. For a dead body himself, however, none of these concepts works. In the present work, while the working of EOLs will be taken as granted, EP-matter of Type II, i.e. the one with attention dominated will be investigated. Also, such a role of consciousness converts physics into the subject of psychophysics.

High Skill Exercises and Projects

6.1 Keeping the wisdom of *SMBG* (cf. verses III.42 and VII.4) in mind discuss and analyse the arrangement of EOLs, WO, B, SE, M, I, E, SO in the form of patomic model. As particular cases, discuss its reduced version and also the fractured patomic model. Elaborate on its applications in daily life.

6.2 It may be mentioned that the enlightened versions of M, I and /or E constitute the so-called "third eye" (wisdom-eye or *jñāna-cakṣu*) in some cults. Explain as how the opening or further enlightenment of the third eye can be achieved and understood in terms of the dressing rules proposed for the trio of M, I and E.

6.3 In the light of the earlier work (Kaushal 2011) write an essay on the viability of patomic model in explaining and understanding the human behaviour and experiences. Also comment on the studies on non-human Beings within this framework.

6.4 In cases of "Type II" SEP-matter, the mind M merges with SO and thus becomes capable of using the entire consciousness assigned, though in a focused manner. Such an attention-dominated mind, when works in or illuminates the worlds of B, SE, I and E or in general that of WO, it does wonders. Keeping the theme of Chapter 9 in mind, write an essay on the acts of such attention carrying (dominated) mind (also, see verse II.67 of *SMBG*):

7

Psychomechanics

Accounting for the Consciousness in Physical Theories

After designing an atom-like (patomic) model for the arrangement of EOLs in an individual in the previous chapter, here we look for still deeper foundations of psychoscience in mathematical terms. In fact, with regard to the human experiences (belonging to spiritual zone) and the actions (belonging to behavioural zone) an understanding of the underlying dynamics of inner EOLs – a backbone for the subject of psychoscience – is desirable. A common man in daily life, while draws pleasure by enjoying sense-objects, an element of peace at mental level also becomes necessary and the same he draws by optimizing the mental potency and by putting a check on the associated mental processes.

In the same way as any discrepancy between the measured truth about the world-3 (cf. Table 3.2) and the perceived truth about the world-2 sets the limits on the modelling processes of objective science, the discrepancies noticed between the perceived truth about the world-2 and the realized truth even by an individual at the level of the world-1, set the limits on the tools of psychoscience (Kaushal 2011), i.e. of psycho-anatomy and/or psychophysiology of the "mind" itself. As a matter of fact, the description of any phenomenon pertaining to world-2 in general would require an account of all the three – space, time and consciousness – on the same footing. The consciousness in the Western schools of thought is considered as an attribute of just "mind". But, in reality, it is not so (Kaushal 2011, 2015), it has rather further details at subtle level in Vedic wisdom. Here, for consciousness we shall introduce a new variable, the so-called "meditation variable" μ, in the theory. Obviously, the variation of μ will account for the entire spectrum of consciousness covering all "islands" of intangible world including the soul – assumed to be the source of consciousness in an individual. As discussed earlier in Chapter 6, some of these islands are: mind (M) – as the faculty of emotions; intellect (I) – as the faculty of decision; self-sense or ego (E) – as the faculty of memory; etc.

First, we outline the linear and non-linear evolutions of an individual with consciousness and then analyse in Section 7.2 the stability of the so-called mindset function, $\mathcal{M}$, associated uniquely with a functional individual. Here, we investigate the stability of $\mathcal{M}$ with respect to space, time and circumstances, and consider an implicit dependence on the consciousness of the three representative variables m, i and e, corresponding to M, I and E. Among other methods to account for the consciousness in physical theories, next we discuss briefly the formal method of classical mechanics in terms of "action integral" in Section 7.3. The emphasis here will be on using a complex Lagrange function. Then, after introducing the notations, terminology and several other concepts for the later development of the subject of psychomechanics, we construct an "effort integral" in Section 7.4 in analogy with the action integral of classical mechanics (see, chapter 2 of Goldstein 1981). Then, using the tools of calculus of variations, psycho-dynamical equations (similar to Euler–Lagrange equations in classical mechanics) for the evolution of the "mindset function" $\mathcal{M}$, are derived in this section. For this purpose, we introduce, perhaps for the first time, several new concepts like the concept of experience-based and event-based space and time durations. Note that here the event-based space–time durations form the basis for the description of world-3. A guide for the use of these equations is suggested in Section 7.5. Finally, concluding remarks are made in Section 7.6.

7.1 Linear and Non-linear Evolution of an Individual with Consciousness

Each of us is born with certain level of development of FOUs, may be due to destiny (*prārabdha*) (cf. Section 4.7) and for the rest we are free to develop here in this birth through education about Nature, society and world-order. Even in the latter part of development only a few and conscious persons succeed in enhancing the level of development of their FOUs. In this process the Being b, as per Vedic wisdom, undergoes several stages of evolution following certain paths to become a man of perfection or to attain a state of liberation (cf. *fig.* 4.3). As a matter of fact, it is the mindset of a person that basically evolves with his increasing attention about world-order and in terms of space, time and circumstances. In particular, it is the focused version of consciousness in the form of meditation or concentration that helps in the evolution of micro-existence of a person. As mentioned earlier, this increasing value (or intensity) of meditation (denoted here by the variable μ) is further translated into the increasing orders of dressing of micro-body (mind, intellect and ego) or of the so-called "mindset function" $\mathcal{M}$ with consciousness. Further, note that this evolution of the mindset function $\mathcal{M}$ could be linear or non-linear depending on the route followed by the practitioner.

The mindset function, $\mathcal{M}$, is something that can be associated uniquely with an individual in given circumstances and at given space and time. Thus, at gross level, no doubt, it is a function of space (q), time (t) and circumstances (σ); but at subtle level, note that it is the consciousness that creates space, time and geometry (a dead body cannot have such feelings) and hence one can write $q = q(t, \mu)$ and $t = t(\mu)$. This suggests a way to account for consciousness in physical theories. We shall also use other methods for this purpose in future sections. Further, recall that there are various routes for the Being b to achieve perfection in the Vedānta philosophy (cf. *fig*. 4.3). In this context, a *bhakti-yogī* offers the example of linear evolution of his $\mathcal{M}$ with consciousness, whereas, both *karma-yogī* and *jñāna-yogī* categories, in fact, undergo non-linear evolution. As a matter of fact, a *bhakti-yogī* directly surrenders himself to the Supreme (God) as far as the roles of his thoughts, actions and speech in his daily life are concerned. For a true devotee, there is no scope of any reasoning or argument and ego or self-sense in the day-to-day activities. He attributes each of his experience and action to God. On the other hand, for a *karma-* or *jnāna-yogī* the evolution of mindset function takes a non-linear route as he has to indulge in reasoning and self-sense at every stage of evolution. In any case, all three categories of persons finally attain stability of mind in their own way. Thus, for mental peace, any variation or fluctuation in $\mathcal{M}$ of b must vanish, or mathematically, $\delta\mathcal{M} = 0$.

7.2 Circumstance-Affected Human Actions: Possibility of a Stable Mindset

While the circumstances σ are the effect of external environment, it is only the mindset of an individual that guides the performance of his actions towards their success. Note that M, I and E in $\mathcal{M}$ in their nascent form are just the instruments ready to be used for their respective purpose. Once they are in operation in a functional Being either at their own or as a result of certain *saṅkalpas* (a decision at the level of highly dressed versions of I and E), then the workings of all the three is beautifully coordinated in terms of space (q), time (t) and circumstance (σ) to give an optimum output through $\mathcal{M}$. If the operative parts of M, I and E are translated into the corresponding variables m, i and e, then one can define the dependence of the later on q, t and σ as

$$m = m(q, t, \sigma) \tag{7.1}$$

$$i = i(q, t, \sigma, m(q, t, \sigma)) \tag{7.2}$$

$$e = e(q, t, \sigma, m(q, t, \sigma),\ i(q, t, \sigma,\ m(q, t, \sigma)). \tag{7.3}$$

On the other hand, the mindset $\mathcal{M} \equiv \{\text{M, I, E}\}$ now becomes an explicit function of m, i and e and it depends implicitly on q, t and σ. Thus, the mindset $\mathcal{M} = \mathcal{M}(m, i, e)$ attains an optimum domain of working not only with respect to the internal variables m, i and e but also with respect to the external variables q, t and σ. Since an individual in general only uses a limited capacity of M, I and E, the variations of m, i and e remain controllable, whereas those of the external variables q, t and σ remain beyond control. For the stability of the mindset $\mathcal{M}$, we shall just demand $\delta\mathcal{M} = 0$ with respect to the variations in q, t and σ. This would define an optimum domain of working of $\mathcal{M}$.

Note the sequential dependence of i on m and of e on m and i in addition to on q, t and σ of all the three m, i and e in eqs (7.1)-(7.3). In principle, one should also have δm, δi and δe is equal to zero separately for $\delta\mathcal{M}$ to be zero, but we shall not demand this here, mainly because the consciousness keeps on dressing M, I and E separately and repeatedly which does not allow m, i and e to attain stable values. However, $\mathcal{M}$ can attain a stability and that too with respect to external variables q, t and σ. Within this framework, we derive here certain conditions which $\mathcal{M}$ has to satisfy towards its stability.

Since $\mathcal{M} = \mathcal{M}(m, i, e)$, this implies

$$\delta M = \frac{\partial M}{\partial m}\delta m + \frac{\partial M}{\partial i}\delta_i + \frac{\partial M}{\partial e}\delta e. \tag{7.4}$$

Now from eqs (7.1), (7.2) and (7.3), we have

$$\delta m = \frac{\partial m}{\partial q}\delta q + \frac{\partial m}{\partial t}\delta t + \frac{\partial m}{\partial \sigma}\delta\sigma \tag{7.5}$$

$$\delta i = \left(\frac{\partial i}{\partial q} + \frac{\partial i}{\partial m}.\frac{\partial m}{\partial q}\right)\delta q + \left(\frac{\partial i}{\partial t} + \frac{\partial i}{\partial m}.\frac{\partial m}{\partial t}\right)\delta t + \left(\frac{\partial i}{\partial \sigma} + \frac{\partial i}{\partial m}.\frac{\partial m}{\partial \sigma}\right)\delta\sigma$$

$$\delta e = \left(\frac{\partial e}{\partial q} + \frac{\partial e}{\partial m}.\frac{\partial m}{\partial q} + \frac{\partial e}{\partial i}.\frac{\partial i}{\partial q} + \frac{\partial e}{\partial i}.\frac{\partial i}{\partial m}.\frac{\partial m}{\partial q}\right)\delta q$$

$$+\left(\frac{\partial e}{\partial t}+\frac{\partial e}{\partial m}.\frac{\partial m}{\partial t}+\frac{\partial e}{\partial i}.\frac{\partial i}{\partial t}+\frac{\partial e}{\partial i}.\frac{\partial i}{\partial m}.\frac{\partial m}{\partial t}\right)\delta t \tag{7.6}$$

$$+\left(\frac{\partial e}{\partial \sigma}+\frac{\partial e}{\partial m}.\frac{\partial m}{\partial \sigma}+\frac{\partial e}{\partial i}.\frac{\partial i}{\partial \sigma}+\frac{\partial e}{\partial i}.\frac{\partial i}{\partial m}.\frac{\partial m}{\partial \sigma}\right)\delta \sigma\,. \tag{7.7}$$

Next we use (7.5), (7.6) and (7.7) in (7.4) and demand the vanishing of the coefficients of δq, δt and $\delta\sigma$ in the resultant expression in order to have $\delta\mathcal{M} = 0$. This would yield the following set of three equations:

$$\frac{\partial M}{\partial m}.\frac{\partial m}{\partial q}+\frac{\partial M}{\partial i}\left(\frac{\partial i}{\partial t}+\frac{\partial i}{\partial m}.\frac{\partial m}{\partial q}\right)$$
$$+\frac{\partial M}{\partial e}\left(\frac{\partial e}{\partial q}+\frac{\partial e}{\partial m}.\frac{\partial m}{\partial q}+\frac{\partial e}{\partial i}+\frac{\partial i}{\partial q}.\frac{\partial e}{\partial i}.\frac{\partial i}{\partial m}.\frac{\partial m}{\partial q}\right)=0. \tag{7.8a}$$

$$\frac{\partial M}{\partial m}.\frac{\partial m}{\partial t}+\frac{\partial M}{\partial i}\left(\frac{\partial i}{\partial t}+\frac{\partial i}{\partial m}.\frac{\partial m}{\partial t}\right)$$
$$+\frac{\partial M}{\partial e}\left(\frac{\partial e}{\partial t}+\frac{\partial e}{\partial m}.\frac{\partial m}{\partial t}+\frac{\partial e}{\partial i}.\frac{\partial i}{\partial t}+\frac{\partial e}{\partial i}.\frac{\partial i}{\partial m}.\frac{\partial m}{\partial t}\right)=0. \tag{7.8b}$$

$$\frac{\partial M}{\partial m}.\frac{\partial m}{\partial \sigma}+\frac{\partial M}{\partial i}\left(\frac{\partial i}{\partial \sigma}+\frac{\partial i}{\partial m}.\frac{\partial m}{\partial \sigma}\right)$$
$$+\frac{\partial M}{\partial e}\left(\frac{\partial e}{\partial \sigma}+\frac{\partial e}{\partial m}.\frac{\partial m}{\partial \sigma}+\frac{\partial e}{\partial i}.\frac{\partial i}{\partial \sigma}+\frac{\partial e}{\partial i}.\frac{\partial i}{\partial m}.\frac{\partial m}{\partial \sigma}\right)=0. \tag{7.8c}$$

In principle, the solution of these simultaneous equations for $\partial M/\partial m$, $\partial M/\partial i$ and $\partial M/\partial e$ in terms of m, i and e, can be obtained in the form of three coupled partial differential equations whose integration with appropriate initial conditions would provide the function $\mathcal{M}_0(m, i, e)$ which defines the optimum mindset. In practice, it is going to be a difficult task; therefore, we shall demonstrate the use of (7.8) to some specific human actions where some of the variables are absent and this will make life simple. However, a general condition for the existence of an optimum mindset can be derived as follows: For this purpose we write eqs (7.8a)-(7.8c) in the form

$$a_1x + (b_1 + ca_1)y + (d_1 + fa_1 + gb_1 + gca_1)z = 0 \tag{7.9a}$$

$$a_2x + (b_2 + ca_2)y + (d_2 + fa_2 + gb_2 + gca_2)z = 0 \qquad (7.9b)$$

$$a_3x + (b_3 + ca_3)y + (d_3 + fa_3 + gb_3 + gca_3)z = 0, \qquad (7.9c)$$

where the variables x, y, z are identified as

$$x = \left(\frac{\partial M}{\partial m}\right), y = \left(\frac{\partial M}{\partial i}\right), z = \left(\frac{\partial M}{\partial e}\right), \text{ and } a_1 = \left(\frac{\partial m}{\partial q}\right), a_2 = \left(\frac{\partial m}{\partial t}\right), a_3 = \left(\frac{\partial m}{\partial \sigma}\right)$$

$$b_1 = \left(\frac{\partial i}{\partial q}\right), b_2 = \left(\frac{\partial i}{\partial t}\right), b_3 = \left(\frac{\partial i}{\partial \sigma}\right)\square d_1 = \left(\frac{\partial e}{\partial q}\right) d_2 = \left(\frac{\partial e}{\partial t}\right), d_3 = \left(\frac{\partial e}{\partial \sigma}\right)\square$$

$$c = \left(\frac{\partial i}{\partial m}\right), f = \left(\frac{\partial e}{\partial m}\right), g = \left(\frac{\partial e}{\partial i}\right).$$

Further, note the condition for the existence of non-zero solutions of these simultaneous algebraic equations is that the determinant of the coefficients in eq. (7.9) must vanish, viz.

$$\begin{vmatrix} a_1 & (b_1 + ca_1) & (d_1 + fa_1 + gb_1 + gca_1) \\ a_2 & (b_2 + ca_2) & (d_2 + fa_2 + gb_2 + gca_2) \\ a_3 & (b_3 + ca_3) & (d_3 + fa_3 + gb_3 + gca_3) \end{vmatrix} = 0, \qquad (7.10)$$

which on simplification leads to a simpler version as

$$\begin{vmatrix} a_1 & b_1 & d_1 \\ a_2 & b_2 & d_2 \\ a_3 & b_3 & d_3 \end{vmatrix} = 0 \qquad (7.11)$$

or $\quad a_1 (b_2 d_3 - b_3 d_2) - b_1 (a_2 d_3 - a_3 d_2) + d_1 (a_2 b_3 - a_3 b_2) = 0. \qquad (7.12)$

The condition (7.12) in original notations takes the form

$$\frac{\partial m}{\partial q}\left(\frac{\partial i}{\partial t}.\frac{\partial e}{\partial \sigma} - \frac{\partial i}{\partial \sigma}\frac{\partial e}{\partial t}\right) - \frac{\partial i}{\partial q}\left(\frac{\partial m}{\partial t}.\frac{\partial e}{\partial \sigma} - \frac{\partial m}{\partial \sigma}\frac{\partial e}{\partial t}\right)$$

$$+ \frac{\partial e}{\partial q}\left(\frac{\partial m}{\partial t}.\frac{\partial i}{\partial \sigma} - \frac{\partial m}{\partial \sigma}\frac{\partial i}{\partial t}\right) = 0. \qquad (7.13)$$

This requirement, in fact, restricts infinitely many choices in which the mind, intellect and ego depend on space, time and circumstance to a particular choice which in turn supplies a feedback for the optimum mindset in the form of the solution of (7.9a)-(7.9c) for $\left(\frac{\partial M}{\partial m}\right), \left(\frac{\partial M}{\partial i}\right), \left(\frac{\partial M}{\partial e}\right)$. Reduction of (7.10) to a simpler version (7.11) implies the self and mutual-cancellation of a number of intermediate processes taking places inside the human Being before the mindset with regard to particular action is prepared. Such an observation is, in fact, supports the Vedānta philosophy of *guṇā guṇeṣu vartantu* (cf. *SMBG* III.27 and III.28).

7.3 Psychomechanics and the Hamilton Principle of Least Action

7.3.1 ACTIONS OF A CONSCIOUS HUMAN BEING: CASE OF A REAL LAGRANGIAN

In earlier work (cf. chapter 8 and Appendix E of Kaushal 2011), we have considered the role of consciousness in classical dynamics by introducing a meditation variable μ on par with the time variable t in the Lagrange function L. The coordinate q and the velocity p of the EP-matter particle now depend rather implicitly on both t and μ. We accordingly define the derivatives, $\dot{q}$ with respect to t, and $\bar{q}$ with respect to μ and write the Lagrangian as $L = L(q, \dot{q}, \bar{q}, t, \mu)$, where $\dot{q} = (\partial q/\partial t)$ and $\bar{q} = (\partial q/\partial \mu)$. The action integral J (Goldstein 1981), now takes the form

$$J = \int_{t_1}^{t_2}\int_{\mu_1}^{\mu_2} L(q, \dot{q}, \bar{q}, t, \mu)\, d\mu\, dt. \tag{7.14}$$

Here, J pertains to the action performed by a conscious observer on the object placed at q and moving with physical velocity $\dot{q}$. The object identified with position q is also dressing up with the consciousness at a rate of $\bar{q}$. Note that J, a measure of conscious action, is a complicated quantity in the sense that it represents now the outcome of a variety of processes taking place inside the conscious (observer) Being. However, these processes become effective only when the role of μ comes into play, not only in locating the object at q but also in realizing its existence and the other details. As t and μ evolve (which is necessary for establishing the existence of the object in the physical Universe or in the field of WO and also for realizing its existence in SO), both outer (B and SE) and inner (M, I and E) EOLs of the person become active. As a matter of fact the variable t is in response to the physical device (like the light ray, etc.) used to detect q and the variable μ is in response to the consciousness used to realize q by the observer. As μ increases, the self-interactions or the interactions inside the Being come into existence and the Being realizes other details about the object in addition to its position and velocity.

Note that the trajectory of the particle followed with respect to t may not be the same as the one followed with respect to μ. The physical trajectory, in fact, could be one possibility out of a large number of possibilities which existed in the mind of the observer. However, as and when the observer focuses his consciousness (μ increases), these possibilities end up in one physical trajectory along with the higher-order dressings of inner EOLs (cf. Section 4.2). Note that in the action integral (7.14) the variable μ is responsible for efforts made by an individual in performing the action. This parameter will, however, depend on the intensity of thinking process or on the degree of concentration achieved by the individual (again on the orders of dressing of inner EOLs in the language of Section 4.2). We shall return to such details later. Using the standard method of calculus of variation, *space-time-consciousness (STC) evolution equations* (in analogy with the Euler-Lagrange equations) are derived from the action integral (7.14) (cf. Appendix E in Kaushal 2011) as

$$\frac{\partial L}{\partial q}-\frac{\partial}{\partial t}\left(\frac{\partial L}{\partial \dot{q}}\right)-\frac{\partial}{\partial \mu}\left(\frac{\partial L}{\partial \bar{q}}\right)=0 \tag{7.15}$$

for the case of a real Lagrangian.

7.3.2 ACTIONS OF A CONSCIOUS HUMAN BEING: CASE OF A COMPLEX LAGRANGIAN

Although it depends on as to how one introduces the complexity in physical theories in mathematical terms, efforts have also been there to identify the role of imaginary parts with the mental world and/or mental processes (Kaushal 2009, 2016b) and that of real parts with the physical world. Keeping such possibilities in mind, a case of complex Lagrangian $L\,(q, p, t, \mu)$ is also considered, where q and p now given by q

$$q\,(t, \mu) = q_1(t) + iq_2\,(\mu) \qquad (7.16a)$$

$$p\,(t, \mu) = p_1(t) + ip_2\,(\mu) \qquad (7.16b)$$

and the complex Lagrangian L as,

$$L = L_1\,(q_1, p_1, q_2, p_2\, t, \mu) + I\, L_2\,(q_1, p_1, q_2, p_2\, t, \mu), \qquad (7.17)$$

where $p_1 = \dot{q}_1$ and $p_2 = (\partial q/\partial \mu) = \bar{q}_2$. Corresponding to L_1 and L_2 in (7.17), one can write under certain assumptions, the conscious action J of eq. (7.14) as the sum of physical and non-physical aspects of the system, viz.

$$J = J_{ph} + I J_{nonphy}\,. \qquad (7.14')$$

In other words, the real parts q_1 and p_1 of q and p correspond to the case of physical reality associated with the object and the imaginary parts q_2 and p_2 are the measures of non-physical reality and in turn account for the role of consciousness in the process of realization of the given object. In spite of the fact that $I^2 = i^2 = -1$, we have used different "I" and "i" with the imaginary parts in eqs (7.16) and (7.17). This is mainly because there is no reason as to why the dreaming of an object be the same as the dreaming of the action performed by it. They might belong to different imaginary planes, particularly when the environment and circumstances leave different impacts in the two situations in real life, or when the observer carries different mindsets in the two situations. In mathematical terms, we are considering different imaginaries with a complex number system and with the mapping on it. This, in fact, has been done at the cost of analyticity property of the complex function L. Moreover, since the consciousness, like time, cannot be fragmented, this non-analyticity of L in some sense becomes imperative in the present case.

For the Lagrangian (7.17) we list the results (cf. Appendix E of Kaushal 2011) corresponding to two cases, viz. when "I" ≠ "i" and when “I” = “i”.

Case I: When “I” ≠ “i”, the STC evolution equations in component form become

$$\frac{\partial L_1}{\partial q_1}-\frac{\partial}{\partial t}\left(\frac{\partial L_1}{\partial p_1}\right)=0;\quad \frac{\partial L_1}{\partial q_2}-\frac{\partial}{\partial t}\left(\frac{\partial L_1}{\partial p_2}\right)=0 \qquad (7.18a, b)$$

$$\frac{\partial L_2}{\partial q_1}-\frac{\partial}{\partial t}\left(\frac{\partial L_2}{\partial p_1}\right)=0;\quad \frac{\partial L_2}{\partial q_2}-\frac{\partial}{\partial t}\left(\frac{\partial L_2}{\partial p_2}\right)=0 \qquad (7.18c, d)$$

$$\frac{\partial L_1}{\partial q_1}-\frac{\partial}{\partial \mu}\left(\frac{\partial L_1}{\partial p_1}\right)=0;\quad \frac{\partial L_1}{\partial q_2}-\frac{\partial}{\partial \mu}\left(\frac{\partial L_1}{\partial p_2}\right)=0 \qquad (7.18e, f)$$

$$\frac{\partial L_2}{\partial q_1}-\frac{\partial}{\partial \mu}\left(\frac{\partial L_2}{\partial p_1}\right)=0;\quad \frac{\partial L_2}{\partial q_2}-\frac{\partial}{\partial \mu}\left(\frac{\partial L_2}{\partial p_2}\right)=0 \qquad (7.18g, h)$$

Case II: When “I” = “i”, the STC evolution equations in component form turn out to be

$$\frac{\partial L_1}{\partial q_1}-\frac{\partial}{\partial t}\left(\frac{\partial L_1}{\partial p_1}\right)=0;\quad \frac{\partial L_2}{\partial q_1}-\frac{\partial}{\partial t}\left(\frac{\partial L_2}{\partial p_1}\right)=0 \qquad (7.19a, b)$$

$$\frac{\partial L_1}{\partial q_1}-\frac{\partial}{\partial \mu}\left(\frac{\partial L_1}{\partial p_1}\right)=0;\quad \frac{\partial L_2}{\partial q_1}-\frac{\partial}{\partial \mu}\left(\frac{\partial L_2}{\partial p_1}\right)=0 \qquad (7.19c, d)$$

A comparison of equations in the sets (7.18) and (7.19) reveals that the four equations of Case II are already present in the eight equations of Case I and the remaining four equations, viz. (7.18b), (7.18d), (7.18f) and (7.18h), are the outcome of non-analyticity property of L. Thus, the non-analyticity requirement of L is more informative (as it provides more equations to employ) as far as the application of these results to human behaviour is concerned. In view of our assumption, the appearance of imaginary part of L, i.e. L_2 in eqs (7.18) and (7.19) represents the effect(s) of non-physical action (i.e. the dreaming or imagination) in the STC evolution of the system. Similarly, the terms in which the imaginary parts of q and p, viz. q_2 and p_2 appear in these equations, account for the non-physical aspects associated with the perception process of an element in WO. As argued earlier (Kaushal 2011), some of the terms in these equations have their origin purely in the domain of consciousness and some have purely in the domain of physics and a good number of them have their origin in the domain where space, time and consciousness coexist pairwise or otherwise. For example, eq. (7.18a), in spite of its implicit dependence on μ, describes exclusively the evolution of physical aspect and eq. (7.18h), in spite of its implicit dependence on *t*, describes exclusively the non-physical aspect – the two extreme situations with regard to the evolution of the system. The remaining eqs (7.18b)-(7.18g) however describe the evolution of a system in the mixed situations in which all three space, time and consciousness play their roles in certain proportions.

In what follows we discuss eq. (7.15) and each of eqs (7.18) along with some examples from human behaviour and actions in day-to-day life.

It may be reminded that not only the location of P-matter particle at *q* but also the actions performed on it towards the realization of some of its features (like the charge, mass, size and shape) undergo changes with respect to both time and consciousness. In other words, the object dresses up with respect to *t* of "wrist watch" (termed as "t-evolution") and hence activates the outer EOLs like SE and B to perform the action and thereby making them $\tilde{S}\tilde{E}^{(1)}$ and $\tilde{B}^{(1)}$, (cf. eq. (8.1) of Kaushal 2011). On the other hand, at the same time, it also dresses up with respect to consciousness (translated into μ) and activates the inner EOLs, viz. M, I and E (termed as "μ-evolution") and thereby making them $\tilde{M}^{(1)}$, $\tilde{I}^{(1)}$ and $\tilde{E}^{(1)}$ (cf. eq. (8.1) of Kaushal 2011). For physical aspects of a system, the variations with respect to *q* (termed as "*q*-evolution") and *t* while continue according to the standard Euler–Lagrange equations corresponding to the given system and without accounting for the μ-evolution, for non-physical aspects, however, an account of μ-evolution is absolutely necessary. Again, the μ-evolution takes place differently from *q*- and *t*-evolutions. It appears that physicists who resort to account for consciousness in physical theories

(Goswami 2013; Jammer 1974; Penrose 1994; Stapp 2009) do not go beyond the first-order dressing) of the EOLs. But, the framework suggested here takes us much ahead in this direction through *tri-karaṇa* rule for inner EOLs and *dvi-karaṇa* rule for outer EOLs. At a crude level, while this can be carried out for real (conscious) actions through the evolution (eq. 7.15), a fine-tuning of the same actually manifests through a complex (conscious) action and via eqs (7.18). Although a relative comparison of the terms in eq. (7.15) can also throw some light on non-physical aspects of an action, an analysis of eq. (7.18) offers further subtle details. (For further details, see Kaushal 2011.)

7.4 Psychomechanics and the Effort Integral

7.4.1 NOTATIONS AND TERMINOLOGY

(i) Note that for a conscious person, the variable μ is never zero but it can be infinity for a liberated individual. We shall consider μ at par with the time variable t in spite that $t = t(\mu)$ and the space variable, q is now, $q = q\,(t, \mu)$, in implicit form. As a matter of fact, in this experience-based world, the "space variable" q is no more a directional quantity (as is the case in the event-based world), rather, it is a distribution in the space of t and μ. This is what one experiences during the initial stages of meditation. In some sense, we want to restore "matter over mind" or "bottom-up" approach (see chapter 4 of Kaushal 2015) to account for the psyche of an individual.

(ii) *Consciousness energy and the mindset function*: In analogy with the energy functions like Lagrangian and Hamiltonian of classical mechanics, we introduce here consciousness-energy (abbreviated here as "c-energy" or termed as "cenergy") function, $\mathcal{M}$, also called as "mindset function". As mentioned before, the state of mind at any stage of meditation is characterized by this "mindset function" $\mathcal{M}$. Further, its evolution with reference to a particular task can be considered with respect to space (q), time (t) and/or meditation variable μ. Note that in general $\mathcal{M}$, in given circumstances, is not only a function of q, t and μ, viz. $\mathcal{M} = \mathcal{M}(q(t, \mu), t(\mu), \mu)$ but also of the respective derivatives of q and t, namely of, $\dot{q} = (\partial q/\partial t)$, $\bar{q} = (\partial q/\partial \mu)$ and $\bar{t} = (\partial t/\partial \mu)$. Thus, $\mathcal{M} = \mathcal{M}(q, \dot{q}, \bar{q}, t, \bar{t}, \mu)$. Unless and otherwise mentioned, the dependence of q and $\bar{t}$ on their arguments remains only implicit. Here $\bar{q}$ and $\bar{t}$, in some sense, belong to the experience-based world of space–time, and q represents a compactified version of space as far as the concept of physical dimensions is concerned. We shall avoid such possibilities in this work.

(iii) *Thinking fast and slow: Gross and subtle components of* $\mathcal{M}$: With reference to the psychology of an individual, the Nobel Prize winner Daniel Kahneman, in his bestseller book *Thinking, Fast and Slow* (2011), emphasized the two aspects of human thinking process, viz. fast and slow. In fact, the "two selves" introduced by Kahneman through "system 1" and "system 2" in his theory of economic science respectively are in accordance with the gross component $\mathcal{M}_g$ and subtle component $\mathcal{M}_s$ of Vedic literature. (For details, see Appendix B of Kaushal 2018b and Section 5.4 in Kaushal 2017a). In view of these considerations, it is not difficult to consider the mindset function $\mathcal{M}$ as consisting of two parts, viz. conscious or active (here referred to as "dynamic") part that corresponds to the gross component $\mathcal{M}_g$ and subconscious or passive (here referred to as "static") part that corresponds to the subtle component $\mathcal{M}_s$. Thus, it is reasonable to write the function $\mathcal{M}$ as the sum of dynamic and static parts in analogy with the "kinetic" and "potential energy" terms in the Hamiltonian function of classical mechanics (Goldstein 1981).

Further note that the dynamic part in $\mathcal{M}$, primarily depending on $\dot{q}$, $\bar{q}$, $\bar{t}$, is positive definite since an individual always makes an effort and also has a tendency to survive in this world through his active mind. The passive or static part, on the other hand, defines his attitude towards the world-/cosmic-order in general. It could be negative to convert $\mathcal{M}$ into a Lagrangian function of classical mechanics or could be positive to retain $\mathcal{M}$ as Hamiltonian

(Goldstein 1981). While such details might be useful in solving specific problems of human behaviour, in any case $\mathcal{M}$, however, represents the cenergy. At times, it is the environment that forces one to take the positive or negative attitude at subtle (subconscious) level, otherwise everything goes well in positive spirit at the conscious level. Thus, $\dot{q}$, $\bar{q}$ and $\bar{t}$ though derived from q and t, but can be considered as independent variables in the spirit of canonical momenta that could be derived accordingly from $\mathcal{M}$.

Note that in psychomechanics, like in classical mechanics (Goldstein 1981), the conserved quantities can be defined and traced with respect to both μ and/or t. As far as the physics relevance of these conserved quantities is concerned, clearly, those with respect to t will correspond to the physical world-3, those with respect to μ will belong to world-1 and those with respect to both μ and t will correspond to world-2. For example, many behavioural facts are found (see, chapter 8 of Kaushal 2015) to be universal, particularly with reference to the personality of an individual, whereas, some facts are realized universally but hard to express them through limited means of speech, letter or actions. We refrain ourselves from going into these details here but refer to our earlier works (Kaushal 2011, 2015, 2017a).

iv. *Meditation variable and the intensity of meditation:* When a person sits in meditation, the depth or the degree of achieving a focused attention on a thought is characterized by μ. In some sense, μ is a collective representation of the parameters responsible for the roles of inner essences of life, viz. mind, intellect and ego, in a decision-making process towards the success of a task. Note that μ can never be zero for a living person but it can be infinite for a super enlightened person, i.e. for the *yogī*-category of persons (see Glossary). For a common man, however, μ lies between zero and infinity. As a first step towards the quantification, our common experience reveals that the intensity of meditation is (A) inversely proportional to the frequency f of life-breaths, (B) directly (inversely) proportional to the number of positive (negative) thoughts N_+ (N_-), (C) inversely proportional to the time duration τ assigned to complete the task, and (D) directly proportional to the capacity C of controlling the mind by an individual from its running into the sense-objects.

Symbolically, one can write the intensity of meditation or of focused attention μ as

$$\mu = \frac{\kappa C N_+}{\tau f N_-}, \tag{7.20}$$

where κ is a constant of proportionality. About the formula (7.20), the following remarks are in order:

a. The proportionality constant κ in general is a function of circumstances, σ or of the mental set-up affected by the environment.

b. The linear dependence of μ on C is rather an ideal and simplified situation; otherwise C in general could be replaced by a complicated function of C, say $f(C)$. This is mainly because that there are five categories of stimulants which can affect the turbulence of mind in different proportion and style. As a matter of fact, in this contemplative state the senses become so inhibited that the individual does not hear, smell, taste or see, nor does one experience touch. During this single-mindedness, the ideas revolve around the object of meditation. As a result, sensory stimuli are excluded, the mind ceases to imagine and the time slows down (Vrobel 2011).

c. Note that the life-breathing frequency f and the assigned time duration τ, themselves have mutual dependence in the sense that if the assigned time is less, then for a common man f increases with reference to the conscious mind (or the gross component of $\mathcal{M}$). This kind of dependence of μ on τ, on the other hand, also supports the "incomprehensibility principle" noticed by Fraser (2013) according to which the intensity of one's consciousness (attention or meditation) and the duration for which it is applied seriously affect the outcome of observation, i.e. they are inversely proportional.

7.4.2 EXPERIENCE-BASED AND EVENT-BASED SPACE AND TIME INTERVALS

In formula (7.20) note that τ denotes the real time duration and such a dependence of μ on τ was noticed by Fraser during his assignment as the editor of CERN courier. In reality, the time duration may arise with reference to both mental (virtual) and physical (real) worlds. The former actually deals with the experience-based time and the latter with the event-based time. In order to have an experience, naturally the experiencer has to have an element of consciousness and the latter in some sense is the creator of time. Such a thing, in fact, is missing in the event-based time. Further, in the event-based case, there is some sort of "internalization of the exterior" whereas in the experience-based case there is "externalization of the interior" and here one talks of the "subjective" time. In fact, whatever is true for the time durations, the same is true for the space intervals. As a matter of fact, a common experience reveals that the experience-based space and time intervals (durations) are contracted (i.e. they fly like anything) if the experiences are pleasant or appealing and they are elongated if the experiences are otherwise (unpleasant or not favourable). Susie Vrobel (2011), while investigating the fractal time, has recently advanced several new concepts in this connection, particularly about the texture of time in Nature.

What Vrobel emphasizes is that even in the event-based time duration there could be an experience-based part which is either not detected by the physical instrument or accounted through the so-called personal errors in the measurement. To this effect, Vrobel introduces the concepts of "length" and "depth" of time in the given interval, which, respectively correspond to "the duration" and "the now" and accordingly characterize the "succession" and "simultaneity" of events during observation. It is "the now" part of the time interval that is subjective and the same can be identified only by a conscious observer and also not unique for each observer. On the other hand, in the experience-based time interval the whole interval is a subjective time – there could be a slow or fast flow of time, or the time is dragged or flies of, etc. For example, one notices the flying of time during suitable enjoyment or dragging of the time during the adverse conditions.

In what follows, we list some phenomena and common experiences involving consciousness and belonging mainly to the world-2:

i. When one crosses an unusually crowded road at zebra mark or when one drives through a crowded lane without divider, all three – space, time and consciousness play – comparable roles in decisions.

ii. As mentioned before, in the observation by Fraser (i.e. the product of intensity of attention and the time span during which the attention is applied is a constant) it is the event-based time duration that appears (cf. eq. (7.20)).

iii. *Time sharpens the mind*: Akin to the incomprehensibility principle of Fraser (2013), this is another common-man experience. In fact, as the time of delivering a speech or lecture or taking an examination approaches, the inner faculties of learning (including that of memory and decisions) become more and more efficient or sharp.

A simple model for the consciousness evolution with event-based time duration can perhaps offer an explanation to this phenomenon. To this effect, we assume that (Kaushal 2017a) at any time t the rate of increase of μ is given by

$$(d\mu / dt) \propto \frac{1}{t_0 - t} \quad \text{or} \quad \frac{d\mu}{dt} = \frac{\lambda}{t_0 - t}, \tag{7.21}$$

where λ is the constant of proportionality and t_0 is the time allotted to complete the task. The integration of (7.21) leads to

$$\mu(t)=\mu_0-\lambda\ln\left(1-\frac{t}{t_0}\right), \tag{7.22}$$

which, in the case when $t \ll t_0$, reduces to

$$\mu(t)\simeq\mu_0+\frac{\lambda t}{t_0}, \tag{7.23}$$

which implies a slow attention on the task at the initial stages. Such considerations can possibly suggest a link between the experience-based (Δt_{ex}) and event-based (Δt_{ev})) time durations (cf. phenomenon (v) below) .

iv. *Chevreul handheld pendulum* : About 180 years ago, French Chemist Chevreul tried to demonstrate that the role of consciousness can be noticed in the handheld pendulum experiment when the variations in time period are analysed in different situations. Recently, an experiment to this effect is proposed (2016b) by the author. For the details on Chevreul pendulum, we shall return in the next chapter.

v. *Weber–Fechner law*: This law quantifies the perception of change in a given stimulus. The perception process as such has roots in consciousness or in the intensity of attention. The law states that the perceived intensity (loudness/ brightness) (I_p) is proportional to the logarithm of actual intensity (I_a), viz.

$$I_p \propto \ln I_a \quad \text{or} \quad I_a = e^{Ip/k}, \tag{7.24}$$

where k is the constant of proportionality, it however depends on the type of the perceived sense-object, viz. touch, taste, seeing, hearing or smell, and also on consciousness or on the strength of meditation μ. Without any loss of generality one can as well use the Weber–Fechner law (7.24) to connect the experience-based (perceived) time interval (Δt_{ex}) and the event-based (nascent or actual) time interval (Δt_{ev}) to give a relation of the form

$$\Delta t_{ev} = A \exp(\Delta t_{ex}/k). \tag{7.25}$$

Note the possibility of understanding Weber–Fechner law (7.24) or the relation (7.25) in the simple model (7.22), of course, after some dimensional considerations. As a matter of fact, the relation (7.22) would be more appropriate when Δt_{ex} and Δt_{ev} are replaced by the corresponding time density as defined by Vrobel (2011). (Note that the number of succession ("length" of time) and simultaneous ("depth" or "the now") events in an interval Δt define the "density" of time.) Here, k can be negative or positive depending respectively on the pleasant or unpleasant experiences that one notices during Δt_{ex}, or when the time-flying or time-dragging situations are there, and A is a dimensional constant. For example, while watching a movie or in touch with a lover, time flies like anything. On the other hand, during the period of waiting for a beloved one or in touch with a hot plate, time is dragged.

vi. *Feeling of plurality of consciousness of the self or of another person*: (a) A metallic ball placed between the two adjacent twisted fingers, when set in motion, gives a feeling of two balls (a case of division of the same consciousness); (b) when the other person itches your body, it gives a different, perhaps enjoyable feeling that makes you laugh, as compared to the case when you yourself itch the same part of the body (a case of interaction of two consciousnesses).

One can trace many such phenomena in day-to-day life that belong to world-2. Using a relation similar to eq. (7.25) for the space interval Δq, we discuss further viability of the Weber–Fechner law in the present context in Appendix E.

7.4.3 THE PRINCIPLE OF MINIMUM EFFORT: PSYCHO-DYNAMICAL EQUATIONS

In mathematical terms, here we look for an explanation of a common experience that we all have, namely, we all want "to do less and accomplish more" or each of us wants to put least effort towards the success of a task. Note that the concept of the word "effort" here is different from that of "action" used in physics in the sense that the former sounds an element of one's mental capability which again has roots in the individual's consciousness. Keeping in mind the preliminaries discussed in Section 7.4.1, here we employ the tools of calculus of variation to obtain the extremeness of the functional of "effort integral", K, defined here as

$$K = \int_{t_1}^{t_2}\int_{\mu_1}^{\mu_2} \mathcal{M}(q,\dot{q},\bar{q},t,\bar{t},\mu)\, d\mu\, dt. \tag{7.26}$$

This we carry out in analogy with the "action integral",

$$I = \int_{t_1}^{t_2} L(q,\dot{q},t)dt. \tag{7.27}$$

of classical mechanics (Goldstein 1981). As mentioned before, $\mathcal{M}$ here is the measure of energy in the same way as the Lagrangian L in classical mechanics.

Next, we introduce two arbitrary parameters α (corresponding to the t-variable) and β (corresponding to the μ-variable) and write (7.26) as

$$K(\alpha,\beta) = \int_{t_1}^{t_2}\int_{\mu_1}^{\mu_2} \mathcal{M}(q(t,\mu,\alpha,\beta),\dot{q}(t,\mu,\alpha,\beta),\bar{q}(t,\mu,\alpha,\beta),\bar{t}(\mu,\beta),\mu)\,d\mu dt. \tag{7.28}$$

Note that the varying paths, characterized by the parameters α and β, are now in the three-dimensional space of q, t, μ. The conscious Being (b) (a capsule of functional consciousness present and works in all individuals (see appendix A of Kaushal 2011) until their death) follows such trajectories in this space between two states of mind, characterized by the point 1 and point 2 in this space. The arbitrary parameters α and β are such that they vanish at these end-points of the path. Further, note that for the effort K to be an extremum, one should have

$$\left.\frac{\partial K}{\partial \alpha}\right|_{\alpha=0,\beta=0} = 0 \quad \text{and} \quad \left.\frac{\partial K}{\partial \beta}\right|_{\alpha=0,\beta=0} = 0. \tag{7.29a, b}$$

These conditions, when used in (7.28), will give the following pair of equations:

$$\int_{t_1}^{t_2}\int_{\mu_1}^{\mu_2} \left[\frac{\partial \mathcal{M}}{\partial q}\cdot\frac{\partial q}{\partial \alpha} + \frac{\partial \mathcal{M}}{\partial \dot{q}}\cdot\frac{\partial \dot{q}}{\partial \alpha} + \frac{\partial \mathcal{M}}{\partial \bar{q}}\cdot\frac{\partial \bar{q}}{\partial \alpha}\right] d\mu dt = 0. \tag{7.30a}$$

$$\int_{t_1}^{t_2}\int_{\mu_1}^{\mu_2}\left[\frac{\partial \mathcal{M}}{\partial q}\cdot\frac{\partial q}{\partial \beta}+\frac{\partial \mathcal{M}}{\partial \dot{q}}\cdot\frac{\partial \dot{q}}{\partial \beta}+\frac{\partial \mathcal{M}}{\partial \overline{q}}\cdot\frac{\partial \overline{q}}{\partial \beta}+\frac{\partial \mathcal{M}}{\partial \overline{t}}\cdot\frac{\partial \overline{t}}{\partial \beta}\right.$$

$$\left.+\frac{\partial \mathcal{M}}{\partial t}\cdot\frac{\partial t}{\partial \beta}\right]d\mu dt=0. \tag{7.30b}$$

Now, after noting that

$$\frac{\partial \dot{q}}{\partial \alpha}=\frac{\partial}{\partial t}\left(\frac{\partial q}{\partial \alpha}\right);\frac{\partial \overline{q}}{\partial \alpha}=\frac{\partial}{\partial \mu}\left(\frac{\partial q}{\partial \alpha}\right);\frac{\partial \dot{q}}{\partial \beta}=\frac{\partial}{\partial t}\left(\frac{\partial q}{\partial \beta}\right);$$

$$\frac{\partial \overline{q}}{\partial \beta}=\frac{\partial}{\partial \mu}\left(\frac{\partial q}{\partial \beta}\right);\ \frac{\partial \overline{t}}{\partial \beta}=\frac{\partial}{\partial \mu}\left(\frac{\partial t}{\partial \beta}\right),$$

and using these results in (7.30a) and (7.30b), perform the integration of the corresponding terms by parts with respect to t or μ as the case may be (except for the first terms, in eqs (7.30a) and (7.30b)). For example, the second term in (7.30a) yields (Goldstein 1981)

$$\int_{t_1}^{t_2}\int_{\mu 1}^{\mu_2}\frac{\partial \mathcal{M}}{\partial \dot{q}}\cdot\frac{\partial}{\partial t}\left(\frac{\partial q}{\partial \alpha}\right)d\mu\, dt$$

$$=\int_{\mu_1}^{\mu_2}\left[\frac{\partial \mathcal{M}}{\partial \dot{q}}\cdot\frac{\partial q}{\partial \alpha}\right]_{\substack{\alpha=0\\ \beta=0}}d\mu-\int_{\mu_1}^{\mu_2}\int_{t_1}^{t_2}dt\left[\frac{\partial}{\partial t}\left(\frac{\partial \mathcal{M}}{\partial \dot{q}}\right)\frac{\partial q}{\partial \alpha}\right]d\mu$$

$$=0-\int_{\mu_1}^{\mu_2}\int_{t_1}^{t_2}\frac{\partial}{\partial t}\left(\frac{\partial \mathcal{M}}{\partial q}\right)\frac{\partial q}{\partial \alpha}dt\, d\mu.$$

Performing similar operations on each term in eqs (7.30a) and (7.30b) (except for the first terms) and then the subsequent use of conditions (7.29) yields

$$\int_{t_1}^{t_2}\int_{\mu_1}^{\mu_2}\left\{\left[\frac{\partial}{\partial t}\left(\frac{\partial \mathcal{M}}{\partial \dot{q}}\right)+\frac{\partial}{\partial \mu}\left(\frac{\partial \mathcal{M}}{\partial \overline{q}}\right)-\frac{\partial \mathcal{M}}{\partial q}\right]\left(\frac{\partial q}{\partial \alpha}\right)_{\alpha=\beta=0}\right\}dt\, d\mu=0. \tag{7.31a}$$

$$\int_{t_1}^{t_2}\int_{\mu_1}^{\mu_2}\left\{\left[\frac{\partial}{\partial t}\left(\frac{\partial \mathcal{M}}{\partial \dot{q}}\right)+\frac{\partial}{\partial \mu}\left(\frac{\partial \mathcal{M}}{\partial \overline{q}}\right)-\frac{\partial \mathcal{M}}{\partial q}\right]\left(\frac{\partial q}{\partial \beta}\right)_{\alpha=\beta=0}\right.$$

$$+ \left[\frac{\partial}{\partial \mu} \left(\frac{\partial \mathcal{M}}{\partial \bar{t}} \right) - \frac{\partial \mathcal{M}}{\partial t} \right] \left(\frac{\partial t}{\partial \beta} \right)_{\beta=0} \Bigg\} d\mu\, dt = 0. \tag{7.31b}$$

Next, we make use of the "fundamental lemma" of calculus of variation (Goldstein 1981; Hilderbrand 1965) after writing the Taylor expansions of the functions $q(t, \mu, \alpha, \beta)$ and $t(\mu, \beta)$ as

$$q(t,\mu,\alpha,\beta) \simeq q(t,\mu,0,0) + \alpha\eta_1(t,\mu) + \beta\eta_2(t,\mu)$$
$$t(\mu,\beta) \simeq t(\mu,0) + \beta\zeta(t),$$

where the functions η_1, η_2 and ζ are the arbitrary and independent functions of their arguments. They vanish at the end-points of the paths which essentially vary for a particular parametric family. Then the lemma, in the present case, states that (Goldstein 1981):

$$\iint M(x,y)\eta_1(x,y)\,dxdy = 0$$
$$\iint M(x,y)\eta_2(x,y)\,dxdy + \iint N(x,y)\zeta(y)\,dxdy = 0$$

and hence implies $M = 0$, $N = 0$. This will result into a pair of equations, viz.

$$\frac{\partial}{\partial t}\left(\frac{\partial \mathcal{M}}{\partial \dot{q}} \right) + \frac{\partial}{\partial \mu}\left(\frac{\partial \mathcal{M}}{\partial \bar{q}} \right) - \frac{\partial \mathcal{M}}{\partial q} = 0. \tag{7.32a}$$

$$\frac{\partial}{\partial \mu}\left(\frac{\partial \mathcal{M}}{\partial \bar{t}} \right) - \frac{\partial \mathcal{M}}{\partial t} = 0. \tag{7.32b}$$

Equation (7.32a) describes the evolution of the cenergy function with respect to all the three – space, time and consciousness – whereas eq. (7.32b) describes the evolution with respect to time and consciousness. In general, both the equations need to be explored for the complete solution of the problem, but it depends on the nature of the phenomenon under study to use (7.32a), (7.32b) or both. Equations (7.32a) and (7.32b) are termed as *psycho-dynamical equations of motion* and are analogous to Euler–Lagrange equations in classical mechanics.

Cyclic Coordinates: Next, we analyse the case of "cyclic coordinates" in analogy with the classical mechanics (Goldstein 1981). In fact, in case when $\mathcal{M}$ does not depend explicitly on q and/or t, then one can derive some conserved quantities for the system which, in turn, will help in solving the problem.

Case (i): When $\mathcal{M}$ does not depend explicitly on t, then $(\partial\mathcal{M}/\partial t) = 0$ and eq. (7.32b) gives

$$\frac{\partial}{\partial\mu}\left(\frac{\partial\mathcal{M}}{\partial\bar{t}}\right) = 0 \text{ or } \left(\frac{\partial\mathcal{M}}{\partial\bar{t}}\right) \equiv C_\mu$$

$$= \text{constant (with respect to } \mu\text{).} \quad (7.33)$$

We term C_μ here as the conjugate cenergy of the system, which in some sense defines the asymptotic limit of one's meditating capacity. This perhaps is the constant that appears in the incomprehensibility principle of Fraser (2013) (cf. Section 7.4.1).

Case (ii): When $\mathcal{M}$ does not depend explicitly on q, then $(\partial\mathcal{M}/\partial q) = 0$ and eq. (7.32a) gives

$$\frac{\partial}{\partial t}\left(\frac{\partial\mathcal{M}}{\partial\dot{q}}\right) + \frac{\partial}{\partial\mu}\left(\frac{\partial\mathcal{M}}{\partial\bar{q}}\right) = 0$$

$$\text{or} \quad \frac{\partial}{\partial t}\left[\frac{\partial\mathcal{M}}{\partial\dot{q}} + \bar{t}\frac{\partial\mathcal{M}}{\partial\bar{q}}\right] = 0$$

$$\text{or} \quad \left(\frac{\partial\mathcal{M}}{\partial\dot{q}} + \bar{t}\frac{\partial\mathcal{M}}{\partial\bar{q}}\right) \equiv P_t = \textit{constt.} \text{ (with respect to } t\text{)} \quad (7.34)$$

$$\text{also} \quad \frac{\partial}{\partial\mu}\left[\frac{1}{\bar{t}}\frac{\partial\mathcal{M}}{\partial\dot{q}} + \frac{\partial\mathcal{M}}{\partial\bar{q}}\right] = 0$$

$$\text{or} \quad \frac{1}{\bar{t}}\frac{\partial\mathcal{M}}{\partial\dot{q}} + \frac{\partial\mathcal{M}}{\partial\bar{q}} \equiv P_\mu = \textit{constt.} \text{ (with respect to } \mu\text{).}$$

We call P_μ as the "conjugate c-momentum". In this case it turns out to be a conserved quantity provided $(\partial\bar{t}/\partial t) \simeq 0$ or, when the variation of experience-based time with event-based time is negligibly small.

7.4.4 CONSTRUCTION OF THE CENERGY FUNCTION $\mathcal{M}$

Following the terminology of Section 7.4.1(iii), the function $\mathcal{M}$ consists of two parts: "gross part" ($\mathcal{M}_g$), an analogue of kinetic energy term and "subtle part" ($\mathcal{M}_s$), an analogue of potential energy term. Naturally, the gross part $\mathcal{M}_g$ is needed for the immediate use in daily life (corresponds to a fast and immediate efforts) and depends explicitly on $\dot{q}$, $\bar{q}$, $\bar{t}$, whereas the subtle part $\mathcal{M}_s$ is needed for the "second thought" (corresponds to slow and later efforts) and in general could be a function of q, $\dot{q}$, $\bar{q}$, $\bar{t}$, t, μ and is denoted by $V(q, \dot{q}, \bar{q}, \bar{t}, t, \mu)$. Here, however, we restrict to the case when the potential energy analogue is $V(q, t, \mu)$ – a function of the variables in the q-t-μ space. As a matter of fact at subtle level the roles of $\dot{q}$, $\bar{q}$ and $\bar{t}$ are very much there in taking decisions and using memory but it is internally consistent with the self and the same occurs at such a fast pace that it goes unnoticed in the outer world. Thus, in analogy with the energy function of classical mechanics, we can postulate a structure of $\mathcal{M}$ (= $\mathcal{M}_g + \mathcal{M}_s$) as

$$\mathcal{M} = a\dot{q}^2 + b\bar{q}^2 + c\bar{t}^2 + V(q, t, \mu). \tag{7.35}$$

Here, a, b and c are suitable dimensional parameters adjusted keeping in mind that the function $\mathcal{M}$ restores the dimensions of energy. Further, note that the potential term V here can be positive or negative depending on the attitude of the individual. In fact, if a person follows the systematic of positive pursuit with respect to the world-order, then the V-term in (7.35) is positive; otherwise this term can be considered as negative. For such a choice of $\mathcal{M}$, eq. (7.32) yields the following psycho-dynamical equations for the evolution of the system:

$$a\ddot{q} + b\bar{\bar{q}} - (1/2)\frac{\partial V}{\partial q} = 0; \quad c\,\bar{\bar{t}} - \frac{1}{2}\frac{\partial V}{\partial t} = 0, \tag{7.36a}$$

where

$$\ddot{q} = (\partial^2 q / \partial t^2), \bar{\bar{q}} = (\partial^2 q / \partial \mu^2), \bar{\bar{t}} = (\partial^2 t / \partial \mu^2). \tag{7.36b}$$

It may be mentioned that unlike the space–time mediated dynamical variables in physical theories, the variables q, $\dot{q}$, $\bar{q}$, t, $\bar{t}$, μ here are not ideally isolated or independent; they rather do have interdependence. This is mainly because of the plurality character of consciousness which, immediately after the switching on, becomes all-pervading and also the creator of space and time. This sets the limitation on the use of eq. (7.36a, b).

7.5 A Guide for the Applications of Eqs (7.36) and (7.32)

As far as the applications of psycho-dynamical eq. (7.36) (or for that matter of their generalized version (7.32)) is concerned, individual's personality appear in the applications. Besides the way in which an individual is involved in the consciousness-manifesting phenomena his attitude or psychology towards the world- or cosmic-order also matters and accordingly the role of "potential term" in $\mathcal{M}$ is considered. As how one reacts in the circumstances created by his own consciousness with regard to emotions, thinking and/or memory, is highly subjective and as such it is not easy to quantify. Still one can attempt to solve eq. (7.36) for some typical cases may be under some simplifying assumptions.

A word of caution regarding the use of eq. (7.36) is necessary. In fact, here q is considered as a simple function of variables t and μ. But in reality it is not so, when one plans a task at a given point in space his consciousness constantly undergoes through all sorts of time and/or consciousness channels as a part of decisions. As a result, q becomes a complicated functional of functions of t and μ, viz. $q = q(u(t), v(\mu))$, even at the initial stages of planning. Such considerations will however help in setting the boundary conditions for the solution of (7.36) or of (7.32). In fact, in this case, the boundary conditions need to be fixed in accordance with initial and final stages (or mindsets) of the task.

Even for the choice of V as $V = V(q, t, \mu)$ in (7.35), the solution of eq. (7.36) is not easy. However, we demonstrate the viability or effectiveness of these results for some representative cases. Note that the role of the potential term V in (7.36) disappears in either of the cases, viz. when (i) $V(q, t, \mu) = 0$, or (ii) $V(q, t, \mu) = V(\mu)$. In these cases eq. (7.36) takes the form

$$a\ddot{q} + b\overline{\overline{q}} = 0, \qquad c\overline{\overline{t}} = 0. \tag{7.37a,b}$$

Equation (7.37b) admits the solution

$$t(\mu) = d\,(\mu - \mu_0), \tag{7.38}$$

where d is a constant and $\mu = \mu_0$ at $t = 0$. Note that (7.38) is the solution of (7.37b) for the ideal case when $V = 0$; otherwise for a realistic situation, equation (7.36a, b) should be solved for the forms

$$a\ddot{q} + b\bar{\bar{q}} - W_1(t, \mu) = 0, \quad c\bar{\bar{t}} - (1/2)\, W_2(\mu) = 0, \tag{7.39a, b}$$

which, in general, will admit very complicated solution depending on the forms of V or of W_1 and W_2. We restrict ourselves from going into further details here. For the solution of the partial differential eq. (7.37a) we discuss the method of the separation of variables (Pipes and Harvill 1970). Such solutions are obtained in Appendix B by considering it as an analogue of Laplace equation in two dimensions.

In Appendix B, the solutions of eq. (7.36) are discussed corresponding to the cases when the subtle component $V(q, t, \mu)$ in $\mathcal{M}$ is either absent or has mild dependence on its arguments. These solutions can however offer a basis for developing the perturbation solution of the problem, if the necessity arises for certain forms of $V(q, t, \mu)$.

From the applications point of view, one can notice some relevance of the solution (B11) of eq. (7.36). Note that under the separable-assumption of the solution $q(t, \mu)$ for t and μ-variables, the solution

$$q_m(t,\mu) = B_m \exp(-m\pi\mu(a/b)^{1/2}/\tau)\sin\left(\frac{m\pi t}{\tau}\right), \tag{B11}$$

describes the space variation with μ and t in a particular mode m and mood (mindset). Further, note that the time and consciousness themselves adjust in such a way that the space q_m in this particular mode is optimum. For a car driver in a crowded lane or for a person crossing a crowded road such different mindsets arise and finally result into the net path $q(t, \mu)$ (cf. eq. (B12)).

7.6 Concluding Discussion

In addition to Chapter 4, note that this chapter too adds another flower to the garland of mathematization scheme of psychoscience in the sense that classical mechanics itself is one of the backbones of modern theoretical physics. With a view that the imaginaries of mathematical world will account for the mental world and associated processes (and so are the real parts would account for the physical world and associated processes), a complex form of "conscious action integral" is revisited here (cf. Section 7.3). While the details are referred to earlier works, the viability of the derived Euler–Lagrange equations is once again highlighted for the dynamics of an EP-matter particle. Here we have used the concept of complex configuration (coordinate-velocity) space rather than perhaps a better choice of complex phase (coordinate–momentum) space. The latter will, however, be considered in the next chapter to investigate the psychophysics of Chevreul pendulum.

This chapter is an attempt to give still deeper foundations to the subject of psychoscience in rigorous mathematical terms, particularly with reference to the phenomena belonging to world-2. After all, it is a necessity of modern times when other soft disciplines like sociology and economics are trying to marry with physics to give birth to the subjects of sociophysics (see, for example, Galam 2012) and econo-physics (see, for example, Doyane Farmer et al. 2005), then why psychology should be left untouched from this kind of development. No doubt, further applications of the psychodynamical equations derived (cf. eqs (7.32) and (7.36)) here are due but some demonstrated in Section 7.5 and Appendix B, will pave new ways to understand the human behaviour and personality better.

With a view to accounting for the consciousness in physical theories or to understand the role of mental processes in physical phenomena, several ways and methods have been proposed in the past (see, for example, Bruneberg et al. 2018; Kaushal 2009; Mlodinow 2012; Penrose 1994; Samuel et al. 2019; Stapp 2009) in different contexts. Susie Vrobel (2011) discusses several such phenomena and tries to understand them through fractal time. An important concept about time advanced in the work of Vrobel is that of "length" and "depth" of the time interval. This concept seems to have a close connection with the concept of experience-based and event-based space–time intervals discussed in Section 7.4.2.

In recent years, Karl Friston and his group (see, for example, Bruneberg et al. 2018; Samuel et al. 2019, and the references therein) have also advocated a free energy (variation) principle to tackle the hard problem of consciousness related to a society. However, their variation method, based on Bayesian statistics, is different from the one used here in the sense that psycho-mechanics here is investigated as a formal extension of the grand theory of classical mechanics. The importance of the concept of using different imaginaries for the elements of the set and for the mapping on the set (see Kaushal 2009, 2011) is particularly noticed in psychoscience. The approach followed here is however more elegant and perhaps easy to extend to the quantum domain.

Note that the derived psycho-dynamical equations (7.32) require further investigation with reference to different consciousness-manifesting phenomena belonging to world-2. An interesting feature one can note from the solution (B9) of eq. (7.37a) is the symmetry of the solution $q(t, \mu)$ with respect to the interchange of t and μ along with the change in the sign of constant, viz. $k^2 \rightarrow -k^2$. This perhaps is the outcome of the assumption of treating μ-variable at par with t-variable in the trio of space, time and consciousness. We have dealt with the typical case of $V = 0$ in Appendix B. The separable-assumption for the solution of (7.37a) has further simplified the solution of the problem of zigzag path for a person in a crowded lane. Note that the detailed features of the movement are still not clear from the solution (B9) or (B11). In reality, one should look for the solution of (7.39a) and (7.39b) together for certain ansatz for the potential functions $W_1(t, \mu)$ and $W_2(\mu)$.

High Skill Exercises and Projects

7.1 Compare, discuss and comment on the underlying philosophies used in the optimization of the following constructs: (i) the mindset function in the form of $\mathcal{M} = \mathcal{M}(m, i, e)$, where m, i, e have a complicated dependence on q, t, σ (cf. eqs (7.1)-(7.3)); (ii) the conscious action J of eq. (7.14) with real Lagrangian and its real arguments; (iii) (a) the conscious action J of eq. (7.14) with complex Legrangian and its complex arguments with $i = I$, (b) the conscious action J of eq. (7.14) with complex Legrangian and its complex arguments with $i \neq I$; (iv) the "effort integral" K of eq. (7.26). Further, comment on the intricate dependence of t on μ as considered in the construct eq. (7.36).

7.2 Are the space (q), time (t) and consciousness (μ) variables independent in various cases listed in Exercise 7.1? If not, then discuss this issue in each case.

7.3 Comment on the definition of the focused attention (μ) as discussed through eq. (7.20). Explain in detail as to how μ gets affected by its dependence on τ and C.

7.4 Write a Note on the concepts of experience-based and event-based space and time intervals vis-à-vis the processes of "externalization of the interior" and "internalization of the exterior". What do you mean by the "length" and the "depth" of time?

7.5 *Sports of high jump and long jump*: Make an attempt to solve psycho-dynamical eq. (7.36a, b) for sports of high jump and long-jump with appropriate choices of $V(q, t, \mu)$; for example for $V(q, \mu, t) \sim V(\mu)$ or, in particular when (i) $V(\mu) \sim \mu$, and (ii) $V(\mu) \sim \exp(a\mu)$, where a is a constant, the two extreme cases. How the trajectories will get affected due to this kind of dependence as compared to the parabolic path for an inanimate object?

7.6 Investigate the application of eq. (7.36a, b) to the case of Chevreul handheld pendulum of Chapter 8.

7.7 Keeping the discussions of Appendix E in mind and in continuation of Exercise 7.4 define an experience-based quantity like "happiness" and its associated measure like "happiness index". Further, discuss its possible links with Weber-Fechner law and the corresponding transformation.

8

Psyche and the Conscious Pendula

8.1 Introduction

8.1.1 PENDULUM IN PHYSICAL SCIENCES: SOME BRIEF REMARKS

THE role of pendulum, in particular that of "simple" pendulum in theoretical physics and mathematical sciences, is the same as that of a wheel in the daily life of a person. In fact, the pendulum in the former case has made the understanding of difficult and involved concepts of physics simple, the use of wheel in the latter case, on the other hand, has made life comfortable and luxurious. Again the concept of "simple" pendulum in physics is a mathematically idealized picture in the sense that

i. the string used is assumed to be massless,

ii. the suspended mass (known as "bob") is assumed to be a point mass, and on the top of these two assumptions there is a third one, viz.

iii. during oscillations the restoring force on the point mass at any instant is (linearly) proportional to its displacement q from the mean position.

For such a system, one describes the motion through a differential equation,

$$\frac{d^2q}{dt^2} = -\omega^2 q, \tag{8.1}$$

which admits a periodic solution with angular frequency ω, where $\omega = 2\pi\nu$, and time period $T = (2\pi/\omega)$, or

$$T = 2\pi \sqrt{(l/g)}, \tag{8.2}$$

where l is the length of the string and g is acceleration due to gravity. Such an idealized picture of the pendulum when used to explain a variety of phenomena, whose occurrence in Nature ranges from micro (atomic) scales to mega and giga (cosmic) scales, has provided highly satisfactory results at least in the lowest order vis-à-vis experiments. As far as the use of this mental construct at different space–time scales is concerned, the same has been carried out on the basis of structural analogy (cf. Section 12.1 and Kaushal 2003).

Departures from such a simplicity of the "physics pendulum" have been discussed (Kaushal 2005) from school-level to research-level studies on all the three fronts or ingredients of the pendulum, viz. related to the type of the string, type of the bob and the nature of the motion (linear or otherwise). Perhaps for the conscious pendulum, besides the other factors, it is the gravity force appearing through g that needs to be questioned! An easy way to have a conscious pendulum is by replacing the rigid support (of physics pendulum) by a handheld support to the string used to suspend the bob.

8.1.2 PENDULUM IN METAPHYSICS, OCCULT SCIENCES AND PSYCHOLOGY

In the seventeenth century, while Sir Isaac Newton was busy in developing the mathematical theories for the motion of inanimate objects including that of physics pendulum, certain components of society were also busy (since earlier days) in the divination of the pendulum. In this context, in somewhat less educated society the handheld pendulum was used in two distinct ways: In one case, the handheld pendulum of convenient length was used to mesmerize/hypnotize a person by performing fast oscillations in front of his face possibly in varying environments. In the second case, the handheld pendulum was used as a personality predictor of ideomotor performance (see, for example, Olson et al. 2017) of a person or to answer some personal or hypothetical questions by studying the changes in the nature of motion of the pendulum.

As a matter of fact, for centuries, people have asked questions to handheld pendula and interpreted their movements as responses from the divine. These movements occur due to "ideomotor effect" wherein priming or thinking a motion causes muscle movements that end up in the swinging of pendulum. By associating particular swinging movements with "yes" and "no" responses, one investigates whether the pendulum can aid in decision making or which personality traits correlate with this performance (movements). As a whole, it turns out to be a complicated process from the point of view of a scientific analysis since the consciousness of several persons directly or indirectly is involved in drawing any meaningful conclusion.

In fact, there was a common belief in society that a (good or bad) "spirit" manifests through the hands of the holder of the pendulum, provided the holder himself is an unbiased (a novice or an innocent) person, like a child. Again the change in the nature of motion in varying environments helped in making "convenient" prophecies. Such uses of pendulum, based mainly on a belief system or on the ignorance of people, continued for centuries (or perhaps still in practice), however does not fit in any scientific framework whatsoever. On the other hand, scientists are also afraid of treading into the zone of consciousness, as they have not yet understood this aspect of human life besides the laws of motion for inanimate objects. No doubt, there is a possibility of reflection of the mindset of the holder of the string in the time period or through the nature of motion, but the question is as to how to account for its role in the "physics" theory of the pendulum.

In the next section we discuss possible types of conscious pendula in the light of simple pendulum and emphasize that it is only the handheld conscious pendulum that can give some clue about the role of consciousness in physical theories, if any, or a justification for its use in psychological studies. In Section 8.3, we attempt to analyse various possible interactions in a handheld pendulum and in the language of physics. Assuming that the mental processes are accounted through the imaginaries of complex numbers and/or of corresponding functions of mathematical physics, we analyse the case of a simple pendulum with complex frequencies in Section 8.4. Here, the neuroscience involved is discussed in a top-down approach. Next, in view of these studies, we comment on certain phenomena of occult sciences, like hypnotization and in analogy of physics we propose a possible generalization of this phenomenon in the form of the so-called "*K*-effect" in Section 8.5. With a view to establishing the divination of the handheld pendulum, a laboratory experiment with laser beam is suggested in Section 8.6. Finally, concluding remarks are made in Section 8.7.

8.2 Various Types of Conscious Pendula

Note that a simple pendulum with all possible corrections, viz. for a massive string, extended bob and/or for non-linear oscillations still remains a physical (inanimate) pendulum, particularly when an instrument (like a photo cell or laser beam) measuring the time period. In fact, a mild consciousness of spectator nature appears in the system when a person directly measures the time period. A conscious pendulum, on the other hand, means that the consciousness (or its source) is very much present in either one, two or in all the three components (viz. string, support and bob) of the pendulum. From this point of view, one can think of the following types of conscious pendula with corresponding examples:

(A) *Zero-conscious (physical or inanimate) pendula:* The pendulum of Section 8.1.1, even after accounting for all possible corrections for various departures from the simplicity, comes in this category.

(B) *Mono-conscious pendula:* When consciousness manifests only through one component of the pendulum: Various situations which arise in this case are:

(B1) conscious support but inanimate string and bob, e.g. the case of a handheld (Chevreul) pendulum;

(B2) rigid support, inanimate string but bob is conscious, e.g. an alive bird is suspended from rigid support, or a swinging girl, suspended from rigid support and with a rope, performing oscillations; and

(B3) rigid support, inanimate bob but conscious string, e.g. a snake holding a dead rat in its mouth downward, suspended from a rigid support and performing oscillations.

(C) *Bi-conscious pendula:* When consciousness manifests through two components of a pendulum: Various possibilities in this case are:

(C1) conscious support, conscious bob, but inanimate string, e.g. a person holding a snake from its tail, snake also holds a dead rat in its mouth downward, and performing oscillations;

(C2) conscious support, inanimate string, but conscious bob, e.g. a person holding the string in his hand and allowing the oscillations of an alive bird at the other end; and

(C3) rigid support, conscious string and conscious bob, e.g. a snake suspended from tail across a rigid support and he holds an alive rat in his mouth downward and performing oscillations.

(D) *Tri- and multi-conscious pendula:* When all the three components, viz. the support, string and the bob, are conscious, e.g. a person holding a snake from its tail and the snake holds an alive rat in its mouth downward, performing the oscillations. Multi-conscious pendulum cases can arise, for example, through the analogy of double or triple pendulum in physics in which two, three or even more children chainwise holding successively the feet of one by the hands of the other and so on, and performing oscillations, as in a circus. In this context (as it normally happens in a circus while displaying amazing events for the viewers), one can imagine several other types of multi-conscious pendula which, in fact, can involve other living species as their component(s).

(E) *Some special classes of multi-conscious pendula: The effect of self-organizing forces*: Under the above categories, it is worthwhile to list some more interesting cases:

(E1) For example, in case (B2), if a thirsty bird is performing the oscillations and a boy with a water-bowl is standing near the mean position to offer water to the bird, then naturally the amplitude or the time period of motion will get affected.

(E2) A mother is swinging and she wants to breast-feed her hungry and crying child, standing nearby (preferably near the mean position or the end-points), again the nature of motion will get affected. Such examples are good enough to study the role of emotions through a multi-conscious system.

(E3) A girl suspended from a rigid support and preparing her mind to swing, but does not have any support whatsoever, is left alone at her own. Naturally, she will use her self-organizing forces to generate amplitude and subsequently motion. Starting with negligibly small amplitude she slowly creates motion of sufficiently large amplitudes. Many such examples can be traced in daily life when self-organizing forces appear and control the movements. The examples (E1) and (E2) display the coupling or tuning of consciousness through self-organizing forces.

Some further remarks about this type of classification of conscious pendula are in order:

i. It may be mentioned that while it is difficult to understand the phenomenon of consciousness (cf. Chapter 2), it is even more difficult to understand a multi-conscious pendula. Still some cases, like the case (B1) of Chevreul handheld pendulum as used in occult sciences, offer a simpler situation as far as the analytical studies of this grand phenomenon are concerned.

ii. From the study point of view, note that there is a lot of differences between the cases (B1) and (B2) in spite of the fact that they both belong to mono-conscious category. In case (B1), while consciousness mostly flows in a directed and focused manner through the hand and fingers of the holder, in case (B2), it is the whole set of EOLs that can come in action irrespective of whether it is the case of a swinging bird or a girl. In the latter case, however, both free will and willpower and hence the self-organizing forces of the bob can play a dominant role in motion. In fact, it is the case (B1) that can give some clue towards the computation aspect of consciousness.

iii. As a matter of fact, the interference of two or more than two consciousnesses (or for that matter bifurcation or trifurcation of the same consciousness through different body parts) makes the studies increasingly difficult. From this point of view, the experimental studies of case (E) may be interesting but developing a theory for this case is a tedious task.

iv. No doubt, the Chevreul handheld pendulum offers an ideal experimental device to investigate the role of consciousness in physical theories, but with a rider that the system is no more a closed one; however, it can be treated as nearly closed.

v. These modest attempts to classify consciousness and to list a few examples are based on the picture of a simple pendulum; otherwise in Nature there are infinitely many situations where many sources of consciousness interact and interfere and sometimes the same consciousness bifurcate, trifurcate, etc. in spite of the fact that they all belong to the same source of cosmic consciousness field of Chapter 4.

8.3 Accounting for Interactions in a Handheld Pendulum: A Physicist's Approach

The Hamiltonian function, H (a function of coordinates and momenta) is a measure of energy or interaction associated with a given (closed!) system in motion. We use the same symbol to identify various types of interactions here, but with distinct subscripts, indicating the nature of interaction or the interacting objects. For a conscious pendulum, we write the Hamiltonian H in a very general manner as the sum of physical (H_{phys}) and non-physical ($H_{\text{non-phys}}$) parts as,

$$H = H_{\text{phys}} + H_{\text{non-phys}}. \tag{8.3}$$

For the so-called simple pendulum, we write H_{phys} as,

$$H_{\text{phys}} = H_o + H_{\text{int}}, \tag{8.4}$$

where H_0, in the small-oscillation limit, is given by

$$H_0 = (1/2)\, p^2 + (1/2)\, \omega^2 q^2 \tag{8.5}$$

with angular frequency, $\omega = 2\pi/T$ and T is the time period given by (8.2). Further, for the case of simple pendulum when a person is measuring the time period, H_{int} can be written as

$$H_{\text{int}} = H_{b\text{-}P} + H_{P\text{-}PA} + H_{b\text{-}PA}. \tag{8.6}$$

Here $H_{b\text{-}P}$ and $H_{b\text{-}PA}$, respectively correspond to human Being (b)-pendulum (P) and human Being (b)-physical apparatus (PA) interactions. Both of these terms basically are the non-physical parts and normally neglected in physical theories as compared to the gravity force, particularly for the external observer. So is the case with the pendulum–physical apparatus interaction, $H_{P\text{-}PA}$.

No doubt, the interactions $H_{b\text{-}P}$ and $H_{b\text{-}PA}$, responsible for the consciousness of the observer, are negligible in the above case, but in reality, their account is necessary through the patomic model of human Being (cf. Chapter 6). In fact, for the categories (B)-(E) of the conscious-pendula and for each participating person, a full structure of b in terms of EOLs, as b = {WO, B, SE, M, I, E, SO}, need to be used. This will suggest a new form of $H_{b\text{-}P}$-term in (8.6) even after neglecting the last two terms in it. In fact, for the mono-conscious case and for the patomic picture of b (cf. Chapter 6) H_{int} in (8.4) can be written as:

$$H_{\text{int}} \equiv H_{b\text{-}P} = H_{WO\text{-}P} + H_{B\text{-}P} + H_{SE\text{-}P} + H_{M\text{-}P} + H_{I\text{-}P} + H_{E\text{-}P} + H_{SO\text{-}P}, \tag{8.7}$$

where various terms correspond to the interactions of each EOL with the pendulum. This full form of interaction (8.7) is, in fact, applicable for the case (B2) of a swinging girl. However, for the handheld case, particularly for the case (B1), while H_{WO-P} will contribute to a perceptible environment, H_{B-P} and H_{SE-P} will just help in taking a fixed physical posture by the holder of the pendulum. Thus, the interaction (8.7) for the handheld case (B1) takes the form,

$$H_{\text{int}} \equiv H_{b-P} = H_{M-P} + H_{I-P} + H_{E-P} + H_{SO-P} . \tag{8.8}$$

It can be noticed that the first three terms on the right-hand side of (8.8) contribute to the mindset of the holder. If the holder is novice or unbiased, then any one of the terms in (8.7), in conjunction with the last term H_{SO-P}, will manifest through the pendulum motion. On the other hand, if the holder is matured, experienced or a biased one, then there are chances of manifesting the effect in pendulum motion, of two or all the three terms, viz. H_{M-P}, H_{I-P}, H_{E-P} in (8.8). Naturally, this situation will make the predictions of the pendulum motion questionable, even if the holder is working with a focused attention.

Recall that the personality is the outer garment of the character of a person (cf. Chapter 11) and the character is shaped by the mental processes involving mind, intellect and ego (or self-conscience). Thus, by calibrating the nature of motion of the pendulum with the data obtained from M-, I- or E-dominated mindset out of some selective holders, one can as well use the pendulum to predict and analyse the personality traits present in the personality of a new holder of the pendulum.

Note that for the bi-conscious or multi-conscious pendula (cf. cases (C)-(E)) the non-physical interactions become very complicated. For example, for the bi-conscious case (C) the non-physical (or H_{int}) – part in (8.3) becomes $H_{b1-b2-P}$, where each b_i (for i = 1, 2) is now described by the patomic model, viz. $b_i = \{WO, B_i, SE_i, M_i, I_i, E_i, SO\}$. Thus, from the point of view of analysis or for drawing any meaningful conclusion about the consciousness or about the nature of pendulum motion, the structure of $H_{b1-b2-P}$ in analogy with (8.7), turns out to be a complicated one.

Here we have analysed the conscious pendula through eq. (8.3), i.e. by attributing the non-physical part to an alive component of the conscious pendulum. In fact, out of these various choices, it is only the handheld pendulum (cf. case (B1)) that can provide some meaningful results about the consciousness and the personality traits of a person and in view of the structure (8.8) it justifies its use in occult sciences and psychology. Next, we plan to explore an alternative way to investigate the mental processes again by using the handheld pendulum in the spirit of Chevreul. In this case, we shall attribute the imaginaries of mathematical physics arising through the complex numbers and complex functions to mental processes, whereas the real parts will remain attached with the real world of physics.

8.4 The Chevreul Handheld Pendulum

In 1833, the French Chemist Michel-Eugene Chevreul (1833) wrote a remarkable paper on the experiments and interpretation of the "magical" or handheld pendulum (hereafter termed as "Chevreul pendulum"). In fact, when a pendulum consisting of a heavy body (say an iron ring) attached to one of the ends of a flexible thread and of which the other end is held by an unmoving hand is allowed to oscillate above certain substance (say water, a piece of metal or a living Being), then the presence of the latter induces the pendulum's oscillation in spite of the fact that the arm of the holder remains immobile. What has been found is the unusual property of the inanimate objects like the ones that the pendulum swings back and forth or in a circular path depending upon what the holder is thinking, i.e. the nature of thought reflects in the mode of oscillation. Chevreul, in fact, arrived at several interesting conclusions (and the same were communicated to Ampere) for which conventional physics does not seem to have any explanation whatsoever even today. However, a detailed study carried out by psychologists Ansfield and Wegner (1996) rules out any kind of their mystical explanation. The first complete English translation of this important document along with an open letter written to A.M. Ampere (the top-ranking physicist of that time) has recently been published by Spitz and Marcuard in *Skeptical Inquirer* (2001). Chevreul also highlights several other phenomena of this category in this open letter.

With a view to understanding such consciousness-manifesting phenomena, it appears that an additional dimension of analysis in the mental domain and responsible for the hidden thought-process or for the self-organizing mechanism needs to be incorporated in the theory. This we pursue here by investigating a complex oscillator in an extended complex phase plane.

8.4.1 EXTENDED COMPLEX PHASE SPACE APPROACH TO CLASSICAL OSCILLATOR

With a view to accounting for the consciousness in the handheld pendulum, we analyse a complex version of H_0 in (8.5) and the same can be produced on an extended complex phase plane. For this purpose, we use the following complex transformation (cf. eq. (5) of (Kaushal 2009) and the references therein)

$$q = q_1 + ip_2, p = p_1 + iq_2 \tag{8.9}$$

and also consider the frequency ω as complex, viz. $\omega = \omega_1 + i\omega_2$. This yields eq. (8.5) in the form

$$H_0 = H_1 + iH_2, \tag{8.10}$$

where the real and imaginary parts of H_0 are given by

$$H_1 = \frac{1}{2}\left[p_1^2 + (\omega_1^2 - \omega_2^2)\, q_1^2\right] - \frac{1}{2}\left[(\omega_1^2 - \omega_2^2)\, p_2^2 + q_2^2\right] - 2\omega_1\omega_2 q_1 p_2 \tag{8.11a}$$

$$H_2 = \omega_1\omega_2(q_1^2 - p_2^2) + (\omega_1^2 - \omega_2^2)\, q_1 p_2 + p_1 q_2 . \tag{8.11b}$$

Regarding the constructions (8.9)-(8.11) the following remarks are in order:

a. As an assumption, we proceed by treating imaginary parts of all (parameters, variables and functions) quantities to describe the dynamics of mental world (the world which we perceive and denoted by W_2) and the same, in fact, is embedded in the field of consciousness. The real parts, on the other hand, describe the dynamics of the physical world (the world which is modelled, denoted by W_3) subject to a measurement by an inanimate apparatus only. In transformation (8.9) the fictitious variables q_2 and p_2 although introduced here in an ad hoc manner (as they belong to the mental world) but like q_1 and p_1 in the physical world, they do form a canonical pair (Kaushal and Korsch 2000) in the mental space. These two sets of canonical pairs jointly describe an analogous two-dimensional (2-D) coupled oscillator system. Note that out of several complexification methods listed (in Kaushal 2009), the transformation (8.9) is capable of generating an in-built coordinate–momentum coupling in the new equivalent 2-D system or in the two worlds. The choice of frequency parameter ω as a complex further adds to this feature, but on different footing.

b. Note that the Hamiltonian H_0 in (8.5) now becomes a function of two complex variables (cf. eq. (8.9)) and for its analyticity feature, H_1 and H_2 now need to satisfy two pairs of Cauchy-Riemann conditions. This, in turn, implies that the Poisson bracket of H_1 and H_2 vanishes (Kaushal and Korsch 2000) and hence suggests that H_1 and H_2 though coupled, are involutively independent. This means that the analogous 2-D system is integrable (Kaushal 1998).

c. Above two mathematical features, viz. the canonicity of the pairs (q_1,p_1) and (q_2,p_2) and the integrability of the equivalent 2-D system as a whole ensures one not just to have only a transparent and consistent description of the two worlds but also an integrated one.

d. In (8.11) while H_2 basically accounts for the different types of couplings in the two worlds, H_1 when written as

$$H_1 = H_{1P} + H_{1M} - 2\omega_1\omega_2 q_1 p_2 \tag{8.12}$$

however describes twin oscillators, out of which the physical oscillator corresponds

$$H_{1P} = (1/2)p_1^2 + (1/2)(\omega_1^2 - \omega_2^2)\, q_1^2 \tag{8.13a}$$

and the mental one corresponds to

$$H_{1M} = -(1/2)(\omega_1^2 - \omega_2^2)\, p_2^{\,2} - (1/2)\, q_2^2$$
$$= (1/2)(\omega_2^2 - \omega_1^2)\, p_2^{\,2} + (-1/2)\, q_2^2. \tag{8.13b}$$

Here H_{1P}, in fact, deals with an angular frequency square as $(\omega_1^2 - \omega_2^2)$ and follows the potential energy curve as a standard parabola for $\omega_1 > \omega_2$, the mental oscillator described by H_{1M}, however, attains a fictitious mass $(\omega_2^2 - \omega_1^2)^{-1}$ rolling on an inverted parabolic potential from inside below the q_2-axis. This latter feature is understandable in view of the fact that the person holding the string has to do some mental work (rather judiciously) on the system to maintain the outside oscillations of the physical world and again in a periodic fashion.

e. With regard to the couplings generated in the present approach and in the equivalent 2-D system (8.11) of (8.5), one can clearly note that they are of the following four types:

   i. Coupling by construction through the transformation (8.9);

   ii. dynamical couplings appearing through pure q_1p_2-, p_1q_2 - and/or $(q_1^2 - p_2^2)$ - type terms in (8.11) which in some sense are the consequences of (i) and also of the nature of H_0 in (8.5);

   iii. pure parametric coupling arising due to the real and imaginary parts of the parameter ω as a result of its complexification (such a coupling somehow does not appear in the present model); and

iv. mixed coupling arising from the combination of both parameter and dynamical couplings like the last term in (8.11a) and the first two terms in (8.11b).

Before analysing further the working of these twin, coupled oscillators, described by the Hamiltonians H_1 and H_2, we briefly remark on some recent works carried out on the study of consciousness and the related brain activity.

8.4.2 CONSCIOUS INTENTS AND BRAIN FUNCTIONING: TOP-DOWN AND BOTTOM-UP STUDIES IN BRAIN SCIENCES

One important aspect of these studies is the selective attention which in some sense is synonym of "meditation" of Vedic science (cf. Section 7.4). In fact, the meditation normally is with reference to the inner essences of life, viz. mind, intellect and ego, whereas its another counterpart, i.e. concentration (of mind) is with reference to the interaction of a human Being with the outer (physical) world. As a matter of fact, according to Vedic science selective attention, meditation and concentration are all manifestation of the same consciousness which makes the "human machinery" functional (Kaushal 2011). According to psychologists, attention is "the taking possession by the mind in clear and vivid form of one out of what seen several simultaneously possible objects or trains of thoughts" (Fell et al. 2003). Focused or selective attention, on the other hand, allows selection of certain items from the stream of information processing. Clearly, the word "selection" brings in the role of "intellect" and that too out of a treasure of information. The latter brings in the role of ego (self-conscience) – the "faculty of memory" in accordance with the Vedic science. While consciousness makes the entire "human machinery" (including both inner and outer EOLs (cf. Chapter 6)) functional, conscious intentions are the outcome of consciousness through mind and that too in an alive human Being. Note that a dead body cannot have conscious intents or a functional brain. In other words, it is the same consciousness which creates intents on the one hand and also makes the brain sites functional on the other.

With a view to reducing the gap between the top-down (consciousness vs psychic processes) and bottom-up (brain functioning vs psychic processes like emotions, feelings and intelligence) studies, brain scientists in consultation with psychologists and neuroscientists have accepted the challenge of identifying the brain sites responsible for some of these psychic phenomena and also for other sensory features. In particular, in this context the study of a neural coupling mechanism through the synchronization of neuronal gamma activity has been carried out to explore the role of selective attention in the synchronized gamma oscillations (Angel et al. 2001; Fell et al. 2003). Studies have shown that the sensory-feature-binding in the brain is accomplished by phase synchronization of induced neuronal gamma activity corresponding to a (30-80) Hz electromagnetic signal. In other words, our conscious intentions are closely linked to this frequency range of synchronous oscillations of the electromagnetic field at many well-separated brain sites. As to how the conscious intentions influence the brain activity or bodily actions in the functionally appropriate way, has been investigated recently by Stapp (2009) and his coworkers (Schwartz et al. 2005). For this purpose Stapp uses a simple solvable model of the dynamical coupling between a person's classically described perceptions and his quantum mechanically described brain within the framework of a mechanism based on the quantum-Zeno effect. In his model, however, this coupling is introduced from outside as a perturbation.

In the model of Stapp, it is the arbitrarily introduced coupling that is expected to make the world W_3 different from W_2. In fact, it is the observer who creates the perceptible world (W_2) and the physical world (W_3) out of the same (abstract) world (W_1) which exists in reality even in the absence of the observer. Moreover, the world W_2 is highly observer-dependent and assigning only one type of quantum character to it in terms of Planck constant is not justified in view of the incomprehensibility principle of Fraser (2013). As a matter of fact, before jumping to the quantum description or to quantum corrections in case of psychophysical systems, other possibilities in the classical description itself need to be explored. For example, we have accounted for the complex extension of the phase space by introducing "iota" in the physical variables (cf. eq. (8.9)). At the next stage, one can as well proceed with different imaginaries in the variables and in the functions of the corresponding complex variables, i.e. by resorting to the choice of a non-analytic complex Hamiltonian for such psychophysical phenomena which basically deal with open systems due to the presence of consciousness. This, in turn, will suggest a variety of possibilities for the analysis. For further details, we refer to our earlier works (Kaushal 2009, 2016b).

8.4.3 TWIN OSCILLATORS: THE ROLE OF DYNAMICAL COUPLING AND ISLANDS OF STABILITY

As mentioned above while H_2 in (8.11b) accounts for the various types of couplings, H_1 in (8.11a) describes twin oscillators — one belongs to the physical world and described by H_{1P} and other belongs to mental world described by H_{1M}, along with a coupling term between the twins (cf. eq. (8.12)). As a matter of fact, an understanding of these dynamical couplings (coupling due to dynamical variables) and parametric couplings (coupling due to parameter(s), like ω) between the two oscillators helps in taking judicious decisions with regard to the tight-holding of the string by the holder in practical terms. In philosophical terms, however, it also connects with the uncertainty principle in quantum mechanics on the one hand and with a possibility of explaining the phase synchronization of induced neuronal gamma activity corresponding to a 30-80 Hz electromagnetic signal in this framework, on the other.

Heisenberg uncertainty principle in quantum mechanics while setting a limit on the simultaneous measurement of a canonical pair of variables, this, in some sense, serves as an example of dynamical coupling in implicit form at micro-level. On the other hand, the examples of explicit forms of dynamical coupling even in the quantum domain arise when one accounts for certain types of interactions (in-built or external) in quantum systems. One can as well analyse another uncertainty principle in the present context that reflects from the incomprehensibility principle postulated recently by Gordon Fraser (2013) on the basis of a practical experience of every one, i.e. the intensity of attention (consciousness) multiplied by the (time) span (during which the attention is applied to complete a task) cannot exceed some fixed value.

It appears from this principle that the canonicity feature of the pair of physical variables in the uncertainty relations of Heisenberg, reflects only in a restricted albeit ideal sense; otherwise, in general, it has to do something with an in-built dynamical coupling in the system and that too at the micro level between certain preferred (canonical) variables. Alternatively, this canonicity feature at the classical level translates itself into the complexity of the phase space used in the present work or in general that of the function space (Kaushal 2009). It could very well be the common factor of consciousness at the root of all such in-built dynamical couplings, which in turn manifest through the uncertainty relations in the quantum domain or through the complexification of physical variables in the classical domain. In other words, it is the consciousness, when switched on to perceive the physical world that creates another domain of canonical variables in an imaginary space and subsequently contributes to the in-built coupling in the twin system.

To investigate the islands of stability in the phase space of twin oscillators (or to look for the values of q_1, p_1, q_2, p_2, for which the holder of the pendulum will finally feel comfortable in holding the string vis-à-vis the frequency management), one can use the prescription of (Kaushal and Singh 2001) to analyse the equations of motion

$$(dq_1/dt) = 2p_1; \quad (dp_1/dt) = -2aq_1 + 4bp_2 \tag{8.14a}$$

$$(dq_2/dt) = -2ap_2 - 4bq_1; \quad (dp_2/dt) = 2q_2 \tag{8.14b}$$

where $a = \omega_1^2 - \omega_2^2$ and $b = \omega_1 . \omega_2$ are real and $a + 2ib = \omega^2$, $a - 2ib = \omega^{*2}$. Further, a stability analysis of these equations (see, for example, chapter 6 of Kaushal and Parashar 2008) suggests four but interdependent fixed points and the same correspond to the following eigenvalues of the stability matrix (Kaushal 2016b):

$$\lambda_1 = 2i\omega^* \equiv 2(i\omega_1 + \omega_2); \quad \lambda_2 = 2i\omega \equiv 2(i\omega_1 - \omega_2);$$

$$\lambda_3 = -2i\omega^* \equiv -2(i\omega_1 + \omega_2);$$

$$\lambda_4 = -2i\omega \equiv -2(i\omega_1 - \omega_2).$$

Here note that $\lambda_1 = \lambda^*_4$ and $\lambda_2 = \lambda^*_3$. Thus, it is not difficult to note that an unstable spiral evolves with time in the $q_1 - p_2$ sector of the phase space since λ_1 and λ_4 have the same positive real part ω_2. On the other hand, an asymptotically stable spiral appears in the $p_1 - q_2$ sector of the phase space. As far as the contribution from $q_1 - p_1$ or $q_2 - p_2$ sectors is concerned, it is only towards the instability of the system as the real parts in the corresponding pair of eigenvalues are of opposite sign. In view of the fact that only the $p_1 - q_2$ plane contributes to the stability, one can say that the consciousness or attention combined with the "dynamism" of the external world implies stability in the psychophysical system; otherwise, its combination with the "statism" of the outer world supports the instability in general. In other words, the distraction of attention of the holder of the pendulum is expected more when the pendulum is in motion and/or when the eyes of the holder are open. In this case, in fact, extra efforts need to be made by the holder to restore the planar vibrations of the bob.

In the next section, we briefly comment on some exotic phenomena of occult sciences in the light of the above studies.

8.5 Hypnotization and the K-effect

8.5.1 THE K-EFFECT

Before proceeding further we mention here an illustrative analogy from physics. Recall that an atom in itself has intrinsic electricity and magnetism and the corresponding fields inside, but when placed in an external electric or magnetic field it shows abnormal behaviour in the form of Stark, Zeeman or Faraday effects. In the same way, a conscious individual who himself has "soul" or "spirit" and hence the spiritual energy (cenergy) field (which, in some sense, is translated into the mindset $\mathcal{M}$), when placed in an external "soul" or "spiritual" energy field, is bound to undergo a change in terms of its mindset or the behaviour thereof. The later phenomenon is abbreviated as "K-effect" (or "Kaushal-effect", meaning thereby "skill-in-action-effect") (for details see, Appendix F of Kaushal 2011). Note that in the case of an atom the electric or magnetic field inside and outside the atom is in no way different as far as its fundamental features in space–time are concerned. The only thing is that these two categories of fields are separated again by space–time boundary to term them as "inside" and "outside" fields and what appears in the observed data is the resultant effect of the interactions between the two. On the other hand, when an individual undergoes an intense or specially designed psychic zone, then a variety of phenomena with regard to the behaviour of the individual, are bound to appear as a result of interactions. In the latter case, however, each – the external psychic zone and the psychic zone associated with the individual – has a number of interacting participants like M, I and E. Therefore, there is a possibility of appearance of a variety of phenomena as a result of interactions in the K-effect.

This effect, no doubt, can be noticed in the above context but basically, it is a change in the mindset of one person by the counselling of the other and this change in the first person is noticed by a third person. In some sense, in the language of Chapter 10, this is the case of three interacting persons (like three business partners, etc.) in which the effect of interaction between any two is noticed by the third person as a spectator. The exchanges here are not balanced and are unidirectional in certain subdomains. In the K-effect however the affected individual (who is also a living Being) himself acts as an instrument and his behaviour as noticed by a third normal person, becomes an observable in terms of abnormality. Note that this abnormality in his behaviour appears from the point of view of a normal person.

8.5.2 HYPNOTIZATION

"Hypnotism" is basically an induced state of mind, like the deep sleep, in which an individual (called "subject") acts on external suggestions and/or commands.

Example 8.5.1: When the pole of a permanent magnet is rubbed on a small piece of iron rod for a certain period of time, the latter starts exhibiting the similar magnetic properties as of the permanent magnet. This is what actually happens in the process of hypnotization.

As a matter of fact, in the process of hypnotization the subject starts acting on the command of the counsellor, particularly when the brain washing is done for a certain period of time. In some methods of hypnotization, a handheld pendulum is also used to impart the spiritual energy to the subject. In this case, the holder performs appropriately fast oscillations using a pendulum of appropriate length and in front of the face of the subject. Perhaps, a matching of frequencies of mindsets of the holder and of the subject is sought in this case through an intermediary instrument like a handheld pendulum; or a frequency difference of about 30-80 Hz (corresponding to the expected neuronal gamma activity) between the two mindsets needs to be created with the help of the external agency like handheld pendulum.

8.6 A Laser Beam Experiment to Investigate the Divination of the Handheld Pendulum

In order to have an idea of the frequency difference between the twin oscillators of Section 8.4.3, we propose here an experiment with laser beam. The experiment needs to be performed in two parts by way of maintaining ideally the same external conditions in the two cases. In the first part, just allow the free vibrations of small amplitude of a simple pendulum (SP) suspended from a rigid support. Then project a laser beam (S) of circular cross-section normal to the plane of vibration of the bob. The beam is of reasonably high intensity and width and projected from across the vibrating thread on a horizontally movable photographic plate

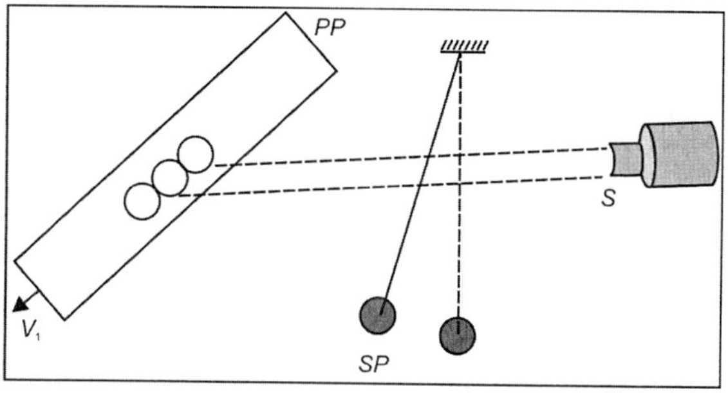

fig. 8.1: Experiment with simple pendulum (*SP*)

(*PP*) such that the beam cross-section leaves a circular mark on *PP* placed on the other side of the thread (cf. *fig.* 8.1).

Adjust the speed of *PP* in such a way that the distance traversed by *PP* is exactly equal to the diameter of the circle formed by the mark of the beam cross-section on *PP*. Also note that this is the time interval during which the bob/thread returns to the mean or initial beam crossing position from one of the extreme end-positions. The important point to be kept in mind in this setting is that the marked circles of the beam cross-section on *PP* should remain exactly in touch with the next adjacent one in the sequence. Let the velocity of *PP* at which this situation is achieved be $V_{1.}$

In the second part of the experiment, replace *SP* by the handheld pendulum (*HHP*) in which the thread of exactly the same length as in the first part, is tightly held between the thumb and the index finger. Rest of the settings of the beam *S* and the photographic plate *PP* remains the same (cf. *fig.* 8.2). Naturally, the pattern of the adjacently touching circles on *PP* will not remain the same as before since the time period of *HHP* is expected to be different. Therefore, next arrange the new speed V_2 of *PP* such that the circles again become in adjacently touching position to create the same pattern as before. Note that in the present case with *HHP*, the holder of the pendulum has to make some efforts to maintain the planar vibrations of bob like that in case of *SP*.

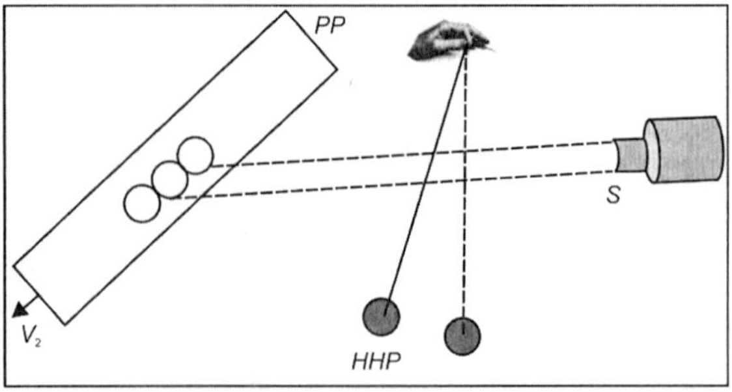

fig. 8.2: Experiment with handheld pendulum (*HHP*)

Analysis of Results: Let $2R$ be the diameter of the circular cross-section of the beam; T_1 and T_2 be the time periods in the two cases, viz. with *SP* and *HHP* respectively, and V_1 and V_2 be the velocities of the movable *PP* needed in the two cases to restore the same pattern. Then note that

$$T_1 = (4R/V_1), \quad T_2 = (4R/V_2),$$

and hence

$$\omega_1 - \omega_2 = \frac{2\pi}{T_1} - \frac{2\pi}{T_2} = \frac{\pi}{2R}(V_1 - V_2).$$

Note that the role of consciousness here manifests through the difference of frequencies, $(\nu_1 - \nu_2)$, and the same is given by

$$\nu_1 - \nu_2 = \frac{1}{4R}(V_1 - V_2). \tag{8.15}$$

Further, note that the difference in frequencies so obtained could as well be an indication of the above 40 Hz frequency of electromagnetic signal found in the neuro-science experiments (Angel et al. 2001; Fell et al. 2003).

As a matter of fact, this simple experiment, particularly the second part, can be repeated in several different situations and the prominence of the role of consciousness or of varying mood of a person in the data can be investigated. For example, the cases of interest could be

i. repeating the second part of the experiment with closed eyes; in this case, extra efforts by the holder will be spent maintaining the same planar vibrations perpendicular to the laser beam;

ii. repeating the experiment while the holder of the pendulum is undergoing deep and normal breathings; and

iii. when the base of the vibrating bob varies, i.e. when the bob vibrates over and above a wooden block, water bucket or a metal sheet.

Even a slight diversion of attention of the holder may result in non-planar vibrations as compared to the case of *SP*. (Recall the case of asymptotically stable spiral in $p_1 - q_2$ plane due to dynamical coupling.)

8.7 Concluding Discussion

After having the picture of "simple" pendulum of physics in the background, attempts are made here, perhaps for the first time, to classify various types of conscious pendula. Such efforts, in fact, are expected to pave the way for academic pursuits of the complicated phenomenon of consciousness (cf. Chapter 2). To this effect, no doubt, a variety of conscious pendula are proposed here in a realistic sense, but the fact is that the most suited for this purpose is found the mono-conscious one. Even among this category, as argued and established differently, the handheld pendulum (cf. Case (B1)) offers an ideal set-up to investigate the effect of consciousness, if any, in physical theories.

As far as the use of handheld pendulum in occult sciences or in studying the phenomenon of consciousness in general is concerned, one can note the following from the above survey:

i. Handheld pendulum is the simplest device that can be used to study the mindset of the holder or to make predictions about one's personality,

ii. if one wants to study the phenomenon of consciousness purely in a scientific spirit, then the handheld pendulum appears to be a better device,

iii. note that the role of mindset of the holder can manifest through both the time period and also through the nature of motion, and

iv. there is a clear support to the belief of divination of this pendulum. In fact, a simple account of interactions involved in this system in physical terms, clearly reveals this fact (cf. eq. (8.8)).

Against the common belief that the role of human consciousness in physical theories can be explored only through the quantum systems or through the studies in quantum measurement, here the possibility of such studies in the classical domain has been explored. For this purpose, the findings of the century-old Chevreul handheld pendulum are revisited in the modern context and a simple pendulum on an extended complex phase plane is investigated to this effect. The complexification of the phase space in the present method yields a pair of coupled (or the so-called twined) oscillators in which the dynamical and/or parameter coupling appears in a natural manner rather than accounting for them from outside, as in the work of Stapp (2009). While these couplings are responsible for the balance between the mental efforts to tightly hold the pendulum on the one hand, they also help in adjustment with the external world on the other, as an outcome of the same consciousness. A plausible experiment to this effect with laser beam is suggested here (cf. Section 8.6).

The complexification method investigated in this work through the handheld pendulum, in some sense, seems to unify the philosophies of the East and the West, when the latter are translated respectively into the top-down (externalization of the interior through intangible EOLs) and the bottom-up (internalization of the exterior through tangible and measurable entities) approaches with regard to the brain studies. To this effect, an analysis of the twin oscillators with dynamical coupling (cf. Section 8.4.3), clearly suggests a close connection between these two approaches. An analysis of the associated complex uncertainty relation in this case (cf. Appendix C) further sets the limit on the simultaneous use of these two approaches towards the understanding of absolute reality in terms of this magical (!) pendulum. As it can be noticed from Appendix C, this will require the introduction of a Planck-like constant (g) in the theory of consciousness.

Finally, it is worthwhile to make a few pertinent remarks about the complexification method used in this work. In fact, the richness of such methods has already been known in physical theories now for a quite some time. Using these methods, several experimentally verifiable results have been predicted in different branches of physics, particularly in nuclear, particle and condensed matter physics. The method employed here through eq. (8.9), however, has already shown (Kaushal 2001) its viability in the context of newly developed fields of PT-symmetric quantum mechanics (see, for example, Bender 2005) and integrability of classical dynamical systems (Kaushal and Korsch 2000; Kaushal and Singh 2001).

High Skill Exercises and Projects

8.1 What makes the swinging pendulum as a simple (or mathematically ideal) one? Write a Note on the varieties of conscious pendula? Explain as to how the Chevreul handheld pendulum offers an ideal device to study the role of consciousness in physical theories.

8.2 List all possible physical and non-physical interactions related to an oscillating pendulum watched by a conscious observer.

8.3 Discuss the types of couplings between the simultaneous working of twin oscillators – one at the level of physical world and the other in the mental domain of the observer.

8.4 Explain as to how the complete understanding of the working of twin oscillators will reduce the gap between top-down (from psyche to brain science) and bottom-up (from brain science to psyche) approaches to study the consciousness-manifesting phenomena.

8.5 What is "K-effect"? Discuss the role of handheld pendulum in the process of hypnotization. Can the results of proposed laser beam experiment in Section 8.6 give a clue to the divination of the handheld pendulum?

9

Physics of Attention-Dominated Matter, Waves, Energies and Processes

9.1 Introduction

WITH a view to understand the role of attention in the working of a human Being with reference to the physical world and associated processes, we briefly recollect here the concepts of EP-matter (cf. Section 4.1) and that of internal processes (cf. Section 11.4.2) in the present context. Also, recall that a functional human Being b is basically a polluted version of SO (cf. Section 3.2). In this chapter we analyse further as to what happens when a Being in general or a human Being in particular, is placed in the cosmos consisting of *pañca-mahābhūtas.* A concept of mind waves in this top-down approach, as an extension of brain waves in the bottom-up approach, will be introduced. This concept will be further used to explore a common framework to understand several interconnected subjects like Āyurveda, naturopathy, teletherapy, astrology and certain phenomena of occult sciences.

9.1.1 HUMAN BEING IN COSMOS: "THERE IS NO SUCH THING AS AN INDIVIDUAL"

The Western philosophy by and large revolves around the individual and hence it may be a bit different for the followers to digest the above phrase. On the other hand, in the Indian context there exists a deep Vedic wisdom (cf. Chapters 3 and 4) that supports the above phrase at the most fundamental level, particularly when the Being b appears as a second quantized (discretized) version of the cosmic consciousness field Φ_{CC} in which a variety of epi-fields like that of cosmic mind, intellect and cosmic memory including that of five cosmic elements (cf. Chapter 4) are embedded in "seed-like" forms. Of course, this kind of discretization yields identical field quantum of SO in all Beings, which at a later stage, gets polluted by differently dressed epi-fields of different categories with consciousness (cf. Section 4.2). Thus, the later role of consciousness, in fact, makes non-identical Beings or individuals in the Universe. Also, on the basis of the past history of evolution of outer EOLs B and SE not only in the space–time but also in terms of the order of dressings of inner EOLs M, I and E makes each of us as a distinct individual, otherwise, at the level of SO, there is no such thing as an individual. Individuality, in fact, starts manifesting when b starts residing in any one of the E, I, M, SE and B states of the patomic model (cf. *fig.* 6.1), while enjoying the same WO. At this stage, it is reminiscent of a beautiful example cited by Indian saint and poet Kabīr only a few centuries ago.

With regard to the existence and the individuality of a Being in this Universe Saint Kabīr emphasizes that it is the same situation as that of a clay pot filled with seawater and placed again in the water of sea. As and when the boundary of the pot is broken, it becomes the same seawater all over and there is no concept of inside–outside with reference to the pot-boundary. Exactly the same is the case with Beings in the all-pervading field of cosmic consciousness. One can say that the water inside the pot may be the polluted one, then so what? Sea itself is the best purifier and purifies the pollution appropriately according to its nature. Similarly, cosmic consciousness field Φ_{CC} takes care of *vāsanā*s and *saṁskāra*s of the Being through the readjustment of epi-fields in terms of their orders of dressing. Further lessons one can have from the above example and from the discussions in Chapter 4 are the following:

i. There is no such thing as individual at the SO level, but the individuality starts due to different orders of dressing of EOLs of each individual or as and when SO starts getting polluted.

ii. One can overcome or minimize the dirt of pollution of SO by constant meditation (self-observation) and subsequently by realization of the realities of the world and cosmic orders and thereby establishing cosmic connections and b-V (Being-*Virāṭ Puruṣa*) correspondence.

iii. It is only on the basis of past history of evolving EOLs, not only in space–time but also in thinking that allows one to be considered as individual as long as b resides in any of B, SE, M, I, E states or in their substates (cf. *fig*. 6.2).

9.1.2 FUNCTIONAL HUMAN BEING AND THE EP-MATTER

First we analyse as to how the pure SO gets polluted to give rise to its polluted version, termed as the Being b. In fact, the localized version SO, as a part (or as a second quantized version) of Φ_{CC}, when illuminates (enlightens) both inner and outer EOLs and works through them in the field of WO, makes them functional, in the same way as the flow of electricity through an electric gadget makes the latter functional. Becoming functional of EOLs means, they start interacting not only among themselves but also with WO. At the first stage, this happens through the grouped version of EOLs, i.e. among $\mathcal{M}$, $\mathcal{G}$ and WO (as the existences S and $\mathcal{N}$ of b are now embedded in the WO itself of the patomic model). At the second stage, b works directly through EOLs E, I, M, SE and B and again in the field of WO. Since each EOL now directly works with reference to the working of the world and cosmic orders, it is successively wrapped with conscious experiences as a result of Nature-born three tendencies (*guṇas*) and thus appears in three shades; at the third, further subtler stage, b works through these distinctly wrapped EOLs with consciousness and coloured differently with *guṇas*. Such is the fine working of the cenergy of SO. As a matter of fact, WO as a physical matter while always existed as inert, now becomes perceptible to b and also the dynamic as well in space and time, particularly after being illuminated by the cenergy of SO. Such a physical matter, in general, is now termed as the "epi-physical" (EP)-matter.

In the light of above considerations, one can further note the following characteristics of b:

i. As per Vedic wisdom, it is called *Jīva* (life principle). Truly speaking it is a life principle as it has roots in SO on the one hand, and not only as a composite unit but also as a complex system it interacts with WO, on the other. Thus, b acts as a consumer of cenergy from the source SO on the one hand, and as a supplier of cenergy to the sink WO, on the other.

ii. As far as the types of EP-matter is concerned it has two distinct categories; first, when cenergy illuminates WO and makes it perceptible by a "composite" as well as "fragmented" b and second, when the same cenergy illuminates each EOL, B, SE, M, I and E (during meditation) and separately enables them to perceive and realize the same WO through this localized version SO. This latter role of cenergy makes the biological body B of the Being as a special, to be termed it as "special epi-physical (SEP-) matter" since the source of cenergy is also contained in it. Note that for most of the time we shall deal with the focused version of consciousness.

9.1.3 FOCUSED CENERGY IN THE FORM OF MEDITATION/ATTENTION

It may be mentioned that the three words "meditation", "attention" and "concentration" though related to the focusing of cenergy, yet are not synonym of each other at deeper level. The word "meditation" while sounds as the inward (towards SO) focusing of cenergy, the word "concentration" refers to its outward (towards WO) focusing in the patomic model. In fact, both these processes, in general, do not proceed unless they are initiated by another focused form of cenergy, i.e. "attention". Thus, attention drags cenergy on both ways inward and outward but mostly remains attached with meditation as it may be done to explore the intangible world. Moreover, the attention-loaded focusing of cenergy defines its intensity as well.

In practical and computable terms, the intensity of the focused cenergy through meditation is expressed by the meditation variable. Its meaning is elaborated in Section 7.1.1 and its role in the process of realization will be elaborated in Section 11.4.2 (cf. *fig.* 11.4). In view of *fig.* 11.4 and our earlier works (Kaushal 2011, 2015), the following remarks about the process of meditation are in order:

i. Meditation basically is the focusing of cenergy by adjusting the dynamics of inner EOLs (viz. of M, I and E). This is done mainly by regulating the traffic of thoughts on their two thresholds – one from $\mathcal{G}$ to $\mathcal{M}$, i.e. by controlling the mind and senses from their involvement in sense objects and second from $\mathcal{M}$ to $\mathcal{C}$ by suppressing the subtle form of ego E. While it is relatively easier to cross the first threshold with little practice, it is equally or more difficult for the practitioner to cross the second threshold even with concerted efforts.

ii. As μ increases the capacity of resolving and realizing the subtlety of gross features of an external object, belonging to WO decreases, i.e. a practitioner follows the sequence, WO $\rightarrow \mathcal{G} \rightarrow \mathcal{M} \rightarrow \mathcal{C}$ (cf. *fig.* 11.4).

iii. Since cenergy is synonym of life (or consciousness) each of us is born with some minimum μ, say μ_{min}, and so is the case with the level of development of one's FOUs with reference to the maintenance of world and cosmic orders.

iv. Meditation is capable of revealing/projecting (may be for a few experts or super-experts) the past and future incidents of a person not only pertaining to his present life but also of his past and future lifespans by way of establishing a cosmic connection in true sense.

v. As far as recent studies in brain sciences are concerned, scientists have yet to understand the holograms of conscious thoughts formed as a result of synchronous firing of electric signals by brain neurons in large number. In fact, the role of cosmic connections in these studies is yet to be investigated.

vi. *"Soft" and "hard" processes:* Depending upon whether the attention softly or hardly (or, lightly or heavily) loads a process, this accordingly divides the processes into "soft" and "hard" categories. For example, for the functional outer EOLs, SE and B, the "perception" of the sense-objects of the outer world is somewhat easier even with limited, attention-dominated concentration. On the other hand, for the process of "learning" or "realizing" by inner EOLs, M, I and E, even the highly intense or attention-dominated meditation sometimes becomes insufficient. (No doubt, the "realization" takes place in the $\mathcal{C}$-domain but its path is through $\mathcal{M}$-domain and that too after an intense initiation by the EOLs M, I and E). Further, the perception process while knowingly or unknowingly goes on in a natural way, the "learning"/"realization" needs some extra efforts in terms of attention. To visualize this divide of "soft" and "hard" processes look at *fig.* 11.4. As argued earlier (Kaushal 2011), there is a "crossover" of three continuous lines at $\mu = \mu_c$ corresponding to some critical dressings of M, I and E with consciousness. This critical order of dressing depends on the loading of attention on meditation and initial interactions (for $\mu < \mu_c$) between $\mathcal{M}$ and $\mathcal{G}$, and final interactions (for $\mu > \mu_c$) between $\mathcal{M}$ and $\mathcal{C}$ through different *tanmātras*. Thus, for $\mu < \mu_c$, the processes are termed as "soft" whereas they are "hard" for $\mu > \mu_c$. Perhaps for similar reasons, "soft" and "hard" disciplines are defined in the education curriculum.

For $\mu < \mu_c$, note that there is yet another perception process (soft or hard) adopted by an objective scientist. In this case, no doubt, the process is loaded with attention but without the carrier wave of consciousness (cf. Section 9.4). The role of consciousness is generally neglected or not accounted for while framing the laws/theories or modelling the phenomenon as such. On the other hand, the results of perception passed to the brain through senses and nerves for the purposes of their further analysis but by conscious brain cells (or brain neurons) as the brain cells of a dead body do not work. Perhaps for such reasons the objective sciences provide only partial truth about Nature. Further, note that the consciousness-carrier-waves loaded mildly with attention and corresponding to $\mu < \mu_c$, in general, account only for materialist-mind (body-conscious) personalities whereas those with heavily loaded attention and corresponding to $\mu > \mu_c$ describe the spiritual-mind (soul-conscious) personalities.

In what follows, while the consciousness-carrier-waves will remain in the background, we shall investigate here the attention-dominated matter, waves, energies and the processes with an eye on the practical applications in the daily life of a common man. Under the heading of attention-dominated matter, in the next section, we investigate and analyse the worship of *pañca-mahābhūtas* in different cultures. In particular, as to how the idol worship in an Indian temple adds to the positive thinking of a devotee, is analysed here. In Section 9.3, we study some attention-dominated waves and energies with reference to matter waves in quantum physics, brain waves in neuroscience and the newly-introduced concept of "mind waves". The role of mind waves is discussed in Section 9.4 with reference to some non-physical processes and exotic phenomena, like teletherapy and reiki. Further, with a view to give still deeper foundations to the subject of Āyurveda, the concept of dressing of *tridoṣas*, viz. *vāta*, *pitta* and *kapha* (the so-called pillars of the Āyurvedic studies), with consciousness, is introduced through a *tri-karaṇa*-type rule. Finally, concluding remarks are made in Section 9.5.

9.2 Attention-Dominated Matter and Worship of an Idol

9.2.1 WORSHIP OF PAÑCA-MAHĀBHŪTAS IN DIFFERENT CULTURES

A common man is born with some minimum or finite potency of both inner and outer EOLs but with a degree of freedom to enhance this potency to any extent if he so desires or the situation arises. Due to this finite potency, at times, it becomes difficult for him to digest the bewildering scenarios of Nature that appear in different forms and often damages/imbalances the natural resources of his survival. While man becomes helpless during these natural calamities, a genuine fear is generated in his mind with regard to the question of his survival. Such unexpected damages (e.g. due to earthquakes, floods and cyclones, storms, torpedos and tornados, forest and ocean fires) are possible due to all five cosmic elements (*PMs*) which separately or jointly carry infinite potency to damage the things beyond one's imagination. As a result, one starts worshipping these *PMs* or their Ultimate Controller for blessings. This Ultimate Controller or Superpower in different cultures is termed by different names. (After all, there has to be a muscle man (power) to look after or to take care of the colony consisting of both Beings and non-Beings.) In spite of the fact that this Superpower works at his own terms, conditions and whims, the persons with some selective personality start worshipping Him in this very intangible form, whereas some others personify this power in their own way. There are still some (but in a large number) who do not bother about this unmanifest, but worship it in a convenient manifest version or directly in the form of *PMs* in the same way as one cannot see the expert person working behind the curtain of puppet show but see only the actions of the puppets on the front. Invariably, some or all five cosmic elements, viz. earth, water, air, fire and ether, are worshipped almost in all ancient religions and cultures of the world.

Even in modern times, the *PMs* in one physical form or the other are worshipped, particularly in those religions which give relatively more weightage to rituals and methods of worship as compared to the philosophy of life if contained in them. In fact, it is the philosophical (mainly spiritual knowledge) content in a religion that makes the religion sustainable (cf. Chapter 13); otherwise, the rituals and related methods of worship are the function of space, time and circumstances; they do not survive very long. The latter, however, also survive longer if they have some scientific basis or logic in them; otherwise, their philosophical meanings can always be traced, mainly to convince the intellectual component of the followers. As far as the common man is concerned, he is often guided by the wisdom of old persons or by the priest of the place of worship in this regard. Although all the five cosmic elements collectively play a role in the survival of Beings and non-Beings not only on this planet but all across the Universe (by considering "earth" as standing for all solids, "water" as for all liquids, "air" as for all gases, "fire" as for all plasmas and "ether" as a container of the remaining four elements), still some plausible reasons for worshipping them are worth highlighting here as follows: (i) Earth is the main basis of vegetation and plant kingdom; (ii) water and air as the main causes of plantation; (iii) fire (sun) as another important cause for (i) and (ii); and (iv) ether as the main cause for providing space for (i)-(iv).

9.2.2 IDOL WORSHIP IN DIFFERENT CULTURES AS FIRST STEP TOWARDS SPIRITUALITY

In *SMBG*, the Lord emphasizes on the worship with love in the verse:

> *teṣāṁ satatayuktānāṁ bhajatāṁ prītipūrvakam* ।
> *dadāmi buddhiyogaṁ taṁ yena māmupayānti te* ॥ – X.10 (9.1)

> On those ever united through meditation with Me and worshipping Me with love, I confer that *yoga* of wisdom by which they come to Me.

Clearly, the Lord not only prescribes the method of worship, but accepts those who worship Him with love, i.e. they follow an attention-dominated process of worshipping and not just a mechanical one. Whether this worship is of an embodied idol (*bhakti-yoga*) or just through meditation (*jñāna-yoga*), in either case, it has to be with love (or with an attention-dominated process). The Lord designates this as *buddhi-yoga* (or the *yoga* of wisdom), i.e. an element of experience need to be added in the process.

A person may be a believer or religious one but may not be spiritual. To become spiritual or to remain in the spiritual zone forever, it requires a lot of efforts and practice on the part of aspirant. On the other hand, if one resorts to be an idol worshipper in true sense, then it is at least his first step towards the spirituality. The following dialogue, in fact, emphasizes the importance of worship in a temple. In Indian context, a non-believer asked a believer the following question, "once you say that God is everywhere, then why there are so many temples all around to adore Him?" The believer then replies, "you know that air is everywhere, but still one feels its obvious existence only under a fan if he so desires". We take this conversation as a guide to elaborate the reason, methodology and the spirit behind the idol worship in an Indian temple, if constructed as per scriptural instructions. Moreover, the worship of an idol in a temple is mainly for the realization of the (unmanifest) Supreme within and that too with the help of the manifest outside.

Depending upon whether the devotee's mindset is world-conscious, body-conscious, mind-conscious or soul-conscious (spiritual), his desires will accordingly vary over a wide spectrum ranging from WO to SO in patomic model in the sequence $\mathcal{N} \rightarrow \mathcal{S} \rightarrow \mathcal{G} \rightarrow \mathcal{M} \rightarrow \mathcal{C}$ in terms of his existences. In the same order, the devotee will expect the blessings from deity (idol) for his well-being and happiness, viz. respectively in terms of material gain, health-fitness, mental peace, over all happiness, or the salvation, irrespective of the type of idol or deity, particularly at the end-point of his contemplation. In the beginning, one needs an idol, but slowly and slowly one starts having cosmic connections and, at the end, one does not need any idol or external (physical) agency including a master. In the light of five existences of a human Being, the possible five steps, which one has to climb up during meditation as a part of worship to reach the Primal Deity from a deity, are as follows:

i. Thinking of the location, material, beauty, type and environment of the temple and idol (mainly in the zone of WO and $\mathcal{G}$);

ii. type of the personality and the history pertaining to and embodied in the idol (mainly in the zones of $\mathcal{G}$ and $\mathcal{M}$);

iii. connecting the embodied virtues and the past character of the idol with the world and society (mainly in the zones of $\mathcal{N}$ and S);

iv. connecting and realizing the embodied virtues and the past character of the idol as part of the cosmos, i.e. via cosmic connections (mainly in the zones of S and $\mathcal{N}$); and

v. thinking beyond Nature and society and residing in the field of cosmic consciousness Φ_{CC} (in the zones of all five existences present in their seed-like form in Φ_{CC}).

Such is the purpose of worship in true sense that can be fulfilled anywhere and anytime, but preferably in a temple, *āśrama* or in solitude. If temple (or for that matter the sacred place of worship of any religion) is constructed keeping scientific spirit in mind and so is the case with the installation of an idol in it, meaning thereby as per Vedic scriptures, then it becomes an asset for the devotee to attain the Ultimate rather speedily, of course, only after concerted efforts and contemplation.

9.2.3 WORSHIPPING IN AN INDIAN TEMPLE: INCULCATION OF POSITIVE ENERGY IN A DEVOTEE

Positive and negative energies here are defined in the context of preparing a mindset and accordingly thinking and performing all actions towards the maintenance and sustainability of both world and cosmic orders. In other words, the "positive energy" means to develop the potency and to learn the art of accepting and respecting the maintenance and sustainability of both the orders. Like the downstream flow, the negativity is natural due to the involvement of the Being in WO and thereby having a craze for the sense-objects. On the other hand, some efforts are needed to attain the positivity, like swimming against the stream-flow. While this positivity is a must in the spiritual path, the worship of any kind, in fact, should be aimed at gaining such positive energy. While the lap of Nature in some sense provides a God-made environment for this purpose, the temples or other sacred places of worship, on other hand, do offer a man-made environment. These are only the humans who can think of positive/negative energies; otherwise non-humans do not have any temple or instinct to worship even though they also share the same *PMs* for their survival. Somehow God has made their life cycle in such a way that their existence does not affect much the sustainability of the world and cosmic orders.

According to Vedic wisdom, the sole purpose of worship is to activate and excite the seven *cakras* (plexus or cluster of nerves) assumed to be situated all along the spinal cord (vertebrate) and the same are responsible for a sequential spiritual evolution of a person. What a great foresightedness our Vedic seers had that they designed the construction of temples keeping all such realities in mind. Not only this, there is also an element of scientific truth in this age-old wisdom.

Modern brain science makes it clear that any information (concerning the biological body, like feelings of pleasure and pain, hot and cold, etc.) are passed to the brain through a process, called "nerve impulse propagation". The neurons present in the brain cells are supposed to recognize that information (translated now into feeling, thinking, memory, etc.) by way of firing some particular type of electric/magnetic signals in synchronization. The latter phenomenon produces distinct patterns (i.e. (3 + 1)-dimensional holograms) in space corresponding to given information and the brain as a whole then recognizes these patterns. Obviously, only a conscious brain can do this job and not that of a dead person.

Knowing very well that the consciousness of the person is important in this process, the brain scientists are still afraid of bringing in the role of consciousness in their analysis (cf. Chapter 2). Now the question is as to how to modify the frequency of firing of electric/ magnetic signals by neurons so as to have a feel for positive energy through actions. One possible way is by visiting temples, if they are designed in accordance with Vedic prescriptions. In what follows, we briefly outline and analyse as to how the temple-site is identified, how the idols are installed in it, or how a devotee has to perform, etc.

i. It is known that the earth has magnetism and the magnetic lines of forces emerge from the geomagnetic north (geographical south) pole and merge into the geomagnetic south (geographical north) pole all along the globe. While the vertical (perpendicular to the earth surface) component of this field dominates in the pole region, the horizontal (parallel to the earth surface) component dominates in the equatorial region and note that the Indian continent lies close to the equatorial region.

ii. With regard to the choice of temple site, the geometry of the land piece has to be such that the maximum of the earth's magnetic flux, i.e. geomagnetic north–southward lines of forces must pass through it.

iii. While these prescriptions are followed, it may be mentioned that at the time of construction of a temple and the installation of the main idol, a large quantity of copper (in the form of blocks, slabs and sheets) is placed little deep into the earth and just beneath the position of the main idol.

iv. Once such preparations are done, then the desired idol, made up generally of a specific metal or of stone, is installed at the designated place and after so many rituals performed with the recitation of varieties of Vedic *mantras*. (A *mantra* basically is a sacred syllable that needs to be recited with their meaning as originating from the core of the heart.) The important point to be noted here is that the idol has to face eastward or towards the eastern gate of the temple.

v. Among other supplementary planning one needs to take care of in constructing a temple are:

   a. to suspend heavy ring-bells in the main hall of prayer in such a way that they remain just above the head of the devotee, and

   b. a round place for free movement of the devotee all around the idol needs to be provided.

vi. The devotees by and large are allowed to enter from the eastern gate and thus facing the idol right from the entry point and also travelling relatively a longer distance to reach the idol. In what follows, we discuss as to how the visit of such a planned temple can enhance the positive thinking of a devotee.

9.2.4 HOW THE VISIT TO AN INDIAN TEMPLE CAN ENHANCE POSITIVE THINKING OF A DEVOTEE?

As mentioned before, the main aim of visiting a temple is to activate and stimulate seven *cakras* to attain the highest in the path of spirituality. A common man, however, visits the temple to fulfil his worldly desires or at the most to seek blessings of the Lord towards his mental peace and happiness. Here we discuss as to how this is possible in scientific terms keeping in mind the above planned construction of an Indian temple. For this purpose, note that a person (devotee) carries electric/magnetic charges in his self, howsoever small they may be, say of the order of micro-coulomb (cf. ballistic galvanometer experiment). Further, note that as soon as a devotee decides to visit a temple, a certain degree of positivity enters in him and brain-neurons start firing electric signals to form a pattern corresponding to this thought. Such an object, when enters the temple from eastern gate and starts moving towards the idol, he becomes the source of disturbance in the geomagnetic field lines coming from his left. As a result, there is a change in the flux that causes to produce induced emf (electromagnetic force) in the copper sheets, blocks and slabs placed underneath the idol, howsoever small the induced field it may be.

On the other hand, note that in addition to this, there is a generation of eddy currents in the copper blocks and sheets lying permanently underneath the idol in the same geomagnetic field of about 0.3 Gauss. This also gives rise to an additional induced emf or magnetic field as a result of the eddy currents almost of permanent nature. In fact, the radiation of that induced magnetic field due to eddy currents causes a distinct environment around and in the premises of the temple, which, in turn, also affects the frequency of firing of electric signals by brain neurons of the devotee and hence affects his thinking or the thought process as well.

Other factors, which also contribute to this kind of enhancement of positivity through the thought process, are also there in the temple. They, for example, are:

a. When the devotee rings the ring-bell placed just above his head in the main hall and in front of the idol, its sound then helps in unifying the left and right parts of the brain by way of creating a kind of resonance between the two parts for a few seconds. This makes the brain relatively more sensitive to receive the induced flux or electric/magnetic signals.
b. When the devotee takes a round around the idol in the designated place, it also causes a change in the magnetic flux but of different nature. This is mainly because the devotee now moves in the resultant of the two magnetic fields, namely, earth's magnetic field and the induced magnetic field due to eddy currents (which at times can be more intense, depending upon the quantity of copper placed underneath and the orientation of the copper slabs or sheets so placed).
c. Not only this, the trajectory a devotee now traverses by moving in clockwise direction (with respect to the idol)

turns out to be a stable spiral in the language of non-linear mathematics (cf. chapter 6 in Kaushal and Parashar 2008), meaning thereby the trajectory has the tendency to merge into the centre, i.e. in the idol. (In fact, the attention of the devotee is now focused possibly maximum on the qualities, virtues and glories of the embodied idol. In this way, the gravity energy also helps in establishing the faith in the idol.) Also, this rounding about the idol further modifies the frequency of firing of electric signals by brain neurons and thereby strengthening and improving the resolution of the desired ideas in the thought process of the devotee.

9.3 Attention-Dominated Waves and Energies

Any disturbance in a medium causes the formation of waves in the latter and wherever there is a wave it carries certain type of energy associated with it that helps in its propagation. In general, the disturbance can also be space and/or time dependent. If the medium as such does not contribute, then the energy associated with the wave is also a measure of the intensity of disturbance. There may be exceptions, but normally the disturbing agent has to be hard enough (in terms of rigidity) or of sufficient intensity (in terms of the applied force) to produce a wave in the given medium. A wave is basically characterized by its amplitude (a), frequency (υ), velocity (v) and phase (φ) with some simple relations among them, viz. $\upsilon = (1/T)$, (T is time period); $v = (\upsilon.\lambda)$, (λ is wavelength) for "linear" phenomenon (here linearity is in terms of the nature of the corresponding differential equation for the disturbance); otherwise, for the "non-linear" case, such relations turn out to be very complicated.

As far as the classification of waves is concerned, scientists and engineers have identified only a few for their use and studies; otherwise, for a person sitting along a seashore (i.e. close to an infinite medium and with all sorts of disturbances) there are infinitely many varieties of waves – starting from longitudinal, transverse to solitary waves, etc. Most of them, in fact, correspond to non-linear phenomena in Nature.

9.3.1 PHYSICAL AND NON-PHYSICAL COMMUNICATION VIS-À-VIS BRAIN AND "MIND" WAVES

At elementary level, while waves are classified as longitudinal and transverse, at the advance level, however, they are classified as mechanical, electromagnetic and matter waves. Further, mechanical waves travel through terrestrial media in the form of solid, liquid and gases, the discovery of electromagnetic waves is one of the wonders of modern science, not only for communication in space and universe but also as a tool for other modern researches like the laser technology. The matter waves, on the other hand, have dragged the mind of scientists into the philosophical domain by identifying the fact that the matter particle at micro-level has dual nature, i.e. it can behave as a wave and also as a matter particle with reference, of course, to a detector that could be an instrument or a conscious observer. In case of conscious observer, the role of consciousness is tactfully avoided by advancing a probabilistic interpretation to the quantum wave function Ψ. This is one of the interpretations of modern quantum mechanics and found to work successfully in a variety of microscopic systems, starting from molecules to quarks. As far as the communication between and among objects is concerned, all three mechanical, electromagnetic and matter waves have been in use, particularly after the advent of quantum computers.

In the preceding section, we have seen that as to how the specially designed Indian temples can activate the firing frequency of electric impulses by brain neurons which, in turn, can affect the formation of synchronized patterns in the brain corresponding to a particular sensation or mental process. An important alternative to this kind of activation of brain cells is through an intense meditation or by way of creating highly intense or attention-dominated brain waves/energies. This is possible by way of focusing more and more consciousness towards the production of the so-called "mind" waves as a result of conversion of brain physical energy into a non-physical (cenergy) one.

What Brain Science has to Tell about the "Mind" Waves

It may be mentioned that an individual behaviour, emotions and thoughts are the result of communication among brain neurons within our brain in the varying frequency of electric impulses, the so-called "brain" waves. Further, all brain waves are produced by synchronized electric signals fired by masses of neurons communicating with each other. The brain waves occur at various frequencies (in Hz or cycle per second) and the brain scientists have classified them into five electro-encephalogram (EEG) bands, viz. delta, theta, alpha, beta and gamma characterized by the frequency ranges as follows: Delta (1-3 Hz); slowest but with highest amplitude, experienced when we are asleep. In general, different levels of awareness (attention) are associated with dominant brain wave states; theta (4-7 Hz) represents a day dreamy state of mind associated with mental inefficiency, activity is at very slow levels – a very relaxed state between the waking and sleep; alpha (8-12 Hz); slower but with larger amplitude, associated normally with relaxation, represents brain shifting into an idling gear, waiting to respond when needed; beta (13-38 Hz); small, faster, associated with a state of mental/intellectual activity; gamma (39-42 Hz); they are fastest, most subtle brain waves, gamma rhythms module, and relates to perception and consciousness.

Each of us however always has some degree of these brain-wave bands present in different parts of the brain. Delta brain wave also occurs when certain areas of brain go "offline". Important point to be noted here is that the brain waves learn to rework connections with positive re-enforcement through a neuronal feedback mechanism, i.e. there is a possibility of enhancing the frequency range of gamma synchronous activity that is found to be a window for the domain of consciousness or for mind waves. While there is an experimental support to this activity of brain cells (Angel et al. 2001; Fell et al. 2003), theoretical studies on conscious intents and brain functioning (cf. Section 8.4) have also been carried out (see Kaushal 2016b; Stapp 2009). With regard to the gamma–synchronous-activity frequency of about 40 Hz, we recall the Chevreul handheld pendulum experiment of Section 8.6. In this experiment, if one finds a frequency difference in the two situations more than 40 Hz, then naturally this will be attributed to a new type of synchronous activity or possibly open a window for "mind waves", whose explanation will be found in the exchange of rather more subtle *tanmātras* (cf. *fig*. 11.4) between brain cells rather than through brain neurons, firing electric signals. Recall that a *tanmātra* in Vedic science is the subtlest quantum of interaction between a sense and its associated *mahābhūta*, and possibly here it will be a case of sound–ether correspondence (cf. entry 3 in Table 9.1).

9.3.2 MIND WAVES IN Φ_{CC} AND COSMIC CONNECTIONS OF AN INDIVIDUAL HUMAN BEING

Here the word "mind" needs to be understood as micro body $\mathcal{M}$ of a human Being consisting of three faculties, viz. emotions, thinking and memory, in the increasing order of their subtlety. Interestingly, these three intents are also the objects of study of brain scientists through brain cells; otherwise as we shall see that the mind waves in general are going to be little more complicated objects when loaded with so much information. As discussed above, the gamma synchronous activity of brain cells at about 40 Hz indicates a window for consciousness studies. Now the question arises as to how to broaden this window upward in the frequency range? or, as to how to peep deep into this window for any further clue about the consciousness. Of course, intense meditation is one such method, foresighted by Vedic seers, to peep into this murky path of consciousness and to go beyond the spatiotemporal world. As discussed in Section 4.6.1, the infinitely dressed versions not only of EOLs M, I and E, but also of cosmic elements E_a, W, A, F and E_t with consciousness (i.e. in their seed-like form) constitute the different sectors of epi-fields in the cosmic consciousness field Φ_{CC}. While the infinite dressing of these entities with consciousness qualifies them to become part of Φ_{CC}, their partially dressed versions are also present in Φ_{CC} at every instant and everywhere.

Recall that Φ_{CC} is the purest and subtlest version of the all-pervading consciousness continuum (field). It is the seed of cosmic desire ($\tilde{E}^{(\infty)}$) that creates a disturbance in Φ_{CC} and the same propagates in the already quiet Φ_{CC} without any concept of velocity or of any type of infinity in it. When this disturbance passes through various sectors of epi-fields present in their seed-like forms, the latter upload the concerned information with this disturbance (or on the carrier wave of pure consciousness). The agencies which upload the information (or convert the carrier wave into a heavily modulated wave) in the order of their increasing subtlety are the sectors Φ_{CEL}, Φ_{CM}, Φ_{CI}, Φ_{CE} (or more precisely, $E_a \rightarrow W \rightarrow A \rightarrow F \rightarrow E_t \rightarrow M \rightarrow I \rightarrow E$). Even the nature of modulation and its varieties are controlled by the cosmic desire. Such a highly multifold-modulated carrier wave is termed as "mind" wave. Other specific characteristics of these waves are:

i. There is no question of velocity of these waves in spatio-temporal terms.

ii. Since epi-fields in their seed-like or partially dressed forms are ever present in Φ_{CC}, there are infinitely many possibilities and ways of modulation of the carrier (pure consciousness) wave.

iii. The process of dressing of EOLs and of cosmic elements with consciousness as a result of meditation at individual level and that of unwrapping of consciousness of corresponding epi-fields during the propagation of the disturbance across these fields in Φ_{CC} are the equivalent and similar processes and their matching at a certain stage in Φ_{CC} is bound to be there. This defines the beginning of realization of cosmic connections.

iv. Once cosmic connections are established by a practitioner, the latter becomes qualified to participate in several attention-dominated processes like reiki, telepathy, etc. at individual level.

v. In electronics, the phenomena of amplitude and frequency modulations are well known. Here in the case of mind waves, however, the cosmic (eightfold) modulation of the carrier wave is highly complicated as both the amplitude and the frequency remain undefined. (In fact, eightfold modulation is in accordance with eight components of insentient mode of Nature as per *SMBG* VII.4). With regard to the ordering of modulation of (or loading on) the carrier wave with cosmic essences associated with the respective epi-fields in Φ_{CC} (viz. e_a, w, a, f, e_t, m, i and e corresponding to E_a, W, A, F, E_t, M, I and E), and their demodulation at the level of an individual during meditation the sequences followed are just opposite to each other. For example, for the demodulation it occurs as: $E_a \to W \to A \to F \to E_t \to M \to I \to E$, i.e. first E_a uploads, etc. In other words, during modulation, the essence of every "epi-field" is attached with the carrier wave in the order of its subtlety, i.e. first that of $\tilde{E}^{(n)}$, then $\tilde{I}^{(n)}$, then of $\tilde{M}^{(n)}$ and so on, and in the end that of $\tilde{E}_a^{(n)}$.

vi. In fact, these eight varieties of epi-fields including their partially dressed versions need to be loaded on a carrier wave. While this number is in accordance with *SMBG* VII.4, they provide a set of minimal for the creation of Universes in Φ_{CC} (cf. Chapter 4) on the one hand and a clue for understanding the details of these creations by an individual on the other. As per Vedic wisdom, this is the case with a perfect mind wave; otherwise the imperfect mind waves also always prevail in Φ_{CC}. It depends on the capacity of the receiving instrument (e.g. human Being who is said to be a perfect creation) to receive these perfect (fully loaded) or imperfect (partially loaded) mind waves.

vii. The role of mind waves starts at a stage where that of brain waves ends, i.e. it could well be beyond the gamma synchronous activity in brain science.

viii. These are the mind waves associated with the individual husband and wife which transcend and interact at the time of conception in addition to other physical environment. It is this phenomenon that is responsible for the germination of personality seeds and traits in the life of the new born baby and the same perhaps translated later into his *saṁskāras* and destiny.

9.4 Attention-Dominated Processes

At times many of us have noticed some peculiar phenomena that occur in the domain of consciousness but cannot be explained within the framework of space–time-mediated objective science. Such exotic phenomena have been in use for centuries in different cultures and form the part of the so-called "occult science". Some of these phenomena, no doubt, are not taken in good taste by the society but still some contribute towards one's happiness provided the person concerned has a belief in them. Earlier, we have tried (see appendix F of Kaushal 2011) to find explanation of some of these phenomena in a limited scientific spirit and within the framework of patomic model, here, however, we analyse a few more such phenomena involving attention-dominated processes, viz. telepathy, teletherapy and reiki, in the present scheme of study. In particular, the role of mind waves discussed earlier will be highlighted in understanding some of these processes.

9.4.1 PHYSICAL AND NON-PHYSICAL PROCESSES: ROLE OF MIND WAVES

Note that the mind waves (in the form of their fully-loaded version with all the eight cosmic essences or as partially loaded with some limited essences) are around all over in the all-pervading cosmic consciousness field Φ_{CC}. In general, they are eightfold modulated waves with respect to a perfect detector, practitioner or an aspirant of highest degree; otherwise only a few essences transcend in an individual during meditation. Now the question arises as to how one or who receives and perceives these mind waves when each individual has the potency to this effect? As a matter of fact, it is the degree or the intensity of one's meditation that decides the transcending of these essences. While the modulation of essences in Φ_{CC} takes place in the order E, I, M, E_t, F, A, W, E_a (or the corresponding essences e, i, m, e_t, f, a, w, e_a associated, respectively with their epi-fields in Φ_{CC}) their demodulation for the practitioner however takes place in the reverse order but in accordance with their subtlety. It is perhaps for this reason the master always advises the disciple to uplift his self during meditation first from the worldly objects, then from the senses and sense objects (i.e. the domain of *pañca-mahābhūtas*), and then from mind, intellect, and in the end from ego, in order to enter into the domain of consciousness or to realize the sentient mode of Nature.

A Notation for Mind Waves and Remarks about their Modulated and Demodulated Versions

We use the notation "(*CCW*)" for the mind wave(s) as they basically are consciousness carrier waves which, after passing through various epi-fields present already in Φ_{CC} in their seed-like form, get multifold modulated (loaded) with essences e, i, m, e_t, f, a, w, e_a corresponding to ego, intellect, mind, ether, fire, air, water and earth. These essences are labelled as superscript on (*CCW*). Next, we display the ordering of essences during the processes of modulation and demodulation as superscripts on (*CCW*), viz. for the modulation in cosmos we have the process,

$$\Phi_{CC} \Leftrightarrow (CCW) \underset{desire}{\overset{cosmic}{\rightarrow}} (CCW)^{e} \underset{intellect}{\overset{cosmic}{\rightarrow}} (CCW)^{ei} \underset{mind}{\overset{cosmic}{\rightarrow}} (CCW)^{eim} \underset{ether}{\overset{PM}{\rightarrow}} (CCW)^{eime_t}$$

$$\underset{fire}{\overset{PM}{\rightarrow}} (CCW)^{eme_t f} \underset{air}{\overset{PM}{\rightarrow}} (CCW)^{eime_t fa} \underset{water}{\overset{PM}{\rightarrow}} (CCW)^{eime_t faw} \underset{earth}{\overset{PM}{\rightarrow}} (CCW)^{eime_t fawe_a} \qquad (9.2)$$

and for the demodulation in an individual practitioner, we have the process

$$(CCW)^{eime_t fawe_a} \underset{PM,\, earth}{\rightarrow} (CCW)^{eime_t faw} \underset{PM,\, water}{\rightarrow} (CCW)^{eime_t fa} \underset{PM,\, air}{\rightarrow} (CCW)^{eime_t f} \underset{PM,\, fire}{\rightarrow}$$

$$(CCW)^{eime_t} \underset{PM,\, ether}{\rightarrow} (CCW)^{eim} \overset{cosmic}{\underset{mind}{\rightarrow}} (CCW)^{ei} \overset{cosmic}{\underset{intellect}{\rightarrow}} (CCW)^{e} \overset{cosmic}{\underset{ego}{\rightarrow}} (CCW) \Leftrightarrow \Phi_{CC} \quad (9.3)$$

that takes place side by side and thus leads finally to *mokṣa* in the limiting case. The matching of the two processes at a certain stage corresponds to the realization of cosmic connections at that stage. Other pertinent remarks about the characteristics of mind waves are as follows:

i. Note that these are the five essences corresponding to the five cosmic elements that are loaded on (*CCW*) in addition to the essences of another three corresponding to inner EOLs M, I and E. Further, the permutations and combinations of these eight essences along with their individual characters finally give rise to the entire world, worldly objects and the stimuli as well.

ii. It appears that the five EEG bands discovered thus far in neuroscience, corresponding to delta, theta, alpha, beta and gamma-synchronous frequencies, represent only the downloading of essences associated only with five cosmic elements in the mind wave. The main reason for such a claim lies in the fact that the human behaviour features, like inertia, activity and dynamism noticed with these bands, also appear in the personality of a person. This similarity of behavioural features in Vedic science can be considered as an effect of three Nature-born tendencies (*guṇas*) on human traits. This later aspect is also linked with the domination of any one or more *mahābhūtas* when they are considered as responsible for producing the three *doṣas*, *vāta*, *pitta* and *kapha* (cf. relation (9.4)), of Āyurveda. This striking similarity opens the possibility of connecting the health (both mental and physical) well-being of a person with his neuro-scientific data.

iii. *How one mind wave can differ from another*: Note that the carrier wave (*CCW*) of pure consciousness remains common in the background of different modulations. The main source of modulating essence is the undressing of an epi-field (present in Φ_{CC}) out of its infinitely dressed version with consciousness. As it happens with different epi-fields in Φ_{CC}, this leads to infinitely many varieties of differently loaded mind waves. We use this feature to call the mind wave as the "charged" one with consciousness, whether heavily or lightly depending upon the intensity of meditation.

iv. As the definition of any kind of infinity in Φ_{CC} is meaningless, the mind waves travel with an imaginary, limitless velocity not only in its unmodulated version but also even in the loaded version with essences e, i, m (corresponding E, I and M). However, they start gaining space–time features in increasing order when loaded respectively with e_t, f, a, w and e_a (corresponding to E_t, F, A, W and E_a). In fact, at this later stage physical fields like gravitation, electromagnetic, weak and strong also start appearing as a result of uncountable infinite permutations and combinations of the undressing mode of *pañca-mahābhūtas* with any highest but finite limit, if any, on the velocity in the space–time domain.

v. *A mind wave propagates as a packet of cenergy*: In some sense, a mind wave, particularly in its modulated version, is a kind of packet of cenergy with many (maximum eight) covers over it. While it always existed in Φ_{CC}, it is also free to propagate anywhere. In the attention-dominated situation by a practitioner, it however finds a direction to propagate. In order to understand its propagation one can as well analogously use the Eherenfest Theorem in quantum mechanics (see, for example, Schiff 1968) concerning the matter waves. According to this theorem, it is reasonable to expect the motion of a wave packet to agree with the motion of a corresponding classical particle, whenever the potential energy changes by a negligible amount over the dimensions of the wave packet. Note that by definition there is no question of presence of any potential energy field in Φ_{CC}, then what to say of any change in it. This theorem, no doubt, will act as a guide for any kind of mathematical formulation of mind waves; it, however, assigns a wave packet feature to them and also explains the role of occult scientists in giving a direction of propagation to a mind wave using their attention-dominated meditation, particularly in the form of packets of cenergy in classical sense. This, in turn, offers a basis for the occurrence of processes like telepathy and teletherapy.

vi. Note that there are certain categories of mind waves which remain functional in the overlapping domain of essences corresponding to *PMs* and corresponding to micro-body. This domain, in fact, is useful for the occult scientists. The velocities in this domain can perhaps lie between the velocity of light and the limitless velocity in Φ_{CC}. Further, note that while *mokṣa* corresponds to the merging of (*CCW*) in Φ_{CC}, the practitioners who attain increasingly higher degree of meditation, distinctly correspond to the following different categories of mind waves, viz. $(CCW)^{e}{}_{a}{}^{wafe}{}_{t}{}^{mie}$,$(CCW)^{wafe}{}_{t}{}^{mie}$, ... $(CCW)^{ie}$, $(CCW)^{e}$.

As far as the objective scientists are concerned, they outrightly reject the role of consciousness while analysing physical process in spite of the fact that their inner conscience is always working not only in collecting data but also in their analysis and thereby in developing models for extracting the absolute reality, if possible. As they often get wonderful matching between theory and experiments by this procedure, for them the role of consciousness is required. Interestingly, the results so obtained and the conclusions drawn therefrom are not only space–time invariant under the given circumstances and under the assumptions made in the theory, but are also experience-based invariant. While such studies for physical processes are going on, there are a very large number of non-physical processes in human behaviour and experiences where the role of consciousness predominates, particularly in the form of attention. In order to understand this latter class of processes the concept of mind waves as introduced above can play an important role.

What a funny game an aspirant or a truth seeker of absolute reality is playing! As an objective scientist exploring the world of *pañca-mahābhūtas* (i.e. first five essences modulated on the mind wave) or the creations of the five senses of knowledge using the instruments of psychoscience (mind, intellect and ego), i.e. the last three essences loaded on the carrier wave. On the other hand, as an occult scientist, one explores the world of psychoscience, i.e. the last three essences loaded on the carrier wave using the *pañca-mahābhūtas* including the biological body of a human Being. None of them, however, is able to derive the complete truth in Nature. Such a role of mind waves in the process of meditation helps both objective and occult scientists in establishing cosmic connections.

9.4.2 EXOTIC PHENOMENA AND THE ROLE OF MIND WAVES

(a) *K-effect and "mind"-"mind" interaction:* With regard to the K-effect, first we briefly remind the illustrative analogy discussed earlier in Section 8.5 and in Appendix F of Kaushal (2011). Recall that an atom in itself has intrinsic electricity and magnetism, and the corresponding fields inside, but when placed in an external electric or magnetic field it shows an abnormal behaviour in the form of Stark, Zeeman or Faraday effect. In the same way, a conscious individual who himself has EOLs including the soul and hence the consciousness energy (cenergy) fields (the same is also translated into a functional mindset $\mathcal{M}$), when placed in an external cenergy field of another individual, is bound to undergo a change in his mindset and also in behaviour. The latter phenomenon is abbreviated as "K-effect" (cf. Section 8.5). Another situation which can be added to such an analogy from physics is that a piece of magnetic material (say, an iron bar), when constantly rubbed by the pole of a permanent magnet, the former starts showing the magnetism or becomes a magnet, may be of somewhat less intensity. Note that, in case of an atom the electric or magnetic fields inside and outside, or in case of magnetized iron bar the magnetic field produced in it and the one present in the rubbing magnet are in no way different as far as their fundamental properties in space–time are concerned. However, only the resultant effects of the fields observed by a detector or an external observer could be different.

In fact, the above two phenomena offer lessons to study the human behaviour in two distinct situations. In the first case, it is all action-at-a-distance (AAD) effect that gives rise to a resultant effect, whereas, in the second case, it is both AAD plus contact type forces that are involved. In terms of human interactions, it is the $\mathcal{M}_1 - \mathcal{M}_2$ type interaction in the former case and it is $\mathcal{M}_1 - (\mathcal{M}_2 + \mathcal{G}_2)$ type one in the latter case. Also, in the former it is all smooth and unprovoked action and in the latter it is forced and under pressure. Thus, the brain-wash or mind-transformation of a person by another could be smooth (as through the classroom-type education or through sermon delivering process) or could be under pressure and fear (as for prisoners in a prison, etc.). While the $\mathcal{M}_1 - \mathcal{M}_2$ interaction, which we shall study in detail in Chapter 10, will be a guide in analysing these cases, in the language of mind waves, however, it is the flow of cenergy from a highly-charged mind wave to a lower-charged mind wave. Further, this gradation of charging, as discussed above, is in terms of orders of dressing/undressing of epi-fields through consciousness in Φ_{CC} besides the hierarchy of EOLs M, I and E (cf. *fig*. 10.3) in terms of their subtlety.

(b) *Mind waves and exotic phenomena:* It is worthwhile to recall a few exotic phenomena related to individual's behaviour but whose explanation does not lie in the domain of space–time-mediated objective science. These phenomena, in fact, lie in the domain of the trio of space, time and consciousness and a plausible explanation of them perhaps can be sought in terms of the mind waves. Naturally, here the forces of AAT- and AADT-type are involved and all three – space, time and consciousness – play a comparable role. In addition to the phenomena investigated earlier (see appendix F of Kaushal 2011) some other of particular interest are teletherapy, remote viewing, remote sensing, unexplained acoustics, telepathy (tele-empathy), reiki, hydrotherapy, etc. These processes basically are the epi-physical processes with highly dominated attention.

It is a common experience of many of us that, at times, telepathy works, blessings of an individual or of a collection of individuals do miracles, particularly in the remedy of a disease. Also, note that a believer (theist) gets quickly or better cured as compared to a non-believer (atheist) for the same disease and in the same given circumstances, etc. Here lies the role of consciousness or of attention-dominated waves or of the mind waves charged appropriately with the necessary essences.

What we have discussed earlier is the origin and the embedding of mind waves in Φ_{CC} but the fact is that an individual's consciousness can also produce the mind waves at secondary level or can modify the ones present already in Φ_{CC}. This is not possible for a common man but the practitioners with sufficiently intense meditation are capable of doing all this. Not only this, the quality of charge on a mind wave can also be modified as a result of constant recitation of certain *mantras* (sacred syllable/words dominated with attention).

In Table 9.1, we supply some necessary inputs for such interdisciplinary studies from both objective sciences and Vedic wisdom with a view to bringing the subject of occult science on par with the mainstream of science. In particular, in this summary table, we attempt to identify the conventional physics and other disciplines with the *tanmātra* and the corresponding *mahābhūta* of Vedic science at a crude level, i.e. without really touching the roles of m, i and e essences in a mind wave.

(c) *Epi-fields of secondary nature in Φ_{CC} and teletherapy:* With a view to understand certain exotic phenomena like teletherapy and reiki,

Table 9.1: A Correspondence Between the Conventional Physics Disciplines and Other Modern Subjects and the Pañca-mahābhūtas of Vedic science*

Conventional Physics and Other Disciplines	*Possible Sense and Sense-objects Associated*	*Cosmic Element(s) Associated*	*Associated Exotic Phenomenon*	*Essence (Charge) Loaded on Associated Mind Wave*
1. Heat	Skin – touch	Air	Teletherapy	(CCW) loaded with e, i, m, a and e_t
2. Optics	Eyes – light	Fire	Remote viewing	(CCW) loaded with e, i, m, f and e_t
3. Acoustics	Ear – sound	Ether	Unexplained acoustics	(CCW) loaded with e, i, m and e_t
4. Magnetism	Human – aura		K-effect, as an example	Mind–mind interaction through all essences
5. Geology, geography and environment	Nose – smell	Earth	Remote sensing	(CCW) loaded with e, i, m, e_t and e_a
6. Water management & hydrology	Tongue – taste	Water	Hydro-therapy	(CCW) loaded with e, i, m and w
7. Psychology	Mind, intellect, ego, experiences	Mind waves	Telepathy, tele-empathy	(CCW) loaded with all essences

* This is carried out in terms of *tanmātras* (or sense-objects) and the corresponding perceptions by human senses of knowledge. The necessary essences to be loaded on mind wave are also indicated.

we have to consider the presence of secondary epi-fields in Φ_{CC} in addition to the primary ones. (Note that the primary ones are the infinitely dressed, seed-like versions of five cosmic elements and those of mind, intellect and ego with consciousness.) For this purpose, we have to rely on the Āyurvedic wisdom (see, for example, Gaur 1990) where the *tanmātras* with their successively increasing and added gross features are linked with *pañca-mahābhūtas* through certain type of correspondence relations like sound $\Rightarrow$ ether (E_t); sound + touch $\Rightarrow$ air (A); sound + touch + light $\Rightarrow$ Fire (F); sound + touch + light + taste $\Rightarrow$water (W); sound + touch + light + taste + smell $\Rightarrow$ earth (E_a), where, sound, touch, light, taste and smell respectively correspond to Sanskrit words *śabda, sparśa, rūpa, rasa* and *gandha.*

On the other hand, certain combinations of five cosmic elements E_t, F, A, W and E_a give rise to the trio of *vāta* (ν), *pitta* (π) and *kapha* (κ) via a new type of *pañcīkaraṇa* rule, which, symbolically, can be expressed in the lowest order of dressing (since a functional trio of ν, π and κ can exist only in an alive body and not in a dead one) with consciousness as,

$$\tilde{\nu}^{(1)} = a_1 E_t + a_2 F + a_3 A + a_4 W + a_5 E_a$$
$$\tilde{\pi}^{(1)} = b_1 E_t + b_2 F + b_3 A + b_4 W + b_5 E_a$$
$$\tilde{\kappa}^{(1)} = c_1 E_t + c_2 F + c_3 A + c_4 W + c_5 E_a, \tag{9.4}$$

where a_i, b_i and c_i (for i = 1, ..., 5) account for the weightage given to a *mahābhūta* or *mahābhūtas* in a particular combination. For example, in $\tilde{\nu}^{(1)}$, the *mahābhūtas* A and E_t, in $\tilde{\pi}^{(1)}$, F and W and in $\tilde{\kappa}^{(1)}$, E_a and W are dominant. Further, note that all three in this trio of the so-called *doṣa* in Āyurveda, basically, are the intangible objects and they form the basis of all kinds of studies in Āyurveda.

As far as the higher-order dressing of $\tilde{\nu}^{(1)}$, $\tilde{\pi}^{(1)}$ and $\tilde{\kappa}^{(1)}$ with consciousness as a result of individual's meditation is concerned, they can be obtained using a kind of *tri-karaṇa* rule (in analogy with the one we had for the trio of M, I and E in $\mathcal{M}$ in Section 4.3), which symbolically can be expressed through recurrence type relations, viz.

$$\begin{aligned}\tilde{\nu}^{(2)} &= (1/2)\,\tilde{\nu}^{(1)} + (1/4)\,\tilde{\pi}^{(1)} + (1/4)\,\tilde{\kappa}^{(1)};\\ \tilde{\pi}^{(2)} &= (1/2)\,\tilde{\pi}^{(1)} + (1/4)\,\tilde{k}^{(1)} + (1/4)\,\tilde{\nu}^{(1)};\\ \tilde{\kappa}^{(2)} &= (1/2)\,\tilde{\kappa}^{(1)} + (1/4)\,\tilde{\nu}^{(1)} + (1/4)\,\tilde{\pi}^{(1)},\end{aligned} \tag{9.5}$$

for the second-order dressing. Similarly, for the nth-order dressing, one writes:

$$\tilde{\nu}^{(n)} = \frac{1}{2}\tilde{\nu}^{(n-1)} + \frac{1}{4}\tilde{\pi}^{(n-1)} + \frac{1}{4}\tilde{\kappa}^{(n-1)} \quad , \tag{9.6}$$

and similar expressions for $\tilde{\pi}^{(n)}$ and $\tilde{\kappa}^{(n)}$. In the limit, when $n \to \infty$, the objects like $\tilde{\nu}^{(\infty)}$, $\tilde{\pi}^{(\infty)}$ and $\tilde{\kappa}^{(\infty)}$ form the seeds of secondary epi-fields in Φ_{CC} and thereby they help in creating life in the Universe. As such, they are not loaded on (*CCW*) but they are gradually formed in due course and in given circumstances favourable for the creation of life at the time of conception. Thus, the concept of secondary epi-fields, while seems to offer a plausible answer to the question of origin of gross body out of Φ_{CC} in philosophical terms, a detailed chemistry for this purpose can be developed by analysing *tridoṣas*. Such considerations will further help in understanding the phenomenon of teletherapy or reiki.

As a matter of fact, the framework of mind waves outlined here does offer an explanation of a variety of phenomena. For example, whether it is remote viewing, remote sensing, unexplained acoustics, telehydrotherapy or, in general, teletherapy, in either case the concept of mind waves offers explanation. For this purpose, one just has to load the carrier wave with appropriate essence(s) corresponding to specific *mahābhūta*(s) as indicated in Table 9.1 and direct the wave towards the true and deserving receiver (patient/ disciple) with an attention-dominated meditation. This kind of loading of carrier wave, in fact, needs to be done after a concerted and intense meditation on the part of the master, of course, with appropriately chosen essences and with still subtler ones out of m, i, e. While all this goes on towards the curing of mental health of the patient, towards his physical health, however, teletherapy in terms of secondary epi-fields need to be initiated. These secondary epi-fields υ, π and κ or their dressed versions basically are the constructs of *pañca-mahābhūtas* (cf. relations (9.4) and (9.5)) and are present already in Φ_{cc} in a seed-like form. While *pañca-mahābhūtas* are directly used in the treatment of diseases in naturopathy (Kaushal 2011a), their combinations in the form of *tridoṣas* υ, π and κ (cf. relations (9.4)) indeed form the backbone of the Āyurvedic system of medicine.

9.5 Concluding Discussion

This chapter, in continuation of Chapters 2-5, offers another step towards the understanding of the phenomenon of consciousness but mostly in the realm of behavioural and physical reality and again in a top-down manner. To this effect, the role of cenergy in the form of intense meditation or attention-domination is analysed to seek explanation of some non-physical processes and phenomena. In particular, the epi-physical version of the physical matter with reference to the idol worship, mind waves (as a step further in brain waves) along with associated energies and processes that fall into the domain of occult sciences are investigated. In fact, while the normal consciousness-manifesting processes (the so-called "soft" ones) proceed in a natural manner, the attention-dominated processes (the so-called "hard" ones) require some special efforts of varying nature towards the success of an action.

It is argued that the idol worship performed in an Indian temple, that is constructed in accordance with ancient Indian wisdom, definitely accelerates the process of thinking in a devotee, whether it is positive or negative, depending upon his attitude or intentions towards world and cosmic orders. Not only this, a positive environment (as an effect of induced magnetic field) surrounds the temple premises which, in the long run, might add to maintaining both these orders through the actions of a devotee.

It may be emphasized that the role of mind waves, as an outcome of the top-down approach, starts at a stage where the role of brain waves of bottom-up approach ends. The mind waves exist and are created in the cosmic consciousness field as a result of cosmic desire. They are multifold (in particular, eightfold as per Vedic wisdom) modulated waves. These constructs basically are the carrier waves of pure consciousness and are loaded with the essences of all eight types of epi-fields present initially in Φ_{CC} in seed-like forms. The modulation starts with subtlest ego, then with lesser subtle intellect, mind, ether, fire, air, water and in the end with the least subtle earth-essence. On the other hand, as a result of intense meditation by a practitioner, these essences of various dressed epi-fields unwrap themselves in a mind wave in the reverse order, i.e. first the grossest essence e_a unwraps and in the end the subtlest essence e unwraps. In view of the similarity of personality traits noted as predictions of neuroscience and the one available in Vedic wisdom, it is suggested for the brain scientists to look for three more EEG bands in addition to the already discovered five ones, viz. delta, theta, alpha, beta and gamma-synchronous activity. In fact, for mind waves there is no concept of velocity or even of infinities as they belong to a domain beyond space–time. It is for the future studies to explore these waves which, at present, seems to be of pure experiential nature and as such their role, particularly in occult sciences, cannot be denied.

Modern researches in cognitive and brain sciences have shown that the human thinking and behaviour are the outcome of constant firing of electric signals by brain neurons in the brain space. To this effect, a possible way of enhancing the frequency of this firing by brain neurons is discussed in Section 9.2 through the idol worship in an Indian temple, mainly as an attribute of geomagnetic field. In fact it is not difficult to extend the discussion to accommodate the effect of electric/magnetic fields (howsoever small they may be) coming constantly from the sun and other planets on the brain neurons. Such studies, in conjunction with the concept of mind waves of Section 9.4, will perhaps open new dimensions of study of astrology, which otherwise is considered as a science but with poor predictions.

In a nutshell, the studies pursued in this chapter clearly indicate that in cosmos there is nothing like an (isolated) individual entity, whether it is living or nonliving one. Each entity, in fact, is not only a part of but also embedded in an all-pervading cosmic consciousness field Φ_{CC}. While some super humans (may be rarest of the rare) develop capacity of realizing these cosmic connections, rest are forced (!) to exist, maintain and to survive only with these connections but without their cognizance. The concept of mind waves, introduced here perhaps for the first time in the light of Vedic wisdom, turns out to be an important tool to explain both physical and non-physical communication between and among entities. In the non-physical case, however, an explanation of variety of exotic phenomena including teletherapy with reference to both physical and mental health of a person can be sought. In this context, the phrase, "Without meditation, all medicine is incomplete" by Osho (2020) is justified, mainly through the Āyurvedic system of medicine.

High Skill Exercises and Projects

9.1 "Perceiving the worldly objects (WO) through senses as sense-objects is an easy task (soft process), whereas the learning or realizing about these objects is a difficult task (hard process)." Comment on this statement with reference to modern soft and hard disciplines of knowledge and in the light of *fig.* 11.4.

9.2 Keeping the present knowledge of brain science in mind, write an essay on the idol worship in an Indian temple constructed as per Vedic norms. Explain in detail as to how the method of worship in conjunction with the construction of the temple adds to the positive thinking of a person, even if the idol is not placed in the designated place.

9.3 Positive energy in a person corresponds to his positive thinking and in the spirit of the maintenance of both world- and cosmic-orders. Explain as to how the essence of this statement is retained in the worship that starts initially with an idol and later followed in the sequence of five existences, viz. natural, societal, gross, micro, causal and end up with cosmic connections in the fifth existence. Further, elaborate on as how the worship in an Indian temple becomes an asset as far as the attainment of peace is concerned.

9.4 Explain as to how the *aṣṭāṅga prakṛti* (*SMBG* VII.4) loaded on the ripples in cosmic consciousness field (*puruṣa*) Φ_{cc} leads to the formation of "mind" waves. List five properties of these waves. Discuss as to how these waves in conjunction with the dressings of embedded epi-fields in Φ_{cc} act as an "information" carrier with reference to an appropriately tuned mindset of the practitioner.

9.5 In view of the theory of mind waves presented in this chapter, comment on the claim that "the role of mind waves in brain science starts at the stage where that of brain waves ends, i.e. it could be well beyond the gamma synchronous activity".

9.6 Explain as to how and why does a temple constructed as per Vedic traditions turns out to be a special place for worship?

9.7 Take up a project to establish the emergence and justification for the disciplines like (i) naturopathy, (ii) Āyurveda in terms of *vāta, pitta* and *kapha*, (iii) telepathy and teletherapy, (iv) reiki, and (v) astrology, out of the same fundamental theory of procreation discussed in Chapter 4 and the concept of mind waves presented in this chapter. In particular, discuss as to how the concepts of (a) dressing rules for PMs and inner EOLs M, I and E; (b) mind waves and their modulation and demodulation; and (c) "K-effect", etc. play roles in these theoretical developments.

10

Psychochemistry and the Science of Human Interactions and Relations

10.1 Introduction

LIKE the theory of a single atom or of a nucleus, the characteristics corresponding to an individual Being or to his associated conscious interaction are investigated in Chapters 6-9. In this chapter, we investigate the systems of two or more interacting Beings in the spirit of the two or more interacting atoms or nuclei.

10.1.1 PSYCHOPHYSICS AND PSYCHOCHEMISTRY

The subject of physics basically deals with the theories of existence of matter, its structure and substructures, and the associated interactions (energy) to this effect at different space–time scales. The subject of chemistry, on the other hand, deals with the theories of coexistence not only of different species of matter but also of their constituents. All this pertains to the inanimate matter, describable successfully in terms of space–time structure of Nature. Note that for the description of living Beings (animate matter), who do have an extra dimension of consciousness, one needs to evolve different aspects of physics and chemistry from that for the inanimate matter as far as the question of their existence/coexistence is concerned. These new types of physics and chemistry considerations have to come either from independent source (in the "top-down" approach) or could be modifications of the existing subjects for the additional concept of consciousness (in the "bottom-up" approach). Naturally, in the former case, a full-fledged formalism, based on the entire gamut of human experiences and capable of coping with modern trends of these subjects, is required; whereas, in the latter case some possible modifications for the phenomenon of consciousness have been pursued, which can only offer a piecemeal solution of the problem. In fact, the Vedānta philosophy is found to offer an elegant framework for the description of the first case (see, for example, the *Kaṭhopaniṣad*, *Śvetāśvataropaniṣad*, *SMBG* and other related literature) and the same will form the basis for the present chapter.

Even among the living Beings, the human Being has a special status for being a perfect creation of God, as its inner essences of life (EOLs), viz. mind, intellect and ego or self-sense are capable of attaining unlimited potency to show wonders in the world. This trio of inner EOLs, in the presence of consciousness, constitutes the micro body of a person (cf. Chapter 6) and the same prepares a seed for actions performed in the outer world. These EOLs, in conjunction with the biological body and senses of knowledge and action of a person, in fact, are responsible for all sorts of interactions and establishing relations thereof with other entities. While such studies are desirable today, the seers in Vedic literature had already suggested such wisdom for a harmonious society thousands of years ago. In fact, while *SMBG* offers the best possible philosophy for the vertical development of personality of an individual, Upaniṣads (like the opening and closing verses in the *Kaṭhopaniṣad* and *Śvetāśvatropaniṣad*) also offer wisdom for the coexistence of individuals. For example, with reference to the teacher–taught interaction, note the *śāntipāṭha* as:

> *auṁ sahanāva vatu* । *saha nau bhunaktu* । *saha vīryaṁ*
> *karavāvahai* । *tejasvināvadhītamastu* । *mā vidviṣāvahai* ॥
> *auṁ śāntiḥ* ! *śāntiḥ* !! *śāntiḥ* !!! ॥

> Oh God! do take care of both (teacher and taught) of us towards our coexistence or togetherness; you nurse and nurture both of us together; we both attain (physical and mental) power to work together; we both attain an enlightened intellect together; we both remain away from mutual envy. Let there be peace inside us, in the family and society, and in the world.

10.1.2 RELATIONS AND INTERACTIONS AMONG HUMAN BEINGS

The word "interaction" (also a synonym of "force") means some resultant effect in intangible form that appears when two or more objects are present in close (!) vicinity or they coexist. These objects could be living or non-living ones. For inanimate objects, these interactions, in ideal sense, are mediated through space–time structure of Nature and again at different space–time scales, whereas for animate objects, in general, they could be mediated by space, time and consciousness. In fact, it is the presence of consciousness that makes the studies of interacting animate objects somewhat difficult, yet realistic.

Recall that the four fundamental interactions identified in physics are: gravitation, weak, electromagnetic and strong, in the order of their increasing strength. These interactions, in general, are characterized by their range and strength. With regard to the range, the strong and weak interactions are of short range while the electromagnetic and gravitation are of infinite range. Unlike the contact force in classical physics, all these four interactions display a common feature of action-at-a-distance (AAD), but not the features of action-at-a-time (AAT) or of action-at-a-distance-time (AADT) (Kaushal 2011). The latter, namely AAT and AADT, feature work mainly for animate objects. Further, this huge difference in the strengths (of several orders of magnitudes) allows us to study a particular system in physics in isolation with reference to a particular interaction, i.e. by neglecting the effect of other interactions, if present. For animate objects, however, this is not the case. The plurality and all-pervading or all-covering character of consciousness comes in the way in this case. The presence of the additional AAT- and AADT-type forces between living objects, particularly between human Beings, makes the studies of human interaction further complicated (Kaushal 2011). No doubt, the "conscious" interactions among the human Beings are of infinite range and of varying strength in physical space–time, but they have the property of converging or diverging or, in general, of all-pervading in the meditation (spiritual) space of consciousness itself. In the lower strata, while the consciousness is capable of creating physical space–time, however, at higher strata of spiritual zone, it goes beyond the physical space–time and it does wonders. Attaining the art of living in the higher strata of spiritual zone always and everywhere is not an easy task for everybody. Depending upon whether a person is body-conscious, mind-conscious or soul-conscious, his interactions with the world or with other Beings change accordingly.

Note that in the background of an interaction, there is always an exchange of energy in a discretized (quantum) form. (In the sense of physics, they are the matter or field particles, whereas in the sense of psychoscience, they could be constituents of interacting objects or *tanmātras*.) In fact, the quality of exchanged energy also defines the characteristic of the interacting objects towards their identification. We shall return to these details in Section 10.2. It may be mentioned that all known physical forces are still gross, they are not as subtle as the subtlest possible cosmic consciousness field (Kaushal 2018a) or the cosmic essence of Vedic science. Even the recently established Higgs field, responsible for the generation of mass towards the gravitation field, is not as subtle as the consciousness field. In case of two interacting animate objects, it is the consciousness that offers the background for conscious interactions of inner (mind, intellect and ego) or outer (biological body, and senses of knowledge and action) EOLs.

Both interactions and relations among human Beings are binary operations (see, for example, Simmons 1963). The former is composite, subtle and hierarchical whereas the latter is gross and unique. Both follow certain symmetries but in a restricted sense. The former appears natural, whereas the latter is by assignment. In general, while both refer to coexistence of objects, the relations additionally refer to the existence of an external observer. Recall the RST-category of binary relation (**R**) for the elements a, b, c, ... of a set **S** (an abstract system) in pure mathematics. In particular, these properties are defined as:

i. Reflexivity (R): a **R** a, for every element a belonging to **S**.
ii. Symmetry (S): If a **R** b, then b **R** a, for all a, b belonging to **S**.
iii. Transitivity (T): If a **R** b, b **R** c, then a **R** c, for all a, b, c belonging to **S**.

The only example for this category of relations is R = "is equal to" or in practical terms twin, triplet, quadruplet children of the same sex are the possible examples; otherwise, once the husband–wife relationship between two persons of opposite sex is established, other dozens of relations automatically follow in the two families in the Indian context oftentimes as a reality or sometimes as an extrapolation. However, the nomenclature changes in different cultures.

In the next section, we highlight the basic difference between a chemical and psychochemical reaction in view of the patomic model of human Being (cf. Chapter 6). With a view to demonstrate the concepts and the methodology of analysis, we discuss the psychochemistry of two human-Being interactions in Section 10.3. The exchanged *tanmātras* are analysed at both crude and hyper-fine levels. While the details of three and many human-Being interactions are already investigated earlier (cf. Chapter 9 of Kaushal 2015; Sharma et al. 2020), here in Section 10.4, we briefly remark on these systems, mainly to give a feeling of the underlying complexity in the study of these systems in terms of possible exchanges and sharing. The effect of environment on these psychochemical reactions is discussed in Section 10.5 in terms of the dressed versions of EOLs of reactants with their respective consciousness. In Section 10.6, we discuss love and affection as binding forces between and among human-Being systems and, accordingly, attempt to search a plausible force-law for love between human Beings. In fact, this category of interactions, not only helps in assigning the relations but also in quantifying the human interactions in practical terms. Finally, concluding remarks are made in Section 10.7.

10.2 Psychochemical Reactions, Reactants and Products: Lessons from Physical Theories III

Symbolically, a "reaction" or a "process" in physical sciences, depicted on a board or on a piece of paper and further going on in the mind of a scientist, is represented conventionally by

$$A+B \underset{condition}{\overset{physical}{\rightleftarrows}} C+D. \tag{10.1}$$

The objects A and B on the left are termed as "reactants" and C and D on the right as "products". Note that this is the simplest and the first step to understand a complicated underlying reaction mechanism. This also represents a variety of processes taught in different branches of physics and chemistry, except for the fact that the meanings of reactants and products, the nature of underlying reaction mechanism and interactions, and energy scales at which these processes occur keep on changing in different disciplines. They appear mostly in an analogous manner. To be more specific,

i. the "objects" A, B, C, D change with regard to their nature, shape, size, structure, etc.

ii. the "rules of the game" change with regard to the nature of interaction between and among A, B, C, D in terms of their strength and range, and

iii. the "scales" change with regard to space and time, and at the level of mind of the scientist as well (for details, see chapter 5 of Kaushal 2003).

Other remarks about the process (10.1) that are relevant in the present context are as follows:

a. The arrow towards right (left) in (10.1) is the "time arrow" representing the process in the forward (backward) direction. The phrase(s) above and/or below the arrows represents the physical conditions (like temperature, pressure, etc.) favouring the occurrence of the process.

b. Only two objects in the initial and final states are shown in (10.1), mainly for simplicity; otherwise one can as well have more than two objects in either of the initial or the final states. Some particular cases of process (10.1) are the "production" process in which either D or C is absent, and (10.1) becomes "decay" process where either B or A is absent.

c. Note that the objects A, B, C, D can be composite as well and their constituents can also participate in the process. In that case, one can question the elementarity of the objects A, B, C and D, and also the fundamentality of the process as the compositeness leads to several other subprocesses which, in turn, correspond to different types of interactions and energy scales.

d. It may so happen that the reactants and products could be the same but are in different (excited) energy states after the reaction, viz. $A + B \rightarrow A^* + B^*$.

e. Whether such a process occurs in physics or in chemistry, the interactions involved are the space–time-mediated ones, i.e. they could be gravitational, weak, electromagnetic or strong. In other words, these interactions are generated only out of space and time, and not from anything beyond like consciousness; second, their nature is considered only as an AAD-type or at most contact type in case of the physical contact of the participants. Participating members in the process, in fact, are assumed not to carry any memory, i.e. there is no scope of any AAT- or AADT-type forces.

f. At certain energy scales and for certain class of reactants, the process (10.1) can also be expressed as Feynman-like diagram (Perkins 1987) as shown in *fig*. 10.1.

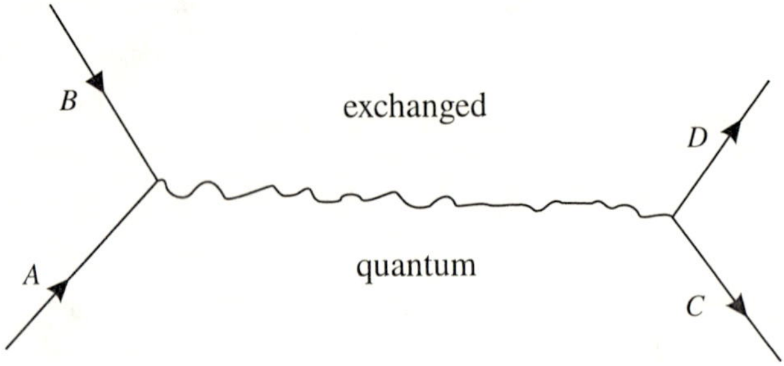

fig. 10.1: At certain energy scales and for certain class of reactants the process (10.1) can also be represented by a Feynman-like diagram

g. In view of remark (e), the entire process consisting mainly of inanimate (participating) objects proceeds as a "closed" system, i.e. it does not interact with the surroundings except for those factors which are accounted for in the process.

As lessons from the above concepts of physical science, we rewrite below all the seven remarks for the case of two interacting human Beings, which are now identified with the objects *A*, *B*, *C* and *D* of (10.1) and each of them is described by the patomic model:

a'. The place of "time arrow" is now taken by the meditation variable, μ, which accounts for the evolution of consciousness of each of the participants. For a common man the processes, however, remain irreversible.

b'. For simplicity, we consider the interaction between two persons. Husband and wife trying to conceive a baby or a mother giving birth to a baby can be considered as examples of "production" or "decay" respectively in the present context.

c'. Note that each participating member *A*, *B*, *C* and *D* is now composite: at crude level in terms of gross, micro and causal bodies and at subtle level in terms of detailed EOLs of each. Note that the interactions are going to be different at different levels of description.

d'. In physical appearance, the process, $A + B \rightarrow A^* + B^*$ for human Beings, is always effective but A^* and B^* can now differ from A and B in infinitely many ways due to a variety of exchanges possible and also the orders of dressings of their different EOLs with consciousness as a result of interactions and hence putting A and B into different enlightened states (cf. *fig.* 6.2).

e'. In addition to the contact and AAD-type forces, the possibility of AAT- and AADT-type forces is always there for conscious participants.

f'. Feynman-like diagram can still be drawn but with reference to the μ-variable (Kaushal 2019), instead of the time variable. As a result, there arises a new class of *tanmātras* (the quanta of interaction) in addition to the ones postulated in Vedic science for the interaction of a human Being with *PMs* (Kaushal 2011).

g'. As the consciousness associated with an individual cannot be localized, the interacting system in the present case always remains an "open" system. Therefore, there is no question of using existing physical laws as such in the present case in view of Remark (e').

Before proceeding further, we elaborate here on the word *tanmātra*, as a remark on the Remarks (f) and (f').

Tanmātras alias Quanta of Interaction

In Vedic literature the word *tanmātra* is used (Ādi Śaṅkara 1962; Shukla 1992) in the context of interaction of five cosmic elements with five senses of knowledge, viz. nose–earth, tongue–water, skin–air, eyes–fire and ears–ether (denoted respectively in this work as τ_{ea}, τ_w, τ_a, τ_f, and τ_{et}). A multiple use of this word and a generalization of this notation to different situations require a word of caution here. For, the

i. interactions inside the human Being τ is labelled with $\mathcal{MG}$ or $\mathcal{MC}$, corresponding to $\mathcal{M}$–$\mathcal{G}$ and $\mathcal{M}$–$\mathcal{C}$ type interactions (Kaushal 2011, 2015) or with their interacting constituents,

ii. interactions of two and three human Beings are described by τ again and the latter is labelled with two and three subscripts, and, where again each of b_i's ($i = 1, 2, 3$) consists of the set $\{\mathcal{G}_i, \mathcal{M}_i, \mathcal{C}_i\}$ with $i = 1, 2, 3$, and thereby giving rise to a variety of *tanmātras*.

iii. At the next stage of the use of this notation, τ is also labelled with the elements of the sets $\mathcal{G}$, $\mathcal{M}$ and $\mathcal{C}$, viz. $\mathcal{G}$ = {B, SE}, $\mathcal{M}$ = {M, I, E} and $\mathcal{C}$ = {SO}. Further, note that the *tanmātras* and the corresponding notations also differ for the cases of dressed and undressed versions of EOLs with consciousness or with the level of development of faculty of understanding of participating Beings in the interaction.

Charged-ion Exchange and Tanmātras

Whether it is the Coulomb-charge-ion of atomic chemistry or the colour-charge-ion of quark chemistry, in either case, certain units of Coulomb- or colour-charge undergo exchanges between reactants to give rise to new products. In human chemistry, however, certain types of *tanmātras* undergo exchanges between and among b_i's ($i = 1, 2, 3$), which could qualitatively belong to different scales of consciousness mainly because of the plurality character of consciousness or of the c-charge on τ.

We shall use patomic model of Chapter 6 for each of the interacting persons *A*, *B*, *C*, *D* in (10.1) and account for the exchanges arising thereof, first due to their causal, micro and gross existences (the so-called crude level interactions) and then, at the next stage, due to the EOLs working through these existences (the so-called fine and hyperfine level interactions). In this scheme of study, we have investigated earlier (Kaushal 2011, 2015; Sharma et al. 2020) the details of two, three and many human Beings interactions in the spirit of physical theories. Here, however, we shall restrict mainly to two human Beings interactions just to demonstrate the underlying methodology. A brief summary of results with some applications will however be given for three and many human Beings cases.

10.3 Interactions between Human Beings

It is a common experience that when a single person is left in the field of *PMs* or in general that of WO, he alone feels and realizes the interactions with them, first through *B* and SE and later through M, I and E depending upon the development of his FOU. However, when two or more than two persons are present in a given environment, then in addition to individual's feeling and realization, there is also a tendency for sharing these feelings and realizations with other persons about the same WO. If the sharing persons are strange to each other (i.e. they are not biased or prejudiced), then the same sequence of interactions follows; otherwise, the interactions get initiated at any subtle level and the same depends on the development of FOUs of the sharing persons. Although the interactions initiate at the most fundamental level through EOLs (bare case), the presence of *PMs* or of WO in the form of environment just dresses them up (dressed case). This enables the interactions to become more effective and the same leads to a success of the outwardly action. With a view to classifying and quantifying these interactions, we employ here the patomic model of human Being.

10.3.1 INTERACTIONS AT THE CRUDE LEVEL

Consider two human Beings b_1 and b_2 each of them having described in terms of gross, micro and causal bodies (i.e. by the reduced version of patomic model of Section 6.1.1(b)), viz. $b_1 \equiv \{\mathcal{C}_1, \mathcal{M}_1, \mathcal{G}_1\}$, $b_1 \equiv \{\mathcal{C}_2, \mathcal{M}_2, \mathcal{G}_2\}$. These persons are now placed within the range (!) of interaction. Unlike the physical forces, the range here is not defined in the space–time domain; rather, it is characterized by the meditation variable μ. (In reality, the meditation variables associated separately and jointly with participating persons need to be considered in the study, but in view of all-pervading, all-covering and plurality character of consciousness, we restrict the discussion here only to a single variable μ, which, in fact, belongs to the observer). In fact, they have to have something common in their thinking in order to interact with each other. For example, the persons sitting next to each other in a train or bus may not interact for hours or even days unless the environment forces them to do so. On the other hand, the persons living far apart (distance-wise) can interact with each other either through thought process or through the material means like phone calls. Similar is the case with the time variable. Persons sitting together may or may not go in the past or future but, if they wish, they can as well share their experiences of infinite past or infinite future (even though rare but it might include their past or future births provided they are capable enough) depending on the development of their FOUs. In case of distant persons, while M, I of $\mathcal{M}$ play the important role, it is E of $\mathcal{M}$ which plays the role in the case of persons sitting together.

The interactions between b_1 and b_2 are shown in *fig.* 10.2 within the framework of reduced version of patomic model and with meditation variable μ in the upward direction. While the consciousness of each of the interacting person is separately evolving through their corresponding variables μ_1 and μ_2, the variable μ accounts for the evolution of consciousness of the observer (Reader!). Before analysing the possible quanta of exchanges in this figure, following points are worth noting:

i. Since $\mathcal{C}_1$ and $\mathcal{C}_2$ represent the second quantized versions of the same all-pervading cosmic consciousness field Φ_{cc} (Kaushal 2018b), they separately or jointly will only provide the background for a cognitive b_1–b_2 interaction in general.
ii. In view of (i), $\mathcal{M}_i$, $\mathcal{G}_i$ jointly or separately for i = 1 and 2 are active in the presence of $\mathcal{C}_1$ and $\mathcal{C}_2$, respectively.
iii. In view of (i) and (ii) above, for the interaction of $\mathcal{M}_1$ with $\mathcal{M}_2$ or $\mathcal{G}_2$, or of $\mathcal{G}_1$ with $\mathcal{M}_2$ or $\mathcal{G}_2$ (or vice versa), $\mathcal{C}_1$ and $\mathcal{C}_2$ separately remain in the background. Similarly, for the interaction of $\mathcal{G}_1$ with $\mathcal{G}_2$ (or of $\mathcal{G}_2$ with $\mathcal{G}_1$), $\mathcal{M}_1$ (or $\mathcal{M}_2$ in the reverse case) remains in the background (since the subtlety increases as one proceeds from $\mathcal{G} \rightarrow \mathcal{M} \rightarrow \mathcal{C}$).

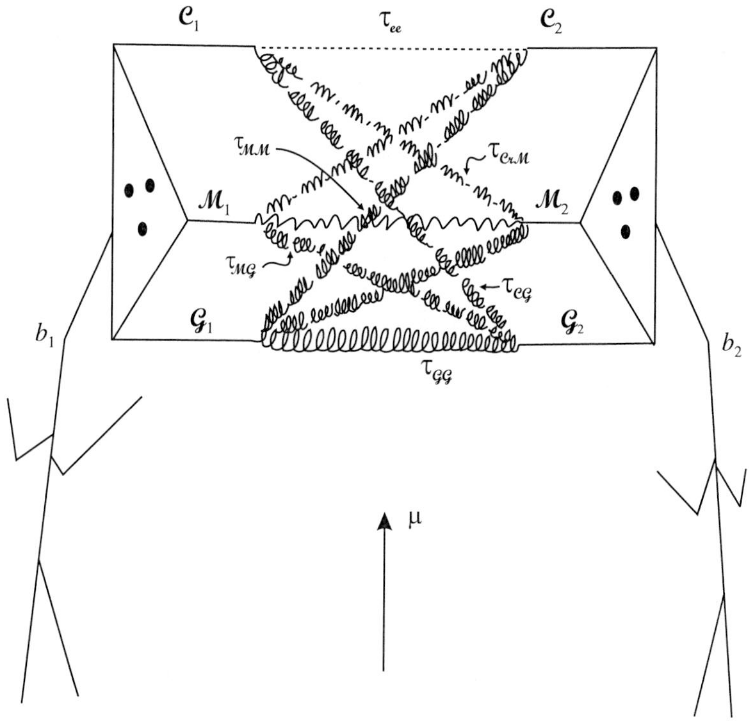

fig. 10.2: Interactions between human Beings at the crude level, i.e. at the levels of $\mathcal{C}$, $\mathcal{M}$ and $\mathcal{G}$

iv. Note that $\{\mathcal{C}_i, \mathcal{M}_i, \mathcal{G}_i\}$ for $i = 1$ and 2, separately constitute individuals who can be in general in different mindsets. For a noticeable interaction between them, there has to be an overlap in certain domains.

In general, there are nine quanta of interaction (*tanmātras*) which can exchange between b_1 and b_2 and at crude level, viz. $\tau_{\mathcal{C}1\mathcal{C}2}$, $\tau_{\mathcal{C}1\mathcal{M}2}$, $\tau_{\mathcal{C}1\mathcal{G}2}$, $\tau_{\mathcal{M}1\mathcal{C}2}$, $\tau_{\mathcal{M}1\mathcal{M}2}$, $\tau_{\mathcal{M}1\mathcal{G}2}$, $\tau_{\mathcal{G}1\mathcal{C}2}$, $\tau_{\mathcal{G}_1\mathcal{M}_2}$ and $\tau_{\mathcal{G}1\mathcal{G}2}$. Further, universality of $\mathcal{C}1$ and $\mathcal{C}2$ implies $\tau_{\mathcal{C}1\mathcal{C}2} = \tau_{\mathcal{C}_2\mathcal{C}_1} = \tau_{\mathcal{C}\mathcal{C}}$. In view of (iv) and because of peculiar features of cosmic consciousness field Φ_{cc} in which the concept of forward or backward processes is irrelevant (mainly because there is no "cause and effect" distinction in Φ_{cc} at the level of its quantized version SO), it is reasonable to assume

$\tau_{\mathcal{M}1e2} = \tau_{e1\mathcal{M}2} = \tau_{e\mathcal{M}}$; $\tau_{\mathcal{G}1e2} = \tau_{e1\mathcal{G}2} = \tau_{e\mathcal{G}}$; $\tau_{\mathcal{M}1\mathcal{M}2} = \tau_{\mathcal{M}2\mathcal{M}1} = \tau_{\mathcal{M}\mathcal{M}}$; $\tau_{\mathcal{G}1\mathcal{M}2} = \tau_{\mathcal{M}1\mathcal{G}2} = \tau_{\mathcal{G}\mathcal{M}}$; $\tau_{\mathcal{G}1\mathcal{G}2} = \tau_{\mathcal{G}2\mathcal{G}1} = \tau_{\mathcal{G}\mathcal{G}}$. Such symmetry considerations thus imply existence only of six quanta, viz. τ_{ee}, $\tau_{e\mathcal{M}}$, $\tau_{e\mathcal{G}}$, $\tau_{\mathcal{M}\mathcal{M}}$, $\tau_{\mathcal{M}\mathcal{G}}$ and $\tau_{\mathcal{G}\mathcal{G}}$ for *b*–*b* interaction. Out of these six, τ_{ee} (denoted by dotted line in the figure) will not contribute in view of the universal character of soul. Thus, there remain only five *tanmātras* to account for the *b*–*b* interaction. While $\tau_{\mathcal{G}\mathcal{G}}$ and $\tau_{\mathcal{M}\mathcal{M}}$ shown by spring-like and wave-like lines in the figure, $\tau_{e\mathcal{M}}$, $\tau_{e\mathcal{G}}$ and $\tau_{\mathcal{M}\mathcal{G}}$ are respectively shown by correspondingly mixed line segments.

Note that while the human Beings b_1 and b_2 will interact accordingly to their own μ_1, μ_2 parameters (or, the levels of development of their FOUs), the observer will evaluate this interaction according to his own μ or the development of his own FOU, essentially remaining only as a spectator. Further remarks about the exchanged quanta between b_1 and b_2 are as follows:

i. The *tanmātra* τ_{ee} may correspond to *turīya* state (a state of the human Being beyond the three commonly known aspects of consciousness on the substratum of Self, viz. awakening, dreaming and deep sleep).

ii. The *tanmātrās* $\tau_{e\mathcal{M}}$ and $\tau_{e\mathcal{G}}$ correspond to the case when the micro- or gross-body of b_1 is in direct communion with the SO of b_2 or vice versa. Similarly, $\tau_{\mathcal{M}\mathcal{M}}$ and $\tau_{\mathcal{M}\mathcal{G}}$ correspond to the cases when the micro body of b_1 is in communication separately with the micro and gross bodies of b_2, or vice versa, i.e. when b_1 can imagine/dream of the gross body actions of b_2.

iii. In the *b*–*b* interaction, it is the $\tau_{\mathcal{G}\mathcal{G}}$-type exchanges that lie within the purview of physical and/or biological sciences; otherwise as μ increases any or all non-physical interactions corresponding to $\tau_{\mathcal{M}\mathcal{G}}$, $\tau_{\mathcal{M}\mathcal{M}}$, $\tau_{e\mathcal{G}}$ and $\tau_{e\mathcal{M}}$ start manifesting and eventually come into existence as a result of fine-tuning of the interaction in the lowest order.

iv. Only good practitioners can realize the dynamics arising out of the higher-order fine-tuning, which is attributed to the constituents of $\mathcal{M}$ and $\mathcal{G}$ of each of the interacting persons. We demonstrate this in the next subsection.

In summary, the conscious mind of one person is capable of activating different EOLs of the other person. As a matter of fact, the mindsets of b_1 and b_2 as a function of their individual μ_1 and μ_2 play a crucial role in the whole process of interaction in addition to the μ of the external observer.

10.3.2 FINE AND HYPERFINE-TUNING CORRESPONDING TO b–b INTERACTION

Next we use the finer details of $\mathcal{G}$, $\mathcal{M}$ and $\mathcal{C}$ as $\mathcal{G} \equiv$ (B, SE), $\mathcal{M} \equiv$ (M, I, E) and $\mathcal{C} \equiv$ (SO) to analyse the "reaction" (or, the interaction process),

$$b_1 + b_2 \rightleftarrows b_1' + b_2' + \tau_{b_1 b_2} \tag{10.2}$$

essentially in the spirit of *fig.* 10.1. Here b'_1 and b'_2 are the enlightened versions of b_1 and b_2 after the interaction(s). The *tanmātras* τ satisfies $\tau_{b_1 b_2} = \tau_{b_2 b_1}$ for the reasons given before and correspond to the earlier composition of b as $b \equiv \{\mathcal{C}, \mathcal{M}, \mathcal{G}\}$ will now correspond to the composition of each of the Being b as $b \equiv$ {B, SE, M, I, E, SO}. This will lead to twenty varieties of interactions mediated through $\tau_{B,B}$, $\tau_{B,SE}$, $\tau_{SE,SE}$, (correspond to $\tau_{\mathcal{G}\mathcal{G}}$); $\tau_{B,M}$, $\tau_{B,I}$, $\tau_{B,E}$, $\tau_{SE,M}$, $\tau_{SE,I}$, $\tau_{SE,E}$ (correspond to $\tau_{\mathcal{G}\mathcal{M}}$); $\tau_{B,SO}$, $\tau_{SE,SO}$ (correspond to $\tau_{\mathcal{G}\mathcal{C}}$); $\tau_{M,M}$, $\tau_{M,I}$, $\tau_{M,E}$, $\tau_{I,I}$, $\tau_{I,E}$, $\tau_{E,E}$ (correspond to $\tau_{\mathcal{M}\mathcal{M}}$); $\tau_{M,SO}$, $\tau_{I,SO}$, $\tau_{E,SO}$ (correspond to $\tau_{\mathcal{M}\mathcal{C}}$). Note that the interactions of the type $\tau_{SO,\,SO}$ do not form the part of this classification since it provides the basis for all the above interactions as argued earlier for $\tau_{\mathcal{C}\mathcal{C}}$. Further, each of these twenty interactions accounts for a certain aspect of behaviour arising out of the interaction of two human Beings. In Table 10.1, we further elaborate on the nature of quanta of exchanges at hyper fine level with an eye on application aspects.

It is worthwhile to remind ourselves of an analogy here from nuclear physics. At the first stage of study of nuclear forces, their origin is considered due to the exchange of pions between nucleons (Yukawa theory). At the next substructure level, their origin is

Table 10.1: Quanta of Exchange of Awareness (Consciousness) between Human Beings b_1 and b_2 ($\tau_{b_1b_2}$) and Their Role at Different Levels of Subtlety in b–b Interactions

Quantum of Consciousness Exchange	*Fine-tuning of the Exchange*	*Nature of Interaction: Remarks and Examples*
1. $\tau_{\mathcal{GG}}$	$\tau_{B,B}$	Body–body interaction without prejudices; certain instances in the wrestling of two wrestlers, meeting of husband and wife or of two drunkards.
	$\tau_{B,SE}$	Body-senses (of knowledge and actions) interactions without prejudices; many examples in a family in day-to-day life, like kissing and blessings.
	$\tau_{SE,SE}$	Senses–senses (of knowledge and action) interaction without prejudices; many examples like shaking hands, interacting through eyes, etc.
2. $\tau_{\mathcal{GM}}$	$\tau_{B,M}$	Body–mind interactions without the roles of I, E or SE (only emotions); many examples, but ideal one is that of mother–baby or at times of husband–wife interactions.
	$\tau_{B,I}$	Body–intellect interaction without the role of M, E or SE; a scientific intellect analysing the body of a person or of a patient in dream or in imagination.
	$\tau_{B,E}$	Body–ego (memory) interaction without the roles of M, I or SE; imaginary verbal duel or anger of a person over the other.
	$\tau_{SE,M}$	Senses (of knowledge and action)–mind interaction: a person inducing the emotions in the other, through his SEs mono-acting of mother–baby as viewed by a viewer.
	$\tau_{SE,I}$	Senses (of knowledge and action)–intellect interaction: A person initiating the analysing power in the other through his SEs, mono-acting of jokers or dialogue as viewed by a viewer.

Quantum of Consciousness Exchange	*Fine-tuning of the Exchange*	*Nature of Interaction: Remarks and Examples*
	$\tau_{SE,E}$	Senses (of knowledge and action)–ego (memory) interaction: A person inducing the memory aspect in the other through his SEs; mono-acting of a historical event as viewed by a viewer.
3. $\tau_{\mathcal{G}e}$	$\tau_{B,SO}$	Body–soul interaction: A person in *samādhi* receiving the salutation of another person.
	$\tau_{SE,SO}$	Senses (of knowledge and action)–soul interaction: A person in *samādhi* enjoying the offered prayer by his devotee.
4. $\tau_{\mathcal{M},\mathcal{M}}$	$\tau_{M,M}$	Mind–mind interaction: Imagination of or dreaming the emotional exchanges between two persons like weeping of a lady as she watches the other weeping lady.
	$\tau_{M,I}$	Mind–intellect interaction: Imagination of as if the emotions of one person are analysed by the other, as in screen play or in drama.
	$\tau_{M,E}$	Mind–ego (memory) interaction: Imagination of that the emotions of one person are inducing the joy or anger in the other.
	$\tau_{I,I}$	Intellect–intellect interaction: Imagination of or dreaming the intellectual exchanges between two persons.
	$\tau_{I,E}$	Intellect–ego (memory) interaction: Imagination of analysis by one person of the anger or joy of the other.
	$\tau_{E,E}$	Ego (memory)–ego (memory) interaction: Imagining or dreaming the exchange of memory-mines between two persons.
5. $\tau_{\mathcal{M}e}$	$\tau_{M,SO}$	Mind–soul interaction: A person in *samādhi* noticing the emotions of the other.
	$\tau_{I,SO}$	Intellect–soul interaction: A person in *samādhi* noticing the decisions of the other.
	$\tau_{E,SO}$	Ego (memory)–soul interaction: A person in *samādhi* noticing the anger or joy of the other.

attributed to the gluon exchanges between the quarks; when both pion and nucleon are considered as composed of quarks. For details, we refer to chapter 9 of Kaushal (2011). In the same spirit, although we are using the same symbol τ here for the exchanges at the crude as well as at the fine-tuning levels but the fact is that these exchanges occur at different scales of meditation, even for the same pair of human Beings. Corresponding to each of the five cases of gross *tanmātras*, several examples are cited from day-to-day living in Table 10.1. In fact, Feynman-like diagrams can be drawn for each of the interactions described therein, but here we elaborate only on τ_{MM} class of exchanges, as shown in *fig.* 10.3.

Keeping the underlying symmetry in mind, *fig.* 10.3 suggests six exchanges, viz. τ_{MM}, τ_{II}, τ_{EE}, τ_{MI}, τ_{IE}, τ_{ME} between b_1 and b_2 at the micro body level. Many examples for this case can be sought in teacher–taught interactions (cf. Section 10.4). Examples can also be sought in intellectual gatherings such as conferences and symposia and religious gatherings, (also see, entry 4 in Table 10.1). Note that the above discussed exchanges are between bare EOLs (not dressed and enriched with environment) of b_1 and b_2. The examples cited above are accommodated only in a crude manner in the scheme of classification. In fact, they suggest the cases of ideal interactions as far as the real life is concerned. In the next section, we shall account for the effect of environment and circumstances on these bare interactions in order to bring them to conform to a more realistic situation.

For animate objects, the process (10.1) in general evolves with respect to space, time and consciousness variables and the latter is accommodated through μ. Here, however, we have proceeded with the evolution of the system only with respect to μ, as the scales of space–time and of non–space–time mediated interactions are quite different. Moreover, the process (10.2) is just a symbolic representation as far as the physics content of reactants and products is concerned.

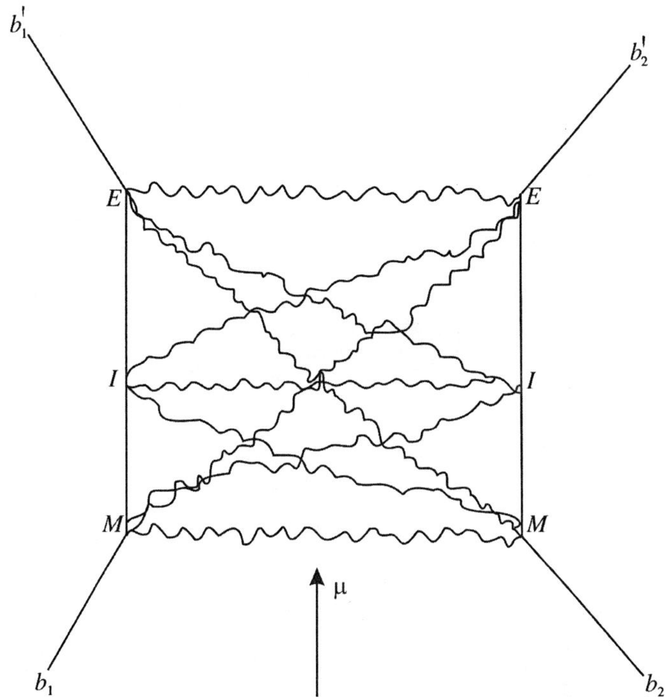

fig. 10.3: An example of fine-tuning of *b*–*b* interaction mediated by $\tau_{\mathcal{M}\mathcal{M}}$. In all, there are six exchanges possible in this diagram after accounting for the symmetry considerations

Lastly, we make a few remarks about the hyperfine-tuning of *b*–*b* interactions. For instance, this feature for the $\tau_{\mathcal{M}\mathcal{M}}$ class of exchanges described in *fig.* 10.3 can be understood as follows. Note that each constituent of $\mathcal{M}$, viz. M, I and E, has subtle and gross components as argued in Section 3.1 of Kaushal 2015. If one considers such subdivisions of M, I and E in the present $\tau_{\mathcal{M}\mathcal{M}}$ class of exchanges, it will further increase the number of exchanges to as many as 36 in general at the next hyper-fine level. However, symmetry considerations will reduce this number to 21. In fact, such hyper fine-tuning of exchanges is also possible for other fine classes of exchanges, viz. those corresponding to $\tau_{\mathcal{G}\mathcal{G}}$, $\tau_{\mathcal{G}\mathcal{M}}$, $\tau_{\mathcal{G}C}$ and

$\tau_{\mathcal{MC}}$ with $\mathcal{G} \equiv \{B, SE\}$. Such details of $\mathcal{G}$ and also that of B (in terms of different inner and outer organs) and that of SE (in terms of different senses of knowledge and of action) will lead to a huge list of exchanges which, in turn, can account for additional finer aspects of two human Being interaction. We restrict ourselves here from going into further details. However, an example pertaining to $\tau_{\mathcal{MM}}$ would suffice in this respect.

Example 10.3.1: If a person has some prejudices against the other, it is all due to the storage of certain past memories in the subtle component of E and this accordingly materializes the interaction between b_1 and b_2. As a result, the person feels either joy or anger out of this interaction depending respectively upon the good or bad memories of the past stored in subtle E.

10.4 Summary of Results for Three and Many Human-Beings Interactions

In analogy with the *b*–*b* interaction discussed above, we briefly discuss here the results of three and many human-Beings interactions investigated earlier (Kaushal 2015; Sharma et al. 2020). Further, unlike the physical theories, note that here the three and many human-Beings interactions are equally important mainly because each participant in the process is equipped with the faculties responsible for emotion, decision and memory. Again, beside the general many human-Beings case, the cases of one-to-many and many-to-one human interactions are of particular interest.

10.4.1 INTERACTIONS AMONG THREE HUMAN BEINGS

No doubt, the methodology in this case remains the same as for the *b*–*b* interaction case but the number of situations to be analysed in terms of exchanged quanta becomes rather large. If one resorts to the pair-wise interactions (by assuming the third person as a spectator) for a three human-Beings system, then life becomes simple as it happens in physical theories (Mitra 1962, 1969), where the contribution of three and higher-body forces (particularly in nuclear physics) are found to be relatively small. However, in case of human Beings this is not the case, three and many human-Beings interactions are equally or even more important, as we are now dealing with an "open" system whose subsystems again are no more the systems that are "closed". In fact, it becomes difficult for a common man to remain spectator but a man of perfection (the person who is living in spiritual (causal body) zone) can be considered as nearly an ideal spectator as possible. Thus, for the three human-Beings case we consider the process,

$$b_1 + b_2 + b_3 \rightleftharpoons b_1' + b_2' + b_3' + \tau_{b_j b_k} + \tau_{b_j b_k b_l}, \tag{10.3}$$

which, in some sense, will suggest a guideline to analyse more realistic situations. Here in the process (10.3) $\tau_{b_j b_k}$ are the quanta corresponding to pair-wise interactions and $\tau_{b_j b_k b_l}$ are the quanta corresponding to three human-Beings exchanges with $j, k, l = 1, 2, 3$; but j is not equal to k and not equal to l in this case.

Further, note that in the language of reduced version of the patomic model each b_1, b_2, b_3, in the subscript of τ can be $\mathcal{C}$, $\mathcal{M}$ or $\mathcal{G}$. However, by legitimately barring only cases like $\tau_{\mathcal{CCC}}$, $\tau_{\mathcal{CMC}}$, $\tau_{\mathcal{MCC}}$, $\tau_{\mathcal{CCM}}$, $\tau_{\mathcal{CGC}}$, $\tau_{\mathcal{GCC}}$, $\tau_{\mathcal{CCG}}$ for the reasons given in the case of b–b interaction in terms of the universality of soul and also that they will not form good examples of three human-Beings interactions, results into twenty possibilities of three human-Beings exchanges, viz. $\tau_{\mathcal{CMM}}$, $\tau_{\mathcal{CMG}}$, $\tau_{\mathcal{CG,M}}$, $\tau_{\mathcal{CGG}}$, $\tau_{\mathcal{M,CM}}$, $\tau_{\mathcal{M,CG}}$, $\tau_{\mathcal{M,MC}}$, $\tau_{\mathcal{M,MM}}$, $\tau_{\mathcal{M,MG}}$, $\tau_{\mathcal{MGC}}$, $\tau_{\mathcal{M,GM}}$, $\tau_{\mathcal{MGG}}$, $\tau_{\mathcal{GCM}}$, $\tau_{\mathcal{GCG}}$, $\tau_{\mathcal{GMC}}$, $\tau_{\mathcal{GMM}}$, $\tau_{\mathcal{GMG}}$, $\tau_{\mathcal{GGC}}$, $\tau_{\mathcal{GGM}}$, $\tau_{\mathcal{GGG}}$, contrary to just the five exchanges for the case of two human Beings interactions, viz. $\tau_{\mathcal{GG}}$, $\tau_{\mathcal{GM}}$, $\tau_{\mathcal{GC}}$, $\tau_{\mathcal{MM}}$, $\tau_{\mathcal{MC}}$. Further, note that out of these twenty possibilities the twelve cases, namely $\tau_{\mathcal{CMM}}$, $\tau_{\mathcal{CMG}}$, $\tau_{\mathcal{CG,M}}$, $\tau_{\mathcal{CGG}}$, $\tau_{\mathcal{M,CM}}$, $\tau_{\mathcal{M,CG}}$, $\tau_{\mathcal{M,MC}}$, $\tau_{\mathcal{MGC}}$, $\tau_{\mathcal{GCM}}$, $\tau_{\mathcal{GCG}}$, $\tau_{\mathcal{GMC}}$ and $\tau_{\mathcal{GGC}}$ qualify as the better choices in the spirit of the spectator model.

Fine- and Hyper Fine-tuning of b–b–b Interactions

Recall that it is the presence of SO (or, of self-awareness or of the source of consciousness) in the background of EOLs of a person that makes the human Being functional. Also, each b_1, b_2, b_3, in terms of

EOLs, is described (cf. Section 6.1) as $b_i \equiv \{SO, E_i, I_i, M_i, SE_i, B_i\}$, with $i = 1, 2, 3$. Note that the EOL SO is the same in all the three because of its cosmic character and the same offers a basis for their interaction. However, other EOLs are different and in general they are different in all human Beings for not completely independent reasons, viz.:

i. each Being has different *saṁskāras* (tendencies) generated out of his *prārabdha, sañcita* and *kriyamāna* components of actions,

ii. each has different levels of development of his FOU, and

iii. each is affected differently by Nature-born three *guṇas* (modes of *Prakṛti*). In principle, one should analyse the *b–b–b* interaction keeping these reasons in mind but it has been found that it is the EOL, M, which acting as a bridge between $\mathcal{M}$ and $\mathcal{G}$, also plays a dominant role in an individual and hence in these interactions. In fact, to whichever SE the mind M is attached, the same SE controls I of that person and accordingly his behaviour gets affected (*SMBG* II.60; II.67).

As for *b–b* interaction, the fine-tuning of *b–b–b* interaction in terms of constituents of each $\mathcal{G}$ and $\mathcal{M}$, corresponding to each interacting person, can also be carried out in principle but as a whole it becomes a very complicated dynamics. In fact, this complexity increases further if one wants to analyse the dynamics of four or more human Being interactions, with the result there is a need to follow other methods (Kaushal 2015) for this case. In analogy with the exchanges shown in *fig.* 10.3, one can have some glimpses of the complexity of *b–b–b* interactions, particularly when one considers the possible exchanges among the constituents of three mindsets $\mathcal{M}_1$, $\mathcal{M}_2$, $\mathcal{M}_3$. In this case, the fine-tuning of interactions associated with the *tanmātra* $\tau_{\mathcal{M}\mathcal{M}\mathcal{M}}$ arises due to the constituents of $\mathcal{M}$ (viz. M, I and E) (Kaushal 2011). Hyper fine-tuning is also possible here by considering the gross and subtle components of each of M, I and E (see section 3.1 of Kaushal 2015) and for each individual.

10.4.2 MANY HUMAN BEING INTERACTIONS

We have seen that the magnitude of complexity of interactions among human Beings increases with increasing number of interacting members. No doubt, for these many human-Being systems, the starting *b–b* interaction, in its general form, still remains in the background but at the same time the environment and circumstances demand many human-Being interactions to be equally important unlike the case with physics – many-body systems. Social, political and economic sciences are full of such examples of interacting many human-Being systems. In fact, the knowledge of *b–b* or *b–b–b* interactions as such cannot be extrapolated to a system of many human-Beings in a straightforward manner. In this context, recall a common experience, "two perfect persons may not be perfect for each other". As a matter of fact, when two or more than two persons perfectly adjust to coexist, several new interactions start appearing and the resulting perfection becomes questionable. The many human-Being features that evolve are coexistence, cooperation, coordination and the like, and the same, at a higher level of description, are more pronounced in the present case than for a physical many-body system where the nature of many-body forces is quite different. However, to analyse an interacting many human-Being system, once again we use analogies from physical sciences and employ the same to the present situation with regard to certain concepts and methodology, of course, after appropriate modifications. In this regard, the viability of core-valence picture for many-body system and the use of some statistical methods is demonstrated. For further details of many human-Being case, we refer to our earlier works (Kaushal 2011, 2015; Sharma et al. 2020).

10.4.3 ONE-TO-MANY AND MANY-TO-ONE HUMAN-BEING INTERACTIONS

Unlike the case with physical systems, here the cases of one-to-many and many-to-one human-Being interactions are interesting.

In this context, the example of teacher–taught interaction (in both one-to-one and one-to-many situations) has been investigated (Sharma et al. 2020) with a view to searching a best performer in a classroom. Here we highlight a few other cases of one-to-many and many-to-one human-Being interactions in daily life.

***Example 10.4.1*:** In fact, when a teacher in the class, a political leader in the masses or a spiritual leader in the meditation class, etc. are showered with questions and queries at the same time from the audience, the situations of many-to-one interaction arise. If this conversation is one-to-one, then life becomes simple for the speaker; otherwise, the speaker becomes puzzled because of the variety of quality of questions posed. Imagine the scene when a truck driver is caught by public over an accident on the road involving his truck, particularly when some casualty has occurred.

***Example 10.4.2*:** *Searching the most beneficiary disciple in a discourse by a spiritual leader*: With a view to achieving happiness, two persons (one with certain negative thoughts and the other with certain positive thoughts) attend the same discourse by a spiritual Master and come out with fullest satisfaction. Now the question is that who is the most beneficiary? Naturally, the answer is the first person. This fact and other details about the underlying process can be understood in terms of the so-called "Saha's ionization formula" (Saha and Srivastava 1931), derived for the ultra-high temperature heating of gases in the early Universe. While the details are referred to our earlier works (Kaushal 2015; Sharma et al. 2020), here we demonstrate the viability of this famous result for the present case as under.

In fact, we use this formula to compute here the evolution (excitation) of a single EOL due to the imposition of a collective thinking expressed by a collective meditation variable, μ_c (on a par with the external temperature in Saha's theory). The fraction α, defined as $\alpha = N_+/N_0$, where N_+ is the number of beneficiaries in terms of evolution of any one of their EOLs (including the sub-levels in *fig*. 6.2) and N_0 is the number of persons in the mob initially ready to undergo such an exposure by a spiritual Master at a given space–time, can be written in the spirit of Saha's ionization formula as (Rumer and Ryvkin 1980),

$$\alpha(\mu_c, \sigma) = -\phi(\mu_c, \sigma) + [\phi^2(\mu_c, \sigma) + 2\phi(\mu_c, \sigma)]^{1/2} \qquad (10.4)$$

with $\phi(\mu_c, \sigma) = \left(\frac{\mu_c}{\mu_c^0}\right)^{3/2} \exp(-x_s^\sigma / \mu_c)$.

Here χ_s^σ is a measure of the (negative) efforts (in appropriate units consistent with μ_c) made by an individual in the given circumstances σ to achieve the sth level in the patomic model (in the spirit of inside–out type interactions (Kaushal 2011)) and μ^0_c is the measure of initial mindset of the human stimulant (transmitter) prevailing and derived by judging the nature of the mob (receiver).

The behaviour of the fraction of beneficiaries in the audience is shown in *fig.* 10.4 as a function of the collective meditation variable μ_c (in the units of μ_c^0) for three typical values of χ^σ_s, viz. solid, dashed and dotted curves correspond to $\chi_s^\sigma = 0.1$, 1.0 and 10.0 respectively, in the units of μ_c^0. Note:

i. In general α increases with μ_c and then slowly attains the value unity rather asymptotically irrespective of the nature of efforts.

ii. For a given μ_c, α is large for small values of χ_s^σ, implying that if μ_c is compatible with μ, i.e. if there is a matching of mindsets of the transmitter and of the receiver, then most beneficiaries are those who have never made an effort (or made negative effort) in the past but now they are conscious to learn or to gain from the given transmitter.

iii. The limiting value of α as unity is an ideal situation and the same is hardly attained by a group of disciples, but for those who have small χ_s^σ, such a limit is achieved rather quickly. From such an analysis, it is not difficult to trace the most beneficiary disciple in the class.

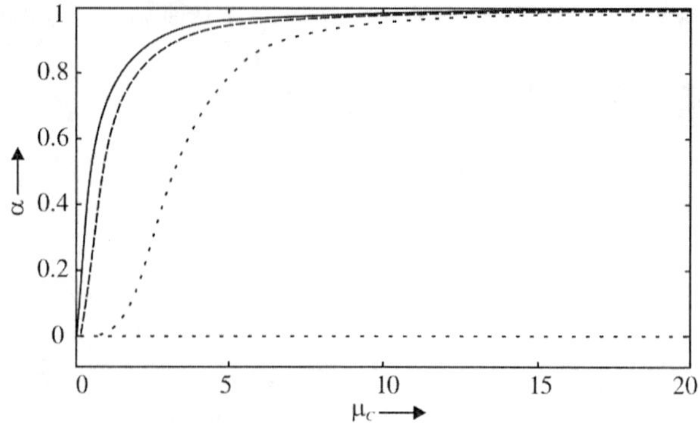

fig. 10.4: Behaviour of α as a function of (μ_c / μ_c^0) for different efforts of individual. Solid, dashed and dotted curves respectively correspond to $\chi_s^\sigma = 0.1, 1.0, 10.0$ (in units of μ_c^0).

10.5 Dressing up of b–b and b–b–b Interactions: Effect of Environment

What has been discussed above (cf. Sections 10.3 and 10.4) are the (bare) *b–b* and *b–b–b* interactions generating basically from the bare EOLs of each Being. These interactions (or, their measure in the form of associated *tanmātras*, viz. $\tau_{b_j b_k}$ or $\tau_{b_j b_k b_l}$) get dressed up in the presence of WO in general or *PMs* in particular. Actually the external environment consists of two aspects, viz. the presence of kith and kin (or a third person) and/or the *PMs*. In either case, the *b–b* and *b–b–b* interactions get modified or dressed up and may enrich the awareness of the participants in terms of the development of their individual FOUs and hence affect the corresponding interactions. Note that the presence not only of *PMs*, but also of a third Being (human or non-human), if that happens to be a relative, a pet or even a stranger, affects the *b–b* or *b–b–b* interaction accordingly. Although, the latter forms the case of three-Being interaction but as long as the third human Being remains a spectator, the *b–b* interaction will only be marginally affected. Thus, in the presence of environment all the five exchanges $\tau_{\mathcal{GG}}, \tau_{\mathcal{GM}}, \tau_{\mathcal{GC}}, \tau_{\mathcal{MM}}, \tau_{\mathcal{MC}}$ (for *b–b* case) or the twenty exchanges (for the *b–b–b* case) get dressed up. It may be mentioned that the "dressing" here means enriching the quota of sharing among, b_1, b_2 and b_3 or enriching the FOU of each of b_1, b_2 and b_3.

Dressing up of b–b interaction, in fact, is a two-step process: In the first stage, each of b_1 and b_2 gets enriched by the presence of WO through the dressed *tanmātras* $\tilde{\tau}_{ea}, \tilde{\tau}_{w}, \tilde{\tau}_{a}, \tilde{\tau}_{f}, \tilde{\tau}_{et}$, associated with the interaction of a human Being with *pañca-mahābhūtas* (Kaushal 2011) and then in the next step such enriched FOUs of b_1 and b_2 interact mutually (Kaushal 2015). Similar is the case with the dressed b–b–b interaction. It may be mentioned that the bare *tanmātras* whether they are τ_i's (with the subscripts $i = ea, w, a, f, et$, corresponding to five cosmic elements, viz. earth, water, air, fire and ether), τ_{ij}'s (with $i, j = b_1, b_2$) or τ_{ijk}'s (with $i, j, k = b_1, b_2, b_3$) type, could be more or less the same for all human Beings but the dressed ones, $\tilde{\tau}_i$'s, $\tilde{\tau}_{ij}$'s, or $\tilde{\tau}_{ijk}$'s, may differ from individual to individual, pair to pair or for trio to trio of human Beings. This is mainly because the EOLs of each of us react with the environment differently even if B and SE may appear to be the same at the gross-level but the personalities are definitely different at the levels of M, I and E. If one also accounts for such differences (which at times are very crucial) then the assumption $\tilde{\tau}_{b_1b_2} = \tilde{\tau}_{b_2b_1}$ breaks down in spite of $\tau_{b_1b_2} = \tau_{b_2b_1}$. Many real-life applications and examples to this effect have already been discussed in the earlier work.

10.6 Love and Affection as Binding Forces among Many Human-Being Systems: Relations

10.6.1 RELATIVE STRENGTH OF BINDING FORCES AND RELATIONS

In view of the fact that human Beings do have extra dimensions of emotions, decision making and memory in considerable proportions, certain b–b and b–b–b systems have achieved special status over others over a period of evolution of human race. For example, the interactions of the type husband–wife, mother–child, father–child, teacher–taught (one-to-one), two best friends, mother-in-law vs daughter-in-law, etc. in the b–b case and father–mother–child, the trio of best friends, the trio of business partners, etc. for the *b–b–b* case can be identified with certain peculiarities in a society. Some of these interactions, in fact, are responsible for assigning and maintaining the so-called human relations.

Like the gravitational force of attraction among inanimate objects, the binding force of love among animate objects too is universal. In fact, the same purest form of love (spiritual version) as the characteristic of soul, when prevails among animates (Beings), manifests mainly in three polluted versions (polluted due to the wrapping of inner EOLs with three *guṇas*), viz. divine, human and demoniacal, depending upon the nature of intention or the motive of the interacting persons. In the divine case, it is all selfless love, in the case of human category the love is mostly with selfish motives and it is mainly barbaric or the forced one in the demoniacal case. Love and affection appear as binding forces not only among humans but also among non-humans. This fact can be noticed from the behaviour patterns of the latter with reference to their kith and kin, their way of colonization, etc. As far as the degree of intensity of love is concerned, it can be adjudged by way of assigning the binary or ternary relations to persons in a family or society. This degree of intensity, in fact, is found to vary from relation to relation, pairwise or otherwise, e.g. it is assumed maximum for mother–infant relation, then somewhat decreases for ideal husband–wife case and for two ideal friends, and other relations, finally becomes constant minimum for the love towards nation or country.

Whether the love between interacting persons is divine, human or demoniacal depends on the nature of the individual. In view of Vedānta philosophy, if the nature of a person is *satoguṇī*, the divine love would predominate, if it is *rajoguṇī*, then human love would predominate and the chances of demoniacal love are maximum for *tamoguṇī* persons. As to how the degree of intensity of love or the quality of love varies from pair to pair in a society in Indian context is displayed in Table 10.2 for some representative cases and in terms of possible exchanged *tanmātras*. In fact, the intensity of

Table 10.2: Some Representative Examples of Relations Showing Varying Intensity of Love between the Participating Persons and Possible Exchanges of (Dominating) *tanmātras* until the Fine-tuned Level. (Recall that here $\mathcal{M}$ = {M, I, E}: $\mathcal{G}$ = {WO, B, SE}, τ_{ee} remains in the background in all cases)

Relation	*Description of Love*	*Possible Exchanges of Dominating Tanmātaras Including Their Dressed Versions*
1. Mother–infant	Mostly one way but perfect and divine	$\tau_{M,B}$, $\tau_{M,SE}$, $\tau_{M,M}$
2. Father–infant	Mostly one way but nearly perfect and nearly divine	$\tau_{M,SE}$, $\tau_{M,M}$, $\tau_{I,SE}$, $\tau_{I,M}$
3. Husband–wife	Both ways, could be perfect, combination of both divine and human love	$\tau_{\mathcal{G}\mathcal{G}}$, $\tau_{\mathcal{E}\mathcal{M}}$, $\tau_{\mathcal{E}\mathcal{G}}$, $\tau_{\mathcal{M}\mathcal{M}}$, $\tau_{\mathcal{M}\mathcal{G}}$, with some selective constituents of $\mathcal{M}$ and $\mathcal{G}$
4. Ideal husband–wife	Both ways, nearly perfect, mostly divine	$\tau_{\mathcal{G}\mathcal{G}}$, $\tau_{\mathcal{E}\mathcal{M}}$, $\tau_{\mathcal{E}\mathcal{G}}$, $\tau_{\mathcal{M}\mathcal{M}}$, $\tau_{\mathcal{M}\mathcal{G}}$, with all constituents of $\mathcal{M}$ and $\mathcal{G}$
5. Two friends	Far from perfect human	$\tau_{\mathcal{G}\mathcal{G}}$, $\tau_{\mathcal{M}\mathcal{G}}$, $\tau_{\mathcal{M}\mathcal{M}}$, and their dressed versions
6. Two ideal friends	Both ways, could be perfect, human love but with the possibility of approaching divine	$\tau_{\mathcal{G}\mathcal{G}}$, $\tau_{\mathcal{M}\mathcal{G}}$, $\tau_{\mathcal{M}\mathcal{M}}$, and their highly dressed versions
7. Teacher–taught	One way could be perfect, a combination of human dominating divine love	$\tau_{\mathcal{M}\mathcal{M}}$, particularly the highly dressed version of $\tau_{I,I}$

love is directly proportional to the quality of exchanged *tanmātras* between EOLs of the participating persons, i.e. it is minimum at the gross-body level and maximum at the soul (causal-body) level.

Note a few clarifications about the terminology used in this table with regard to love.

i. *Perfect love*: When all the exchanges of *fig*. 10.2, along with their fine-tuned constituents take place either one way or both ways.

ii. *Nearly perfect love*: A case when a few exchanges are missing in case (i).

iii. *Far from perfect love*: A case when most of the exchanges are missing in case (i).

It can be noticed from Table 10.2 that (i) relations get stronger and stronger if the exchanges take place between the inner and inner(-most) EOLs or between the levels of description (L) in the patomic model. (In this model, note that in whichever state of an individual, viz. B, SE, M, I, E or SO, the Being *b* resides, the same reflects in the behaviour and personality of that person). The position of these EOLs with reference to WO, defines the level of description, L, of that person. In some sense L is also the measure of level of development of his FOU and the quantum number J of rigid rotator model (cf. eq. (6.2)) also reveals this fact. In certain units, one can as well assign some numerical values to L or J, like L = 1, 2, 3, 4, 5 and 6 respectively correspond to B, SE, M, I, E and SO. Further, note that each EOL in its functional form can appear in three modes, viz. *sattva*, *rajas* and *tamas*, in accordance with three adjective degrees – superlative, comparative and positive (Kaushal 2015). Although between WO and SO, it is all continuum in the space of meditation, but the seers of Vedic science have identified some islands like B, SE, M, I and E in certain succession and the same are responsible for various human processes and intents.

10.6.2 SEARCHING A FORCE-LAW OF LOVE BETWEEN HUMAN INTERACTIONS

At the outset, it may be mentioned that if force-law of love has to be modelled, then it has to be in the domain of the trio of space, time and consciousness as it belongs to the world of psyche and not necessarily to the world of physics. Consciousness or its variants (like meditation and attention) have to appear in it. During love, it is the one's consciousness that is dragged by or springs out towards the other person, only if the other partner is a living Being. Although the intensity of love is experienced by the participating persons, at times it is also judged by a spectator.

Like the gravitation force in physics, the force of love is mostly attractive as long as it prevails in the form of spiritual or divine love, i.e. in its purest or nearly purest version; otherwise, it could as well be repulsive (hatred) for human or demoniacal categories of love, particularly for *rajoguṇī* and *tamoguṇī* persons. It is a common experience that love between isolated, distantly placed persons, besides the intensity of conscious attention, also depends on the distance, time and circumstances. Again for reasons of simplicity we ignore the dependences on time and circumstances, but consider dependence on space. In this regard, it is again a common experience that stronger is the force or the intensity of love for far away participants since certain exchanges of $\tau_{\mathcal{GG}}$ -class which, at times causes of hatred/dislike, are missing. Thus, for simplicity, we postulate power-law type dependences on distance and meditation. In other words, the force of love, $\mathcal{F}$, is directly proportional to

i. the product of levels of description of each participant in patomic model,

ii. certain powers, say p and q, of the meditation variables μ_1 and μ_2 of the two participants 1 and 2, and

iii. certain power, say r, of the physical distance d between the participants.

Symbolically, one can write $\mathcal{F}$ as:

$$\mathcal{F} = \Lambda \frac{L_1 L_2}{\mu_1{}^p \mu_2{}^q d^r}, \tag{10.5}$$

where L_1 and L_2 are the levels of description of participants 1 and 2 respectively; p, q, r are some constant numbers (each could be positive, negative or fraction) and are fixed constants for the given pair (e.g. they could be relatively large for mother–infant case in Table 10.2 and small for two normal friends); Λ is a constant of proportionality which at times show mild dependence on time t and strong dependence on circumstances σ. Circumstances basically are contributed by the attitudes A_1 and A_2 of the participants. In fact, Λ (like gravitation constant) is positive for attraction, it is positive (negative) definite when both A_1 and A_2 are positive (negative); otherwise it could be both positive and negative, depending upon the domination of the either of the attitudes.

10.7 Concluding Discussion

Attempts are made in this chapter to develop the subject of psychochemistry on a par with atomic chemistry of physical science and in accordance with the psychophysics in its new incarnation (Kaushal 2017b). The subject is developed at the most fundamental level within the framework of Vedic wisdom. A basis is sought for assigning the relations and forming the groups, subgroups and castes in a society. Instead of exchange of (coulomb charge) ions as in atomic chemistry or (colour charge) ions as in quark physics (Harari 1983), here the exchange of *tanmātras* (quanta of various human interactions) are considered. A galaxy of these *tanmātras* for two, three and many human-Being interactions are identified and analysed. This enables one to resolve the intricacies of human relations.

With a view to demonstrating the underlying methodology and the intricacies involved therein, two human-Being interactions are investigated in detail not only at crude level but also at fine and hyper fine level. A brief summary of results for three and many human-Being case is given. It is argued that like in physical theories, the three or higher human-Being interactions in a many human-Being system cannot be neglected, rather they become more important. In spite of all this, the viability of certain concepts and tools of many–body physics is demonstrated in the present case. Some important results arrived at in this chapter are as follows:

i. At crude level, there arise five quanta of exchanges (*tanmātras*), viz. $\tau_{C\mathcal{M}}, \tau_{C\mathcal{G}}, \tau_{\mathcal{M}\mathcal{M}}, \tau_{\mathcal{M}\mathcal{G}}, \tau_{\mathcal{G}\mathcal{G}}$ which mediate the interaction between conscious human Beings and are capable of covering their entire gamut of experiences and actions at least in the lowest order. For the pairwise interaction among three conscious persons, this number, however, becomes large. These numbers become even larger, if one also accounts for the circumstances in which the interaction is taking place, in addition to considering the dressed versions of $\mathcal{G}$ and $\mathcal{M}$ with consciousness.

ii. Mainly to demonstrate the underlying complexity in understanding the fundamental processes in human behaviour and experiences, only the fine-tuning of the interactions mediated through $\tau_{\mathcal{M},\mathcal{M}}$ in the *b*–*b* case is analysed and discussed (cf. *fig*. 10.3).

iii. For the simultaneous interaction among the three conscious persons, the number of quanta of possible exchanges (*tanmātras*) is computed at the crude level (i.e. using the reduced version of the patomic model) as twenty in number, and they turn out to be $\tau_{C\mathcal{M}\mathcal{M}}, \tau_{C\mathcal{M}\mathcal{G}}, \tau_{C\mathcal{G},\mathcal{M}}, \tau_{C\mathcal{G}\mathcal{G}}, \tau_{\mathcal{M},C\mathcal{M}}, \tau_{\mathcal{M},C\mathcal{G}}, \tau_{\mathcal{M},\mathcal{M}C}, \tau_{\mathcal{M},\mathcal{M}\mathcal{M}}, \tau_{M,\mathcal{M}\mathcal{G}}, \tau_{\mathcal{M},\mathcal{G}C}, \tau_{\mathcal{M}\mathcal{G}\mathcal{M}}, \tau_{\mathcal{M}\mathcal{G}\mathcal{G}}, \tau_{\mathcal{G}C\mathcal{M}}, \tau_{\mathcal{G}C\mathcal{G}}, \tau_{\mathcal{G}\mathcal{M}C}, \tau_{\mathcal{G}\mathcal{M}\mathcal{M}}, \tau_{\mathcal{G}\mathcal{M}\mathcal{G}}, \tau_{\mathcal{G}\mathcal{G}C}, \tau_{\mathcal{G}\mathcal{G}\mathcal{M}}$, and $\tau_{\mathcal{G}\mathcal{G}\mathcal{G}}$.

iv. Love and affection as binding forces between and among many human Being systems offer a particular class of interactions. They not only help in assigning the relations, but a type of hierarchy noticed among them (cf. Table 10.2) prompts us to frame a force-law of love between participating persons. This is pursued perhaps for the first time and in the spirit of other power law forces in physics.

v. On the application front, the underlying theory suggests a new basis for the socialization of persons in a society at the most fundamental level and within the framework of patomic model of human Being. In fact, in view of the core-valence picture, the formation of various groups, subgroups and further subdivisions of subgroups or those of castes, subcastes, etc. in a society can be understood on the basis of valence-sharing mechanism among the interacting persons (Kaushal 2015).

vi. Further applications of the Saha-like ionization formula for searching the most beneficiary disciple in the discourse by a spiritual Master are demonstrated.

A plausible question that immediately comes to mind is whether the psychochemistry developed here will work for non-human or for physically or mentally challenged people? The answer is yes! The only thing is that in this case one has to use the "fractured patomic model" (Kaushal 2011) and account accordingly for the permissible interactions in the given case to predict or understand the resultant behaviour. Further, the cases may differ on the basis whether the non-humans are pet or wild, or tamed or untamed, etc. In these cases, in fact, the role of the trainer through a spectator type model (Mitra 1962, 1969) also becomes important.

The psychochemistry developed here is capable of explaining many human experiences and of answering many questions of daily life in the most fundamental terms. For example, the meaning of the phrase, "two perfect people may not be perfect for each other" is clearly elaborated in Section 10.4.2 in the present scheme of study. In the same way, one can as well look for the meaning of the phrase like "I love you", or the theories of "first love", "love at first sight", and "the love for the lifetime" between two people, including the search for the theories of processes like "greeting" and "wishing". While some such attempts are already made (Kaushal 2015), further studies are desirable.

High Skill Exercises and Projects

10.1 List the points of difference in the following cases when the reactants and products in the process (10.1) are: (i) inanimate point objects, (ii) inanimate but extended objects,

(iii) animate objects like human Being, and (iv) animate objects like non-humans.

10.2 Using the reduced version of patomic model, argue that there are only five independent conscious exchanges (*tanmātras*) possible in b_1–b_2 (two human Being) interactions. In the light of this classification, analyse and discuss (i) husband-wife, and (ii) two ideal friends interactions. How do these interactions get fine-tuned for the $\tau_{\mathcal{M}\mathcal{M}}$-case, where $\mathcal{M}$ = {M, I, E}.

10.3 Write a Note on three human-Being interactions using the reduced version of patomic model. In particular, analyse the fine-tuned version of $\tau_{\mathcal{M}\mathcal{M}\mathcal{M}}$ -case, for the *b*–*b*–*b* interaction. How do these interactions play roles in (i) husband–wife–mother-in-law, and (ii) three business partner relations, in creating a conducive environment for working.

10.4 Discuss as to how the dressing of EOLs with consciousness (enlightened faculty of understanding) affects the $\tau_{\mathcal{M}\mathcal{M}}$- and $\tau_{\mathcal{M}\mathcal{M}\mathcal{M}}$-exchanges and their roles in the behaviour. Explain as to how the dressed versions of $\tilde{\tau}_i$, $\tilde{\tau}_{ij}$ and $\tilde{\tau}_{ijk}$ for self, b_1–b_2 and b_1–b_2–b_3 interactions differ from person to person, from pair to pair, from trio to trio of persons.

10.5 Discuss in detail as to how the love and affection between and among the relations strengthen the latter by way of acting as lubricating oil. Take up a project to find the constant of proportionality and the powers *p*, *q*, *r* in the force law (10.5), rather empirically. To this effect, carry out a critical analysis of the data so collected on children and adults of different age groups and in different circumstances, particularly by studying their psychology in varying conditions.

10.6 Take up a project to develop the psychochemistry of non-humans or of physically and/or mentally challenged persons on the lines followed in this chapter. [*Hint*: use fractured patomic model of human Being to this effect.]

Part 3
Behavioural Links of Psychoscience

11

Incorporating Spiritual Content in the Personality Theory of Jung

11.1 Introduction

AS FAR as the study of personality and its development in behavioural sciences is concerned, this has always remained a forefront subject of research in psychology. While Western schools of thinking are dominating these studies, the role of Vedic wisdom in these studies has either remained minimum or almost nil. But the fact is that it is this wisdom that actually justifies the causal existence of a person or guides his psyche to the spiritual zone in order to give a humanly touch to all his actions. This chapter, in fact, is devoted to drag the Western thinking into these realities of life.

In new generation, the link of psyche with spiritual zone is becoming weaker, whereas its link with sensual or body zone is becoming rather unduly stronger. In general, one can notice the tendency of a person to become "ego-centric" or "I-centric". Although some of these features in one's personality are individual-based, a general decline of values related to human coexistence in a society can easily be noticed. In such a situation, when the question of judging a person or his personality for an assignment, for a job, for a recognition of his lifetime work, for a recruitment of officers or employees in a given firm or organization, for appointing priests at religious places, etc. arises, the judges are hardly equipped with or the questionnaire concerned barely contains the questions related to search the spiritual content in person. True, judges themselves may not be of spiritual taste/inclination in direct recruitments but the questionnaire in the indirect recruitments can definitely contain such contents which a priori can be supplied by or at a later stage evaluated by experts. Such an attempt will not only generate a spiritual thinking among the employees or recruiters or in an organization in general but in the long run this will encourage masses to imbibe such thinking. Naturally, in the absence of spiritual content in the personality, human values are bound to decline since the scientific advancements are drastically affecting both the lifestyle and the psyche and that too at a fast pace.

No doubt, religious forums are constantly advocating spirituality but for a limited number of persons and more as a faith and often without a scientific basis. Students in the classroom are hardly exposed to any such spiritual teaching, particularly by experts with a scientific background. The psychology taught in the classroom is often the one that is based on Western thinking. The Western thinking, no doubt, talks of spirituality but in a casual way. In it, there is no methodology as to how to achieve it. Very often this thinking ends up at the psyche level. On the other hand, there exists a systematic development of the art and science pertaining to spirituality in the Eastern thinking, particularly in the Vedic wisdom. In fact, there is a timely need to bring this wisdom into the curriculum. The present chapter is an attempt in that direction.

Eastern wisdom, in fact, suggests (Kaushal 2015) a classification of persons in a society into three broad categories: body-conscious, mind-conscious and soul-conscious. Here, the word "mind" stands for the inner trio of essences of life, viz. mind (faculty of emotion), intellect (faculty of decision) and ego (faculty of memory). Out of them, the mind-conscious category can further be of two types: introvert (philosopher) category and extrovert (scientist) category. Note that the level of development of faculty of understanding of a spiritually evolved person is such that he, while conscious of all the three fronts of body, mind and soul, however attempts to dwell always and everywhere in the zone of soul and hence of cosmos through cosmic connections. What we also plan to discuss in this chapter is the relevance and role of individual personality in the working of an organization as a whole. Note that the latter, in the language of physics, is basically a collective version of certain individuals.

In the next section, we attempt to give a broad classification of various types of organizations with an emphasis on the involved individual processes. In Section 11.3, we briefly review the personality theories as they are taught in the classroom with reference to the theory of Jung. "Step-one" modifications in the theory of Jung, as suggested earlier (Kaushal 2016), are summarized here. With a view to searching the spiritual content in a person "step two" and "step three" modifications in this theory are discussed in Section 11.4 again in the light of Vedic wisdom. The search for spiritual content in the personality continues further in Section 11.5. Here we propose a "step four" modification in the theory of Jung in rigorous mathematical terms by way of postulating an appropriate vector space for all the known human virtues (HVs), viz. qualities, characteristics and intents. The personality in general and the spiritual or ideally integrated personality, in particular, turn out to be particular vectors in this space defined over a cosmic consciousness field. Some application aspects of these deep-rooted concepts are discussed in Section 11.6 and finally concluding remarks are made in Section 11.7.

11.2 Individual Processes and Organizational Behaviour

By definition, an organization in the man-made world is the organized body of people with a particular purpose; in particular, the purpose could aim at business, society or association. Other synonyms of organization are: company, firm, corporation, institution, group, consortium, conglomerate, agency, etc. While studying the behaviour of an organization, note that one starts with the study of individual and interpersonal processes. Thus, any account of spiritual thinking at individual level will affect the ideology of the organization as a whole. As a result, its purpose will become value-based and sustainable. On the other hand, if one looks at the processes responsible for the human behaviour and experiences at the most fundamental level (Kaushal 2011), then it can be noticed that the dynamics of EOLs of an individual and the associated interactions between and among the human Beings at different scales do contribute in shaping the nature of attitude (*saṅkalpa*) of an individual at micro level. Such individual personalities, in turn, reflect at the organization level and thereby qualify the purpose of an organization. Such details will form the part of Sections 11.3 and 11.4.

Depending upon the nature of the wisdom available and also of interactions and deliberations that take place among the people of the organized body, one can define the objective and the quality of the output of the latter. In fact, if the objectives are in the positive and constructive spirit towards the society, culture and nation, may be for a limited span of space and time, then the organization is a success; otherwise, it becomes a failure. Note that the organizations with negative and destructive objectives do exist in this man-made world, but they mostly remain hidden. Moreover, the success and failure of an organization are relative with respect to the attitude and perception of beneficiaries or common men. We shall, however, concentrate here on organizations with positive objectives towards the society and nation. At initial stages an organization starts with a group of people in which each person works with full responsibility and limited powers. This is the case of an informal organization. When the success of such an organization is noticed, then the organization is made formal by extending the domain of working of individual and by sharing the success with common mass or beneficiaries. A possible classification of formal organizations with positive objectives is displayed in *fig*. 11.1 more in a philosophical spirit.

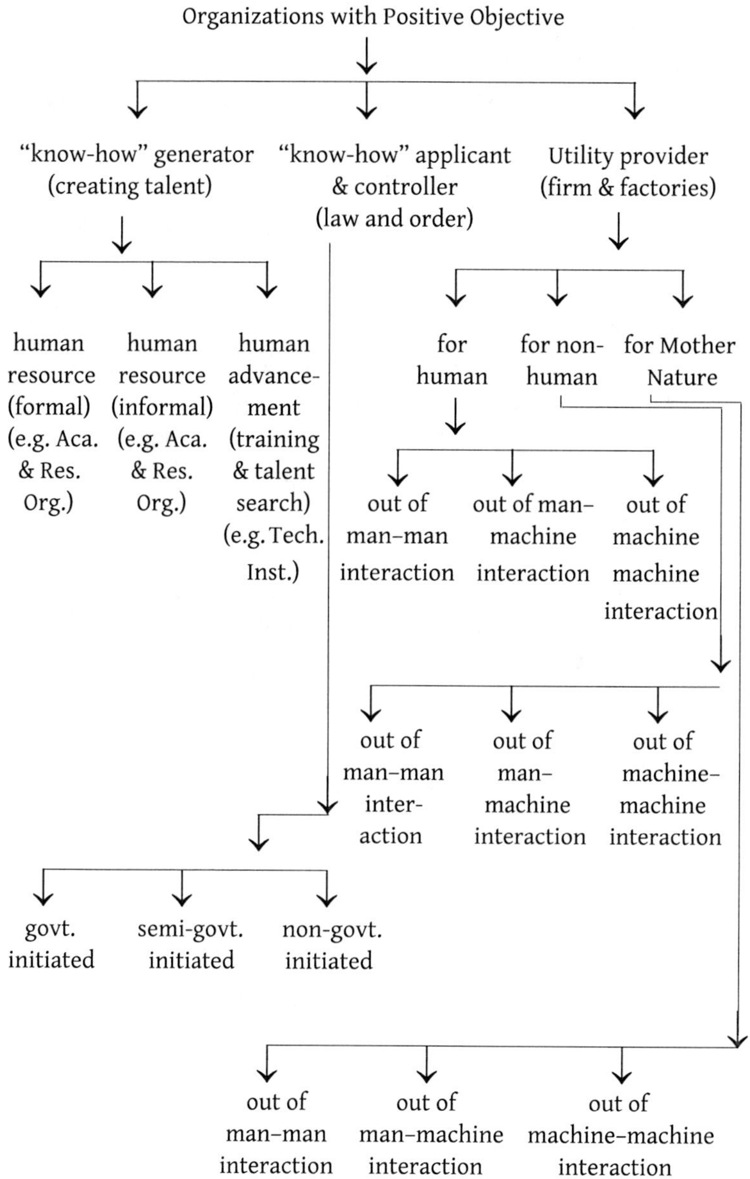

fig. 11.1: A possible classification of organizations with positive objective towards the society, nation and Nature

According to Vedic wisdom (cf. *SMBG* IV.38), the knowledge, in whatever form and type it may be, is the most supreme and purest entity to be achieved in this world. When the question arises of its types, then the knowledge of the "Self" (cf. Chapter 1) is said to be further supreme and pure. Anyway, the first stage classification of organizations is carried out in *fig.* 11.1 on this basis and the broad categories are "know-how" generating, "know-how" applying and controlling, and utility providing. Naturally, only the human Beings can generate the "know-how", not the robot or non-humans. No doubt, this generation and application of the wisdom on all fronts is ever growing and infinite (including on both positive and negative attitudes towards the maintenance of the world and cosmic orders) but these aspects of wisdom need to be curtailed to positive objectives by a body, such as the government. Moreover, the wisdom so filtered need to be used for providing facilities towards the survival of both human and non-human Beings and also to maintain the balances in mother Nature. Such an attitude towards life gives rise to the next stage of classification of organizations. With regard to the utility-provider organizations, note that the next three possible classes correspond to each of the three possible utility fronts, namely the ones related to humans, non-humans and Mother Nature. In fact, the utility can be generated out of man–man, man–machine and machine–machine interactions depending on the product and purpose of the organization. Thus, it is not difficult to put all organizations of this man-made world in this scheme of study. Further, note that the spiritual content of personality in general plays a role only in the cases where man–man or man–machine interactions are involved. Just by supervising the products of machine–machine interaction does not require any such role.

11.3 A Brief Review of Earlier Works

11.3.1 PERSONALITY THEORIES VIS-À-VIS PERSONALITY TRAITS AND DIMENSIONS

An understanding of personality traits and dimensions is important at the time of recruitments for an organization. In fact, the behaviours of employees and of would-be employees in an organization need to be judged with reference to the following five heads:

1. individual processes,
2. interpersonal and group processes,
3. organizational processes,
4. change processes, and
5. environment-based (space–time mediated) processes.

The last one becomes important when an individual thinks of changes at the global level rather than confining only to local objectives of the organization. As emphasized earlier (Kaushal 2016a) in philosophical terms, these are the individual processes and associated interactions taking place among individual's EOLs at the most fundamental level that form the basis for the rest of the four processes. Thus, the personality of an individual while reflects in these processes, however, plays an important role in the inner dynamics of an organization at the same time.

In the Western schools of thinking, the personality theories, by and large, revolve around the definition of personality itself. On the other hand, in the Eastern wisdom, such theories are discussed at a much deeper level through the phenomenon of character building and personality creation mechanism (Kaushal 2015). The latter, in fact, has suggested several intrigue parameters to improve upon the set of conventional personality traits and dimensions. Before highlighting them in the next subsection, we present here a brief survey of the Western theories (Kaushal 2016a; Singh 2010) taught in the classrooms of psychology and management courses.

In this context, following the review by Kavita Singh (2010), some recent works on personality and personality theories are worth mentioning here. According to Engler (1991), the personality of a person represents personal characteristic that leads to conscious patterns of behaviour. Hogan (1981), on the other hand, refers the personality to a relatively stable pattern of behaviours and consistent internal states that explain a person's behavioural tendencies. The personality, in this case, is considered to have both internal and external elements. The internal states here are considered to represent thought, values and genetic characteristics that one infers from the observable behaviours that help in identifying one's personality. According to Hofstede (1980), the culture also plays a role in the personality development. In fact, the cultural-religious framework shapes the personality and assigns the meaning to and the purpose of it. In this case, the behaviour patterns are compared with those of others and then it remains a case of relative studies. Such studies may be good for certain organizations but not for all on an absolute scale.

11.3.2 "BIG FIVE" PERSONALITY THEORY AND THE ASSOCIATED TRAITS AND DIMENSIONS

In order to distinguish different people's behaviour and experiences at a very fine level, the concept of personality factor is introduced in the multidimensional model of personality. Pertaining to human qualities, this personality factor consists of grouping of words, which are semantically similar (synonyms), in a minimal number of sixteen, as antonym pairs. The personality factors so thought over (Singh, 2010) are:

i. apprehensive vs self-assured,
ii. assertive vs humble,
iii. conscientious vs expedient,
iv. controlled vs causal,
v. emotionally stable vs unstable,
vi. experimental vs conservative,
vii. happy-go-lucky vs sober,
viii. imaginative vs practical,
ix. more intelligent vs less intelligent,
x. outgoing vs reserved,
xi relaxed vs tense,
xii. reserved vs warm,
xiii. shrewd vs forthright,
xiv. suspicious vs trusting,

xv. tough-minded vs sensitive, and
xvi. venture-some vs timid.

When the question comes of analysing the personalities, these sixteen factors are further reduced to five, viz.:

a. extraversion (comfort level of individual),
b. agreeableness (individual's behaviour towards others),
c. conscientiousness (extent to which one shows consistent and reliable behaviour while working in an organization),
d. emotional stability (ability to control his emotions at the time of crisis), and
e. openness to experience (ability to be open to any kind of experience that helps him to do his job).

Recall that the personality is the outer garment of the character of an individual. Further, towards the building of his character a person has to train and keep fit all the three, viz. his physical health (gross body), his mental health (micro body) and his spiritual health (causal body) as discussed earlier (Kaushal 2015). No doubt, the spiritual health of a person reflects through his mental health and the mental health reflects through his physical health in terms of patterns of his behaviour, yet when the question of objective assessment of his personality arises, then the fitness of these three types of health must be there in the questionnaire. (Note that this type of search works for a common man; otherwise, for a conscious spiritual aspirant, this sequence is reversed: It is said that the physical fitness of a person offers the ground for the mental fitness and it is only during the mental fitness the seeds of spirituality can be sown.) Truly speaking, for judging the degree of spiritual fitness any kind of questionnaire is inadequate. One should rather go for a constant watching of the way of life of the person concerned rather closely. The questionnaire can only reveal one's intentions and beliefs which at times may be far from reality concerning his spiritual health. As far as the search of spiritual health in a person is concerned, the choice of sixteen pairs of antonyms (or for that matter their reduced version in "big five" form) is insufficient and inadequate and hence requires further exploration. In fact, they are neither systematic nor unique in fundamental terms. They judge only up to mental health and that too partially according to the standards set by the Vedic wisdom. We shall return to some of these discussions later and try to have the meanings of these traits in absolute terms, i.e. independent of race, culture and environment.

11.3.3 PERSONALITY THEORY OF JUNG: FOUR STYLE MATRICES BASED ON COGNITIVE PSYCHOLOGY

The founder of analytical psychology Swiss psychologist Carl Jung proposed a theory of personality based on the cognitive style of psychology. This theory, now about 100 years old and taught in business organizations in spirit, suggests an approach to understand a person at the most fundamental level through a framework that relies on psychophysiology of a person. From the point of view of exploring still deeper role of human psychophysiology in terms of essences of life, this theory suffers on several counts, particularly in the light of Vedic wisdom (cf. next subsection). In a nutshell, the theory of Jung can be described as follows:

At the first stage, Jung divides the personalities into two major categories, viz. extrovert and introvert. Each of them, at the next stage, is further divided into four categories which are generated out of cross-combinations of some four – the so-called "basic human intents", viz. sensation, feeling, intuition and thinking, as shown in *fig*. 11.2. Again, two out of these four basic intents, sensation and intuition are considered responsible for gathering information and the remaining two – feeling and thinking – for evaluating information. Thus, the 2 × 2 matrices, so formed out of the four cross-combinations, viz. sensation thinkers (ST), intuition thinkers (IT), sensation feelers (SF) and intuitive feelers (IF), classify persons into eight categories with sharply defined boundaries. In reality, it is not so. Nature, however, offers a huge spectrum of personalities in society and organizations not only for any of these four cross-combinations but also for other combinations, may be a few, about which the Jung's theory is silent.

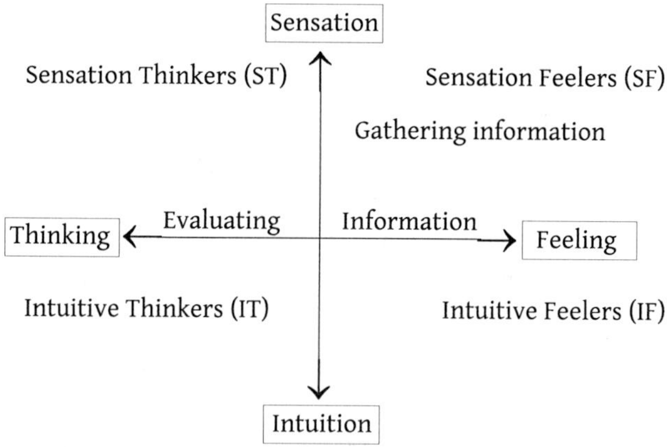

fig. 11.2: The framework of Jung for handling information. In this representation, the four quadrants depict the four cognitive styles of analysing the personality of individuals

11.3.4 A MODIFIED VERSION OF THE THEORY OF JUNG IN THE LIGHT OF VEDIC WISDOM

With a view to understanding human behaviour and experiences at the most fundamental level in terms of some psychophysiological minimas, we remind here, of patomic model of a human Being (cf. Chapter 6). This model, based on Vedic wisdom (*SMBG* III.42), basically derives its utility from the identification and arrangement of EOLs in a person in a particular form. In order to understand the dynamics of inner EOLs M, I, E and the associated interactions at a crude level, a grouped version of these EOLs into three is considered (cf. Chapter 6). This group of three, also called three existences of human Being, are: gross body ($\mathcal{G}$) as $\mathcal{G}$ = {WO, B, SE}, micro body ($\mathcal{M}$) as $\mathcal{M}$ = {M, I, E} and causal or astral body ($\mathcal{C}$) as $\mathcal{C}$ = {SO}, in accordance with the wisdom of *SMBG*. It may be emphasized that the functioning of these EOLs (or for that matter of gross and micro bodies) of a person (except those of SO and WO) towards the maintenance of the world/cosmic orders qualifies itself with three – *sattva*, *rajas* and *tamas guṇas* – in accordance with the Vedic wisdom or the three degrees, viz. best, better and good, of an adjective in grammatical sense.

Further, recall the dressing of these EOLs with consciousness emanating from SO, viz. the *pañcīkaraṇa* rule for *PM*s, the *dvi-karaṇa* rule for B and SE, and the *tri-karaṇa* rule for M, I and E of Chapter 4. In this context, it is worth quoting the recursive relations (4.8) for the nth–order dressing of M, I and E in terms of their $(n-1)^{th}$ order dressings. Thus, one can sharpen the given EOL up to desired level so as to enable it perceiving the outer world with an increasingly better understanding. This is what one actually does during meditation. An interesting aspect of these dressing rules is that one can define the level of development of one's faculty of understanding (FOU) in terms of orders of dressing of inner EOLs. Thus, a nth–order dressed version of $\mathcal{M}$ with consciousness is denoted by $\tilde{\mathcal{M}}^{(n)} = \{\tilde{M}^{(n)}, \tilde{I}^{(n)}, \tilde{E}^{(n)}\}$, where $n = n-1, n-2, ..., 3, 2, 1$ with $\tilde{M}^{(0)} = M$, $\tilde{I}^{(0)} = I$, $\tilde{E}^{(0)} = E$ as the corresponding nascent versions. For the dressing rules of $\tilde{G}^{(n)} = \{\tilde{B}^{(n)}, \tilde{SE}^{(n)}\}$, we refer to our earlier work (Kaushal 2011). In fact, FOU of an individual is a composite version of appropriately dressed inner EOLs with consciousness and the set of orders of dressing of M, I and E with consciousness defines (cf. Chapter 4) the level of development (or degree of evolution) of one's FOU. It is this quantity which not only differs from person to person but also differs for the same person with his space–time varying environment.

With such an understanding of the Vedic wisdom, some possible and plausible modifications are proposed in the personality theory of Jung and the same can be described as follows in three steps in the order of their subtlety.

11.3.5 THE "STEP-ONE" MODIFICATIONS

i. In order that a person should have basic intents like sensation, intuition, feeling and thinking, he must be alive. (Note that a dead body cannot undergo these processes.) Therefore, in addition to these basic intents, a source of consciousness must be there to make the corresponding faculties functional. It is the EOL SO in the present case that solves the purpose. In fact,

Vedic wisdom suggests that EOLs M, I and E are inanimate in themselves; like biological body, B, they become functional only in the presence of SO (cf. *SMBG* VII.4).

ii. In fact, a simple replacement of "sensation" by the biological body combined with senses, i.e. G (= B + SE), "feeling" by the faculty of emotion, i.e. the mind M, "intuition" by the faculty of memory, i.e. the ego E and "thinking" by the faculty of decision, i.e. the intellect I, as shown in *fig*. 11.3, in the theory of Jung (cf. *fig*. 11.2) will give a new and perhaps further deeper foundation to this theory.

iii. Since a person looking for an employment has to be conscious enough of his capabilities, it is worthwhile to consider the dressed versions of his EOLs G, M, I and E with consciousness up to certain orders, say, respectively up to *s*, *m*, *r* and *n* orders (cf. *fig*. 11.3).

iv. Jung calls "thinking" and "feeling" as the opposite ways of evaluating information. But it is really not so; they are rather

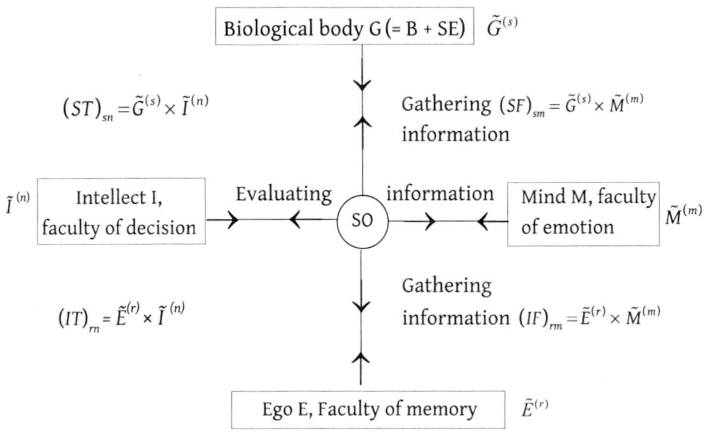

fig. 11.3: Possible modifications to the personality theory of Jung in the light of patomic model of human Being. The matrix formation, which helps in distinguishing the personalities, can clearly be seen in this picture in all the four quadrants complementary to each other. In fact, Nature has made the corresponding faculties to work in an amazing harmony at the subtle level and the same goes unnoticed for a common man. Further, note that this kind of harmony is possible only in the presence of SO. Similar is the case with the pair "sensation" and "intuition" while gathering information.

v. As SO plays a central role in the entire working, not only of EOLs but also of the human Being as a whole, it is worthwhile to put SO in the centre in this schematic picture. Moreover, the effect of the presence of SO in the present case appears through the proposed dressing rules for EOLs G, M, I and E with consciousness.

These are some "step one" modifications in the theory of Jung at crude level. In the next section, we continue with the fine-tuning of these suggestions and discuss "step two" and "step three" modifications with a view to having a deep insight into the human personality.

11.4 "Step Two" and "Step-Three" Modifications in the Theory of Jung

11.4.1 THE "STEP-TWO" MODIFICATIONS

In "step one" modifications, the four basic intents of Jung, viz. sensation, feeling, intuition and thinking respectively, are replaced by the EOLs G(= B + SE), M, E and I with a central place of SO. As far as the formation of four style matrices of Jung – SF, IF, IT and ST – for each of the introvert and extrovert category of persons is concerned, it remains intact except for the fact that now a deeper philosophical meaning is assigned to each of the intent. The role of SO in the functioning of intents is emphasized as an additional advantage like a coordinator and as a foremost need. In fact, it is the induction of SO in the scheme that will help in defining and invoking the spiritual content in a personality, otherwise Jung's basic intents are sufficient to accommodate ethical and moral aspects in a personality. Note that this is the picture with nascent

EOLs. Once we bring in the role of consciousness (an attribute of the EOL, SO) by considering the dressed (or, charged) versions of EOLs with consciousness, this will open new vistas in the theory of personality development.

In "step"-two modifications in the theory of Jung, we in fact replace EOLs G, M, E and I by their dressed versions, $\tilde{G}^{(s)}$, $\tilde{M}^{(m)}$, $\tilde{E}^{(r)}$ and $\tilde{I}^{(n)}$, respectively. Such an entry in the scheme will pave the way to form the four style matrices in the form

$$(SF)_{sm} = \tilde{G}^{(s)} \times \tilde{M}^{(m)}; \quad (IF)_{rm} = \tilde{E}^{(r)} \times \tilde{M}^{(m)};$$
$$(IT)_{nr} = \tilde{I}^{(n)} \times \tilde{E}^{(r)}; \quad (ST)_{sn} = \tilde{G}^{(s)} \times \tilde{I}^{(n)}. \tag{11.1}$$

With regard to these constructs, the following remarks are in order:

i. Each of the four style matrices of Jung now generalized to have infinitely many submatrices or matrix elements but in different space and that too in real mathematical spirit and not just in symbolic sense. This is mainly because the superscripts s, m, r and n are integers (which, in fact, characterize the order of dressing). Here, $s = 0, 1, 2$ and each of m, r and n separately varies from 0 to ∞ (cf. Kaushal 2011, chapter 8).

ii. Note that when each superscripts s, m, r, n has zero value, i.e. when EOLs are in their nascent version, then this case corresponds to the theory of Jung.

iii. Since each subscripts m, r, n now varies from 0 to ∞ (Kaushal 2015), there is a possibility to accommodate infinitely many personalities in this scheme of study (and not just eight as per theory of Jung) starting from a common man to a highly evolved spiritual personality.

iv. Note that both EOLs B and SE belong to the gross body domain. As argued earlier (Kaushal 2011) their second-order dressing according to *dvi-karaṇa* rule is sufficient enough to make them fully functional in the physical world and this suggests $s = 0, 1, 2$.

v. In view of remark (iv), note that most of the matrix elements in (11.1) contribute to a rectangular matrix, particularly for the case of (SF) and (ST) matrices.

vi. Since the "cause and effect principle" of physics also works in certain domains of human behaviour (Kaushal 2011, 2015) at least up to the level E of the patomic model, then it can be noticed that the four style matrices of Jung are non-commutative and also the submatrices introduced in the present work are asymmetric. For example, SF ≠ FS, i.e. a sensation feeler may not behave in the same way as feeling sensitized and $\tilde{G}^{(s)} \times \tilde{M}^{(m)} \neq \tilde{M}^{(m)} \times \tilde{G}^{(s)}$. These features are the attributes of the nature of consciousness. In fact, the conscious-interactions are believed to be of non-local nature in both space and time.

11.4.2 THE "STEP-THREE" MODIFICATIONS

Under the "step three" modifications in the theory of Jung, we discuss as to how the Vedic wisdom can help in identifying the spiritual content in the personality. To this effect, we have already investigated (Kaushal 2011, 2015) the interactions that take place inside the human Being prior to and after the performance of a task. In fact, the effect of these interactions is expected to appear through the higher orders of dressing of the inner EOLs. As shown in *fig.* 11.4, rather schematically, these interactions are the outcomes of dynamics of inner EOLs. Attempts are made in this figure to demonstrate the roles of all the three processes, viz. concentration (defined for the gross body ($\mathcal{G}$) domain), meditation (defined for the micro body ($\mathcal{M}$) domain) and realization (defined for the causal body ($\mathcal{C}$) domain). These processes, in fact, are the manifestations of the same focused and directed consciousness or attention (represented in this figure by the same meditation variable μ) respectively in the three domains of $\mathcal{G}$, $\mathcal{M}$ and $\mathcal{C}$. As to how the spiritual attitude takes over the materialistic attitude with the increase of meditation variable μ is shown in this figure. Further,

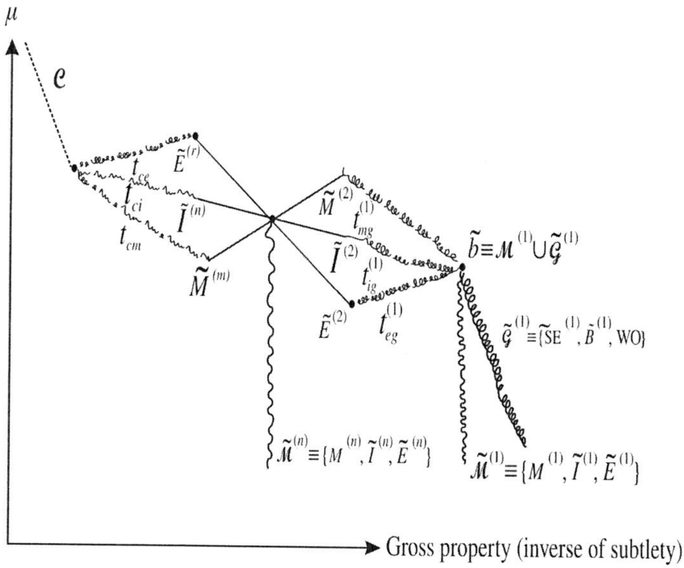

fig. 11.4: Interactions inside the human Being expressed through different sets of "quanta of interactions" or *tanmātras* (Kaushal 2011) between $\mathcal{C}$ and $\mathcal{M}$, and between $\mathcal{M}$ and $\mathcal{G}$ domains

note that the increasing value of μ is a measure of increased orders of dressing of inner EOLs but in the discrete sense (Kaushal 2018). Further, the gross features of material world are on increase as the meditation (or, the self-observation) decreases and at a certain μ it becomes constant with reference to a common man.

As it can be seen from *fig.* 11.4, the trio of inner EOLs when interacts with the gross body or the outer EOLs and the physical world (through *tanmātras* or quanta of interaction), their dressing with consciousness enriches them about the knowledge of latter. On the other hand, when the same trio of inner EOLs is dressed beyond certain order, it withdraws the interaction from the outer world and at the same time initiates the interactions with the astral or causal body through another but subtler set of *tanmātras*. This enriches the trio not only about the innermost existence (SO) and its universality but also about its connections with the cosmos. While such a realization of cosmic connections by an individual, if achieved, supports his existence at the causal body level, it is also an indicator of spiritual content in his personality. In fact, the start of realization of cosmic connections by the finite Self (whatever may be the source of stimuli out of five cosmic elements) with the Cosmic Self (if the same is believed) is the beginning of spiritual health. Note that the manifest gross body existence cannot be dressed infinitely with the consciousness as it is bound by the space–time boundaries, whereas, the same is possible with the micro body existence. It has been argued and shown in Chapter 4 that infinitely dressed any of the inner EOLs is as good as the realization of the Cosmic Self (cf. Section 4.4). Thus, the spirituality can be inculcated through any one, two or all the three ways, viz. action (*karma-yoga*), devotion (*bhakti-yoga*) and knowledge (*jñāna-yoga*).

It may be mentioned that the above three discussed existences, i.e. causal, micro and gross, of a person basically are the God-gifted ones and their evolution with consciousness in an individual forms the part of his character building. In fact, this defines the "vertical" component of his personality. As discussed earlier (see Appendix A of Kaushal 2015), in addition to these three, there are two more existences of a person, viz. societal ($\mathcal{S}$) and natural ($\mathcal{N}$) originating from the facts that (i) the birth of a person is bound to take place in a particular society or culture, and (ii) in certain natural climate and environment.

In some sense, they are the elaborations of the EOL, worldly objects WO, of the patomic model. They do contribute to his personality development and thereby define the so-called "horizontal" component of his personality. Thus, in all, we have five parameters (or dimensions) through which the personality of a person can be judged at the crude or ground level. Also note that during his dwelling in any of the existences, a person can perform actions which can come again in three flavours, viz. *sattva* (*s*), *rajas* (*r*) and *tamas* (*t*). Out of them, only the *sāttvika* actions in the zones of all five existences are supposed to contribute maximum to spiritual content in a personality, viz. $\mathcal{C}_s$, $\mathcal{M}_s$, $\mathcal{G}_s$, S_s, $\mathcal{N}_s$. However in the zone of $\mathcal{C}_s$ there is no scope of any kind of duality and causal effects. Here, the concept of "one in all and all in one" prevails. Therefore, the actions corresponding only to four $\mathcal{M}_s$, $\mathcal{G}_s$, S_s, and $\mathcal{N}_s$ are justified in shaping the spiritual attitude. Moreover, the role of consciousness, as an attribute of SO (or $\mathcal{C}$) appears through the dressing of EOLs and environment. (In the present context by dressing with reference to society and environment means as to how one perceives and reacts with them in the presence of his consciousness.) While it is not difficult to carry out the actual computation of the spiritual attitude, in the next section, we elaborate further on the identification of this built-in (in whatever proportion it may be) basic intent in a person.

11.5 Spiritual Content and an Ideally Integrated Personality

Recall that Jung started with two major classes of personality at the first stage: viz. introvert and extrovert categories. It would be rather more appropriate to replace them here respectively by personalities with spiritual attitude and material attitude. But note that these are the two extremes like theist and atheist or believer and non-believer categories of persons in a society. As a matter of fact, most of us are the combinations of the two – a necessity to become a practical person. If one stretches the analogy of these concepts further, then it is not difficult to identify spiritual, material and their combination attitudes in a person respectively with *satoguṇī*, *tamoguṇī* and *rajoguṇī* personalities of Vedic wisdom in accordance with the three working modes (*guṇas*) of Nature (*Prakr̥ti*). Once we have such identification, then it becomes easy to understand and analyse the above theory of personality in a mathematical spirit.

While the societal and natural existences of a person are the extensions of WO of the patomic model, they, respectively, in turn, offer the ground for the man-made world and the God-made world for a person to live in. Further, note that like the trio in $\mathcal{M}$ (i.e. M, I and E) and the duo in $\mathcal{G}$ (i.e. B and SE), both S and $\mathcal{N}$ (or their constituents, if any, not discussed so far) belong to the insentient Nature according to Vedic wisdom (cf. *SMBG* VII.4). Like any other EOL (except SO), they become functional only in the presence of SO of an individual and also wrapped with three modes (*guṇas*) of Nature.

11.5.1 PERSONALITY AS A VECTOR IN THE VECTOR SPACE SPANNED BY THREE GUṆAS IN NATURE

With a view to have a mathematical perspective of the above concepts, we consider the personality as a vector ($\vec{P}$) in three-dimensional space spanned by the three *guṇas* of Vedic wisdom: *sattva* (*s*), *rajas* (*r*) and *tamas* (*t*), viz.

$$\vec{P} = P_s \hat{s} + P_r \hat{r} + P_t \hat{t}, \tag{11.2}$$

where $\hat{s}, \hat{r}$ and $\hat{t}$ are the unit vectors along the three dimensions. Truly speaking, like $\vec{P} = (P_s, P_r, P_t)$, the existences, $\mathcal{M}$, $\mathcal{G}$, S and $\mathcal{N}$ can also be considered as vectors in the same space, with corresponding components as $\mathcal{M} = (\mathcal{M}_s, \mathcal{M}_r, \mathcal{M}_t)$, $\mathcal{G} = (\mathcal{G}_s, \mathcal{G}_r, \mathcal{G}_t)$, $S = (S_s, S_r, S_t)$ and $\mathcal{N} = (\mathcal{N}_s, \mathcal{N}_r, \mathcal{N}_t)$. While the personality P is a complicated function of existences $\mathcal{M}$, $\mathcal{G}$, S and $\mathcal{N}$, viz. $P = f(\mathcal{M}, \mathcal{G}, S, \mathcal{N})$, its vector version $\vec{P}$, in some sense, can be considered as (a) a linear combination of the vectors $\vec{\mathcal{M}}$, $\vec{\mathcal{G}}$, $\vec{S}$ and $\vec{\mathcal{N}}$ mainly for simplicity, or (b) P as a superset expressed as the union of dressed versions of subsets $\mathcal{M}$, $\mathcal{G}$, S and $\mathcal{N}$ with appropriate weightage to each of them, viz. $P \equiv \tilde{\mathcal{M}} \cup \tilde{\mathcal{G}} \cup \tilde{S} \cup \tilde{\mathcal{N}}$. However, recall that personality is also a function of space and time and this type of explicit dependence should reflect in any representation of $\vec{P}$. In accordance with the choice (a), we write $\vec{P}$ as

$$\vec{P} = b\vec{\mathcal{M}} + c\vec{\mathcal{G}} + d\vec{S} + f\vec{\mathcal{N}} \tag{11.3}$$

where the coefficients b, c, d and f in general are the functions of space (q) and time (t), and they determine the weightage of the corresponding existence in the construction of $\vec{P}$. Note that the component P_s *of* P – a measure of spiritual attitude — can be expressed as

$$P_s = b\,\mathcal{M}_s + c\mathcal{G}_s + \mathrm{d}\mathcal{S}_s + \mathrm{f}\mathcal{N}_s \tag{11.4}$$

along with similar expressions for P_r and P_t. One can as well write (11.3) as:

$$\vec{P} = \vec{P}_I + \vec{P}_{II}\,, \tag{11.5}$$

where $\vec{P}_I = b\vec{\mathcal{M}} + c\vec{\mathcal{G}}$ and $\vec{P}_{II} = d\vec{S} + f\vec{\mathcal{N}}$ are the two-dimensional vectors but in the space of existences. Note that it is in the behavioural or verbal sense in real life that we have called (see Appendix A of Kaushal 2015) $P_\perp$ and $P_{//}$ as the vertical and horizontal parts of personality; otherwise, they appropriately help in grading a personality (Kaushal 2016a).

11.5.2 THE QUESTION OF ASSIGNING WEIGHTAGE TO COEFFICIENT FUNCTIONS b, c, d, AND f IN (11.3)

As to how much weightage be given to a particular existence in (11.3) towards an ideal and integrated personality *P* mainly depends on two factors

1. as which of the existence (or its constituents) of the Being *b* enables him to visualize maximum and the best cosmic connections, and
2. as in which of the existences the Being *b* performs better actions towards the maintenance of the world and cosmic orders, of course, through its constituents.

Next, we identify the functional constituents of $\mathcal{M}$, $\mathcal{G}$, $\mathcal{S}$ and $\mathcal{N}$ for this purpose in a crude sense as follows:.

Clearly, for $\mathcal{M}$ these constituents are M, I and E, i.e. this number is 3 and each comes in three modes; for G, these are B and SE and the latter is of two categories – motor organs responsible for physical action (SEA) number is 5 and five senses of knowledge (SEK) whose actions come in three modes. Thus, the total of functional domains due to $\mathcal{M}$ and $\mathcal{G}$ respectively are $3 \times 3 = 9$ and $1 + 5 + (5 \times 3) = 21$. To identify the functional domain of S, note that for S we have family, society, nation and the world as constituents and each can again come in three modes and this makes $4 \times 3 = 12$ functional domains. Similarly, for $\mathcal{N}$, the first division we have as animate and inanimate; for animate we have two categories as – living creations and plant kingdom and for inanimate we have physical and chemically composite matter. Also, for $\mathcal{N}$ each constituent comes in three modes from the point of view of a conscious observer and this makes the total number of functional domains of S and $\mathcal{N}$ as $(4 \times 3) + (4 \times 3) = 24$. Thus, the total number of possible functional domains due to $\mathcal{M}$, $\mathcal{G}$, S and $\mathcal{N}$ are $9 + 21 + 12 + 12 = 54$. Ideally speaking, this makes the normalizing standard for coefficient functions b, c, d and f respectively as (9/54), (21/54), (12/54), (12/54).

The nature of personality of a person basically is the judgement of an external observer who again will appear in either of the three modes: *satoguṇī*, *rajoguṇī* and *tamoguṇī*. Further, note that these are the senses of knowledge that play a dominant role in creating a personality, mainly because they offer a readily available instrument to act as windows for interaction with the outer world (Kaushal 2011) and thus deserve more weightage in the computation of P. In this way, for judging the individual character (like *satoguṇī*, *rajoguṇī* or *tamoguṇī*) the appropriate fractions respectively for b, c, d and f turn out to be (3/54), (7/54), (4/54), (4/54). Ideally speaking, the questionnaire for the recruitment (Cosentino 2007) should consist of questions of these four categories in the same proportion, viz. 9:21:12:12 or 3:7:4:4, of course, after giving certain leverage to space–time dependence as well.

11.5.3 PERSONALITY AS A VECTOR IN THE VECTOR SPACE OVER A FIELD OF CONSCIOUSNESS

In the language of mathematics, a linear vector space $\mathcal{V}$ over a scalar field $\mathcal{F}$ is the set of elements that satisfy the following two postulates: (i) addition operation is closed, and (ii) the scalar multiplication is defined. This means that, if elements A and B

belong to $\mathcal{V}$, then the element $C = \alpha A + \beta B$, where α and β are the elements of the scalar field $\mathcal{F}$, also belongs to $\mathcal{V}$. Here, the field $\mathcal{F}$ is a set of elements which satisfy nine postulates, namely, $\mathcal{F}$ is a group under both addition and multiplication operations (four postulates associated with each operation) and the distributive property (one, i.e. the ninth postulate). For the postulates of a group, we refer to the literature (Jain 2007).

Note that the cosmic consciousness field Φ_{cc} is such a desired field (cf. Chapter 4) under the assumption that its elements do fulfil all possible known operations in the cosmos (in fact, it is possible in the light of the Vedic wisdom, particularly, the opening verse of the *Īśāvāsya Upaniṣad*: *auṁ pūrṇamadaḥ pūrṇamidaṁ pūrṇāt pūrṇamudacyate*। *pūrṇasya pūrṇamādāya pūrṇamevāvaśiṣyate*।। It means: "That is whole, this is also whole, the whole or fullness originates again from the whole, if one takes away the whole out of the whole only the whole remains") whatsoever, then what to say of the nine mathematical postulates of a mathematical field $\mathcal{F}$. Thus, the scalars α, β, ... belong to Φ_{cc} and they correspond to a certain stage of dressing of vectors of $\mathcal{V}$ with consciousness. Some of them, of course, become the coefficient functions b, c, d and f of (11.3) which also have an implicit dependence on space and time.

In the present context, the elements of $\mathcal{V}$ not only are the existences $\mathcal{M}$, $\mathcal{G}$, S and $\mathcal{N}$ but also are their constituents like M, I, E, B and SE, since the latter also come in three modes of Nature as per *SMBG*. Not only this, $\mathcal{M}$, $\mathcal{G}$, S and $\mathcal{N}$ separately and also in combination with some other vectors, do form the subspaces in $\mathcal{V}$. As a matter of fact *SMBG* suggests several other vectors of $\mathcal{V}$ (see Section 5.3.3, and chapters XVII and XVIII of *SMBG*) which directly or indirectly are linked with these four existences and appear as linear combinations of some other vectors of this vector space. Some such examples of vectors discussed in *SMBG* are

(a) intellect itself (*buddhi*),
(b) faith (*śraddhā*),
(c) sacrifice (*yajña*),

(d) charity (*dāna*) and gift,
(e) renunciation (*tyāga*),
(f) penance (*tapa*),
(g) perseverance (*dhṛti*),
(h) knowledge,
(i) action,
(j) doer of action,
(k) joy (*sukha*),
(l) food, etc.

Note that some of them are as fundamental as the EOLs of the patomic model; whereas, others are composites of these EOLs in varying proportions. However, all of these vectors in the space of three *guṇas* as listed in *SMBG* can be put under the four heads of the existences in one way or the other (cf. Appendix D, Table D.1). As a matter of fact, the trios of *SMBG* in conjunction with the four existences can produce a huge spectrum of personalities. This spectrum becomes even bigger when the designated dressing rules for EOLs are also incorporated. Following Appendix D, one can identify some such vectors discussed in the context of personality theories in recent times. In fact, such sets of human virtues (HVs), listed some of them in Table D.1 of Appendix D, are of particular interest when one is looking for an extended list of personality traits.

11.5.4 "EMOTIONAL INTELLIGENCE" AND "SENSATIONAL CONSCIENCE" IN THE PRESENT SCHEME OF STUDY: "STEP FOUR" MODIFICATIONS IN THE THEORY OF JUNG

Emotional skills or skilful emotions are vital for success. While talking of emotional quotient in personality, it is judged on the basis of emotional intelligence. According to Goleman (1995), "emotional intelligence is the capacity for recognizing our own feelings and those of others for motivating ourselves and for managing emotions well in ourselves and in our relationships". In today's work environment, when people hire and fire people, people rule and control people, people leave people, an understanding of this trait of personality is necessary.

Recall that in the theory of Jung, the four style matrices – (ST), (IT), (IF) and (SF) – (cf. *fig.* 11.2) basically correspond to four quadrants in a plane in this figure which are later modified and generalized as in *fig.* 11.3 in the light of Vedic wisdom. As emphasized earlier, the thinking and feeling here are no more the opposite ways of evaluating information and similarly the sensation and intuition are not the opposite ways of gathering information. Note that each of these pairs of EOLs leads to four planar quadrants and hence to four matrices. In fact, there arises one more pair of matrices as an attribute of space formed out of diametrically opposite placed EOLs which are internally connected through the same SO. As a result, we obtain two additional style-matrices, viz. (TF) corresponding to "emotional intelligence" and (IS) corresponding to "sensational conscience" for which Jung had no account in his theory. In view of Vedic wisdom, the modified and generalized version of these new matrices can be written as before as

$$(TF)_{mn} = \tilde{M}^{(m)} \times \tilde{I}^{(n)}\ ; \quad (IS)_{rs} = \tilde{E}^{(r)} \times \tilde{G}^{(s)}. \tag{11.6}$$

Thus, in addition to the emotional intelligence, an extensively discussed concept in recent times in the theory of personality, one should also account for another interesting trait, viz. "sensational conscience".

To understand the "sensational conscience" trait in a personality, consider a person who is body conscious and is also under the control of sense objects, but devoid either of feeling and decision-making capacities or only has their minimum. Naturally, such a person when sensitized by external stimuli or assigned the job of judging someone will behave differently from a normal case. In this way, the quotient assigned with sensational conscience can be defined as "the capacity of maintaining our own body fitness in physical terms with a strong self-sense and also looking at others with the same attitude". In fact, one can as well define the components and categories of this trait in the same ways as for emotional intelligence at work, depending upon the type of memories (e.g. short or long term, etc.) the person carries and the type of specialty he attains in body actions and performances. An example of this trait that immediately comes to one's mind is that of the behaviour of a wrestler as an individual or with reference to his interactions with others. For another example, one can consider the behaviour of lower-cadre personals in a defence organization for analysis.

11.6 Application Aspects

While the theory of personality, discussed in the preceding sections, is of interest as an academic pursuit in psychology and behavioural sciences, it does have applications in different contexts, particularly in the areas where human component plays a dominant role either directly (as in social studies) or indirectly (as in economic sciences and management courses). It may be mentioned that according to Vedic thinking a human Being is considered as a perfect creation of God and for whom the patomic model was designed and used here in practical terms; otherwise, for the behaviour of non-human Beings, a fractured patomic model proposed earlier (Kaushal 2011) is expected to work in the same spirit. In other words, the psychological aspects discussed here are equally applicable to understand the behaviour of non-human Beings and their society but only after appropriate modifications at different stages. As far as the search of spiritual content in a personality is concerned, in author's opinion it is limited to human race only. Not only this, the use of fractured patomic model will eliminate a considerable part of psychology content in the non-human case depending on the species. Further, when studying the psychology and behaviour of physically and mentally disabled persons, similar modifications in the theory will be required at different stages. In what follows, we briefly discuss some applications relevant to running organizations, academic and financial institutions, societies, etc. In fact, in this case, it is desirable to fix the efficiency, working capacity and dedication to the task with an individual employee and also to frame guidelines for working through a questionnaire prepared in advance, prior to the recruitment process. In the light of present studies note that the questionnaire can also include inquiries about spiritual content in the personality in addition to queries about physical wellness and mental health.

11.6.1 ORGANIZATIONAL BEHAVIOUR: SOME GENERAL REMARKS

Present studies basically offer a guide to personality creation mechanism (Kaushal 2015) for an individual. As mentioned before, in an organization, an individual is supposed to play the role mainly in four but interconnected stages, viz. as an individual, through interpersonal and group interactions and through the interaction of the organization with the world outside. Once the individual attains the best of personality, the same sooner or later will reflect through the remaining three stages and this, in turn, becomes an asset for the organization and its progress. To this effect, the interaction mechanism in terms of EOLs is discussed earlier (Kaushal 2015) at the most fundamental level by way of using analogies from physical theories for many-body interactions.

While the fundamental processes more or less remain the same for different categories of organizations (cf. *fig.* 11.1), these are the objectives, motivation and utility (OMU) that decide the role of a specific EOL in fulfilling the purpose of an organization. For example, if the OMU focuses around the intellectual evolution of individuals, then this normally corresponds to educational institutions, if it moves around the faith and emotions, then this normally corresponds to religious organizations, if it moves around utility like forming the policies for money transaction and circulation, etc. then it corresponds to banking and financial institutions. These are some cases where micro-body domain of a person plays a role. Next category of organizations corresponds to the gross-body domain of working of a person where OMU are fixed in relation to body, senses and sense-objects. This will lead to health- and physique-related organizations and societies. In this way, OMU will also define the existence of various other organizations and institutions. In fact, in present times, these organizations, corresponding to micro and gross existences, are growing like anything for more than one reason. First, to make the life luxurious; and second, to cure the diseases (like physical and mental) caused by such a life. To grow and impart the wisdom related to these organizations, the number of teachers, taught and practitioners is also increasing all over the world.

Note that the best of personality reflects through its spiritual content. No doubt, the ever-growing zones of micro and gross existences of a person are necessary for his meaningful survival but not sufficient from the point of view of attaining the joy and eternal peace of mind. Here comes the role of spirituality – a cognizance of causal existence. But, unfortunately, the teacher, taught and practitioners for this case are rare in true sense and hence the number of organizations of this category is rare. Once spiritual person works through these organizations, the latter will have a different standing in the society. If we find or inculcate the spiritual content in a person, so what! Then what next? The question arises as to how it will benefit the society. In what follows, we shall try to find an answer to this question.

11.6.2 SOCIETY VS ORGANIZATION

In the Vedic way of life, note that a society is personified as having head, chest, stomach and lower organs, and accordingly it is divided into four but interdependent classes, like that of intellectuals, security and defence, utility provider and service provider personnels. In some sense, all organizations can also be classified in the same spirit into four categories pertaining to wellness and personality development (this includes educational institutions and religious organizations), security and defence, utility provider (this includes farming and finance) and service provider (this includes factories and industrial organizations).

While basic processes that run the organization remain the same for all categories, it is the OMU that will differentiate these different categories. Further, note that the wellness and personality development category of organizations involve the human component directly and immediately whereas other categories involve human component in two stages, viz. at the micro level (policymaking stage) and at macro level (implementation or facility providing stage). It is not difficult to visualize that the presence or inculcation of spiritual values in a personality will definitely affect both OMU and the working of an organization and hence on its purpose. In fact, whatever may be the type of organization, an individual and his personality always play a dominant role via individual processes. Recall that a society is a collective version of individuals and hence any characteristic change at the level of individual essentially affects the purpose of an organization. Such studies based on the dynamics of inner EOLs will clearly support a connection between the societal existence *S* of an individual (cf. Section 11.4.2) and the society as a whole and also justify the concept of personification of a society.

11.6.3 UTILITY PROVIDER AND OTHER ORGANIZATIONS

Food, money and assets are interconvertible, and their logical and equitable distribution among the people in a society makes the latter sustainable, harmonious and peaceful. The organizations related to such needs of people do involve human component but in two stages. At the first stage, those who make policies to this effect (micro version) and second those on whom these policies are implemented (macro version). At both stages, the human personality plays a dominant role with regard to the success of the organization concerned. In particular, the role of psyche of common mass has become very important and sensitive in recent times in the studies pertaining to share market, banking and finances including some social phenomena. In fact, the use of physical theories in these studies has made the subject of economics (Doyane Farmer et al.

2005) more viable from the point of view of practical applications. We shall return to some of these details in the next chapter.

11.7 Concluding Discussion

With a view to highlighting the depth and richness of Vedic wisdom several plausible modifications in the personality theory of Jung are suggested in this chapter. These modifications, while suggesting the parameters necessary to judge the emotional and intelligence quotients in a personality, also pave the way to find the spiritual content in a person. It is emphasized that all five existences of human Being, viz. causal, micro, gross, societal and natural, do contribute to the "personality creation mechanism" (Kaushal 2015) and thus define a complete or an ideally integrated personality. It is argued that the first three existences are responsible for the character-building aspect and contribute mainly to the so-called "vertical component" of the personality, whereas, the last two existences are mainly responsible for the personality development in a horizontal manner.

A variety of ways of classifying the personalities are revisited here within the framework of Vedic wisdom. In particular, the proposed psychophysiological model for the human Being (Kaushal 1990, 1994, 2000, 2011), i.e. the patomic model, in conjunction with three Nature-born *guṇas*, viz. *sattva*, *rajas* and *tamas*, suggests a variety of ways for this purpose. In fact, the dressing of inner EOLs with consciousness in different orders is found to provide a method for fine and hyper fine-tuning of the personalities and this enables one to see the different personalities as different at subtle level.

It may be mentioned that the existing personality of a person is only one aspect of study as far as the entire gamut of human behaviour and experiences (Kaushal 2011) is concerned; otherwise the permutations and combinations of various human qualities and characteristics give rise to different personalities of the same person may be at the same or different space–time points. To this effect, an interesting mathematical concept of linear vector space for the personality creation is introduced here. This mathematical entity is basically a set of human qualities and characteristics largely of innate nature that are considered as vectors in the three-dimensional space of (three) *guṇas*. Such qualities are the elements of the vector space and satisfy the closure property; meaning thereby that 2, 3, 4, ... *N* elements of this set give rise to different partitions and their corresponding combination or superposition offers a resultant which again is an element of the same set (vector space) in view of the closure property. The personality in general while is an element of this set, an ideally integrated (or spiritually elevated) personality is also an element of this set, but it is a result of superposition of some specific qualities and characteristics or for that matter of certain components of existences. Such explanations, in some sense, support the self-consistency of the "cause and effect" cycle inherent in the kārmic theory of *SMBG* (cf. *SMBG* III.28, viz.*guṇā guṇeṣu vartantu* ..., i.e. *guṇas* move in the *guṇas*). Further studies in this direction are desirable.

This chapter suggests a roadmap to develop the so-called "winning personality" which requires a person to be physically fit, mentally alert, intellectually sharp and spiritually elevated. With regard to the practical aspect of the theory developed here, note that the search for spiritual content in a person requires the preparation of a meaningful questionnaire in which an appropriate weightage be given to questions pertaining to different existences. Attempts are made here to find such weight factors. In summary, as far as the search of spiritual content in a person is concerned, note that such studies are only necessary but not sufficient. For the sufficiency, however, a continued watch on the behaviour patterns of the person concerned for a certain period of time and in varying environment is necessary.

High Skill Exercises and Projects

11.1 "Spiritual thinking and the associated (*satoguṇī*) human values, when incorporated in individual processes, that makes the personality integrated and sustainable." Comment and justify this statement with some examples from behavioural science.

11.2 Write an essay on the personality traits and the personality theory of Jung. What possible modifications to it are suggested here in the light of patomic model of human Being. Explain in detail as to how this modified version of the theory can account for the spiritual content in the personality.

11.3 Write a summary of possible corrections discussed in four steps in the personality theory of Jung. Explain as to how these step-wise corrections lead to inculcate spiritual content in the personality. Also explain as to how the personality traits like "emotional intelligence" and "sensational conscience" emerge out of these corrections. Discuss these traits in detail with examples.

11.4 Discuss personality **P** as a vector in the vector space spanned by three *guṇas*, viz. *sattva*, *rajas* and *tamas*, over a field of cosmic consciousness, Φ_{cc}. Explain as to how the causal, micro and gross existences of a person are responsible for the vertical development of the personality, whereas the societal and natural ones are responsible for the horizontal development of the personality.

11.5 In the light of the modified personality theory of Jung, revisit and write an essay on the organizational behaviour described through four heads: (i) individual processes, (ii) interpersonal and group processes, (iii) organizational processes, and (iv) change processes. Explain as to how a society will progress and become spiritual by considering it as an organization.

12

Psychoscience and the Emerging Disciplines of Sociophysics and Econophysics

A SYSTEMATIC framework, developed for psychoscience in Chapters 6-10, has very wide applications in humanities, social science and economics beside the ones investigated in previous chapters with regard to management, organization behaviour and personality development. As a matter of fact, in whichever branch of knowledge the human component is involved the role of psychoscience is bound to be there, particularly when one resorts to study quantitative aspects of the underlying phenomenon and that too in the most fundamental terms. Nowadays, it has become a fashion to use the tools of mathematics and the concepts of physical science in soft disciplines like sociology and economics. As a result, several new interdisciplinary subjects like sociophysics and econophysics are emerging. Now the question arises whether these marriages – first of mathematics with other disciplines and now of physics with soft disciplines, are going to be genetically acceptable and stable or else they just are the marriages of convenience to fulfil the timely need. The present chapter is an attempt to look for an answer to such questions more in a philosophical spirit. These interdisciplinary studies by and large are carried out on the basis of analogies or similarities, which, in turn, could occur at various levels like at the level of concept, sequence of concepts, model or the phenomenon as a whole. Before proceeding further, it is worthwhile to understand this concept of structural analogy used frequently in these studies.

While applying the wisdom of one field into other or the vice versa, the concept of structural analogy plays a dominant role in both the situations, viz. in the process of abstraction and also in the process of proliferation of knowledge (Kaushal 2003). Therefore, we first briefly review this concept in the next section. Then, we discuss the psychoscience as a unifying framework to study both the newly emerging disciplines of sociophysics and econophysics, respectively in Sections 12.2 and 12.3. In Section 12.4, we try to look for the foundations of the Kahneman's (2011) work in behavioural economics in Vedic wisdom. To this effect, a plausible link of his theory with the Vedic wisdom is demonstrated. Finally, concluding remarks are made in Section 12.5.

12.1 The Role of Structural Analogy in the Development of a Discipline

Whether it is the process of abstraction or of proliferation of knowledge, in either case, the concept of analogy (or its variants like parallelism, similarity and symmetry) plays a dominant role in the respective studies. Indeed, a generalized concept of "structural analogy" has been found (Kaushal 2003, 2004) to accommodate all these variants of the more or less same philosophical concept including that of metaphor/simile of the grammar of a language. As a matter of fact, this concept has been prevailing equally in both soft (through literary beauty and philosophical interpretations) and hard (through logical concepts and mathematical constructs) disciplines. It may be further mentioned that the abstraction aspect of knowledge while have the tendency to connect with the philosophy of the subject, the proliferation aspect, on the other hand, elaborates the applications of the subject in a down-to-earth style. Here, we present only a nutshell summary of this generalized concept of the so-called "structural analogy".

In the language of pure mathematics, the analogy can be considered as the mapping (or correspondence) of one set of objects to the other in the same or in different mental spaces and with certain features preserved during this process. The features which can be exploited are:

i. The elements of the set (the so-called "objects").
ii. The relations between and among elements or the internal correspondences among subsets of the set, or the mappings on the set as a whole (called "rules of the game"). At the next stage, the characterization either of elements of the set or of mappings on it possibly could be on the basis of their physical, mathematical or philosophical contents.
iii. Further the comparing sets may appear at different scales or at the same scale in terms of space, time and/or their mental pictures.

Schematically, the contents of structural analogy are displayed in *fig.* 12.1a. Further, one can as well define the "order" and the quality q of an analogy within this framework (cf. Kaushal 2003). In the first order, one just has the comparisons of "objects", "rules of game" and scales, and in the second order one carries out the fine-tuning of the first two in terms of physical, mathematical and

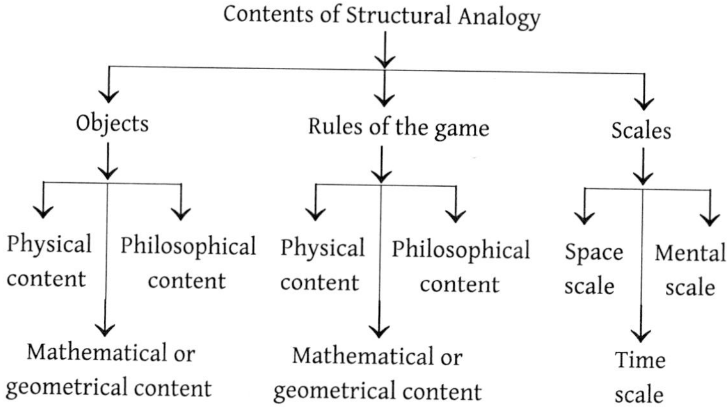

fig. 12.1a: Schematic representation of contents of a structural analogy

philosophical contents and also in terms of space, time and mental scales (cf. *fig*. 12.1a).

As a matter of fact, it is the set of suppositions on the nature of correlations (rules of the game) among objects that bring them together for comparison as far as the explanation/description of the two situations is concerned. However, the analogy is considered to be the best if the number of suppositions (*n*) and the gap (*g*) between the explanation/description of the two situations is minimum. Thus, the quality of analogy (*q*) is inversely proportional to both *n* and *g*, viz.

$$q \alpha \frac{1}{ng} \quad \text{or} \quad q = \frac{K}{ng}, \tag{12.1}$$

where *K*, the constant of proportionality, is a measure of the merit (i.e. the level of development of his faculty of understanding) of the individual user of analogy. These ideas will help in exploring the sustainability of the newly emerging interdisciplinary subjects in recent times.

Structural Analogy of a Phenomenon as a Whole

What we have investigated earlier (Kaushal 2003) and also in the above is the structural analogy of concepts, phrases and sequence of concepts in terms of "objects", "rules of the game" and "scales" in the first order (cf. *fig*. 12.1a). Here, one establishes the correspondence (in terms of similarity) between two sets in terms of their elements and certain operations on them. Nevertheless, there exist several examples in both hard and soft disciplines where the entire phenomenon of one situation can be put for a comparison with the entire phenomenon of the other. In this case, the correspondence (in terms of similarity) between two sets at gross level is investigated not only at level of elements and operations on them but also between the subsets of each set. These subsets of each given set are identified at micro level again on the basis of certain types of characteristics of elements and operation on them including that of subgroup(s). However, the scales in this case remain only the mental ones as the phenomena are perceptible at the levels of mind and intellect. Schematically, we display this situation in *fig*. 12.1b.

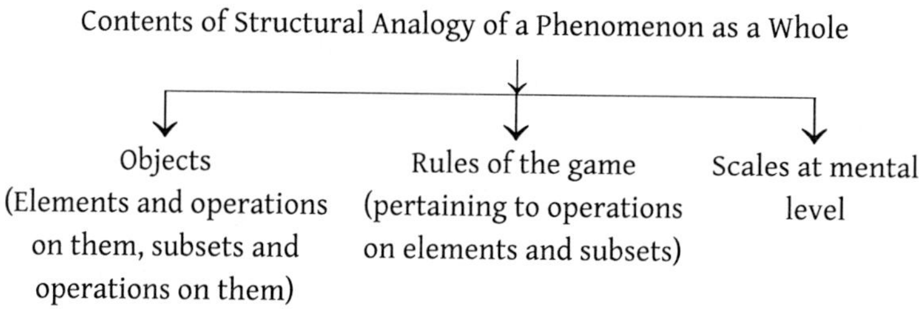

fig. 12.1b: Schematic representation of contents of a structural analogy of a phenomenon as a whole

Corresponding to this category of analogy, we cite two examples from each "hard" and "soft" disciplines. In fact, the examples from hard disciplines describe a part of absolute reality in view of the available experimental support, whereas those from soft disciplines describe the same reality but only at the realization level.

Example 12.1.1*: *Examples from hard disciplines: The two examples already detailed in Section 3.3 are:

1. One concerns astrophysics in which the event of the Big Bang at the time of origin of early Universe is compared with mini bang, i.e. the formation of a "fireball" as a result of relativistic heavy ion collisions, in terms of cooling and space–time expansion, and
2. Other concerns biology in which the evolution of species in the Darwinian theory over a period of billion years is compared with the growth of foetus in the womb of a mother in about nine months.

Example 12.1.2*: *Examples from soft disciplines: The two classic examples, in this case, concern the Indian philosophy:

i. One from *SMBG* in which the immortality of soul is emphasized through an example (cf. verse II.22), viz. *vāsāṁsi jīrṇāni yathā vihāya* ..., meaning thereby "as a man shedding worn-out garments, takes other new ones, likewise, the embodied soul, casting off worn-out bodies, enters into others that are new".

ii. The human body in action is like a moving chariot: Consider the human body as a chariot which is driven by ten horses (five senses of knowledge and five motor organs). The master (soul) is sitting in the chariot and the driver (intellect) is driving the chariot using the rein of mind. To run the chariot rightly (i.e. towards the successful performance of an action) according to the wishes (ego) of the master (soul), charioteer (intellect) has to pull or release the rein appropriately (i.e. to control the mind) so that the movement of horses (senses and motor organs) remains under control.

In these examples one can easily trace the correspondences at the level of both sets and the subsets within them. Such examples, however, are rare and the underlying correspondences is supposed to define a new mathematical concept of mapping which is obviously different from a "function" or "functional". It is this category of analogy that plays a role in these new advancements.

12.2 Sociophysics as an Emerging Discipline

As far as the involvement of physicists in social science and business studies is concerned, it has been there for centuries. Daniel Bernoulli in 1738 introduced the idea of utility to describe people's preferences. Pierre-Simon Laplace in 1812 pointed out that events, that might seen random and unpredictable in daily life, can be quite predictable and can be shown to obey simple laws. Later, these ideas of Laplace were further elaborated by a student of Joseph Fourier, named Adolphe Quetelet, who studied the existence of patterns in different data sets and coined the word "social physics" in 1835. Further, in nineteenth century, Irving Fisher, a student of Willard Gibbs discussed the role of physics in the development of economic theory, mostly on the basis of analogies. Later, famous nuclear physicist, Ettore Majorana in 1938 analysed the viability of statistical physics methods when used in the studies of social phenomena. For an answer to the question as to what extent physical theories can be viable in studying sociology and economics, we refer to recent articles in *Physics Today* (Doyane Farmer et al. 2005; Pimbley 1997).

12.2.1 SOCIOPHYSICS HAS ROOTS IN PSYCHOSCIENCE: THE VIABILITY OF PHYSICAL THEORIES

During the last few decades there has been considerable interest (see, for example, Nowak and Vallachar 1998) in studying the subject of sociology as a dynamical system and, in fact, why should it not be! After all, the ever-growing scientific advancements are drastically affecting the once considered as "static" society. To this effect, a fine-tuning in studies is achieved by using not only the advanced mathematical methods but also the analogies from physical theories (Galam 2012).

In preceding chapters (cf. Chapters 7 and 11) and the earlier works (Kaushal 2011, 2015) we have tried to analyse as to how the dynamics of EOLs of a person play an important role in shaping his action, character and, later, personality. For this purpose, the subject of psychophysics in its new incarnation is developed and the tools so emerged have proven as an asset in understanding the entire gamut of human behaviour and experiences in terms of certain fundamental processes that take place at subtle level among various EOLs. Further, it is noticed that the patomic model of human Being (cf. Chapter 6), also offers a plausible and viable framework to understand the social psychological dynamics, i.e. of a collective version of individuals. Here, we further elaborate on the subject and discuss as to how the communities or subgroups of individuals of different tastes and cultures contribute to the dynamism of a society as a whole. We use again the physics concepts and theories but now for different types of systems and at different scales.

As to how the study of sociophysics emerges from that of psychophysics can be understood from the following analogy: If one wants to understand a gas in terms of molecules or a solid in terms of atoms, where an understanding of molecule or an atom in terms of their structure already exists, then note that the force laws at molecule level or at atom level would be different from those of at their constituent level. In fact, similar is the case when many individuals come together and constitute a society. Note that individual psychology as such does not constitute the collective psychology in a simple additive manner. Like in gases or solids, here too, correlations and, consequently, the forces characterized by their strength and range become different at collective level from that at individual substructure level.

Further note that the forces for physics systems are contact or AAD type and also they are the space–time mediated ones, however, for human-Being-systems it is not so, the forces could be of AAT (derived from the history of society) and/or AADT (derived from both the geography and history of society) type in addition to the contact and AAD type. They can as well involve roles of consciousness and/or of mindsets of people and the same need to be incorporated even in physical theories through a meditation variable (Kaushal 2009). This feature of force laws for human-Being systems, in addition to the fact that they are the "open" (to circumstances and environment) systems, reduces the viability of applications of physics concepts and theories as such to human-Being systems. In such a situation, there are three possibilities:

i. alternative theories need to be developed for social system on the lines of a physical system,
ii. physics theories need to be modified to accommodate "human features" pertaining to consciousness, and
iii. the existing theories of physics can be used with a rider and in the lowest order of predictive power.

The important point is that the strengths and ranges of the forces involved do not change in the present case of many human-Being system unlike in physics. They almost remain the same all throughout when one proceeds from individual to a collection of individuals. In summary, it may be emphasized that physical theories and concepts, developed basically for inanimate objects, cannot be used as such for animate objects like human Beings whether at individual level or for their collection. However, the patomic model in its crude or reduced version (cf. Chapter 6) can prove to be an asset in these studies.

Next arises the question of studying change in a social system with respect to space, time and circumstances. In this regard, recall that a physical system, often assumed to be closed as is generally the case, undergoes changes with respect to a single time scale defined conveniently with reference to the external observer or at the best with reference to the cosmic time scale (Big Bang). The dynamical variables here mostly have intrinsic dependence on time and the explicit dependence on time, if it is there, is often neglected since the available mathematical tools are still inadequate (Kaushal 1998) to account for it. In a social system, however, there are many time scales, besides the ones with reference to the external observer and cosmos. As a matter of fact in a social system the consciousness of each individual subsystem is capable of creating its own time, space and geometry and hence complicates the studies of the system as a whole and also projects the system as a "complex" system. (A complex system is one whose study often deals with a hierarchy of "cause and effect" principles and that too at different scales). Further,

i. subsystems (individuals) are now no more closed systems; then what to say of the social system as a whole and this limits the viability of physical theories for this purpose,

ii. explicit dependence on time is bound to be there and hence the application of physical theories as such is not justified, and

iii. even in an individual, the change can occur at the level of all EOLs, viz. body, senses, mind, intellect and ego, but in the presence of soul.

Some of these difficulties, no doubt, are overcome by using the methods of statistical physics or statistics in general. But in view of the presence of "free will" and "willpower" in the subsystems, the question arises as to how long the rules of inanimate dice will be applicable for a collection of living as well as interacting systems. In a nutshell, in order to develop formal theory for social systems a feedback has to come from the psychoscience of new incarnation (cf. Part 2). An important point to be noted here is that for social systems the change takes place not only with space and time but also with respect to the circumstance created by the mindset (a representative of consciousness) of individuals or of their collection. This constitutes the subject of social psychology. In some sense the situation here is similar to that when the probabilistic interpretation of the quantum wave function was advanced and prompted Einstein to remark that "God never plays a dice".

12.2.2 SOCIAL EXPERIENCES AND RELATED STUDIES

There was a time when societies or social life of a person was almost static for centuries if not for decades; but now, in view of the everyday increasing scientific advancements towards a luxurious lifestyle, both culture and society are undergoing a fast change. This has not only brought the dynamism in the society but has considerably affected the psychology of an individual and also the values in society. Naturally, this type of dynamism is not the same as one studies for physical systems. Here, the subjective element in the psychology of society dominates over the objective one contrary to a physical system. In recent years, there have been several attempts (made on the basis of some limited experiences) to account for this kind of dynamism in a social system (see, e.g. Galam 2012). However, the viability of these rather disconnected and empirical approaches remains highly restricted mainly because they borne out of some limited experiences that are translated into models. Some of these methods used in the studies in recent times are:

a. cyclic phenomena in some social psychological experiences,
b. cellular automata;
c. connectionist models; and
d. social systems as non-linear dynamical systems.

While the choice of the method depends on the nature of the social phenomenon under study, for details, we refer to specialized works as cited in (Kaushal 2017b; Vallachar and Nowak 1994).

12.2.3 DYNAMICAL SOCIAL PSYCHOLOGY: SCOPE OF MATHEMATICAL MODELLING

Keeping above features of a social system in mind and noting the limitations of physical theories regarding their use in soft disciplines in general, it becomes clear that the latter theories cannot be used as such in true sense, but only in an analogous manner. Further recall that an analogy can never be a reality even if it is of finest order (cf. Section 12.1), it can only hint to a reality and that too after showing agreement of the predicted results with experiments. When there is a lack of understanding of consciousness itself or its role in the dynamics of EOLs working through human or social actions in the Western thinking, then how can one expect a good prediction from such theories and models (Galam 2012; Nowak and Vallachar 1998). Truly speaking, the use of physical theories can only describe the space–time evolution and hence only the partial truth about the system. The theories corrected for the role of consciousness or developed independently as an alternative for a human system can however be expected to yield better results. Some glimpses of such considerations are already given in the previous section in terms of the patomic model. As a matter of fact, there appears a timely need to apply these concepts of Vedic wisdom while studying and/or analysing a social system. In this regard, it may be mentioned that Vedic science offers much more than necessary for a social scientist of Western thinking.

It is believed that the most advanced tools, methods and concepts of natural sciences may ultimately have greatest applications in social psychological studies. To this effect, such notions as spatio-temporal chaos, self-organization and unpredictability may find better applications in social sciences than in physical sciences. As far as the use of physics concepts and mathematical modelling in the study of social phenomena is concerned, one can trace some recent works. For example, see Nowak and Vallachar (1998); Bascompte and Sole (1993, 1995) for the applications of theories of network analysis, non-linearities in system behaviour, hysteresis, etc. where the intrinsic beauty and effectiveness of these tools of study are demonstrated.

Thus, there are several factors which resist the study of social psychology in a truly scientific spirit, particularly in the way of physics. The remarkable complexity of human thought, behaviour and relationships makes these studies difficult. As a matter of fact, the success of dynamical system theories in natural sciences is largely due to its ability to provide simple explanation for complex phenomena pertaining mainly to inanimate objects whereas in social dynamics (or for that matter even in behavioural economics) the objects of study are the living (human) Beings and the presence of consciousness and hence free will in them complicates the studies. In reality, in the latter case one would however require a different type of modelling and the dynamics as well.

12.2.4 ROLE OF (INDIVIDUAL) MENTAL DYNAMICS IN SOCIAL ACTIONS

It is true that the mental dynamics of an individual, incorporated through the patomic model (cf. Chapter 6) not only reflects in his actions, behaviour and personality (Kaushal 2015) but also affects the society in which the person lives in, provided such personalities dominate in society. In response to the question as to how to account for this individual's role in the collection of individuals (i.e. society), some methods in analogy with many-body theories in physics are already discussed in Section 10.4 and in Sharma et al. (2020) within the framework of patomic model. In fact, since the Western psychology show limitations (cf. Chapter 11) in this regard, further studies in terms of patomic model are desirable.

Before proceeding further, it is worthwhile to recall the basic difference between the Western and Eastern (Indian) philosophies of human actions performed in this world. In some sense, they respectively correspond to the bottom-up and top-down approaches (Ellis 2005) adopted in recent times to study a complex system. In philosophical spirit, these approaches respectively correspond to "matter over mind" and "mind over matter" styles of thinking. Whenever the role of consciousness in human actions (which cannot be denied from any angle) is talked about, it is just attributed to a philosophical entity called "mind" in the Western way of thinking. This is done again without really understanding as to what this philosophical entity "mind" is? Not only this, the reasoning and memory are also included in addition to emotions among the attributes of mind. Further, the source of these attributes is traced in the structure and the functioning of the "brain" – a material part of the body. Truly speaking, in the Western way of thinking mind is one complex system and whose working once again one tries to understand in terms of another complex system of different category and scale, i.e. brain without really understanding the consciousness and its associated phenomena inside a Being. The latter, in fact, is in the root of working of both mind and brain. A dead body does not have a functional brain or mind. As a matter of fact, it is the same consciousness which makes the brain functional on the one hand and also at the same time creates an environment on the other not only for the mind to work but also to activate other faculties of understanding. These faculties, in particular, are responsible for reasoning and memory in a human Being. Thus, the Western thinking while ends up with the entity mind, the Indian philosophy, on the other hand, goes one step further and clearly and distinctly accounts for the roles of faculties of reasoning (i.e. intellect) and of memory (i.e. ego or self-sense) in human actions. In fact, a great deal of Vedic philosophy revolves around these considerations along with the studies of the source and phenomena of consciousness related to living Beings in general.

Truly speaking, the role of individual mental dynamics in social actions needs to be analysed in two steps – at the first stage, study the individual's behaviour either in isolation or in an environment (consisting of both animate and inanimate surroundings) and then, at the next stage, study the correlation, cooperation, coordination, relationship capacities, etc. of this personality with other person(s). Even physics-based analogous models in this regard show the limitations mainly because of the presence of free will, willpower or consciousness in general in the object of study. Nowak and Vallachar (1998) underline this entire gamut of study under four heads, viz. self-organization of action, coordination of mind, dysfunction in action systems and a dynamical taxonomy of action. It is needless to say that the Vedic wisdom through the methodology of patomic model (cf. Chapter 6) in conjunction with dressing rules (cf. Section 4.3) can add a lot to these studies.

12.3 Econophysics as an Emerging Discipline

12.3.1 STATUS AND ROLE OF PHYSICS IN ECONOMIC SCIENCES

The possibilities of marriage between economics and physics have been discussed in recent articles and books (Doyane Farmer et al. 2005; Mantegna and Stanley 1999; Pimbley 1997). Pimbley (1997), while discussing the status and value of physics and physicists in economic sciences, does accept the existence of creativity element in physicist in handling the core problems of a given subject. However, their insufficient basic training in the subject concerned like economics entails a handicap in the development of the subject. On the other hand, Doyane Farmer et al. (2005) are optimistic and believe that the interdisciplinary training for students/researchers can perhaps yield better results. Doyane Farmer et al. further highlight the solution to certain economic problems using the physics concepts, theories and models. As far as the uses of the latter are concerned, they are carried out mostly in an analogous manner. Note that such applications of physics in economics can no doubt facilitate the solution and handling of the core problems but this will hardly throw any light on the ultimate reality in Nature, mainly because economics itself is a science of utility to mankind and as such is not the science of fundamental nature like physics. After all, the goals and philosophy in the two disciplines are different. The following discussion will further elaborate this point.

Note that the subject of psychophysics is entirely developed for the understanding of the role of human component in soft disciplines and inculcating human values at an individual level. The sociophysics, on the other hand, does involve relatively more external parameters in its dynamics emerging mainly from the constraints of family, society, culture and country. In spite of all this, individual psychology does play a role in building a society and the same is generally accounted for in the studies more in a statistical manner. As far as the subject of economics is concerned, historically, it has always remained an important utility not only at the family and society level but also at the individual level. It is only in recent centuries, particularly after the scientific advancements and industrial revolutions, that the subject of economics is talked about at the national and international levels. The subject of physics, on the other hand, has grown mainly for the understanding of inanimate components in Nature. As mentioned before, its concepts and laws show limitations when applied to living objects. Even then, the methodology and tools developed in physical sciences are so noble and elegant that any soft discipline will be enriched by their use.

Recall that the change in Nature is as true as our existence in the Universe. This change in general, of course at different scales, might take place with respect to some or all the four variables, viz. space, time, circumstances and environment. The subject of physics, in fact, neatly accounts only for the changes with respect to space and time, and that too, for the closed systems. Whether it is sociology or economics, in either case, changes with respect to circumstances and environment dominate the scene as compared to space and time. Hence, the source of dynamism in these disciplines is of different type and it does have branch-root in individual's psychology. In spite of all these changes, certain invariants (universalities or eternal truths) can be traced in the studies of these subjects, which not only encourage these studies but also help in establishing certain values (human or otherwise) in the world order.

In view of these considerations, economics still remains a subject of immense utility (like food technology and fashion designing) and that too only for human society and not even for non-human ones. Again, as history reveals, the whims of rulers, political or religious leaders have been playing a dominant role in its development. Universalities can be traced only in the branch-roots connecting to human element like behavioural economics; otherwise, the economic sciences deal with phenomena which are highly circumstantial and environment-dependent and also spatio-temporal. With regard to the question of economics becoming a part of physical science, note that the two subjects, at present, are having beautiful intertwining analogies of fine (second) order (cf. *fig*. 12.1a) in spite that their goals and philosophies are different in the process of searching the ultimate reality in Nature.

12.3.2 SOME GLIMPSES OF APPLICATIONS OF PHYSICS TOOLS IN ECONOMIC SCIENCES

There are several branches in mathematical disciplines in physics (like classical and quantum mechanics, classical and quantum field theories and statistical mechanics) which do have roots in pure mathematics or they seem to originate from the same abstract mathematical construct. Also, the tools of applied mathematics, at one time, were found to have maximum applications in physical sciences including chemistry and biology through modelling game (see Kaushal 2011, appendix A). These tools, in fact, are very elegant and at times their applications to a phenomenon forces one to think that they are God-made or Nature likes them most in view of their predictive power and subsequent experimental verification of results. For example, the roles of power law functions (e.g. linear, quadratic, inverse square laws), exponential (e.g. simple exponential, $e^{-\alpha x}$, or Gaussian (normal distribution), $e^{-\alpha x^2}$), Fourier transform, second-order ordinary and partial differential equations, random walk theory, group theory, theory of probability, etc. are worth recalling in physics studies.

Truly speaking, these tools can be applied to any discipline of knowledge through the modelling game, but the fact is that it is the quality of analogy/model (cf. Section 12.1) that matters in extracting the knowledge content pertaining to a given phenomenon in terms of universality or absolute reality in Nature. As human-component is involved at a large scale in both social and economic sciences, the viability of these tools in these disciplines is naturally curtailed. No doubt, these tools can still be effective in some situations but the weakness of the underlying assumptions in modelling the situation further weakens the predictive power of the model and agreements of results with experiments remains only spatio-temporal – far from universality. If at all there appears any universality in the results, then it all pertains to the human-element involved in the phenomenon like human behaviour vis-à-vis financial model of a society or behavioural economics, etc. For example, some mathematical tools, concepts and constructs of physics found viable in the studies of economic/finance problems are the

a. use of power laws;
b. use of random walk theory;
c. use of game theory and rational choice; and
d. use of entropy methods, etc.

For further details, we refer to specialized works cited above.

12.3.3 SOME REMARKS ON BEHAVIOURAL ECONOMICS

From the survey in the previous section, it appears that physics will continue to contribute to economics in a big way in solving the problems ranging from macroeconomics to market-microstructure. This, in turn, will also have implications in economic policy making, where arises the role of human component or behavioural economics, and generally accounted through statistical analyses (Smith and Subik 2005).

Behavioural economics basically is the study of (human) psychology with reference to the economic decision-making processes of individuals and institutions. Even in this case, note that there are two distinct and important situations, viz. the cases of short-memory and long-memory processes. In this connection, two questions are normally addressed:

1. Are economists' assumptions of utility or profit maximization good approximations of real people's behaviour?
2. Do individuals maximize subjective expected utility?

Several notable economists have contributed to the answer of these questions and have accordingly been honoured with Nobel memorial prizes in the recent past. For example, Herbert Simon (honoured in 1978) explored the concept of bounded rationality or studied the decision-making processes in economic organizations; Gary Becker (honoured in 1992) looked into the problem of people's motive and consumer market problems and George Akerlof (honoured in 2001) studied the market-behaviour with "asymmetric information". Daniel Kahneman has been honoured in 2002 for his research on prospect theory, in particular, for exploring the concepts of "illusion of validity" and "anchoring bias". The prospect theory basically deals with human judgement and decision-making processes under uncertainty. Recall that economics, historically, has assumed that people act in their self-interest and make rational decisions. Kahneman's research combines psychology with economics to explore as to how people's behaviour may depart from these classical assumptions. In the next section we shall revisit the essence of Kahneman theory in the light of patomic model and suggest some possible modifications in it with a view to having a better human judgement and a fine-tuning of decision-making processes.

12.4 Revisiting the Kahneman Theory in the Light of Vedic Wisdom

12.4.1 SHORT- AND LONG-MEMORY PROCESSES AND THE TWO SELVES OF KAHNEMAN

In some sense, the short-memory and long-memory processes appearing in the market strategies are the outcome of short-term and long-term thinking built in the psychology and behaviour patterns of an individual or a society as a whole. This fact is beautifully exploited by Daniel Kahneman in developing his prospect theory in behavioural economics, particularly in his recent bestselling book *Thinking, Fast and Slow* (2011). In day-to-day life we call these processes as "immediate" and "second thought" reactions towards an event in the outer world. Kahneman, in fact, introduces the characters of a hypothetical story as "system 1" and "system 2". A close observation of the development of the subject matter in the introduction of the book clearly reveals that these two systems of Kahneman basically are two components of the micro body $\mathcal{M}$, denoted here as the gross (conscious) part $\mathcal{M}_g$ and subtle (subconscious) part $\mathcal{M}_s$, respectively. The same will be elaborated in the next section.

According to Kahneman, the system 1 operates automatically and quickly, with little or no effort and no sense of voluntary control. On the other hand, the system 2 allocates attention to the effortful mental activities that demand it, including complex analysis and computations. The operations of the system 2 are often associated with the subjective experience of agency, choice and concentration. A kind of psychodrama of system 1 and system 2 is described in the entire book at a very fine level which finally ends up with the birth of a new economic science in terms of experience and decision utilities and a subject like intuitive statistics. What a great job Kahneman has done by bringing the subjective science of

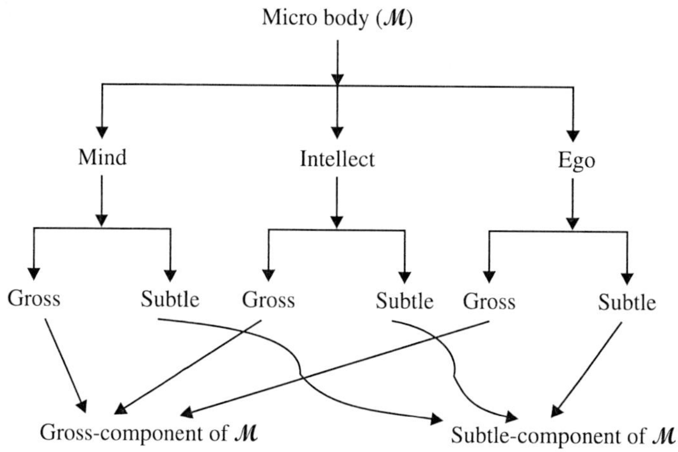

fig. 12.2: Schematic display of as to how the micro body $\mathcal{M}$ of patomic model splits into the gross component $\mathcal{M}_g$ and the subtle component $\mathcal{M}_s$

the Self to the level of most practical modern science of economics, however, without really going into the details of patomic model and the associated dynamics of EOLs (cf. Chapter 6). Next, we elaborate on the connection between the Kahneman theory and the more generalized concepts discussed in the patomic model.

12.4.2 THE TWO SELVES OF KAHNEMAN IN PATOMIC MODEL AND THEIR PSYCHODRAMA

With a view to identifying the system 1 and system 2 of Kahneman in the patomic model of human Being, the constituent of the micro-body $\mathcal{M}$ can be reconstructed (see section 3.1 of Kaushal 2015) as shown in *fig.* 12.2. For this purpose, note that each member of the trio – mind, intellect and ego – is considered as consisting of a gross part and a subtle part. The gross parts of all three combine again to give the gross component of $\mathcal{M}$ (denoted as $\mathcal{M}_g$) and the combination of subtle parts of them gives the subtle component of $\mathcal{M}$ (denoted as $\mathcal{M}_s$) as argued in Section 5.3. Note that these $\mathcal{M}_g$ and $\mathcal{M}_s$ are the system 1 and the system 2 of Kahneman, which at a later stage respectively are termed as "experiencing self" and "remembering self" by Kahneman on the basis of their functions. Further remarks on the work of Kahneman are as follows (cf. Kaushal 2017b):

i. An important outcome of the theory of Kahneman is the frequent demonstration of the connection between the time and the meditation variables in his book (also see Chapter 7 here). From this work it appears that the thinking process is "fast" with reference to system 1 and it is "slow" with reference to system 2 and all this is with respect to the (physical) time variable or the event-based time. However, as per our common experience, the meditation takes us in reverse order, i.e. first it overcomes the constituents of the set $\mathcal{G}$, viz. WO, B, SE and then enters into the realm of $\mathcal{M}$, viz. M, I, E and finally into the realm of $\mathcal{C}$ (cf. *fig.* 12.2). On the other hand, the gross component $\mathcal{M}_g$ (system 1 of

Kahneman) of $\mathcal{M}$ is operative in conjunction with $\mathcal{G}$. Thus, the meditation (variable μ) has inverse/reciprocal dependence on time *t* as analysed in Chapter 7. Note that the intensity of thinking would depend on the (internal) meditation variable μ, whereas the "slowness" or "fastness" of thinking would depend on the external variable *t* but only in the $\mathcal{G}$ and perhaps in the $\mathcal{M}_g$ domains; otherwise in the $\mathcal{M}_s$ or $\mathcal{C}$ domain, there is hardly any role of *t*. In fact, in order to account for the efficiency of systems 1 and 2 or for the intensity of thinking process, one should also consider the evolution of these systems with consciousness. Some glimpses of discrete evolution are given in Chapter 4 and of continuous evolution in Appendix A.

ii. The way in which the thinking process is considered and analysed by Kahneman through the drama of system 1 and system 2, clearly shows that it is a complex process, i.e. it is not just the act of the inner EOL I in the present context, but that of a collective entity to which the contribution does come from other inner EOLs, viz. from M and E. Kahneman, however, seems to attach only the memory aspect to it by calling system 2 as "remembering self". As a matter of fact there are several other aspects of exchanges considered between the system 1 and the system 2 which would require the thinking to be a composite process in the present scheme of study (for details, see Kaushal 2023a).

iii. In the work of Kahneman the set of systems 1 and 2 is studied in isolation. But in reality it is not so, for both are active only in the presence of consciousness that originates from the entity SO. Also, $\mathcal{M}_s$ is linked with $\mathcal{C}$ on the one end and the component $\mathcal{M}_g$ is linked with $\mathcal{G}$ on the other. Kahneman, no doubt, accounts for the linkage of $\mathcal{M}_g$ with $\mathcal{G}$ (i.e. with the outer world) but ignores the linkage with $\mathcal{C}$ completely. As a matter of fact, the consideration of this latter linkage in the theory would definitely bring the spirituality content (cf.

Chapter 11) in the output (i.e. in the behaviour and character of an individual) in the same way as the consideration of the former linkage has provided a better reason for the worldly-living in economic terms.

12.4.3 EFFICIENCY OF THE TWO SELVES OF KAHNEMAN: POSSIBLE MODIFICATIONS IN THE THEORY

According to the theory of Kahneman, the two selves, viz. "experiencing self" and "remembering self" (which, in fact, in the present scheme of study are the gross component $\mathcal{M}_g$ and subtle component $\mathcal{M}_s$, respectively) work at different time scales or in different spatio-temporal zones and so do their actions are defined as "fast" and "slow". But the fact is that their working belongs to different meditation zones or at different levels of attention. (Recall that the attention basically is a directed, channelized or focused version of consciousness that provides the cognizance of working of oneself to the other). Further note that the efforts of an individual are associated with $\mathcal{M}_s$ and his actions mostly with $\mathcal{M}_g$. Moreover, when one talks of the quantification of the efficiency of $\mathcal{M}_s$ and $\mathcal{M}_g$, one needs to understand their ability and limitations in terms of their evolution with consciousness and/or with spatio-temporal circumstances.

As mentioned before, there are two ways to analyse the process of perception of an external stimulus in a given environment. In one case, one proceeds with the dynamics of EOLs and accounts for the environment/circumstances separately, preferably by introducing a parameter for it from outside. In other case, one considers the successive evolutions of EOLs with consciousness either by way of their successive dressing with consciousness (discrete evolution) or by writing a differential equation for the evolution of the constructed mindset function (continuous evolution). These evolutions of EOLs with consciousness will, in turn, enrich the EOLs with the knowledge about the stimuli. Note that $\mathcal{M}_g$ and $\mathcal{M}_s$, which basically are certain combinations of inner EOLs, viz. M, I and E, will also undergo some sort of dressing with consciousness, particularly when one wishes to account for the interplay or the psychodrama between them in view of the external environment. In what follows, we identify the dressed versions of $\mathcal{M}_g$ and $\mathcal{M}_s$ in view of their definitions given above and use the discrete dressing rule (*tri-karaṇa* rule) defined in Chapter 4 through relations (4.7)-(4.8). For this purpose, we write the nth-order dressed version of the micro body $\mathcal{M}$ as $\tilde{\mathcal{M}}^{(n)} = \{\tilde{\mathcal{M}}_g^{(n)}, \tilde{\mathcal{M}}_s^{(n)}\}$with corresponding gross and subtle components as $\tilde{\mathcal{M}}_g^{(n)} = \{\tilde{M}_g^{(n)}, \tilde{I}_g^{(n)}, \tilde{E}_g^{(n)}\}$, $\tilde{\mathcal{M}}_s^{(n)} = \{\tilde{M}_s^{(n)}, \tilde{I}_s^{(n)}, \tilde{E}_s^{(n)}\}$. Here, $\tilde{M}_i^{(n)}, \tilde{I}_i^{(n)}, \tilde{E}_i^{(n)}\,(i = g, s)$, in terms of their $(n-1)^{th}$-order dressings, are given by eq. (4.8). With regard to these mathematical constructs, the following remarks are in order:

i. The orders of dressing of $\mathcal{M}_g$ and $\mathcal{M}_s$, say n and l in $\tilde{\mathcal{M}}_g^{(n)}$ and $\mathcal{M}_s^{(l)}$ in some sense, will define their efficiency of working.

ii. When one talks of exchanges (or psychodrama) between $\mathcal{M}_g$ and $\mathcal{M}_s$, the orders of their dressing with consciousness will matter and constitute a matrix $\tilde{\mathcal{M}}_g^{(n)} \times \tilde{\mathcal{M}}_s^{(l)}$ which, in turn, might offer explanations of a variety of situations discussed by Kahneman in his book.

These remarks, in fact, require further discussion and deeper studies (for details, see Kaushal 2023a).

12.5 Concluding Discussion

Note that it is human component in general and the individual human Being in particular that plays a dominant role in all studies in humanities and social sciences including sociology and economics. As far as the understanding of the human Being and his actions in the outer world is concerned, the subjects of anthropology and psychology in conjunction with philosophy have been explored to a considerable extent in recent times. Still, the success in these endeavours remains limited in the Western school of thought, perhaps due to the lack of identifications of fundamental essences of life responsible for the existence and survival of a person in this world. In this respect, no doubt, Vedic thinking has gone little deeper and the same has been exploited here to explore new and additional dimensions of study of modern sociology and economics.

It is not that we are searching a base of modern developments in soft disciplines in the ancient Indian wisdom here for the first time, rather, there have been several attempts in the past when the foundations of modern physics were sought in ancient Indian and Greek wisdom (for example, see the works of Harrison 1978; Misner and Wheeler 1957: fn. 9a; Schrodinger 1964: 18). Note that in these works the reference to Indian wisdom was made only tangentially but the fact is that the latter is a treasure of a lot of many original ideas. Note that in most of these works analogies of certain order between the two approaches were pointed out with a certain degree of justification. Here, however, we have demonstrated the viability of the patomic model in unifying the studies of both sociophysics and econophysics.

It is true that such interdisciplinary studies, most of the time, are carried out using analogies and analogue models. As far as the understanding of the ultimate reality (whether subjective or objective, depending upon the phenomenon under study) in Nature using such tools is concerned, it again depends on the quality and nature of analogy (cf. Section 12.1) used for this purpose. In order to judge these features in the use of an analogy at a subtle level, a generalized concept of structural analogy is highlighted here. The patomic model itself offers one such a fine example in this case, of course, at a more subtle level than atomic model of matter. Moreover, an analogy can never be a reality, it only hints towards the reality even if there is a support from human/instrument-based observations. The ultimate reality remains a matter of realization only, which in principle is possible for all of us according to the development of our own faculty of understanding. In fact, the quality of knowledge thus acquired through these studies of interdisciplinary subjects like sociophysics and econophysics cannot be underestimated, particularly when one talks of universality, sustainability or invariants in social dynamics or in the changes in financial markets. Among several analogies studied in this context, the use of ideal gas model to understand the kinetic exchange of wealth could be an interesting case. Basically, these aspects of study are the outcome of human interactions with other humans and with the physical world (Kaushal 2011). In fact, the use of patomic model of human Being through the subject of psychoscience definitely offers one such and a new dimension of study also in political science, human geography, environmental science, evolutionary biology, besides behavioural economics and social psychology.

It may be mentioned that while physics mostly deals with the spatio-temporal Cartesian grid and thereby the space–time-mediated interactions through contact and AAD type forces, the appearance of human component in these interdisciplinary subjects would require an entry into the domain beyond space–time and an account of AAT type forces. These features in sociophysics and econophysics, in fact, are already appearing through the studies of short-memory or long-memory processes or through the "thinking, fast and slow". It is not that the physics laws and concepts are used only to glorify the soft disciplines with a view to explore them better but the studies in reverse order can also be meaningful. In fact, some intricate phenomena in sociology and economics, though appearing in the presence of human component, can also inspire physics to carry out a fine-tuning of physical laws or they are capable to provide tools for alternative studies in physics theories. This would require an account of a variety of non-linearities in the equations and that too in higher dimensions. The same was tactfully avoided in the development of physical laws and theories in the last century, perhaps due to the non-availability of sufficient mathematical or computational tools for this purpose in those days. But now the situation has changed and such exact analytical results are desirable, particularly in psychology and economics. Among new tools, the use of graph theory and complex network analysis have proven an asset in these studies in recent times.

With regard to the personalities of agents in financial market or of consumer members in a society, particularly in the context of Kahneman theory, Vedic wisdom does offer (Kaushal 2016a) several new and viable alternatives in studies in terms of three Nature-born *guṇas*: *sāttvika*, *rājasika* and *tāmasika*. This will further fine-tune the dynamics of two selves of Kahneman through $\mathcal{M}_g$ and $\mathcal{M}_s$ with reference to behavioural economics.

After having lessons from psychochemistry of individual in Chapter 10, there seems to be enough scope now to develop the subjects of sociochemistry and econochemistry with reference to various societies and economies of the world and their related interactions/reactions. To this effect, the patomic model already offers fine parameters (Kaushal 2016a) to distinguish between different personalities in terms of dressing of EOLs with consciousness and/or a hierarchy of interactions and scales through $\mathcal{G}$, $\mathcal{M}$ and $\mathcal{C}$. Alternatively, one can as well start with the level of development of one's FOU and accordingly develop these subjects. Such studies, in fact, will help in studying the amalgamation/interaction of two and more societies, cultures or economies in modern times.

High Skill Exercises and Projects

12.1 Discuss the contents and orders of structural analogy. Hence, explain with examples from both soft and hard disciplines as to how the analogy helps in the abstraction and proliferation of knowledge.

12.2 "Whether it is a social system or the case of economic science, in either case, the physical theories, when applied in an analogous manner, can only be useful in the lowest order. For the fine-tuning of the results, however, one has to account for the human (conscious or living) content present in the system." Discuss and argue the justification for these statements.

12.3 If one decides to account for the human content present in a social system or in economic science, then discuss in detail the viability of patomic model in this regard vis-à-vis other available methods in recent times.

12.4 Write an essay demonstrating the advantage of using patomic model of human Being in understanding the dynamical social psychology better on the one hand and the behavioural economics on the other. Discuss as to how the physics theories, laws or even the concepts show limitations when applied to subjects like sociology and economic science.

12.5 Write an essay on the Kahneman theory in behavioural economics that includes the following points: (i) Kahneman concept of "two selves" and Vedic wisdom; (ii) Kahneman concept of "two selves" and their psychodrama; and (iii) the question of efficiency of "two selves" and possible modifications in the theory.

13

Philosophy, Religion and Psychoscience

13.1 Introduction

Since time memorial, there has always been a small fraction of people in a society who constantly think of survival and maintenance of the society in terms of its societal and natural existences. Such thinkers and seers set the philosophy of life and also of the working style of the people with respect to the contemporary world and cosmic orders. To this effect, these selective thinkers set the norms for leading a regulated, peaceful and sustainable lifestyle of the people. Here enters the concept of "religion" mainly to keep the people engaged for twenty-four hours of the day and night. Note that a slight change in the norms, either by an individual thinker or by a group of thinkers in given circumstances, becomes a necessity to give birth to a new religion and accordingly the followers get divided. If this continues, then a time comes when the society gets flooded with religions and there are chances of its becoming a chaotic system rather than a regulated one, since in the limiting case again there is a possibility that each individual becomes a religion in itself! In the absence of such norms there could be chaos, one becomes confused about the boundaries between his personal, professional and public life. Also, the lines become blurred between work, family, friends, society and the self. When all this happens some changes in the norms become desirable and the same take place mainly on the initiative of the ruling component of a society. In this process, however, a subset of norms pertaining to an ideal society remains unaffected.

As far as the origin of these norms at initial stages is concerned, in historical context, one can view three possibilities:

A. an individual out of his own experiences and whims, who happens to be a superhuman Being, established these norms;

B. a group of contemporary high-level thinkers sat together and formulated these norms as per spatio-temporal need of society; and

C. several persons equipped with supernatural powers and cosmic connections realized these norms in their Self during meditation at different space–time points and put them together in words and letters as a cosmic desire.

In any case, note that an individual cannot be an originator of an eternal and sustainable set of norms; he or she can only be a reviver or modifier of the originally existing norms, because human race following certain norms was already there prior to the birth of that individual. Similarly, a group of contemporary individuals also cannot be founder of these norms. The only reasonably acceptable possibility is the third one, in which these norms were transcended from the cosmos and realized by great souls at different space–time points of the history and went only adding them successively to the earlier ones and thus identifying and pruning them later with the human race.

These original norms, framed basically in the lap of Nature, convey the subtlest possible philosophy of life of an individual and of a society in a logical and scientific spirit. As the human race is the same and so are the human intents and virtues, if not all but some of these norms are definitely going to be eternal and universal, i.e. they are independent of time, caste, colour, creed or country. On the basis of these observations, it is worthwhile to list the following remarks at this stage:

i. When one looks for a sustainable set of norms, naturally one looks for the elements of basic goodness (EBGs) (cf. Chapter 3) in them. In this search only the possibility (C) will qualify, since the seers in this case also kept the role of Nature (i.e. the maintenance of world order and cosmic order through cosmic connections) in mind. As a matter of fact, the presence of EBGs in norms ensures an element of spirituality along with a good (!) psyche in the behaviour of the corresponding followers.

ii. When one follows these norms as a routine, in a mechanical manner or as an imposition from outside, this does not solve the purpose. Though with an element of acceptance at the psychic level these norms define a religion, with the elements of both psyche and spirituality, these very norms will define a way of life in totality. Also, an experience with them needs to be added in human contacts for a better and fruitful outcome.

iii. When these norms are followed by generation after generation, they become traditions, and rich traditions of a society always contribute to a sustainable society.

iv. Rich traditions from whatever religion they come, always contribute to happiness and longevity of human race along with a good maintenance of world and cosmic orders. As to what these rich traditions actually are, we shall elaborate it in the next section.

v. In general the rigidity in following these norms is not a good symptom for a progressive society. It is, however, a prerequisite at the spiritual level, somewhat less necessary at the psychic level and still less necessary in the day-to-day working of a person, but when all goes within the limits.

These relaxations, in fact, are the need of time in view of the ever advancing scientific methods and technologies and their use in life.

In the next section, we look for certain criteria to judge the merit and quality of a religion in terms of its components, viz. *jñāna* (J), *upāsanā* (U) and *karma* (K), as per the Vedānta philosophy. An ideally integrated religion, in mathematical terms, is also defined in Section 13.3. In Section 13.4, after having lessons from physical theories, we try to understand the meanings of eternity and universality of a religion. In this context, the concept of experience-based invariants (EBIs) is introduced in Section 13.5, perhaps for the first time, mainly to understand the sustainability of a religion. Corresponding to five existences of a human Being, five categories of EBIs are suggested and their viability with reference to the wisdom in *aṣṭāṅga-yoga* of Patañjali and *SMBG* is demonstrated in Section 13.6. In Section 13.7, we once again comment on the connection of Vedic wisdom and *Sanātana Dharma* in the light of event-based knowledge (K_{ev}) and experience-based knowledge (K_{ex}) components of a religion. Finally, concluding remarks are made in Section 13.8.

13.2 Quality of a Religion vis-à-vis the Maintenance of World and Cosmic Orders

13.2.1 WORLD AND COSMIC ORDERS

Love, affection and other human virtues offer a kind of lubricant in maintaining good relations of an individual not only with other living Beings but also with Nature as a whole. Again, an individual as a member of a family, a society, citizen and netizen of a nation and lastly as a person on the planet earth has certain duties to perform and certain responsibilities to discharge towards a regulated and peaceful working of the entire planet or the man-made world. An ideal working of this entire gamut of working domains defines the "world order". In other words, the human qualities, associated with an individual, matter a lot in maintaining a sustainable equilibrium with regard to this man-made world. In fact, the impact of these qualities does reflect at all the levels starting from the family to the world and the planet. These are only the good deeds and positive thinking of *sāttvika* nature of an individual that will not only introduce one to a divine system of justice, but will also contribute to a sustainable equilibrium of the world order and the same will save the planet from an early decay. As a matter of fact, in view of the advancing technologies and their successive use in making the human life comfortable and luxurious, an attainment of such equilibrium has really become questionable.

Like an ideal world order, the mankind has also to maintain yet another equally important, the so-called "cosmic order" rather ideally for a peaceful, prosperous and sustainable equilibrium with regard to the working of the God-made world and to this effect again the nature of human qualities and virtues matter a lot. In this case too, an individual once again plays a dominant role in taking care of his environment, natural and geographical surroundings, etc. which finally end up not only with a pollution-free planet earth but also the cosmos as a whole.

Vedic science described the external (rather God-made world) in terms of five cosmic elements (*pañca-mahābhūtas*): earth, water, air, fire and ether. For its luxurious life, the human race has been exploiting all these five elements by way of polluting them in one way or the other, and from time to time, particularly after the emergence of modern scientific technologies. For example, the earth is polluted by mining, use of pesticides and fertilizers; water and air are polluted by industrial waste in the form of liquid and gas; fire or light is polluted by different ways of its production, which, in turn, affects plant and animal kingdom, ether is polluted by heavy traffic of aircrafts and satellites in space. Thus, the whole cosmos is affected by modern technology, even though at a slow pace. Recall that a definite proportion of the five cosmic elements is a must for the survival of human race; otherwise, any kind of pollution will disturb this proportion and thus will spoil the cosmic order in Nature.

13.2.2 QUALITY AND CONTENTS OF A RELIGION

Quality of a religion cannot be judged by the number of its followers in the world but by the quality of its contents/norms with reference to providing sustainable pleasure, peace and joy (or, in general happiness) in the life of an individual. Note that the intents like pleasure, peace and joy are subjective, in that they can neither be marketed nor can be imposed from outside on an individual; rather they have to be extracted out of one's own living respectively in the domains of his causal ($\mathcal{C}$), micro ($\mathcal{M}$) and gross ($\mathcal{G}$) existences (cf. Chapter 6). In other words, the philosophy content in a religion, which forms the basis for the formulation of norms of that religion, needs to be rich enough to provide these intents for an individual. Vedic science, in fact, suggests a criterion in this regard.

According to Vedic wisdom, any religion in general is considered to have three components: (i) *jñāna* (J) (knowledge), (ii) *upāsanā* (U) (methodology), and (iii) *karma* (K) (practice). (Coincidently, these three components also constitute a scientific theory, in which the practice component is replaced by experiment. We shall return to these discussions later in Section 13.8). Note that it is the practice or experiment component that gives a feedback to improve upon the knowledge component in the case when the former does not come up to the mark for the practitioner (scientist). But this makes sense for a progressive or dynamic society; otherwise, the system remains static even for centuries. While the J-component of a religion in general is mostly responsible for defining its quality, note that a religion can also survive without it, i.e. only with U and K components, but not for a very long time. Such religions normally are followed by a society under pressure, or fear or by way of imposition. A natural desire to follow it up does not come from within, i.e. from soul, mainly because the norms of such religions lack in these human qualities that are attributes of the soul. As and when the pressure is relaxed (or the fear of death is overcome as a result of an inner desire) people switch on to the "natural religion" (i.e. to the "religion of soul"!).

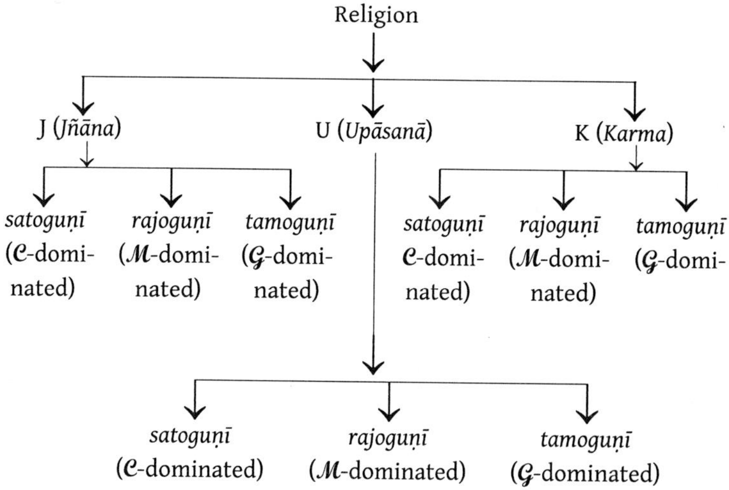

fig. 13.1: The components and sub-components of a religion

It is interesting to note that the contribution to each of the three components of a religion can come in three flavours or shades, i.e. it is wrapped with three Nature-born *guṇas* or the three modes of Nature, *sattva* (*s*) (quality of goodness), *rajas* (*r*) (principle of activity) and *tamas* (*t*) (principle of inertia). This will not only enhance the plurality of sets of norms but also the variety of religions and thereby the groups of corresponding followers. As a matter of fact, these three *guṇas* further divide the followers into subgroups of persons identified by *J*, *U* or *K* domination. This domination of any of them in the life of an individual in conjunction with three existences $\mathcal{C}$, $\mathcal{M}$ and $\mathcal{G}$, suggests a definition of an "ideal religion". Schematically, these considerations are displayed in *fig.* 13.1.

13.3 Religion as a Vector in the Vector Space Spanned by Three Guṇas in Nature

Earlier in Section 11.5, we have discussed the personality of a person as a vector in the vector space $\mathcal{V}$ spanned by three *guṇas* over a scalar field of cosmic consciousness $\mathcal{F}$ and as a linear combination of $\mathcal{M}$, $\mathcal{G}$, S and $\mathcal{N}$, existences of a person. Here, in the same spirit, we analyse a religion as a vector in the same space but as a linear combination of its three components $\vec{J}$, $\vec{U}$ and $\vec{K}$ which are also vectors in the same space. In fact, this will give a clue to define an ideal religion (like an integrated personality) and also a basis for a variety of distinctive religions followed in the world.

In general, the religion vector $\vec{R}$ is also a function of its component vectors $\vec{J}$, $\vec{U}$ and $\vec{K}$, but like the personality vector $\vec{P}$ (cf. Appendix D), we consider this $\vec{R}$ as a linear combination of component vectors, and write it as

$$\begin{aligned}\vec{R} &= \alpha\vec{J}+\beta\vec{U}+\gamma\vec{K} \\ &\equiv R_s\,\hat{s}+R_r\,\hat{r}+R_t\,\hat{t},\end{aligned} \tag{13.1}$$

where $\hat{s}$, $\hat{r}$, $\hat{t}$ are unit vectors along the three-axes of *guṇas* and α, β, γ are the weight functions assigned, respectively to J, U and K components and in general they are the elements of the scalar field $\mathcal{F}$. The vectors $\vec{J}$, $\vec{U}$ and $\vec{K}$ can also be expressed in terms of basis vectors $\hat{s}$, $\hat{r}$, $\hat{t}$ as

$$\vec{J}=a_{js}\,\hat{s}+a_{jr}\,\hat{r}+a_{jt}\,\hat{t}\,, \tag{13.2a}$$

$$\vec{U}=a_{us}\hat{s}+a_{ur}\,\hat{r}+a_{ut}\,\hat{t}\,, \tag{13.2b}$$

$$\vec{K}=a_{ks}\,\hat{s}+a_{kr}\,\hat{r}+a_{kt}\,\hat{t}\,. \tag{13.2c}$$

Here the coefficients (matrix elements) a_{pq} with $p = j, u, k$, $q = s, r, t$, define the fractions of *satoguṇī*, *rajoguṇī* and *tamoguṇī* tendencies present in a religion through the *jñāna*, *upāsanā* and *karma* components. Note that the features of the transformation in (13.2) are characterized by the matrix A, viz.:

$$A \equiv (a_{pq}) \quad \begin{pmatrix} a_{js} & a_{jr} & a_{jt} \\ a_{us} & a_{ur} & a_{ut} \\ a_{ks} & a_{kr} & a_{kt} \end{pmatrix}. \tag{13.3}$$

As far as the *satoguṇī*, *rajoguṇī* and *tamoguṇī* components of a religion are concerned, they can be obtained by comparing (13.1) and (13.2), viz.:

$$R_s = \alpha a_{js} + \beta a_{us} + \gamma a_{ks}, \tag{13.4a}$$

$$R_r = \alpha a_{jr} + \beta a_{ur} + \gamma a_{kr}, \tag{13.4b}$$

$$R_t = \alpha a_{jt} + \beta a_{ut} + \gamma a_{kt}. \tag{13.4c}$$

From these results, the following remarks about the quality and content of a religion are in order:

i. Note that the coefficient functions α, β, γ in (13.1) define the weightage given respectively to knowledge, methodology and practice components in a religion. This weightage, in fact, can change with space, time and circumstances.

ii. The components in R_s, R_r and R_t in (13.1) characterize the religious subgroups in a society dominated respectively by *satoguṇī*, *rajoguṇī* or *tamoguṇī* tendencies and again in the spirit of adjective degrees – best, better and good with regard to the maintenance of world and cosmic orders. As a matter of fact, it is the *satoguṇī* tendency that introduces one to a divine system of justice through world and cosmic orders. However, it may so happen that at certain space–time point in history, the followers of R_r and R_t components become nil and the entire society starts following only R_s, i.e. they become full of *satoguṇī* tendencies, then such a society becomes an ideal one and the corresponding religion with all three *sāttvika* components becomes an "ideal religion". In the Indian context, people imagine such a religion as *rāmarājya* and that existed during the period of great epic *Rāmāyaṇa.*

iii. A religion can survive, though not for very long, without its knowledge component. This normally happens when one does not want to know the logic working behind the methodology followed or the practice carried out. In this case, people just learn the methodology of earning and working accordingly for their livelihood. The questions like how and why are not raised before anyone or before the group of thinkers, if they ever existed in the society.

iv. *Ideally integrated religion*: Like the personality of a person (cf. chapters 9 and 11 of Kaushal 2015) one can as well define an ideally integrated religion. To create such a religion in practice, one has to readjust the norms associated with components *J*, *U* and *K* in an *R*. This can be carried out in two distinct ways:

   a. at crude (macro) level one can readjust the overall weightage given to *J*, *U*, and *K* component guiding groups through coefficients α, β and γ in (13.1) in the light of given circumstances, space and time, and

   b. at subtle (micro) level, one can readjust the fraction of expertise with *satoguṇī*, *rajoguṇī* or *tamoguṇī* tendency, that are present in those groups specialized in *J*, *U* and *K* components, and are responsible for framing the corresponding norms.

In mathematical terms, (b) above would suggest a new choice of basis vector with respect to which the matrix $A = (a_{pq})$ of eq. (13.2) becomes a diagonal one, viz.:

$$A_D = \begin{pmatrix} A_{ss} & 0 & 0 \\ 0 & A_{rr} & 0 \\ 0 & 0 & A_{tt} \end{pmatrix}. \quad (13.4)$$

Note that the set of modified basis vectors, in turn, will constitute the columns of the so-called diagonalizing matrix in the language of mathematics. However, the components *J*, *U*, *K* will now correspond to the diagonal elements A_{ss}, A_{rr} and A_{tt} in (13.4) and the same will give rise to a new form of a religion $\vec{R}$ through (13.1). Such a religion, if designed carefully, will be ideally integrated for each component of the society, i.e. *satoguṇī*, *rajoguṇī* and *tamoguṇī* nature, but with a new kind of balance among them – leading perhaps to a sustainable religion.

v. As far as the search of new basis vectors in (iv) is concerned, it is not a difficult task. In fact, in (13.2) we expect a person to be ideally associated with *satoguṇī, rajoguṇī* or *tamoguṇī* tendency, but in practice it is not so; rather most of us are born with mixed tendencies and one can easily find persons of a desired and dominating tendency in the lot or in the subgroup. These are the additional efforts to be made by the group of thinkers in a society to establish a sustainable religion.

13.4 Eternity and Universality of a Religion

13.4.1 LESSONS FROM PHYSICAL THEORIES: EXPERIENCE-BASED INVARIANTS (EBIs)

In order to explore the eternity and universality of a religion, we seek guidance from physical theories. In fact, it is the character of physical theories in terms of conservation laws and invariance principles that makes the subject of physical science easy and understandable in spite of the fact that it describes only the partial truth in nature. While the scientology of physical sciences mostly rely on the space- and time-mediated processes and interactions, that of human sciences basically relies on the trio of space-, time- and consciousness-mediated processes and interactions. This fact is largely explored in Chapter 7 in the context of psychomechanics.

As a matter of fact, the above character of physical theories transcribes the symmetries built already in the (closed) physical system and the same, in turn, simplifies the understanding of the system. Other features of a physical system to be added towards its simplified description are linearity, harmonicity, centrality, integrability, etc. which in turn restrict the domain of understanding of the system vis-à-vis the absolute reality. Also, the study of an idealized system in physics is useful as it at least shows the path to reach the real system, maybe in asymptotic limit. In reality, not only a physical system, rather whole physical world, is asymmetric, non-linear, anharmonic, non-central and non-integrable as far as its understanding using limited tools of science or of a finite human Being is concerned. A complete understanding of this grand creation is perhaps possible only by an Infinite Supreme. These features of a physical theory, in whatever domain they work, undoubtedly make it eternal and universal in philosophical terms.

It may be noted that if a quantity Q in this continuously changing world and cosmos is eternal, then this implies that it is time (t) invariant; if it is universal, then it is space (q)-invariant. In fact, the quantity Q can as well be experience-invariant (i.e. it is a kind of invariance that takes place with respect to the meditation variable (μ) and pertains to mental or spiritual domain). Recall that only a conscious object will have experience and the consciousness of this conscious object, when translated into the meditation variable μ, play a dominant role in unveiling the whole process, for certain phenomenon in psychophysics. In mathematical terms, these concepts can respectively be transcribed as

$$(dQ/dt) = 0, \quad (dQ/dq) = 0, \quad (dQ/d\mu) = 0. \qquad (13.5a, b, c)$$

Here, μ is meditation variable (its intensity, in fact, is a measure of dressing order of an inner EOL or of a *PM* with consciousness in discrete evolution (cf. Chapter 4)).

A few remarks about these equations and the quantity Q are in order:

i. Note that the science (objective) is valued mainly due to the universal character of its laws, maybe for a closed or other type of assumed systems. Therefore, eq. (13.5b) is generally redundant.

ii. The quantity Q in general is a function of q, t and μ in psychoscience, but in the two limiting cases, it can account for the phenomena pertaining to pure objective science or materialism (particularly, when the variable μ is absent or zero) and pertaining to spirituality (particularly, when Q is a function of μ alone or the variables q and t are zero or absent);

otherwise, in psychoscience it remains a function of all the three variables q, t and μ.

iii. While eq. (13.5a) is explored in great detail in physics in different contexts (cf. Kaushal 1998), eq. (13.5c) needs to be explored in the context of psycho and spiritual sciences. We plan to pursue this in the forthcoming sections.

iv. For the viability of eq. (13.5a), note that the quantity Q itself could be a dynamical variable (like energy, momentum and angular momentum) leading to conservation laws in physics. In fact, Q can as well be a function of dynamical variables leading to the so-called "integrable" systems (cf. Kaushal 1998) in physics. In the same vein, for the viability of eq. (13.5c), Q can just be a "fact" or an element of basic goodness (or badness) or a human quality, or a collection of such facts, phrases or a theme of spiritual taste as a whole, that could be an experience-based invariant.

v. As μ varies from some minimum value μ_{min} to higher values for a person sitting in contemplation, the resolution of levels of description in patomic model (cf. *fig.* 6.1) starts increasing and they accordingly become sensitive to view the roles of the world and cosmic orders within and without. During this process, experiential knowledge associated with an individual starts exploring the actions pertaining to different existences, viz. from $\mathcal{N}$, S, $\mathcal{G}$, $\mathcal{M}$ and finally from $\mathcal{C}$.

vi. Interestingly, in the process discussed in (v) above, there are certain facts and themes experienced by many and almost at the same stage of meditation and also in the same sequence of experiences, viz. $\mathcal{N} \rightarrow S \rightarrow \mathcal{G} \rightarrow \mathcal{M} \rightarrow \mathcal{C}$. This defines an experience-based invariant (EBI) associated with a given existence. One can categorize these EBIs, e.g. class-I type for $\mathcal{C}$-domain, class-II type for $\mathcal{M}$-domain and so on (cf. Table 13.1) in the order of decreasing subtlety.

vii. For example, for the domain $\mathcal{C}$ while eternal peace, joy, unconditional love, etc. define the EBIs, thirst, hunger, biological clocks, etc. are examples of EBIs for the domain $\mathcal{G}$. For the domain of $\mathcal{N}$ and S existences of a person, note that the EBIs are mostly in the form of experiential knowledge, whereas for the domain $\mathcal{M}$ of psychoscience, the EBIs are in the form of both experiential knowledge of spiritual taste at one end and of behavioural taste on the other.

13.4.2 RANKING OF THE ELEMENTS OF BASIC GOODNESS AND THE TYPES OF EBIs

Keeping the above remarks (particularly, the remarks (v)-(vii)) in mind, it can be noticed that there is an automatic ranking of elements of basic goodness (EBGs) as and when the meditation focuses itself on a given domain of human existence. Accordingly, the type of EBIs gets associated (cf. column (ii) of Table 13.1). In Table 13.1, we list a few candidates for EBIs (i.e. for the elements of basic goodness) corresponding to different existences of a person along with possible applications in the behaviour domain.

These are the elements of basic goodness, when combined with *satoguṇī* tendency at individual as well as at collective (society) levels and pursued in thoughts and actions, which will contribute to establishing a sustainable but ideal religion. While the followers of *rajoguṇī* tendencies always dominate a society and nation, those of *tamoguṇī* tendencies can never be eliminated completely in this ever-changing world. No doubt, the domination of any of these tendencies at any time in a society is a function of space, time and circumstances, but religious scriptures, and their ideals followed, do play an important role in maintaining the sustainability of a religion. A selective choice of EBGs, when incorporated in the norms of a religion, will definitely inspire in producing a role model for an individual or for the society as a whole.

Table 13.1: Some Examples of Elements of Basic Goodness (EBGs) in all Five Existences of a Person*

Existence (EBI-type Associated)	*Examples of EBGs, EBIs*	*Domain of Application*	*Remarks*
1. Causal ($\mathcal{C}$) (class-I type)	Truth, eternal peace, joy, unconditional love and affection, forgiveness, fearlessness, satisfaction, etc.	Origin in spiritual zone but applications in all psychic, behavioural and objective science zones	EBGs help in establishing cosmic connections, in realizing unity in diversity, etc.
2. Micro ($\mathcal{M}$) (class-II type)	Non-violence, control of mind and senses and their withdrawal from sense objects, lack of egoism, etc.	Origin in psychic zone but applications in all other zones	EBGs help in achieving placidity of mind, an urge for meditation and concentration to gain knowledge and wisdom, an urge for character building, etc.
3. Gross ($\mathcal{G}$) (class-III type)	Continence, regulated lifestyle leading to good health and happiness through good deeds, thirst, hunger, biological clock towards fitness, etc.	Origin in gross-body domain and its interactions with WO; body and health maintenance to become a good citizen in ethical zone	EBGs help in shaping personality and its development to become a good citizen and netizen

cont.

Table 13.1: *Cont.*

Existence (EBI-type Associated)	*Examples of EBGs, EBIs*	*Domain of Application*	*Remarks*
4. Societal ($\mathcal{S}$) (class-IV type)	Sustainable relationships and friendship; qualities of coexistence, cooperation, coordination while working in a group or in an organization and in consonance with Nature or with the God-made world.	When a child is born, it automatically becomes a part of the society in which it has born and also becomes a part of the prevailing Natural environment: both affect his existence and lifestyle	$\mathcal{C}$, $\mathcal{M}$, and $\mathcal{G}$ existences, while are responsible for the character building of a person, the existences $\mathcal{S}$ and $\mathcal{N}$ are responsible for his personality development and hence for the character of a society and also of the nation as a whole
5. Natural ($\mathcal{N}$) (class-V type)	The quality of realizing and appreciating Nature and its acts, or of the God-made world in general, including cosmic order.	– do –	– do –

* if identified in a religion, then they qualify the religion for eternity, universality and also for the EBI. Corresponding to these existences, the associated class of EBIs is also indicated

13.5 Further Remarks on EBIs Associated with Human Cognition and Actions

It may be mentioned that the dynamical invariants of physics (cf. eqs (13.5a) and (13.5b)) are also the EBIs but in a restricted sense. In fact, for this case, the expert scientist has to have an analogous experience or realization of the same physical truth (facts) (laws, theory and experiment) prior to its acceptance but within the limits on the measurement process (errors, etc.) and on the extent of quantification (modelling, etc.) of the phenomenon. Here, we plan to investigate EBIs corresponding to eq. (13.5c) which basically belong to the wisdom related to a psychic and/or a spiritual zone. As a matter of fact, when the experience (consciousness) is combined with the material world or with its phenomena (i.e. the world – W_3), then the dressed version of an object in the latter becomes an object of meditation and realization and thus putting it in the psychic and/or spiritual zone. However, the implications of this modified version manifest in practical life but with a sustainable and positive spirit. For example, experience + knowledge $\Rightarrow$ experienced knowledge (wisdom); experience + yogic exercise $\Rightarrow$ experienced *yoga* (*raj-yoga* of Patañjali); experience + dynamical invariant $\Rightarrow$EBIs.

With a view to expanding the concept of the laws and invariants of human cognition, the subject of psychophysics beyond sensation has been investigated in recent years by Kaembach et al. (2016). These studies, pursued in the bottom-up approach and using the tools of brain science and neural network, in fact, help in identifying the domain of psychophysics in this context. Whether it is the study of laws or the concept of invariants, the borrowed analogies from physics still have limitations in these studies as far as the search for a complete truth in Nature is concerned. This is mainly due to the limits on modelling games involved in these bottom-up approaches. It may be of interest to look for a possible connection, if any, between the invariants investigated by Kaembach et al. and the EBIs of the present top-down approach, particularly when both lead to the sustainability of the concepts of psychoscience.

Other type of EBIs worth investigating are the outcomes of psychodynamical eq. (7.32) for the case of cyclic coordinates. In fact, for the case when the mindset function (cenergy measure) $\mathcal{M}$ does not depend explicitly on t or on q, then the constructs identified as the EBIs are the "conjugate c-energy" C_μ, viz.:

$$\left(\frac{\partial M}{\partial \bar{t}}\right) \equiv C_{\mu} = \text{constant (with respect to } \mu) \qquad (13.6a)$$

Or, the "conjugate c-momentum" P_{μ}, viz.:

$$\frac{1}{\bar{t}}\frac{\partial \mathcal{M}}{\partial \dot{q}} + \frac{\partial \mathcal{M}}{\partial \bar{q}} \equiv P_{\mu} = \text{constt. (with respect to } \mu) \qquad (13.6b)$$

Here, symbols have their usual meanings as in Chapter 7. Note that these EBIs do not make much sense as long as the function $\mathcal{M}$ $(=\mathcal{M}_g+\mathcal{M}_s)$ in which the subtle part is identified with the particular form of the "potential function" $V = V(q, t, \mu)$ (cf. eq. (7.35)). However, for the phenomena in which the "potential function" V turns out to be $V(q, \dot{q}, \bar{q}, t, \bar{t}, \mu)$, these EBIs (13.6)) for the form (7.35) yield

$$C_{\mu} = c\bar{t} + (\partial V/\partial \bar{t}) \qquad (13.7a)$$

$$P_{\mu} = (1/2\,\bar{t})\,(2a\dot{q} + (\partial V/\partial \dot{q})) + 2b\bar{q} + (\partial V/\partial \bar{q}), \qquad (13.7b)$$

which, in fact, turn out to be the combination of both slow (corresponding to subtle or subconscious) and fast (corresponding to the gross or conscious) parts of $\mathcal{M}$ (cf. Section 7.4.3).

13.6 EBIs in Indian Philosophy: Examples and Applications

13.6.1 AṢṬĀṄGA-YOGA OF PATAÑJALI: A PERFECT EXAMPLE OF EBI

Who and what contribute to an ideal and sustainable religion at the most fundamental level? These are some questions which need to be addressed in the present context. In the light of what has been discussed thus far, these are the EBGs inculcated in a personality which effectively contribute the most to the society. At the next stage the EBIs, if present in or are used in framing the norms to be adopted by the society, also matter a lot in this respect. Note that the philosophy of a common man in the Indian context generally revolves around the *aṣṭāṅga-yoga* of Patañjali which, in fact, offers a perfect example of EBIs in the following sense.

Aṣṭāṅga-yoga (also called *rāja-yoga*) consists of eight components, viz. (i) *yama*, (ii) *niyama*, (iii) *āsana*, (iv) *prāṇāyāma*, (v) *pratyāhāra*, (vi) *dhāraṇā*, (vii) *dhyāna*, and (viii) *samādhi*. Each of these components has further divisions and subdivisions. Another classification of these eight components is in the form of *bahiraṅga* (external) *yoga* (cf. components (i) to (v)) and *antaraṅga* (internal) *yoga* (cf. components (vi) to (viii)). In fact, several variants of *yoga* are discussed in *SMBG* and other Vedic scriptures but the fact is that the *aṣṭāṅga-yoga* retains its own place mainly because in this *yoga* the entire spectrum of human experiences and actions is covered through these eight components and the same are also in accordance with the three existences of a human Being. For example, components (i) to (iv) correspond to gross existence $\mathcal{G}$, components (v) to (vii) correspond to micro-existence, $\mathcal{M}$, and the component (viii) corresponds to causal existence $\mathcal{C}$. Since a lot of specialized literature is available on this subject under the head *rāja-yoga*, we refrain ourselves from going into details. It may be mentioned that without knowing the deep underlying philosophy behind the ordering of these eight components, the component (iii), i.e. *āsana*, is practised worldwide mostly in the context of health fitness regime. Components (i) and (ii), each having five subdivisions, further add to the list of EBGs in a down-to-earth manner. These subdivisions including the variety of *āsanas*, if inculcated in daily life, will definitely prepare a person as an ideal unit for the society. While the component (iv) *prāṇāyāma* helps in synchronizing gross and micro existences, it does teach the art of meditation, control of mind and senses from their corresponding sense object in conjunction with the component (v) *pratyāhāra*. The components (vi) and (vii), if properly practised, prepare a person to enter in the spiritual zone of $\mathcal{C}$.

It may be mentioned that it is only after remaining in stages (vi) and (vii), not only for years and decades but even for several lifespans (depending on one's attitude towards life and the level of development of his FOUs), that a practitioner becomes entitled to a journey into *samādhi*, i.e. the stage (viii) of *aṣṭāṅga-yoga*. This is the stage when a finite (soul) becomes capable of merging into the infinite (cosmic consciousness field Φ_{CC} of Chapter 4), a state defined as *mokṣa* in Vedic scriptures. If one somehow discontinues these systematic practices at any stage, then, as per Vedic wisdom, nothing is lost. The practitioner with some efforts and practice revives them rather quickly later possibly in the same or in the next lifespan. As this royal method of practising *yoga* remains independent of space, time and circumstances, it is also termed as *rāja-yoga* for this very reason. Interestingly, the practice of each component yields more or less the same or similar results for each practitioner while he resides in his respective $\mathcal{G}$, $\mathcal{M}$ and $\mathcal{C}$ existences. This, of course, offers the example of EBIs of different categories and hence the *aṣṭāṅga-yoga* is a unique and complete example full of EBIs.

Components (i) and (ii) of *rāja-yoga*, prerequisites for any sustainable religion as EBGs, are also the candidates for EBIs in results. The entire set of eight components of this *yoga* represents the spirit of *Sanātana Dharma*, but many religions of the world can be seen as particular cases of the first five components alone. In modern times, several Indian saints have proposed their own short-cuts to this noble method of *rāja-yoga* for eternal peace, but in reality they only provide spatio-temporal peace. We refrain ourselves from going into such details.

13.6.2 EXAMPLES OF EBIs FROM SMBG AND OTHER VEDIC SCRIPTURES

No doubt, some EBIs belonging to the $\mathcal{G}$-domain can be expressed through words and letters and that too only in parts as far as their meanings and understanding are concerned. On the other hand, those belonging to the $\mathcal{M}$- and $\mathcal{C}$-domains by and large, are a matter of meditation and realization. Everyone, whosoever desires, can have a feel for them or has an experience with them. There is, however, no question of any imposition on anyone in this regard. The only prerequisite is that the practitioner should have an appropriate level of development of his FOUs. Several examples to this effect can be cited in the form of proverbs, idioms, sayings, or storytelling. Normally, the literature of a good (!) language is also full of such constructs. In the Indian context, in the following, we cite some examples of EBIs from *SMBG* – a treasure of such experience-based Vedic wisdom. One can classify these EBIs into five, corresponding to five existences, viz. class-I type EBIs corresponding to the $\mathcal{C}$-domain, class-II, class-III, class-IV and class-V types, respectively corresponding to the $\mathcal{M}$-, $\mathcal{G}$-, S- and $\mathcal{N}$-domain EBIs (cf. Table 13.1). In fact, class-IV and class-V type EBIs also belong to WO and again correspond to the man-made and God-made worlds. Note that most of the EBIs of physical and behavioural sciences belong to class-IV and class-V types.

a. *Examples of EBIs of class-III, class-IV and class-V types*: A kind of satisfaction of permanent nature is noticed by each practitioner out of the results of an action performed by a variety of persons in given circumstances but with the same level of development of their FOUs. This is what has been termed as an "EBI". As mentioned before, while *yama, niyama, āsana* and *prāṇāyāma* components of *rāja-yoga* offer examples of class-III type at the gross-body level, such EBIs do leave an impact on both ends, i.e. on the $\mathcal{M}$-domain (class-II type) on one end and on the S- and $\mathcal{N}$-domain (classes-IV and V types) on the other, and thus affecting the corresponding EBIs. Further, note that the $\boldsymbol{S}$- and $\mathcal{N}$-domains not only constitute the WO of patomic model, but they are also responsible for the man-made (the world of science) and the God-made (the world of behavioural science or of consciousness) worlds.

In *SMBG*, the Lord hints at varieties of *yoga* but all lead to the same objective (Absolute) if followed in a true sense. However, the prerequisite that Lord sets in *SMBG* for all types of *yoga* is through the verse VI.17:

yuktāhāra-vihārasya yukta-ceṣṭasya karmasu ।
yukta-svapnāva bodhasya yogo bhavati duḥkhahā ॥ (13.8)

> *Yoga*, which rids one of woe, is accomplished only by him who is regulated in diet and recreation, regulated in maintaining righteous efforts towards the performance of actions and regulated in sleep and wakefulness.

These are a few tips prescribed to become a successful person in life. The person undoubtedly notices their importance in his heart as an EBI. Out of them, note that the diet and recreation are mostly man-made and the corresponding EBIs fall in the societal domain (class-IV type), righteous efforts fall under class-II and class-III categories, sleep and wakefulness, on the other hand, belonging to the God-made world and fall partly under class-V type category of EBIs. There are plenty of situations described in *SMBG* where the occurrences of EBIs of various categories can be noticed. Look at the varying degree of satisfaction derived by an individual by performing actions of different domains. For example, this degree is highest for class-I type and minimum for class-V type EBIs. A good percentage of grand wisdom of *SMBG* is full of EBIs of different categories, but that of class-I type is rare of the rarest from the point of view of practice vis-à-vis the occurrence of such EBIs in the scriptures of other religions. This is what makes the Vedic wisdom distinct from others in the sense of eternity and universality.

b. *Examples of EBIs of class-II type*: As the Lord has to console and provide a mental cure to dejected Arjuna in the situation of war, a great deal of *SMBG* is full of psychological and the related processes therein and so are the occurrences of EBIs of class-II type. Even among the EBIs of class-II type, there are sub-classes – some are close to class-I type at one end, whereas some are akin to class-III type on the other and the remaining are in-between them. In what follows, we cite a few EBIs of these types mainly from the second chapter of *SMBG*:

   i. *The art of crossing two thresholds as one progresses from the $\mathcal{G}$- to $\mathcal{C}$-domain (as examples of EBI):* In the context of kārmic theory, recall the morale hidden in the phrase, "the work is your duty and the reward is not thy concern" (cf. *SMBG* II.47). Naturally, if one practises this moral in his heart, he will have more time to focus on his work and improve the methodology involved in performing the task rather than wasting time on thinking about the fruit (good or bad!) of his task. Fruit is bound to appear with time, once the task is started. Also, this is the way to attain peace of mind and an element of satisfaction as well. Now the question is as to who can deny the experience of this eternal truth. In fact, this moral enables one to retain peace at mental level. In later chapters, the Lord goes one step ahead when He emphasizes on rejecting the feeling of doership of action or suggests to surrender the same to the Lord (cf. *SMBG* V.14). Practising on such a concept in mind, if becomes possible, will definitely take one to the path of eternal joy. For a materialistic mind, though these are difficult steps or sermons to follow but for a spiritual mind it is a question of stepping up further, obviously without affecting the activities performed in the world outside.

It may be mentioned that the two situations cited above basically are the two thresholds to be crossed by a practitioner to enter the spiritual zone. The first is the renunciation of fruit of action that corresponds to the control of mind and senses from the sense objects which, in turn, facilitates the entry from the $\mathcal{G}$- to $\mathcal{M}$-domain and the second, surrendering the doership to the Lord (which is tantamount to suppression of ego) will facilitate the entry of a practitioner from the $\mathcal{M}$- to $\mathcal{C}$-domain.

ii. *The art of experiencing the stability and instability of mind as an example of EBI:* Those whose mind is carried away by flowery speech, deeply attached with the enjoyment of sense objects, and of power, cannot attain the determinate intellect concentrated on higher objects (cf. *SMBG* II.44) – a case of unstable mind. On the other hand, one who discards all cravings and desires and confines to self-satisfaction has a stable mind (cf. *SMBG* II.55). The art of experiencing such realities offers an example of EBI.

iii. *An experience of sequential downfall or uplifting of moral strength as an example of EBI: SMBG* II.62-63 offers a wonderful theory of sequential moral downfall of a person who could not concentrate on higher object but deeply involved in and attached with the enjoyment of sense objects. A person, who is at the verge of downfall or dwelling on the sense objects, develops attachment for them, from attachment springs up desire, from desire (mainly from the unfulfilled ones) causes anger. From anger arises delusion, from delusion, confusion of memory, from confusion of memory, loss of reason and from loss of reason, the person goes to a state of complete ruin. Contrary to this sequence, a self-controlled person (or a person of stable mind), while enjoying various sense objects through his senses which are disciplined and free from likes or dislikes, attain placidity of mind. Such is a wonderful and reasoned experience, if one can have it, as and when he faces a situation. This offers a case of EBI, as anyone, anywhere and anytime can undergo such an experience.

c. *Examples of EBIs of class-I type:* Recall that the capsule of wisdom given in *SMBG* is basically an extraction of the wisdom detailed in various Vedic scriptures. No doubt, it is full of examples of different types of EBIs, but those of class-I type are repeatedly highlighted in different contexts (e.g. chapter 12 of *SMBG*). In fact, there are a few rarest of the rare situations as far as other Vedic scriptures or the texts of other religions are concerned.

Before discussing a grand class-I type case of an EBI from *SMBG*, we remind the reader here of some concepts used analogously in different contexts in mathematics and physics, viz. those of "closure property" and "self-consistency". The concept of closure is well known

i. for the eigenstates of a Hermitian operator in quantum mechanics,

ii. for the elements of a vector space or of a group in pure mathematics.

   A feeling for the concept of self-consistency can be derived from,

iii. the octet model and the bootstrap dynamics in particle physics, and

iv. the use of self-consistent theories in atomic and nuclear physics.

In what follows, we shall use the spirit of these concepts in analysing a case from *SMBG*.

In this regard, note the following verses narrating the highest truth about the working of Nature and also of a human Being:

prakr̥teḥ kriyamāṇāni guṇaiḥ karmāṇi sarvaśaḥ ।
ahaṁkāra-vimūḍhātmā kartāhamiti manyate ।।

– *SMBG* III.27 (13.9)

tattvavittu mahābāho guṇa-karma-vibhāgayoḥ ।
guṇā guṇeṣu vartanta iti matvā na sajjate ।।

– *SMBG* III.28 (13.10)

In fact, all actions are Being performed by the modes of *prakr̥ti* (Primordial Nature). The fool, whose mind is deluded by egoism, thinks, "I am the doer". However, he who has true insight into the respective spheres of *guṇas* (modes of *prakr̥ti*) and their actions, holding that it is the *guṇas* (in the form of senses, mind, etc.)

> that move among the *guṇas* (objects of perception) does not get attached to them, Arjuna.

In order to understand the truth of the highest degree hidden in these verses, recall the concept of two thresholds mentioned in class-II type EBIs (cf. example (b(i)) above). While these verses teach the art to remain constantly in the domain of existence $\mathcal{C}$ as a man of wisdom (*jñāna-yogī*), also supply the logic behind this art of crossing the threshold of ego. For this purpose, the concepts of "closure" and "self-consistency" of physical science are very much relevant. In fact, after experiencing this art with an eye on the underlying logic, the practitioner has every chance to remain in the domain of $\mathcal{C}$ or in the state of *mokṣa*.

To this effect, consider a set of (23 + 1) entities as per Vedic wisdom, viz. *five* cosmic elements: earth, water, air, fire and ether; *five* senses of action or motor organs: hands, feet, speech, anus and copulatory organ; *five* senses of knowledge: eyes, ears, nose, tongue and skin, with corresponding *five* sense objects: light, sound, smell, taste and touch; *three* inner EOLs, mind, intellect and ego, and the last 24th is the Being or the polluted version of soul (cf. Chapter 1). Out of them, each of the first twenty-three entities comes in (or are wrapped with) three flavours (shades) of *guṇas* (modes of *prakṛti)*, i.e. *sattva, rajas* and *tamas*. Such a set of twenty-three entities with *guṇas* forms a fundamental set of entities called *guṇa-vibhāga*; and the set of their mutual interactions, efforts and actions in the outer world defines the so-called *karma-vibhāga* in Vedic science. The important point to be noted here is that an individual as per his composition, efforts and actions does not go out of the domains of these two sets in philosophical terms. Not only this, these efforts and actions are carried out in a self-consistent manner, i.e. without affecting the Being (localized) or the Super Being (cosmic consciousness field Φ_{CC}). Such features of these fundamental sets, in fact, define its closure and self-consistency in the sense that any newly thought entity or its operations does not leave these fundamental sets in their respective domains.

Perhaps for such reasons, the Lord, under the head of "Yoga of Knowledge (*jñāna-yoga*)", summarily conveyed His role in the functioning of both the world and cosmic orders through the verse V.14:

na karttṛtvam na karmāṇi lokasya sṛjati prabhuḥ ।
na karmaphala-saṁyogaṁ svabhāvastu pravartate ॥ (13.10a)

God determines neither the doership nor the doings of persons, nor even their contact with the fruit of action; but it is Nature (in terms of the above two fundamental sets) alone that does all this.

In mathematical terms, first twenty-three entities of the first fundamental set (and so are the operations listed in the second fundamental set) can be considered as the vectors of a vector space spanned by the three *guṇas* (cf. Appendix D) over a (mathematical) field of Φ_{CC}. Thus, all these twenty-three entities including the related operations, like the personality described through the five existences of a person, are vectors of a vector space which, by definition, fulfil the closure property.

13.7 Vedic Wisdom and Sanātana Dharma

Besides the universality (invariance with space) and eternity (invariance with time) concepts discussed in the preceding sections to judge the merit of a religion, another criterion, introduced perhaps for the first time, is the existence and search of the EBI in the tenets of a religion. Although some representative examples in this regard are detailed from *SMBG*, but the fact is that a great deal of the Vedic wisdom conforms to these requirements. As this wisdom concerns the entire lifestyle of a person and thus becomes his way of life, its followers call this wisdom as *Sanātana Dharma* – an eternal way of life.

As a matter of fact, the Vedic wisdom can be considered as consisting of two types of knowledge:

i. Which is transcended directly from the cosmos (cf. Chapter 4) through the minds of great seers of the past, like the one in Vedas, and

ii. the one derived from Vedas and interpreted by superhuman Beings from time to time as per need of space, time and circumstances.

We identify these two types of knowledge respectively as experience-based (K_{ex}) and event-based (K_{ev}). As the original Vedic knowledge or for that matter even the derived one could not remain pure due to the followers of varying tastes and needs, both K_{ex} and K_{ev} have implicit dependence on space (q), time (t) and circumstances (σ). Not only this, the collection of tenets of any religion, Q, does have an implicit dependence on q, t and σ in addition on K_{ex} and K_{ev}. Thus, the quantity to be optimized for practical lifestyle in modern times is $Q = Q\,(K_{ex}, K_{ev})$, where $K_{ex} = K_{ex}\,(q, t, \mu)$, $K_{ev} = K_{ev}\,(q, t, \mu)$. Further note that

i. while K_{ex} remains abstract and compact, K_{ev}, on the other hand, has undergone a lot of proliferation in view of varieties of religions, belief systems and faiths all over the world, particularly after the incarnation of a large number of prophets from time to time, and

ii. in some sense K_{ex} and K_{ev} can also follow a kind of Fechner type (cf. Chapter 7) law, viz. $K_{ex} \propto \ln K_{ev}$.

The variable μ can be understood here as representing the given circumstances in the mental domain.

Next we look for the conditions under which the set of tenet Q attains an optimal value with the variations of K_{ex} and K_{ev} and also with q, t and μ. Thus, for $Q = Q\,(K_{ex}, K_{ev})$ with $K_{ex} = K_{ex}\,(q, t, \mu)$; $K_{ev} = K_{ev}\,(q, t, \mu)$, the three eqs (13.5a-c) for space-, time- and experience-invariance of Q, respectively yield

$$\frac{dQ}{dq} \equiv \frac{\partial Q}{\partial K_{ex}} \frac{\partial K_{ex}}{\partial q} + \frac{\partial Q}{\partial K_{ev}} \frac{\partial K_{ev}}{\partial q} = 0, \tag{13.11a}$$

$$\frac{dQ}{dt} \equiv \frac{\partial Q}{\partial K_{ex}} \frac{\partial K_{ex}}{\partial t} + \frac{\partial Q}{\partial K_{ev}} \frac{\partial K_{ev}}{\partial t} = 0, \tag{13.11b}$$

$$\frac{dQ}{\partial \mu} \equiv \frac{\partial Q}{\partial K_{ex}} \frac{\partial K_{ex}}{\partial \mu} + \frac{\partial Q}{\partial K_{ev}} \frac{\partial K_{ev}}{\partial \mu} = 0. \tag{13.11c}$$

On the other hand, for the stability of Q one should have $\delta Q = 0$. For this purpose, note that

$$\delta Q = \frac{\partial Q}{\partial K_{ex}} . \delta K_{ex} + \frac{\partial Q}{\partial K_{ev}} . \delta K_{ev}$$

$$= \frac{\partial Q}{\partial K_{ex}} \left[\frac{\partial K_{ex}}{\partial q} . \delta q + \frac{\partial K_{ex}}{\partial t} . \delta t + \frac{\partial K_{ex}}{\partial \mu} . \delta \mu \right]$$

$$+ \frac{\partial Q}{\partial K_{ev}} \left[\frac{\partial K_{ev}}{\partial q} . \delta q + \frac{\partial K_{ev}}{\partial t} . \delta t + \frac{\partial K_{ev}}{\partial \mu} . \delta \mu \right]$$

$$= \left[\frac{\partial Q}{\partial K_{ex}} \frac{\partial K_{ex}}{\partial q} + \frac{\partial Q}{\partial K_{ev}} \frac{\partial K_{ev}}{\partial q} \right] \delta q + \left[\frac{\partial Q}{\partial K_{ex}} \frac{\partial K_{ex}}{\partial t} + \frac{\partial q}{\partial K_{ev}} \frac{\partial K_{ev}}{\partial t} \right] \delta t$$

$$\left[\frac{\partial Q}{\partial K_{ex}} \frac{\partial K_{ex}}{\partial \mu} + \frac{\partial Q}{\partial K_{ev}} \frac{\partial K_{ev}}{\partial \mu} \right] \delta \mu . \tag{13.12}$$

Thus, $\delta Q = 0$ would require the vanishing of the coefficients of δq, δt and $\delta \mu$ on the right hand side of (13.12). This, in fact, will yield the same set of equations as (13.11) and the same, in turn, implies that the space, time and experience invariance of a belief system corresponds to its stability in the mind of an individual and also in a society. Further, note that for the cases when μ-dependence in K_{ev} is mild or negligible or when q- and t-dependences in K_{ex} are mild or negligible, eqs (13.11) take some simpler forms. It is worthwhile to investigate these cases further.

Almost all truths prevailing in Vedic scriptures, or in the derived belief systems thereof, are expected to fulfil the three conditions given in (13.11), of course in varying proportions, particularly when analysed in terms of the components, K_{ex} and K_{ev}. No doubt, K_{ex} dominates the scene in the Vedic wisdom, but in the wisdom of other religions, it is the K_{ev} component that dominates the scene. Even in Vedic stream, when question comes to Purāṇas, K_{ev} again starts dominating and K_{ex} component of wisdom *remains* only in the background, sometimes distantly.

13.8 Concluding Discussion

The philosophy behind the prevailing religions is studied in this chapter with reference to their universality, eternity and sustainability features. In analogy with physical sciences, attempts are made here to look for these features in the components of a religion or belief system. In particular, the efforts have been made to look for the criteria in mathematical terms to judge the merit and quality of a religion through its components, viz. *jñāna*, *upāsanā* and *karma*. To this effect, a religion (and so are its components) is considered as a vector in the vector space spanned by three *guṇas* – *sattva*, *rajas* and *tamas* – over a field of cosmic consciousness. With regard to the setting of norms for an integrated religion in terms of its components, macro and micro processes are suggested to find the component experts for this purpose (cf. Section 13.3). In this connection, the diagonal elements of a diagonalized version of the component matrix are expected to help in identifying an "ideally integrated religion".

The universality, in fact, demands the invariance of the set of tenets of a religion with respect to space. Similarly, the invariance of this set with respect to time defines the eternity of the corresponding religion. The newly proposed invariance with respect to the variable μ defines the sustainability or the EBI of the belief system concerned. Corresponding to the five existences of a human Being, viz. causal, micro, gross, societal and natural, five types of EBIs are suggested, viz. class-I type corresponding to the $\mathcal{C}$-domain, class-II type corresponding to the $\mathcal{M}$-domain, and so on (cf. Table 13.1). It is argued that the Vedic scriptures like *SMBG* are full of examples of EBIs. The occurrence of higher and higher rank EBIs in a religion also defines the quality and merit of that religion vis-à-vis their universality, eternity and sustainability. Other alternative mathematical criteria, in analogy with physics, are also investigated (cf. Section 13.7) to establish these features in a religion, particularly in terms of its event-based and experience-based knowledge contents. While Vedic scriptures are full of class-I and class-II type EBIs, it is worthwhile to look for these features in the sacred texts of other religions. In fact, most of these texts are again dominated by class-III to class-V type EBIs.

From the survey of examples listed in Section 13.6.2, it can be noticed that EBIs of class-III to class-V type mainly contribute to the proliferation of knowledge on the initiative of class-II type EBIs. But the fact is that at times they too become a cause of envy and mutual conflict between societies and nations. On the other hand, the class-I type of EBIs, if exists and practised properly in a religion, does encourage one in establishing the harmony and the concept of unity in diversity among people. Unfortunately, only a few religions in the world are gifted with such golden thoughts. If the initiatives of class-II type EBIs are directed towards the class-I type, then this will certainly support the popular slogan of modern generation: "we are spiritual, but not religious".

It may be mentioned that various belief systems offer the case of subjective science directly or remotely. The modern (objective) science which, of course, does not have very old history also offers a kind of belief system in the sense that its working components, viz. theory, methodology and experiments, are exactly the same in spirit as the components of a religion, viz. *jñāna* (J), *upāsanā* (U) and *karma* (K). No doubt the quantification, measurement and predictability are the main concern of objective sciences but the fact is that the scientists who created it in recent centuries do follow similar expertise of components as that of a religion. Their space–time-mediated models and associated interactions are in no way different from the experience-tested set of norms of a religion that are framed for its followers. Also, while the elements of exactness and predictability dominate in objective science, these features somehow appear in poor shape in subjective science and that too in a speculative manner unless the experts of norms have realized the realities of world- and cosmic-order to their finest possible level. A discussion on these intricacies of religion and science will be continued in the next chapter (cf. *fig.* 14.1).

A Case of Infinite Happiness (or Mokṣa) in Vedic Traditions

In continuation of Appendix E, we analyze here the concept of happiness associated with an individual. In accordance with five existences of a person, namely natural, societal, gross, micro and causal, one can say that there could be five (minimal) essential needs (or desires) of an individual which have to be fulfilled for survival after the elimination of the most of them, and they are; (i) housing, (ii) clothing, (iii) food, (iv) breathing, and (v) ego. Let us define the happiness index, h, for an individual as, $h = (x/n)$, where x is the number of possible desires and n is the number of essential desires to be fulfilled. Note that as $n \to 0$, then $h \to \infty$ since x can never be zero in given space, time and circumstances. Further note that it is the intensity of meditation and of *saṅkalpas* that can minimize even the essential needs. Thus, if a person desires, he can discard the need of a house and start living in open or in forest, he can discard clothing and live naked, discard food by living first on water and later on air, discard or minimize breathing by way of having deep or unusually elongated breath, etc. However, an element of ego still remains to justify one's existence in this world (even in the causal zone). In the end, if one discards even this ego, then n becomes zero and so h turns out to be infinite. This state of infinite happiness of a human soul is, in fact, termed as *mokṣa* in Vedic traditions and it is at this stage that our soul is prepared to merge with the cosmic consciousness field Φ_{cc}.

High Skill Exercises and Projects

13.1 "Quality of a religion is defined by the richness of 'elements of basic goodness' present in that religion." Explain as to how such a religion becomes sustainable with reference to the maintenance of both world- and cosmic-orders.

13.2 Discuss religion $\vec{R}$ as a vector in the vector space spanned by three *guṇas* and over a field of cosmic consciousness. Hence, define and discuss an "ideally integrated religion".

13.3 In analogy with physical theories, explain as to how the eternity and universality of norms in a religion make it eternal and global. How does the "*Sanātana* religion" differ from the *Sanātana Dharma*?

13.4 "The presence of different types of 'experience-based invariants in abundance' in Vedic scriptures, makes the *Sanātana Dharma* eternal and global." Cite some examples to support this statement from Vedic literature and also write an essay to justify the same.

13.5 Seek help of contents of Chapter 14 to justify the place value of psychoscience in between the spiritual zone and the behavioural zone. In fact, in the spiritual journey described in this book, there are many side pathways to realize the final truth. List the pathways and write a Note supporting these claims.

14

Summary, Future Prospects and Concluding Remarks

Attempts are made in this book to quantify and to bring out some parts of the ancient Vedic wisdom, related to the psychology of an individual, in the mainstream of modern science, of course, not by way of glorifying the wisdom but by way of presenting its underlying concepts in analytical and computable terms. For this purpose, the newly-coined subject of "Vedic psychoscience" is presented in three parts. After discussing the spiritual hold on psychoscience in Part 1 in the finest and deepest possible philosophical spirit, Part 2 is devoted to develop the subject in accordance with various disciplines of modern science. Attempts are made in Part 3 to extend the derived concepts of Part 2 to a "ready to use" form. Keeping the size of the book in mind, further ground level applications of these concepts are not pursued but are left for the researchers in the field to investigate. In fact, a detailed discussion of psychoscience in its new incarnation, mainly in the top-down manner (that is from spirituality to materialism), is carried out in Part 2 of the book.

It may be mentioned that the Vedic literature is an ocean of wisdom and the author could pick only a few drops from this ocean because of his own limitations. This has further limited the discussions in the book at various places. A flow chart showing the value and place value of psychoscience in the entire spectrum of Vedic wisdom is displayed in *fig.* 14.1. In accordance with the three-world concept (cf. Table 3.2), the spiritual science while deals with the realization of Absolute Reality (world W_1), the psychoscience, in fact, paves the way to achieve this state through the world W_2. The behavioural science, on the other hand, offers a practical ground for both spiritual science and psychoscience. As far as the feedback to spiritual science is concerned, it constantly comes from both psychoscience and behavioural science respectively in the form of subjective and objective realities, of course, via a common thread of methodology as shown in this figure.

Whether it is the proliferation or the abstraction of knowledge, note that in either case the use of structural analogies (Kaushal 2003) becomes an integral part of the study in general and that of the methodology in particular towards the development of a subject. The same in fact could not be avoided in the present case. The analogies of terms, concepts, phrases, or the collection of phrases or of the phenomenon as a whole, are frequently borrowed from the hard disciplines like physics, chemistry and other mathematical sciences.

When different flowers are connected through a thread, then the resultant product is termed "garland" and it is used for different purposes and in a much wider perspective. It matters a lot as to how one connects the flowers or as to how strong the thread is? Similar is the case with the pieces of Vedic wisdom which are distributed among various Vedic scriptures by varieties of names and in different contexts propounded sometimes by different seers. The common thread adopted in the present scheme of study is the natural science along with its time-tested methodology – analytical, mathematical and otherwise. Keeping the ever-increasing scientific progress in mind, it appears that the thread of the garland cannot be stronger than this and the garland so prepared is definitely going to be somewhat more durable.

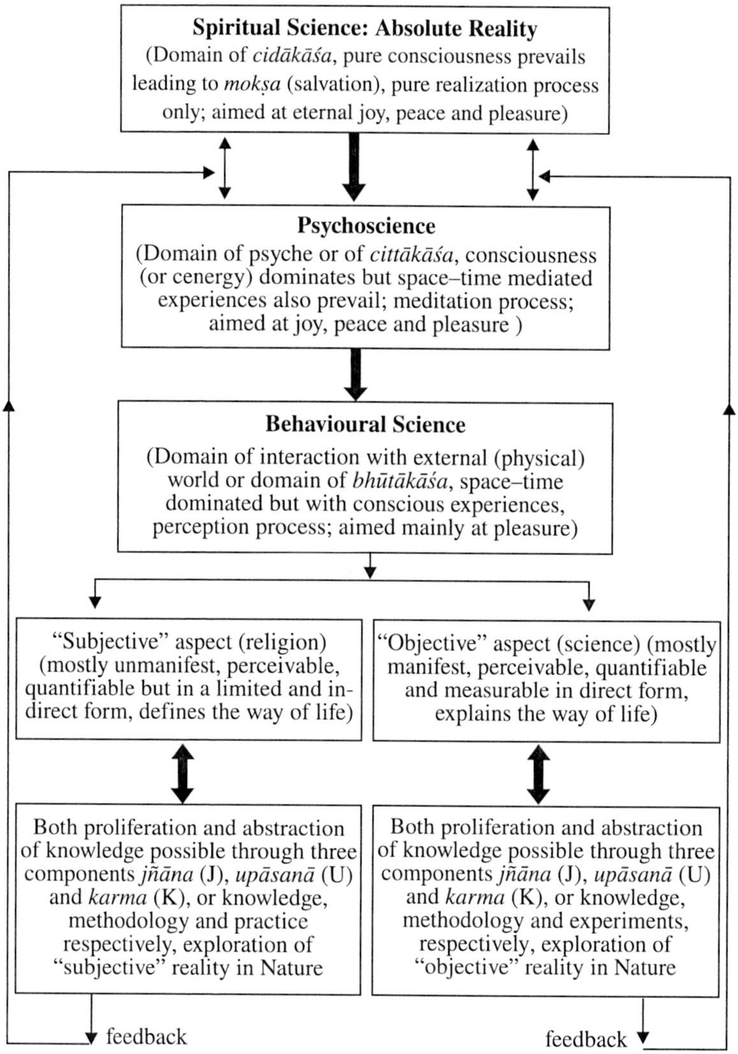

fig. 14.1: The philosophy of life (and in some sense elaborating the theme of the present book). This chart can be used as a guide in fixing the objectives in a scholarly mind

In *fig.* 14.1 we display different paths to Absolute Reality along with the characteristic features associated with each. In fact, the three zones for human existences $\mathcal{C}$, $\mathcal{M}$ and $\mathcal{G}$ are respectively identified here as spiritual, psychic and behavioural zones and are also in accordance with *cidākāśa*, *cittākāśa* and *bhūtākāśa* concepts of Vedic wisdom (Ādi Śaṅkarācārya, in the *Vivekacūḍāmaṇi*). As shown in this flow chart, the applied aspect of psychoscience is in the behavioural domain and the behaviour of an individual, in fact, takes place in the lap of both society and Nature. While the behaviour of an individual residing in a society with other Beings gives birth to soft disciplines including religion or to the subjective science in the spirit of "externalization of the interior", amazing are the ways of working of Nature on the other hand. The latter gives birth to objective science in the spirit of "internalization of the exterior". As a matter of fact, in recent times the knowledge in both these sciences is separately proliferating through their respective components. No doubt, such a proliferation of knowledge continues to give a feedback to update both spiritual science and psychoscience, but at the same time it also suggests their further evolution with time. While this enriches psyche towards attaining peace, it also contributes to spirituality in terms of joy. This process will go on till the spiritual domain becomes stable or sustainable in the limit to a state of what is called *mokṣa* (salvation).

14.1 A Brief Review of the Contents

In some sense, *fig.* 14.1 depicts the theme and content sequence of the book. Chapters 3-5, dealing with the definition and properties of cosmic consciousness field, cover the spiritual zone. Chapters 6-10, dealing with the arrangement of EOLs M, I and E, and their related dynamics, describe the details of new incarnation of psychoscience. Chapters 11-13 highlight some important applications of psychoscience in the realm of behavioural science, in particular with reference, respectively to individual (personality aspect), collection of individuals (society and related economic aspects) and as a mob (philosophy and religion).

While actual contents of the book start with Chapter 2 in Part 1, Chapter 1 introduces one to some fundamentals of Vedic philosophy. Whether animate or inanimate, note that there is nothing like an isolated individual entity in the cosmos. In that, at the most fundamental level, three entities, viz. *Puruṣa, Prakṛti* and *jīva* (for which there are no exact English translations but one can respectively term them as "cosmic essence", "non-Being" and "Being"). In its localized version, the entity *jīva* is again considered as a composite, consisting of soul (SO), senses of knowledge and action, biological body which is placed in the field of worldly objects. Here, while soul, considered as a part of cosmic essence, is denoted by "Self" and all other essences of life including worldly objects (which are abstracted in five cosmic elements (*pañca-mahābhūtas*)) as "non-self" and the Being *b* (self) is a common participator in the whole game of "Self" and "non-self". With these inputs, we try to look for a spiritual science that can work globally and defines a universal scientific religion. In fact, many persons have started claiming that they are "spiritual, but not religious". In order to understand this way of life a distinct clarification among humanity, human consciousness and spirituality is necessary. Not only this, for this purpose, a separate but connected working domains of psychoscience and spiritual science need to be understood. In this way, the sovereign science of spirituality, if emerges, it has to have multifaceted contents including pscychoscience and behavioural science as subsets. Such wisdom in its organized form, if realized and used in daily life, then it would prove to be the best of human existence as far as the survival of a person is concerned. Note that in this whole game, the human consciousness plays a central role.

14.1.1 SPIRITUAL HOLD ON PSYCHOSCIENCE

With a view to understand the role of consciousness in physical and other processes, two approaches are generally used in modern times – bottom-up (i.e. from materialism to spirituality) and top-down (i.e. from spirituality to materialism), Chapter 2 summarizes the work on consciousness studies in the bottom-up approach. In these studies, analogies borrowed from physical theories have played an important role. A survey of the work on "mind"–matter interaction is carried out in two situations, i.e. by treating the matter as a stimulant and also as a participator in the process involving the same "mind" stuff. As an example of the latter case, the "mind"–brain problem is studied in detail with reference to recent studies in brain science. A possibility of convergence of the two approaches with regard to the consciousness studies in brain science is also explored.

Chapters 3-5 are devoted to find a plausible answer of the questions like as to why a person has to be spiritual, or as to how his psyche is linked with his spiritual thinking, etc. In fact, answer(s) of such questions are sought in some Vedic verses including some from *SMBG* by way of tracing their still deeper meanings in the spirit of quantum field theory of modern physics. To this effect, in Chapter 3 we look for a common source of origin of both Beings and non-Beings and again in both modern science and Vedic wisdom. A new interpretation of some of these verses seems to support the concept of "cosmic essence" or of cosmic consciousness field Φ_{cc}. A justification to the commonly known fact that "a human Being is miniature (microcosm) of cosmos" is sought here through these interpretations. It is argued that while consciousness manifests through varieties of ways in living Beings, it manifests through the universality of force laws that govern the structure and dynamism in both animate and inanimate objects. Further, it is the same consciousness that manifests through causal, micro and gross existences of a person.

The *pañcīkaraṇa* rule known for *pañca-mahābhūtas* (*PMs*) in Vedic literature is generalized for their higher-order dressings with consciousness in Chapter 4 as a result of individual's meditation. Many new concepts developed in this chapter, perhaps for the first time, are:

i. higher and infinite order dressing rules for *PMs*,

ii. a *tri-karaṇa* rule for the lowest and higher order dressings of the trio of inner EOLs M, I and E, and

iii. it is shown analytically that in the limit of infinite orders of dressing with consciousness, all eight (five cosmic elements plus three inner EOLs) tend to merge into Φ_{cc} and ever remain present there in seed-like forms.

They are termed as "epi-fields". A theory of procreation is proposed in this chapter. In fact, a deeper look at the meanings of some Vedic verses and the verses of *SMBG* suggests a method similar to the method of second quantization of quantum field theory in physics. Further, the quantization of such a composite consciousness field leads to discrete entities like souls, out of the continuum of the field. Varieties of species are the result of permutations and combinations, not only of eight epi-fields but also of infinite orders of their dressed versions present in the continuum. While the contents of Chapter 5 support the ideas advocated in Chapters 3 and 4, also advance some additional scriptural evidence for the spiritual links of psychoscience. For this purpose, different ways of classifying the human qualities and characteristics are revisited as per wisdom of *SMBG*. Also, some "golden rules" towards the upliftment or downfall of a personality are traced here. In particular, it is argued that the qualities which are of *sāttvika* as well as of divine category take a personality close to the spiritual zone from his psyche. The roles of two barriers, viz. mind and ego, in the form of gross and subtle components of the micro body in the spiritual journey of an individual are highlighted.

14.1.2 PSYCHOSCIENCE IN ITS NEW INCARNATION: VEDIC VERSION

In analogy with the concepts of physics, mechanics, chemistry and other hard disciplines, we develop these subjects respectively in Chapters 6-10, for the case of human psyche which is dominated by the workings of M, I and E. In Chapter 6, we revisit an atom-type model for human Being (termed as "patomic" or "philosophical atom-like" model) designed in analogy with the atomic model of matter and in accordance with the philosophy of *SMBG* (cf. verse III.42). Note that the human Being (*b*) is considered as perfect creation of God and consists of some EOLs, viz. biological body (B), senses of knowledge and action (SE) , mind (M), intellect (I), ego (E) and soul (SO). While the EOLs B, SE, M, I and E are considered as inanimate as well as discrete states for the transitions of the Being *b*, a localized version of the cosmic essence, i.e. "Self" or the soul (SO) is considered as continuum in this model. Further, note that it is the presence of SO that makes all the remaining EOLs functional, particularly when such an arrangement of EOLs is left in the field of worldly objects (WO) (which plays the role of nucleus) (cf. *fig.* 6.1). For the Being *b*, the upward transitions are rare, whereas the downward transitions towards WO are frequent. A multiplicity of states M, I and E is also investigated by analysing their successively higher-dressed versions (cf. *fig.* 6.2). In fact, such a patomic model of human Being has not only helped in understanding deep-rooted ideas of Vedānta philosophy but has also been an asset in explaining varieties of processes related to human behaviour and experiences more in analogy with physical sciences.

In Chapter 7, we first discuss and analyse in mathematical terms the cases of linear and non-linear evolution of the mindset function with consciousness which is now translated into the meditation variable μ. Stability of solutions is studied as a function of μ (cf. Appendix A) in general and as functions of some internal variables in particular. Then, for the case of consciousness manifesting human phenomena and processes in which the trio of space, time and consciousness plays comparable roles, we attempt to formulate, the so-called "principle of minimum effort" (a built-in human tendency) using the methods of calculus of variations and in analogy with the "Hamilton principle of least action" in classical mechanics. For this purpose, in addition to several other inputs, like designing an effort integral, a quantifiable definition of μ (cf. eq. (7.20)) is proposed and the same is treated at par with the time variable t. Similar to the Lagrange equations of motion, the "psycho-dynamical equations of motion" for mental processes are derived here for the mindset function $\mathcal{M}$. With regard to the application of these results, the case of car driving in a crowded lane, as an example, is solved (cf. Appendix B) for its least path. Another new aspect investigated in this chapter is a possible generalization of the Weber–Fechner law of psychology. In the present context, we use this law to obtain connections between experience-based and event-based versions of several measurable quantities like space and time intervals and then try to compute the velocity of conscious interactions. A similar use of Weber–Fechner type law yields a definition of "happiness index" – an experience-based quantity (cf. Appendix E).

The century old problem of Chevreul (handheld) pendulum and its role is revisited in occult sciences in Chapter 8. The use of a complex phase space approach to handle the case of a "conscious pendulum" yields the concept of twin oscillators – one works in the mental space and the other in the physical world. The role of conscious intents is expected to reflect in the difference of time periods in the two cases. While solutions of several phenomena in occult sciences are sought, a feasible laser-beam experiment is proposed to trace the divination, if any, in the handheld pendulum. This experiment is also expected to explain the gamma synchronous frequency of about 40 Hz, observed in brain science studies. The role of handheld pendulum is also discussed in this chapter in the context of occult sciences. Studies of exotic phenomena are further continued in Chapter 9 but using different tools. Here we develop the underlying theories to investigate the features that evolve as a result of the domination of the one's attention during meditation, i.e. the practitioner tries to use his intense or highly-focused consciousness energy with reference to matter, waves, energies and processes. With regard to matter, we trace a theory behind the idol worship in a scientifically planned way and accordingly constructed Indian temples; with regard to waves, we develop the concept of multimodulated mind waves which primarily are generated in the cosmic consciousness field but can carry the effect of eight epi-fields in the form of modulated information. The demodulation of such waves at the end of the appropriately tuned practitioner would convey the information loaded on a mind wave. This is how the attention-dominated energy expected to propagate through the all-pervading cosmic consciousness field. Using such a concept of mind waves, an explanation of varieties of exotic phenomena that occur in the realm of human behaviour and experiences like telepathy, teletherapy, reiki and distant healing is sought. Not only this, in conjunction with the brain science studies, a basis of working of Āyurvedic system of medicine, naturopathy, horoscope science, is sought in this scheme of study.

Once we have an atom-like patomic model of a human being, then it becomes easier to develop the chemistry of interactions of two and more persons in analogy with the chemical (nuclear) reactions in conventional chemistry (nuclear physics). This we pursue in Chapter 10 and develop a theory of human interactions and relations for composite and alive participants in a reaction. For the psychochemistry, the interactions of the trio of M, I and E are studied in detail and through the exchange of a variety of *tanmātra*s (the quanta of interactions in the language of Feynman diagrams). While two and three human-Being interactions are investigated in detail and at the level of all three existences gross, micro and causal, for many human-Being interactions, however, the viability of statistical methods in analogy with many–body systems in physics, is demonstrated in a few sample cases. For example, to understand the teacher–taught or spiritual leader – disciple interaction, the viability of Saha ionization formula is demonstrated. The interactions involved in the cases of mother–child, father–child, husband–wife, two ideal friends, etc. for the two Being case, and mother–father–child, three business partners, three good friends, etc. for the three human Being case, are analysed. The role of love and affection as binding forces between and among human Beings is discussed in detail. In this context, attempts are also made to search a force-law of love between the persons in terms of their levels of description in the patomic model.

14.1.3 BEHAVIOURAL LINKS OF PSYCHOSCIENCE

In Chapter 11, after a brief review of personality theories, the personality theory of Carl Jung, based on cognitive psychology, is investigated in detail using the patomic model or Vedic wisdom. Four style matrices of Jung-type are now constructed by replacing sensation, feeling, intuition and thinking intents respectively by biological body G (= B + SE), mind M, ego E and intellect I, and placing the soul SO in such a way that it plays a central role for the processes of gathering information and evaluating information in the schematic picture of Jung. For the next stage modifications in the theory, note that the patomic model contents in the scheme are replaced by their respective dressed versions (each with an arbitrary order of dressing) with consciousness that is considered as emanating from SO present now in the centre. While such modifications suggest the construction of the existing four style matrices of Jung in a very general and natural manner, also suggest formation of two more matrices. In view of these rather more realistic modifications in the theory, it becomes possible to look for a "spiritual" content in a personality. In addition to the "emotional" and "intelligence" quotients, one can now as well introduce the concepts of "spiritual quotient" and also of a personality trait like "sensational conscience" in analogy with the existing one of "emotional intelligence". An interesting aspect of these studies is that in mathematical terms the personality of a person can be considered as a vector in the vector space spanned by three *guṇas*, viz. *sattva, rajas, tamas*, of Vedic science and over a field of cosmic consciousness. In fact, the closure property of vector space would give rise to the creation of varieties of personalities out of the set of human qualities present already as vectors in the vector space.

It may be mentioned that the tenets of psychoscience, although developed at individual level, however, play an important role in the collection of individuals, i.e. in the case of a society (cf. Chapter 10). This, in particular, happens when a human component is involved in a social or physical phenomenon, or else when matter acts as a stimulant for persons, e.g. in the form of money, property, fame and beauty. From this point of view, we demonstrate the applications of psychoscience to the subjects of sociology and economics in Chapter 12. In particular, the viability of psychoscience in the study of newly emerging disciplines like sociophysics and econophysics is investigated in this chapter. While psychoscience is found to play a dominant role in these subjects in its own right, the development of these disciplines heavily rely on the use of theories and methodologies of physics and, in fact, there is hardly any doubt on the robustness of these physics tools. Here, we look for a unifying framework to study both sociophysics and econophysics via the tools of psychoscience. Keeping the Kahneman theory of "two selves" in mind and thereby having lessons from the distinct roles of slow and fast thinking in human processes, we revisit here the roles of gross and subtle components of micro body in these processes.

In Chapter 13, we attempt to explore the philosophy behind a possible unification of two major factors affecting the change in one's social life, viz. religion and science. Note that these are the qualities and contents of a religion which defines its global acceptance and sustainability. The quality of a religion, in fact, is again judged by the effectiveness of its tenets in the maintenance of both the world and cosmic order. Further, the qualities in the form of "elements of basic goodness (EBGs)" while are common in almost all existing religions, the contents of a religion (R), on the other hand are defined through its three components, viz. *jñāna* (J), *upāsanā* (U) and *karma* (K) as per Vedic wisdom. (EBGs are a set of human virtues and qualities defining the humanism on the one hand and forming the systematic of positive pursuits towards the world order on the other.) In a mathematical language, conditions and criteria are sought in terms of contributions from J, U and K in a religion R, so as to make it an ideally integrated and a sustainable one. The religion R (like the personality P in Chapter 11) along with its component J, U, K is considered as a vector in the vector space spanned by three *guṇas* and over a field of cosmic consciousness. Thus, by using the closure property of a vector space, a variety of religions can be created suitable for a particular society. An alternative route, followed in this chapter, to establish the eternity (invariance with time), universality (invariance with space) and sustainability (invariance with respect to human experiences) of a religion, is by using the tools and methodology of physics with regard to conservation laws and dynamical invariants. Thus, a concept of "experience-based invariance (EBI)" is proposed in this work and this feature for a large number of sacred facts, phrases, sequence of phrases, or a collection of facts, etc. in Vedic literature is discussed. In summary, answers of several questions like "what is *sanātana* in the *Sanātana Dharma*?" or "why is this way of life surviving even after centuries and epochs?" are sought in this chapter purely in a scientific spirit. As a matter of fact, the occurrence of EBGs and hence of EBIs in a religion in abundance, defines its merit and quality. Several examples to this effect from *SMBG* and other Vedic scriptures are analysed in detail.

Five Appendices are added to support the conceptual discussions and mathematical details presented in various chapters. Appendix A offers the practical solution of a non-linear mathematical problem. Here, the stability of mindset function $\mathcal{M}$ (towards the attainment of peace) is investigated for a person who is constantly undergoing positive and negative thoughts during the meditation. Appendix B gives the details of the two-dimensional Laplace equation in the context of principle of minimum effort discussed in Chapter 7. The role of a complex Heisenberg-type uncertainty relation, connected with the twin oscillators of Chapter 8, is discussed in Appendix C. This relation arises as a result of using the complex phase space approach to solve the problem of handheld pendulum. In Appendix D, we elaborate the mathematical concept of vector space used in the context of personality creation mechanism in Chapter 11 and in the context of designing an ideally sustainable global religion in Chapter 13. Based on some limited discussions in Chapters 7 and 13, further possible generalizations of some concepts are suggested in Appendix E. In particular, the concepts related to experience-based and event-based versions of quantities like space and time intervals are discussed here with a view to having their wider applications in mechanics. Attempts are also made here to define an experience-based quantity, like "happiness index", in terms of the number of desires fulfilled and the number of desires that arose.

14.2 Future Prospects

Attempts are being made in this book to develop a kind of formal theory of the subject of human psyche and related processes within the framework of Vedic wisdom. Both value and place value of this subject are identified, discussed and developed with reference to the huge spectrum of human knowledge, thinking and understanding. A "garland-like" object is prepared from knowledge-flowers distributed all over in various Vedic scriptures, of course, constrained by the limitations of the author. The top-down approach, originating basically from the roots in Vedic wisdom, when followed in conjunction with modern scientific and mathematical methods, gives rise to several new aspects and dimensions of study of the subjects of psychology and behavioural sciences.

It may be mentioned that these new concepts and dimensions of study, presented in this book are not the last word on the subject matter but they need to be explored further on both the fronts: development and applications. No doubt, an inquisitive mind can always trace a research problem out of the blue but it is worthwhile to list a few of them here in explicit terms. Such studies, in fact, are desirable in the domain of both soft (psychology, philosophy, management, etc.) and hard (mathematical psychology, mathematical sciences including engineering and brain science) disciplines. Although some such issues are already addressed briefly in the concluding sections of various chapters, still an elaboration of some of them is necessary here at one place and on both development and application fronts. We list some such projects as follows:

1. Only a few selective verses from Vedas and also from *SMBG* are quoted here (cf. Chapters 3 and 4) to support the concept of an all-pervading and finest possible cosmic consciousness field Φ_{cc} and subsequently the theory of procreation. Also, these are again a few verses whose subtle meanings have led to a method like "second quantization" for the discretization of the continuum of Φ_{cc}. This is mainly due to the limitations of the author; otherwise expert scholars can always trace many more evidences out of the ocean of Vedic literature; for example, an extended interpretation of the Nāsadīya Sūkta (*R̥V* X.129.1) and several others (see, for example, S.N. Upadhyaya in *Saṁskāram* (Hindi), 2015, pp. 39-42) can yield similar meanings and results.
2. Keeping in mind the presence of eight epi-fields (corresponding to five cosmic elements and three inner EOLs M, I and E, and in accordance with *aṣṭāṅga prakr̥ti* of Vedic science) in Φ_{cc}, one can think of constructing varieties of living species. For this purpose, one can use different permutations and combinations not only of these eight epi-fields but also of different (in general infinite) orders of dressing associated separately with each of these fields. This will demonstrate the viability of the scheme of study. Also, it is worthwhile to construct some exotic species (the so-called "fractured" ones, in which some of the EOLs are absent) like $\alpha = \mathcal{C} \cup \mathcal{G}$ and $\beta = \mathcal{C} \cup \mathcal{M}$, as the presence of $\mathcal{C}$ is a prerequisite for the existence of a species.
3. With regard to the upliftment or downfall of a personality in terms of the sequence of human qualities, note that only a few "golden rules" are discussed in Section 5.3.3; but the fact

is that a large number of such rules exist in Vedic scriptures and they can be traced and studied at different levels of human existences.

4. In mathematical terms, the complexification in physical theories either of a physical variable or of its functions in general opens new vistas in the study, particularly with reference to their respective imaginary parts. Further, the analyticity property of the corresponding complex functions brings these imaginaries, associated with both variable and functions, at the same platform (Kaushal 2009). Any relaxation in this property, however, makes the treatment of the two types of imaginaries – associated with variables and functions, as different. Keeping this fact in mind and with a view that the imaginary parts in the theory would provide a description of mental world and the real parts as usual will take care of the physical world, in Chapters 7 and 8 we try to develop psychomechanics using different ways of complexification. In Chapter 7, while we give some glimpses of the derived Lagrange-type equations of motion using a complex Lagrange function (or a complex "action integral"), later in the "effort integral", however, a meditation variable μ is explicitly used at par with the time variable t to account for the role of psyche. Although one application of "psycho-dynamical equations of motion", so derived, is explicitly demonstrated, however, further extension of these studies is desirable on several fronts. For example, as discussed in Section 7.4.4, one can explore different possibilities, depending upon the mental process under study, for the potential-like function $V(q, \dot{q}, \bar{q}, \bar{t}, t, \mu)$ and solve the corresponding equations, in particular eq. (7.36).

Similarly, with a view to detecting the divination (or the mental effect), if any, in the time period of handheld pendulum, an extended complex phase space approach is used to solve the problem of Chevreul pendulum in Chapter 8 which results into the problem of twin oscillators – one is considered to belong to mental world and the other to physical world. The proposed laser-beam experiment in this context, still needs to be performed. The role of the proposed complex Planck constant (cf. Appendix C) in the Heisenberg-type uncertainty relation requires further investigation, particularly with reference to a conscious double-slit experiment, in the quantum measurement studies with mind waves (cf. Chapter 9) and/or in the studies where waves/particles are considered to travel faster than light velocity (e.g. the case of tachyons in the special theory of relativity) (also see Appendix E).

5. Chapter 9 leaves a lot of scope for the future development of the subject matter discussed therein. For example,

    a. a precise explanation of the processes like telepathy, teletherapy or telehealing and reiki as a result of modulation and demodulation of the proposed mind waves is desirable, more in analogy with physical science;

    b. note that mind waves are the outcome of top-down approach, whereas brain waves are the outcome of bottom-up approach, (cf. Section 9.3.1). While consciousness transcends in the former, it seems to ascend in the later as speculated on the basis of gamma synchronous frequency data. It would be worthwhile to investigate further the convergence of the two approaches to seek a definite word about the phenomenon of consciousness;

    c. it is worthwhile to look for the foundations of naturopathy through the role of five epi-fields (corresponding to the five cosmic elements) present in Φ_{cc}, in the treatment of diseases using naturopathy;

    d. on the other hand, the role of the secondary epi-fields present in Φ_{cc} in the form of *vāta*, *pitta* and *kapha* (cf.

Section 9.4.2(c)) needs further investigation not only to give still deeper foundations to the subject of Āyurveda but also to justify it as a holistic system of treatment of diseases; and

e. an important observation of brain science highlighted in Chapter 9 is the recognition of human intents through a brain-pattern formation as a result of firing of electric signals by brain neurons in synchronization. This observation has already helped in finding a reasonable scientific theory of idol worship (towards attainment of peace) in an Indian temple constructed in accordance with ancient Indian scriptures.

6. A reasoning similar to the one in (5) above for idol worship in terms of working of brain neurons can also be sought for tracing the foundations of the "science" of astrology, where one talks of the effect of nearby planets and stars on thinking, behaviour, or in general, on life of an individual, provided his space–time coordinates at the time of birth are known. As a matter of fact, the electric and magnetic signals coming from stars and planets, howsoever weak they may be, can permanently affect the firing frequency of electric signals by brain neurons. Alternatively, in terms of the concept of multimodulated mind waves (cf. Chapter 9), ever present and spread all over in Φ_{cc} (space), it is the interaction of two mindsets in a given environment at the time of conception, that will initially affect the mindset of the conceived baby. At a later stage comes the role of electric and magnetic signals coming from individual planet or star to affect the firing frequency of electric signals by brain neurons of the conceived baby by the parents. The later aspect, however, drags one's attention to a still deeper theory of horoscope science and thus makes sense to pursue (also, see Kaushal 2023a).

7. An important concept of linear vector space, spanned by three Nature-born *guṇas* over a field of cosmic consciousness, is discussed in Appendix D mainly to create a variety of personalities (cf. Chapter 11) as a result of closure property of this mathematical construct. The role of this construct is further outlined in Chapter 13 with regard to creating a variety of models of religion, where the latter is expressed through its three components J, U and K. Note that for an ideal society worth living, both an ideally integrated personality of its persons and a global (in terms of its eternity, universality and sustainability) religion (in order to lead a regulated and peaceful life) are a must. With such objectives in mind and to develop science and art to this effect, it is worthwhile to pursue these tools further.

These are the glimpses of a few future projects worth pursuing and the present scheme of study suggests; otherwise one can easily trace and notice several fill-up the blanks in the text.

14.3 Concluding remarks

As mentioned, the contents of the book give a new flavour to the conventional subject of psychology, developed now using alternative but plausible and scientific interpretations of some verses of Vedas, of *SMBG* and of other Vedic scriptures. In philosophical terms, over all attempts have been to explore Absolute Reality as objectively as possible, knowing full well that this otherwise is only a matter of realization. With regard to these efforts, one would wonder as to how science and scientific advancements doing wonders in making one's life luxurious on the one hand, can be helpful in exploring this abstract concept of reality on the other. As a matter of fact, this whole game of human thinking becomes clear from *fig.* 14.2. This figure clearly depicts the case when "unreal becomes manifestly real". In philosophical terms, the objective reality, howsoever fine it may be, ultimately remains an outcome of modelling game at a certain level besides its roots in quantifiable and measurable aspects.

fig. 14.2: Three world concept and absolute truth in Nature; W_1 – the (subjective) truth or reality that actually exists in Nature but only realizable (blurred); W_2– the truth or reality that is perceivable by adjustment of both attitude and data; W_3 – the (objective) reality that is quantifiable, measurable and obtained by modelling the phenomenon but remains unreal. (Unlabelled figure: courtesy, *Times of India*)

In the first phase, the reality marked as "truth" in *fig.* 14.2, is the absolute reality that actually exists in Nature and belongs to the so-called world W_1, inclusive of its cosmic links. In the second phase, the same reality manifests through a limited but expandable apparatus consisting of micro body, biological body and senses, which adjusts themselves with respect to the quality of scientific observations and perceptible intents, describing the world W_2. (An adjustable lens in the figure displays this fact.) An example of adjustment in scientific observations (in order to grasp the underlying subjective reality better) is the concept of "extended apparatus" as discussed by von Neumann (1955) in the context of quantum measurement while accounting for the human component in the bottom-up approach. Similarly, the use of spectacles, hearing aids or in general of various types of sensors, offers the example of "extended senses" with reference to adjustable perceptible intents (in order to grasp the objective reality better) in the top-down approach. It may be mentioned that a model (as long as it is designed using limited assumptions or limited apparatus of micro body, biological body and senses) can never be a reality in spite of the fact that it perfectly describes all measurable data belonging to the world $W_{3.}$ At times, as there is an excellent agreement between the predicted results and the experiments, this forces one to believe that the objective reality as described by science is the ultimate one. But this reality, as a third phase of absolute reality, is only manifestly real but in reality it is "unreal", as displayed in the figure.

Appendices

Appendix A

Analysis of Certain Aspects of Non-linearity in Mental Pocesses

A.1 Introduction

THE purpose of this Appendix is twofold: first, to demonstrate in mathematical terms the continuous evolution of the mindset function $\mathcal{M}$ with consciousness (meditation variable μ), and second, to find a plausible answer to the question as to how a turbulent mind, flooded with negative and positive thoughts, can achieve the stability again in analytical terms. This all relates to the non-linear processes taking place inside a person at mental level, of course, we shall resort here for some particular type of non-linearities while modelling the processes. In some sense, the present studies are in continuation of Chapters 4 and 7 and the terminology used is also the same.

In what follows, we attempt to model two phenomena pertaining to our common experience, viz.:

i. competitive roles of negative and positive thoughts in a cool mind towards the completion of an outward task in a society, and

ii. the experience that many of us have regarding the preparation of a speech and subsequently delivering the same before a gathering or a class.

In the later case, time sharpens the mind in the sense that the preparation/learning for the talk grows rather slowly as the "time to act" arrives (in spite that the learning faculty acts sharply) and after the task is over, it is noticed that the heap of knowledge decays rather fast unless one has keen passion for it. For the first phenomenon while we resort to a Voltera–Lotka type model, a van der Pol kind of equation is solved for the latter. This we pursue in the next two sections. Finally, concluding remarks are made and the outcome of studies is discussed in Section A.4.

A.2 A Competitive Role of Negative and Positive Thoughts Towards the Performance of a Task

A.2.1 THE MODEL

Let a conscious person calmly sit to decide about a successful completion of a task in a cool environment. The person is a common man in the sense that he wants to account for both positive and negative aspects of values prevailing in the society. All sorts of pros and cons come to his mind and the thoughts evolve as he concentrates on the details of the performance of the task. In this process, the dynamics of his inner EOLs is guided by his *saṅkalpas* (partly related to the seed of action) in the light of systematic of positive, negative or both pursuits, depending upon his personality.

Let N_+ be the number of positive thoughts and N_- be the number of negative thoughts that evolve at a given stage of meditation and the same, in turn, will eventually lead to SPP and/or SNP. Note that for a common man living in a society neither N_+ is zero (as it will lead to a *bhogī* person deeply involved in the worldly objects WO) nor N_- is zero (as it will lead to a *yogī* or a man of perfection) in the same way as in the prey–predator problem none of the species completely extinct – while considering the dynamics of their survival with respect to the time variable. In general, N_+ and N_- evolve with the meditation variable μ in a non-linear fashion (cf. Kapoor 1985: 11), viz.:

$$\frac{dN_+}{d\mu} = N_+ g_1(N_+, N_-) \tag{A1}$$

$$\frac{dN_-}{d\mu} = N_- g_2(N_+, N_-), \tag{A2}$$

where g_1 and g_2 are the functions of their arguments chosen in a variety of ways depending upon the physical environment as in the prey–predator problem. To give some glimpses of the ongoing competition between the numbers of positive and negative thoughts here, however, we resort to some simple forms of the functions g_1 and g_2, and write (A1) and (A2) in the form

$$\frac{dN_+}{d\mu} = N_+(a_1 - b_1 N_-) \tag{A3}$$

$$\frac{dN_-}{d\mu} = N_-(-a_2 + b_2 N_+), \tag{A4}$$

where a_1, a_2, b_1, b_2 are positive real constants. (In general, these constants can also depend explicitly on μ, but we ignore such a situation.)

The critical (equilibrium) points of the system (A3)-(A4) are at $(N^*_+, N^*_-) \equiv (0, 0)$, $(a_2/b_2, a_1/b_1)$ (Kaushal and Parashar 2008). The eigenvalues of the stability matrix, λ_1, λ_2 at these points turn out to be $\lambda_1 = a_1$, $\lambda_2 = -a_2$ at (0, 0), representing an (unstable) saddle point S, and $\lambda_1 = i\sqrt{a_1 a_2}$, $\lambda_2 = -i\sqrt{a_1 a_2}$ at $(a_2/b_2, a_1/b_1)$ representing a (stable) centre C as shown in *fig.* A.1.

A.2.2 REMARKS ON THE MODEL

For a common man, although it depends on as from which of his mental state the Being *b* is working (cf. *fig.* 6.1), in general, the positive thoughts are known to dominate the scene since they basically are the attributes of soul and also work through its attribute – consciousness. In fact, it is a prerequisite for the working of a conscious person. In other words, N_+ prevails over N_- unless the Being *b* works from B or SE states in accordance with the *saṅkalpas*.

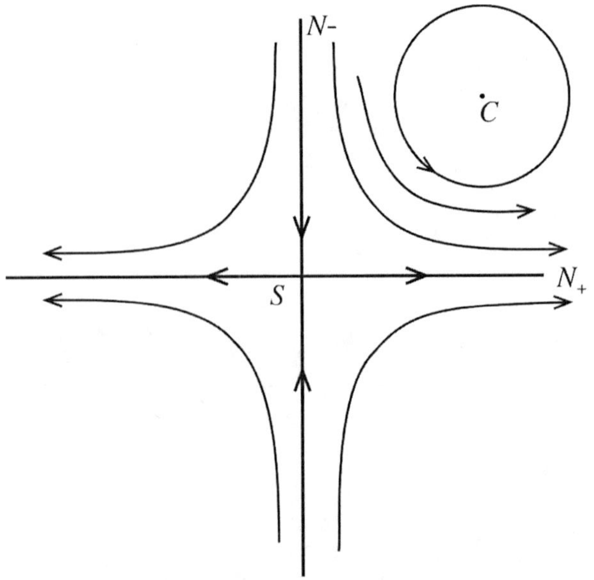

fig. A.1: Stable and unstable equilibrium points in the Voltera–Lotka system

In analogy with the prey–predator problem, recall the roles of parameters a_1, b_1, a_2 and b_2 in eqs (A3) and (A4). While a_1 is responsible for an increase of N_+ during the meditation, b_1 defines the "negative increase" owing to the fact that positive thoughts are being destroyed by the negative ones during their encounters. Further, note that in the absence of positive thoughts, negative thoughts also do not play any role as far as a judicious outcome of the task is concerned and thereby their destruction "rate" dominates over their "birth rate" (characterized by the a_2-term in eq. (A4)). At the same time, however, the compensating growth of negative thoughts still remains proportional to the encounters with the positive thoughts (characterized by the b_2-term in (A4)). This is how the eqs (A3) and (A4) are designed.

As the thought process evolves with μ, there also emerges an ideally unstable equilibrium between the populations of positive and negative thoughts (cf. saddle S in *fig.* A.1, characterized by the parameters a_1 and a_2) during their competition. However, as populations increase, an ideal stability (cf. centre C in *fig.* A.1) also emerges between the positive and negative thoughts and in general it is characterized by the values of all the four parameters a_1, b_1, a_2 and b_2 in eqs (A3) and (A4), leading to a successful performance of a task. Note that this latter stage can be achieved quickly either by increasing the parameters b_1 and b_2 or by decreasing a_1 and a_2. This all depends on the way in which an individual reacts with the external changes due to the environment and/or circumstances. Further, if the success of the task lies in the domain of gross body $\mathcal{G}$ (like the satisfaction from a feast, etc.), this will provide (sensual) pleasure; if it lies in the domain of micro body $\mathcal{M}$ (like the satisfaction from an intellectual task such as interview and examination), then this will provide peace and if it is in the domain of causal body $\mathcal{C}$ (the satisfaction from a spiritual discourse, etc.) then it will be the source of joy (*ātmānanda*) to an individual.

In fact, the quality of thoughts also matters in achieving the hierarchy of the outcome out of the same process of competition between N_+ and N_-. In some sense, this can be understood from the nature of solution curves derived from eqs (A3) and (A4) by writing them in the form

$$\frac{dN_-}{dN_+} = \frac{(-a_2 + b_2 N_+) N_-}{(a_1 - b_1 N_-) N_+}.$$

After integrating this equation, one obtains (Jordan and Smith 1988)

$$a_2 \ln N_+ - b_2 N_+ + a_1 \ln N_- - b_1 N_- = k \qquad \text{(A5)}$$

or

$$F(N_+) + G(N_-) = k, \qquad \text{(A6)}$$

where k is an integration constant – a parameter whose values, in turn, will provide different family of curves (hierarchy of outcome perhaps corresponding to different domains of EOLs), however, for the same functional forms of F and G and independently for N_+ and N_-.

With regard to the nature of trajectories in the neighbourhood of the equilibrium points *S* and *C*, the respective solutions of (A3) and (A4) are given by (see, e.g. Kaushal and Parashar (2008)):

$$N_1 = N_+ - N_+^* = N_{10}\, e^{a_1 \mu}; \qquad N_2 = N_- - N_-^* = N_{20}\, e^{-a_2 \mu} \tag{A7}$$

around *S*, and

$$N_1 = N_+ - N_+^* = b_1 a_2 r_0 \cos(\omega\mu + \phi_0), \;\; N_2 = N_- - N_-^* = \omega b_2 r_0 \sin(\omega\mu + \phi_0) \tag{A8}$$

around *C*. Here, $\omega = \sqrt{a_1 a_2}$, and r_0 , ϕ_0 are arbitrary constants. Note that eq. (A7) represents different open curves, whereas eq. (A8) represents closed curves.

A.3 A Slow Growth and Fast Decay Model for the Mindset Function

A.3.1 THE MODEL

Here, we consider the evolution of the mindset function $\mathcal{M}$ with the meditation variable μ under certain specific situations. For example, when a teacher is preparing himself for a lecture series, a student is preparing for a series of examinations or a politician is preparing for speeches in public, but every time on different topics during elections and the like that, this function evolves rather slowly during the preparation part of the process but decays fast after the task is over. Note that during the process the person undergoes a kind of both encouragement and discouragement as and when he thinks of the success in the task. These features of the phenomenon respectively are analogous to the positive and negative damping in a classical dynamical system. For such a situation, one can express the μ-evolution of the mindset function in general by a non-linear equation of the form,

$$\mathcal{M}'' + f(\mathcal{M}, \mathcal{M}')\, \mathcal{M}' + g(\mathcal{M}) = 0, \tag{A9}$$

where, $\mathcal{M}' = (d\mathcal{M}/d\mu)$, $\mathcal{M}'' = (d^2\mathcal{M}/d\mu^2)$. For the Lienard case, however, when the function $f(\mathcal{M}, \mathcal{M}')$ becomes the function of $\mathcal{M}$ alone and both $f(\mathcal{M})$ and $g(\mathcal{M})$ satisfy certain conditions (see Kaushal and Parashar 2008: chap. 7) for the stability of solutions of this non-linear equation, we resort to a simpler van der Pol version of eq. (A9) as

$$\mathcal{M}'' + \varepsilon(\mathcal{M}^2 - 1)\,\mathcal{M}' + \mathcal{M} = 0, \qquad \text{(A10)}$$

where ε is a positive parameter.

Equation (A10) describes a relaxation–oscillation system corresponding to a slow build-up and a fast discharge of the bulk of knowledge with regard to a particular task. In fact, the values of the parameter ε in eq. (A10) play a crucial role with regard to the stability of the solutions, when it is studied as a function of μ. Further, note that the region $|\mathcal{M}| < 1$ corresponds to the discouragement (depression) and $|\mathcal{M}| > 1$ corresponds to the encouragement on the $\mathcal{M}$–$\mathcal{M}'$ plane. (Note the modified terminology used here as compared to the one that prevails in the dynamical system theory where the phrases like negative and positive damping are used for the negative and positive contributions of the $\mathcal{M}'$-term in eq. (A10)). For example, for the value of ε as 0.1, there exists a stable close curve called "limit cycle" in the $\mathcal{M}$–$\mathcal{M}'$ plane as shown in *fig.* A.2.

A.3.2 REMARKS ON THE MODEL

While the consciousness is constantly pouring into the system (i.e. the meditation μ is increasing), the function $\mathcal{M}$ (a measure of the bulk of knowledge or the level of understanding) oscillates between two values (say $\mathcal{M}_1$ and $\mathcal{M}_2$) and with two periodic values of μ, say μ_s and μ_f corresponding to the slow growth and the fast decay parts of the process. During μ_s, $\mathcal{M}$ slowly attains the (higher) value $\mathcal{M}_2$ (i.e. $\mathcal{M}$ increases and undergoes a kind of relaxation) and during μ_f it decays (decreases) rather fast to the (lower) value $\mathcal{M}_1$. This process with varying (oscillating) $\mathcal{M}$ continues for the subsequent preparations until the role of $\mathcal{M}'$ term in (A10) in conjunction with the value of ε becomes crucial. Finally, for some critical values of ε, μ_s and μ_f, a stability in the system (in the form of limit cycle) is achieved and note that it is this stage when the mindset $\mathcal{M}$ is fit for the success of the task of course without much wear and tear.

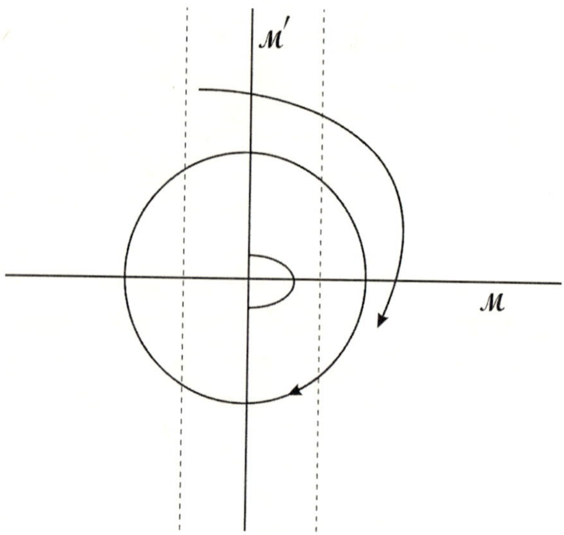

fig. A.2: Limit cycle in the van der Pol system for $\varepsilon = 0.1$

A.4 Concluding Discussion

With a view to carrying out an analytical study of certain processes taking place inside the human Being towards the performance of a task in the outer world, attempts are made here to quantify both, the basic participants and the underlying mechanism involved in these processes. While the possibility of modelling a couple of phenomena pertaining to human experiences is demonstrated here through some examples, at the same time, the viability of some tools of non-linear dynamics in obtaining a plausible solution of some problems in psychology, is shown. In fact, while the use of these non-linear methods in the study of other soft and hard disciplines has become a fashion these days (Huys and Jirsa 2011; Kapoor 1985; Murray 1993; Sulis and Combs 1996; Vallachar and Nowak 1994), then why the subject of psychology should be left behind. It is argued that such an understanding of the dynamics of inner EOLs towards the completion of a task, when becomes available to an individual even in its crude form, can help him not only in his judicious decisions but also in attaining some pleasure and/or peace out of his day-to-day actions. No doubt, these processes for many of us often go unnoticed, but for a conscious person, their knowledge at times could be of immense help in crucial situations.

While the different values of k in eq. (A6) can characterize the nature of satisfaction in terms of pleasure, peace and joy (*atmānandas)* out of a successful performance of the task, these three stages in turn could be in accordance with restless, imperfect and perfect equilibria as discussed in Parthasarathy (1992).

Appendix B

Solution of Equation (7.37a)

HERE, we present the solution of eq. (7.37a) by writing it in the form (as an analogue of Laplace equation in two dimensions),

$$\frac{\partial^2 q}{\partial x^2}+\frac{\partial^2 q}{\partial y^2}=0, \tag{B1}$$

where $x=t/\sqrt{a}, y=\mu/\sqrt{b}$. Next, we choose a separable form of the solution (see, for example, Pipes and Harvill (1970)) of (B1), viz. $q(x, y) = u(x).v(y)$. Using this form of q, eq. (B1) can be written as:

$$\frac{1}{u}\frac{d^2 u}{dx^2}=-\frac{1}{v}\frac{d^2 v}{d\mu^2}. \tag{B2}$$

Note that the left-hand side of this equation is a function of x alone, whereas the right-hand side is of y alone. Hence, each of the expression in (B2) must be independent of x and y and should be a constant (say, $-k^2$). Thus, (B2) is equivalent to a pair of equations of the form

$$\frac{d^2 u}{dx^2}=-k^2 u, \quad \frac{d^2 v}{dy^2}=+k^2 v, \tag{B3, B4}$$

whose solutions can be written immediately as:

$$u(x)=A_1\cos kx+A_2\sin kx \tag{B5}$$

$$v(y)=A_3 e^{ky}+A_4 e^{-ky} \tag{B6}$$

Thus,

$$q(x, y) = e^{-ky} (B_1 \cos kx + B_2 \sin kx) + e^{ky} (B_3 \cos kx + B_4 \sin kx) \tag{B7}$$

or

$$q(t,\mu) = e^{-k\mu/\sqrt{b}} \left(B_1 \cos\frac{kt}{\sqrt{a}} + B_2 \sin\frac{kt}{\sqrt{a}} \right) + e^{k\mu/\sqrt{b}} \left(B_3 \cos\frac{kt}{\sqrt{a}} + B_4 \sin\frac{kt}{\sqrt{a}} \right), \tag{B8}$$

where A_i's and B_i's (for i =1, ..., 4) are the arbitrary constants to be fixed after using the boundary conditions.

For choosing the boundary conditions, recall the nature of the variable μ. Ideally speaking, when $\mu = \infty$, the roles not only of q and t but also of $u(t/\sqrt{a})$ and $v(\mu/\sqrt{b})$ disappear.

Hence, in (B8) we should have $B_3 = B_4 = 0$. On the other hand, we also have $q = 0$ for $t = 0$. This implies that we cannot have a cosine term in the solution and hence $B_1 = 0$. Thus, an acceptable solution turns of to be

$$q(t,\mu) = B_2\, e^{-k\mu/\sqrt{b}} \sin(kt/\sqrt{a}), \tag{B9}$$

which, for the form (7.38), automatically satisfies, $q = 0$ at $\mu = \mu_0$, otherwise for an arbitrary $t(\mu)$ as the solution of (7.39b), one should have $q = 0$ at $t = \tau$ (say) and $\mu = \mu_0$ and thus requiring from eq. (B9) that

$$\sin (k\tau/\sqrt{a}) = 0\,. \tag{B10}$$

This suggests the values of k as $k = \frac{m\pi\sqrt{a}}{\tau}$, where m = 0, 1, 2 .... Finally, the solution of (7.37a) takes the form

$$q_m(t,\mu) = B_m e^{-m\pi\mu\sqrt{(a/b)}/\tau} \sin\left(\frac{m\pi t}{\tau}\right), \tag{B11}$$

where B_m is an arbitrary constant for given m. In fact, m accounts for different modes that cover the net path $q(t, \mu)$, now given by

$$q(t,\mu) = \sum_{m=0}^{\infty} q_m(t, \mu). \tag{B12}$$

Note that in a realistic situation $q(t, \mu)$, as the solution of eq. (7.37), is not separable in t and μ.

Appendix C

Twin Oscillators and Complex Uncertainty Relation

Dynamical coupling vis-à-vis uncertainty relations in quantum mechanics

Heisenberg uncertainty principle in quantum mechanics while setting a limit on the simultaneous measurement of a canonical pair of variables, this, in some sense, is the example of dynamical coupling in implicit form and at micro-level. On the other hand, the examples of explicit forms of dynamical coupling even in the quantum domain arise when one accounts for certain types of interactions (in-built or external) in quantum systems. It is worthwhile to comment on another uncertainty principle discussed in Chapter 7 and the same reflects from a incomprehensibility principle (Fraser 2013).

It appears from this principle that the canonicity feature of the pair of physical variables in the uncertainty relations of Heisenberg, reflects only in a restricted or ideal sense; otherwise, in general, it has to do something with an in-built dynamical coupling in the system and that too at the micro level between certain preferred (canonical) variables. Alternatively, this canonicity feature at the classical level translates itself into the complexity of the phase space used in Section 8.4.1 (or, in general that of the function space (Kaushal 2009)). It could very well be the common factor of consciousness at the root of all such in-built dynamical couplings, which in turn manifest through the uncertainty relations in the quantum domain or through the complexification of physical variables in the classical domain. In other words, it is the consciousness, when switched on to perceive the physical world that creates another domain of canonical variables in an imaginary space and subsequently contributes to the in-built coupling in the twin system.

In view of the above discussions and the choice of transformation (8.9), it may be of interest to analyse a complex uncertainty relation with, let us say a complex Planck constant $\hbar^*(= \hbar + ig/2\pi)$, viz.:

$$\Delta q \cdot \Delta p \geq \hbar^*,$$

or

$$\Delta(q_1 + ip_2) \cdot \Delta(p_1 + iq_2) \geq \hbar + ig/2\pi. \tag{C1}$$

Here, g is another Planck-like constant needed to account for the role of mental world in the quantum description of a psychophysical system like the handheld pendulum. Note that this constant ($g/2\pi$) like $\hbar$ is not a universal constant but varies slowly from person to person due to his limitations on the development of his own essences of life or his faculty of understanding. Equation (C1) implies a pair of uncertainty relations, viz.

$$\Delta q_1 \cdot \Delta p_1 - \Delta q_2 . \Delta p_2 \geq \hbar. \tag{C2a}$$

$$\Delta p_2 \cdot \Delta p_1 + \Delta q_2 . \; \Delta q_1 \geq g/2\pi. \tag{C2b}$$

Thus, in the quantum description of a psychophysical system, effective Planck constant turns out to be somewhat smaller than that for a physical system (cf. eq. (C2a)). This happens at the cost of the appearance of another uncertainty relation (C2b) and another constant ($g/2\pi$). In fact, the constant g is an attribute of dynamical coupling between the two physical and non-physical (mental) worlds.

Further remarks about the relations (C2) are as follows:

i. Note that constant $g/2\pi$, like $\hbar$, also has the dimensions of (energy × time) and the same can be recovered by considering the transformation (8.9) in the form $q = q_1 + i\alpha p_2, p = p_1 + i\beta q_2$, where α and β are dimensional constants, viz. dim (α) = time (mass)$^{-1}$ and dim (β) = mass (time)$^{-1}$.

ii. The $(\Delta q_2 \cdot \Delta p_2)$-term in (C2a) is an attribute exclusively of the mental world. The two terms $(\Delta p_2 \cdot \Delta p_1)$ and $(\Delta q_2 \cdot \Delta q_1)$ in (C2b) are the results of coupling between the two worlds.

iii. In some sense, the relation (C2b) speaks of the "incomprehensibility principle" of Fraser in view of remark (ii) above. This is mainly because the process of comprehension itself is the case of interaction between the two (mental and physical) worlds. Now the question is what value be assigned to g? While future studies will throw some light on its mean value in general as the answer to this question, one thing is clear that it is an observer-dependent constant. In some sense, it is a measure of departure from the mathematically idealized situations, viz. canonicity of pairs of dynamical variables, analyticity of functions of these variables and/ or the property of closedness of the physical system under consideration.

Appendix D

Personality Vector Space, Personality Creation Mechanism and Inner Transformations

In continuation of Section 11.5, we elaborate here on the concepts of personality vector space, personality creation mechanism and the associated transformations that take place inside the human Being during the period of personality development. Personality development is basically a change in or an evolution of behaviour patterns of a person with respect to space and/or time and consciousness. This change takes place generally for a positive pursuit or with a positive attitude towards the social and/or world order. For this purpose, an individual inculcates one or more human virtues (HVs) in his character out of the available sea of the same (see Table D.1). In Table D.1, some representative, HVs (qualities, characteristics and intents) are listed corresponding to the four domains of human existences and most of them as per *SMBG* are wrapped with three *guṇas*. Note that some of the HVs are common to different existences but they occur at different conceptual scales. For example, the HV renunciation could be at the level of both gross and micro existences, but the former is in the physical sense and the latter is at the mental level.

Table D.1: Some Representative Examples of Human Virtues (Qualities, Characteristic and Intents) That Are the Functions of and Getting the Incentive from the Four Existences. Also, they are the Elements of the Corresponding Subspace in the Personality Vector Space. Note that Each HV Is Wrapped with Three Nature-born *Guṇas* That Form the Basis for the Vector Space

Micro Existence (*$\mathcal{M}$*)	*Gross Existence* (*$\mathcal{G}$*)	*Societal Existence* (*$\mathcal{S}$*)	*Natural Existence* (*$\mathcal{N}$*)
1. Feeling (M)	Body actions (B)	Charity (*dāna*)	Forgiveness (*kṣamā*)
2. Thinking (I)	Actions: senses of knowledge (SEK)	Gift (*bheṅṭa*)	Patience (*dhairya*)
3. *Saṅkalpa* (S)	Actions: motor organs (SEA)		Love for all living and non-living entities
4. Memory (E)	Food		
5. Faith (*śraddhā*)	Renunciation (*tyāga*)	Sacrifice (*yajña*)	Realization of cosmic connections in Nature
6. Firmness (*dhṛti*)	Austerity		
7. Penance			

Though these HVs and their inculcation methods are independent at the grass-root level, there is a definite mechanism for this purpose in view of the hierarchy of inner EOLs (cf. patomic model). To this effect, a mechanism – personality creation mechanism – is already discussed (cf. chapter 9 of Kaushal 2015). While we assume the linearity of the personality vector space, certain tricks (like the *tri-karaṇa* rule for the dressing of inner EOLs with consciousness and subsequently generating their higher-order dressed versions) to this effect are used to handle the underlying non-linearity of inner transformations. It is the meditation variable μ that will characterize the directed and focused component of consciousness – in some sense also defines one's attention. Also, certain types of non-linearity's in the mental processes are investigated (cf. Appendix A) with respect to this variable using the methods of non-linear dynamics (see, chapter 6 of Kaushal and Parashar 2008).

D.1 Personality Vector Space

The personality– as an outer garment of the character of a person manifests in the outer world on different fronts of human actions and is assessed in an organization through several parameters based on human virtues (HVs) (the so-called personality traits and dimensions). As ingredients of personality, some of these HVs or human qualities, characteristics and intents are listed in Table D.1. Some remarks about these HVs are as under:

i. These HVs or their combinations create a personality but only in the presence of consciousness.

ii. As each of these HVs is wrapped with the three Nature-born *guṇas* (*sattva* (*s*), *rajas* (*r*) and *tamas* (*t*)), the latter are considered to form the basis vectors, $\hat{s}, \hat{r}, \hat{t}$ of the vector space $\mathcal{V}$.

iii. Note that a given personality can be created in manifest form by permutation and combination of one and more of these HVs, this implies a closure feature of the set $\mathcal{V}$ in the spirit of mathematics.

iv. The basis vectors $\hat{s}, \hat{r}, \hat{t}$ span the entire space including the subspaces of human existences. These subspaces could be of both types – proper and improper – in the sense that any one of the existences is capable of giving salvation to the Being as per Vedic wisdom.

v. In spite that the human Being is considered as a perfect creation of God, most of us remain imperfect creations mainly because we are unable to inculcate all these intents at the same space–time point. To become a successful person, it requires a basis formed out of the present basis vectors (cf. Section D2). Further, the internal transformations (cf. Section D3) are linked to the so-called personality development.

As examples, we display below the superposition (in symbolic form) of dominating (but the domination is in decreasing order as far as the role of the corresponding HV in an action is concerned) HVs to produce a particular type (or desired) personality, viz.:

B + SE + E + austerity ⇒ Physical personality

M + B + SE + E + penance ⇒ Emotional personality

I + M + B + SE + E + penance + ... ⇒ Intellectual personality

E + I + M + B + SE + penance + .. ⇒ Spiritual personality

Note that each of these personalities can appear in three distinct flavours *s*, *r*, *t* or their mixed version depending on the choice of basis vectors and the associated inner transformation (cf. Section D3).

vi. An interesting feature one can notice from the construction of the above vector space, in analogy with physics, is that of the symmetries associated either with the elements of $\mathcal{V}$ or with the transformations on $\mathcal{V}$, of course, under some given physical and/or mental conditions. The invariants so associated with these symmetries (as in physics), in fact, will form a basis for the eternity-nature of human values prevailing in Vedic wisdom and survived during the evolution of human race (cf. the concept of *Sanātana Dharma* in Vedic thinking).

D.2 Personality Creation Mechanism

This mechanism, based essentially on the Vedic wisdom, suggests a way out to develop one's own personality just by having self-observation regularly and analysing periodically the actions so performed. In fact, in this mechanism, the inner EOLs, M, I and E constantly undergo some sort of charging (dressing) with consciousness as a result of meditation or self-observation and the set of these EOLs – the so-called "mindset function" (cf. Chapter 7) – evolves with space, time and meditation (μ) mainly in a non-linear fashion. Such an evolution of mindset function in conjunction with *saṅkalpa* results into a desired personality. Here, we only outline the underlying philosophy of the mechanism and for details we refer to our earlier work (cf. chapter 9 of Kaushal 2015).

In this mechanism, the concept of *saṅkalpa* (i.e. a highly dressed version of E, of course, in the presence of SO and in conjunction with M and I generates a quality of self-determination towards the performance of actions in the outer world), S, plays a dominant role in shaping a personality. As a matter of fact, the examples of personality, listed in Section D1 above, are the outcome (Kaushal 2011) respectively of such combinations of S with G(= B + SE), S with M, and S with I (Kaushal 2015).

Note that the EOL intellect plays a central role in creating a personality. In view of this, an alternative method for this purpose is also proposed. In this case, each of the three P, S and I is considered as a 3×3 matrix in the space of three Nature-born *guṇas* s, r, t, viz. $P = S \otimes I$. The three diagonal and six off-diagonal elements of P thus respectively define the integrated and non-integrated personalities with respect to the basis vectors, $\hat{s}, \hat{r}, \hat{t}$. However, it was emphasized that ideally integrated personalities (i.e. the spiritual ones) are obtained by diagonalizing the personality matrix P, of course, with a new set of basis vectors which turn out to be the superposition of $\hat{s}, \hat{r}, \hat{t}$. Thus, for an ideally integrated personality an appropriate consummation and culmination of the three *guṇas* is a must. Also, the diagonalizing matrix required for this purpose must be born out of other suitable intents of Table D.1 depending upon the circumstances.

D.3 Inner Transformations

Once we have the concept of personality vector space, then note that the concept of transformations on it automatically follows. In fact, it is the (psycho)chemistry of inner EOLs M, I and E or of their dressed versions with consciousness along with their respective attributes that participate in these transformations. While these EOLs actively participate in the personality-creation mechanism, they are also responsible for personality development. Further, note the two important factors, viz. self-observation and *saṅkalpa*, that play dominant roles in these processes mainly through the process of meditation. The latter is quantified here in terms of the meditation variable μ (cf. Chapter 7).

In mathematical terms, a transformation is characterized by the change of basis vectors (or by rotation of axes). Here, it is the meditation (μ) that will generate these changes mainly from *tamas* to *rajas* and then to *sattva* ($t \to r \to s$) for the personality development in positive spirit. This means a resetting of the basis vectors is a must. Thus, the system or the mindset function (cf. Chapter 7) evolves with the intensity of meditation or μ. This evolution of mindset function ($\mathcal{M}$) can be investigated in two distinct ways: (i) as discrete evolution, and (ii) as continuous evolution. While the dressing rules highlighted in Chapter 4 (and also see, Kaushal 2011, 2015) are the examples of discrete evolution of EOLs, the case of continuous evolution of mindset function is discussed in Appendix A and in Kaushal 2017a with reference to some non-linear mental processes.

Appendix E

Further Remarks on Experience-Based and Event-Based Space–Time Mediated Phenomena

E.1 Experience- and Event-Based Space–Time Intervals

HERE we elaborate on certain concepts developed in Section 7.4.2 with a view to finding a basis for the well-known Fechner transformation. In fact, if one goes with the concept of Vrobel (Vrobel 2011) of "time density" in terms of "the length" and "the depth" or of "the succession" and "the now" of a time interval Δt and uses a similar concept for the space interval Δq as well in terms of "the succession of the steps (or space slices)" and "the here", then there is a possibility to obtain a new type of space–time transformation for the happenings in the world-2 and the world-1 (cf. Introduction to chapter 7). This transformation, no doubt, has to be a non-linear (logarithmic) one (unlike the Galilean or the Lorentz transformation in physics which connects the events in two moving reference frames) but also has roots in the Weber–Fechner law. We demonstrate here a new type of kinetics that emerges out of these concepts and is relevant for further application of eq. (7.32) or (7.36).

As mentioned in the text $\dot{q}, \overline{q}, \overline{t}$ in (7.35) are not independent; they are rather connected in view of the fact that $q = q(t, \mu)$ and

$t = t(\mu)$. This, in turn, implies that

$$dq = \frac{\partial q}{\partial t}dt + \frac{\partial q}{\partial \mu}d\mu$$

or

$$v(\mu) \equiv \frac{dq}{dt} = v_{ph} + v_d, \qquad \text{(E1)}$$

where $v_{ph} = (\partial q/\partial t)$, is the physical velocity that corresponds to the world-3 and $v_d = (\bar{q}/\bar{t})$ is the additional derived velocity that emerges out of consciousness dependence in the system. Note that the contribution of v_{ph}-term in the (E1) could be positive or negative depending on the pleasant or unpleasant experience by an individual. Although v_d is not fixed, there is an upper bound on v_{ph} due to the velocity of light c, i.e. $v_{ph} \leq c$, which implies that

$$v(\mu) \leq c + v_d. \qquad \text{(E2)}$$

Whether it is the case of pleasant and unpleasant experiences or of the functioning of conscious and subconscious minds towards an experience, in either situation, the same $v(\mu)$ plays a dual role depending on the magnitude of the ratio $(\bar{q}/\bar{t})$ or of v_d. In fact, for the experiences of the conscious domain $\mathcal{M}_g$, $\bar{q}$ and $\bar{t}$, and hence the ratio $(\bar{q}/\bar{t})$ has mild (or at times hardly any) dependence on μ, whereas in the subconscious domain, $\mathcal{M}_s, \bar{q}, \bar{t}$ and also the ratio $(\bar{q}/\bar{t})$ have strong dependence on μ.

Alternatively, one can derive $v(\mu)$ in a crude way using Weber–Fechner law (7.24) written for space and time intervals, viz.:

$$\Delta q_{ex} = k_1 \ln(\Delta q_{ev}/A_1), \quad \Delta t_{ex} = k_2 \ln(\Delta t_{ev}/A_2).$$

Obviously, k_1 and k_2 here are the dimensional constants of proportionality and also are the functions of μ. Thus, we have

$$v(\mu) = \frac{\Delta q_{ex}}{\Delta t_{ex}} = \frac{k_1(\mu)}{k_2(\mu)} \cdot \frac{\ln(\Delta q_{ev}/A_1)}{\ln(\Delta t_{ev}/A_2)}. \qquad \text{(E3)}$$

Here, (k_1/k_2) while defines the "velocity" v_d, the remaining factor can be linked with v_{ph} but in a complicated way, perhaps some simplifying assumptions regarding Δq_{ev} and/or Δt_{ev}, can help in obtaining these results.

Next, we employ this concept of experience- and event-based perceptions to analyse a common man's query as to what is the connection between the happiness (an experience-based concept) and the fulfilment of one's desires (an event-based concept).

E.2 Happiness vs Fulfilment of Desires

In this context, we analyse an assertion made recently by Hasmukh Adhia (2020), "Why Zero Desire Equals Infinite Happiness?" In fact, the logic behind this assertion is the use of an oversimplified definition of happiness by the author, viz. the happiness is a ratio of the number of desires fulfilled divided by the total number of desires one has. Naturally, for zero desires, the number of fulfilled desires is also zero and Adhia assumes this ratio of zero is divided by zero as infinity. But in reality it is not so, in mathematical terms, it is an indeterminate quantity that can lie anywhere between zero and infinity. On the other hand, it is believed (since the author has not yet realized that state) that during the state of *mokṣa* when the finite soul merges with the infinite (cosmic) consciousness, then it is all infinite happiness. Now the question arises is that as who is the experiencer of that infinite happiness in that state. The answer is none. Thus, it is all the polluted version of SO, i.e. the Being *b* or the *jīva* that experiences the happiness in the space time domain and that too in its lower strata of existences, viz. in $\mathcal{M}$, $\mathcal{G}$, $\mathcal{S}$ and $\mathcal{N}$ existences but in the presence of causal existence $\mathcal{C}$. As a matter of fact, as long as there remains an element of space–time in the actions, the number of fulfilled desires can never be zero. They rather get multiplied from the involvement of *b* in other existences at the same time and soon after the fulfilment of some old ones.

No doubt, desires originate from and are the objects of mind but their variety and accordingly the fulfilment can vary over various human existences. For example, the desire of *mokṣa* belongs to the $\mathcal{C}$ domain, the desires related to livelihood belong to the $\mathcal{G}$ domain and those related to mental peace belong to the $\mathcal{M}$ domain, those related to name and fame belong to the S domain, or the desire, for example, for the fresh air belongs to the $\mathcal{N}$ domain, etc. Broadly speaking, desires can be of two types: necessity-based and luxury-based. While the fulfilment of the former type desires is a must for survival, of course within some minimal, that of the latter type at times becomes the main cause of one's unrest and also disturbs his peace of mind. Further, it is not difficult to fulfil the former type desires, but there is no end of fulfilment of the latter type of desires; they rather keep on multiplying unless one learns the "art of living" in this world. In fact, in this world, there is enough for need but not enough for greed.

The happiness or the satisfaction one obtains after the fulfilment of desires is a function of space, time and circumstances. Thus, the fulfilment of desires is also temporal. An individual, however, remains ignorant about this fact and tries to retain this happiness forever and at all cost. As a matter of fact, the attained happiness is the outcome of the fruits of all the causes of an action, viz. *prārabdha*, *sañcita* and *kriyamāna*. One can while easily regulate the *sañcita* and *kriyamāna* causes to this effect, the *prārabdha* is undoubtedly beyond ones control. This subtle role of *prārabdha* in actions also controls, first the fulfilment of desires and later the degree of happiness. A kind of satisfaction is the only way to come out of such pairs of opposites like pleasure and pain and heat and cold. While desires can run over all the five existences, their fulfilment is there mostly in the corresponding domains. Further, the happiness out of these domains while remains only additive, the desires, on the other hand, are multiplicative.

Next, we define a quantity, the so-called "happiness index $h_i(q, t, \sigma)$" as,

$$h_i(q,t,\sigma) = \frac{\text{number of desires fulfilled in given space, time and circumsances}}{\text{total number of desires arose during given space, time and circumsances}}.$$

Here, the word circumstances also accommodates the state of mind corresponding to a particular existence i in which the Being *b* resides and that too at a given space–time. The subscript $i = 1, 2, 3, 4, 5$ respectively correspond to $\mathcal{C}, \mathcal{M}, \mathcal{G}, S$ and $\mathcal{N}$ existences. Thus, the resultant happiness index h_r is given by $h_r = h_1.\ h_2.\ h_3.\ h_4.\ h_5$ and the corresponding resultant happiness $H_r\ (q, t, \sigma)$ so obtained can be assumed to follow a Fechner type law, viz.:

$$H_r(q,t,\sigma) = \ln h_r(q,t,\sigma) = \sum_{i=1}^{5} H_i(q,t,\sigma)$$
$$= \sum_{i=1}^{5} \ln h_1(q,t,\sigma).$$

Note that both H_r and h_r always remain a function of q, t and σ until the Being *b* merges with $\Phi_{cc,}$ i.e. in the limit when $\mu \to \infty$ and not only q, t and σ as such but also their concepts tend to zero, then $H_r\ (q, t, \sigma) \to H_{eternal}$, or one attains eternal happiness.Odiasi venihic te eum sus dellitiunt que quia non prem adiscipisqui bla iusciis dolecepe vid et eristius dolo maior sedit eatem suntio volut pratur?

Im quatur si bererum eosamus, quis et diciliquod et aut idionse rnatiunturit quidusania aut venistin comniendel erecaborera conecab orehenimint ab iur aliquodis am eari dolum as adis voluptatis que et facitatur modis ne nonserum nem aute plit faceat.

Dolorem quiduci millabo. Licaborerrum rem quo cus vit in peribus doles volo omnitio in preprate laut as dolor autem nullabo. Et ut porroreici te volores idi dolor atus maiorem qui omnimpelia doluptas ut excest aut eosant laceped et, occum aliquo esti dolupta erchilisquis explibus asitae doluptia sa dis quam fugia volores tendiatur?

Udis autem nihicienis aliquae verum, quas vidusda ectaquident est, ut qui odit voluptatem sumquam susae renia que incipit ipsanti bustori onsequas adit, sunt.

Millenimaio cus. Arit que veles est, omni aut molumquo dis aut qui si con rempor seque cum iunt aut is dent re pera doluptat fugiat volo tentis nulparum excerch itassin reium esciis aboriat estiasperum solum eumeneces delibus tiatend ipsunt fugiam auditiu mquibus.

A Glossary of Words, Terms and Phrases Used in the Text

HERE we present detailed meanings of certain words, terms and phrases used in the text for their ready reference in alphabetic order.

Analogy: A concept which generally helps in understanding the unknown in terms of known. In some sense, it is the generalized version of the concepts like simile, metaphor and parallelism used frequently not only in literature but also in other disciplines of knowledge depending upon the phenomenon under study. Further, the analogies can be of different orders or categories, for details, see Kaushal (2003).

Basis of actions performed: As per Vedic science, there is a basis of all actions performed by an individual and of the fruits obtained thereof. On this basis, three categories of actions are *prārabdha*, *sañcita* and *kriyamāna*. Destined due to previous (past) birth(s) are the *prārabdha*, accumulated in this birth itself are *sañcita* and the ones performed in present are the *kriyamāna* actions.

Biological body (B): Biological body of a human Being including both inner and outer organs.

Broad classification of actions (need to be performed): These are of four categories: *nitya* (daily routine), *naimitika* (social obligation), *kāmya* (by choice or desire) and *niṣedha* (prohibited or immoral). Man is free to perform *karma* (actions), particularly in *kāmya* category. In fact, a person must perform *nitya karma* but he must not perform *niṣedha karma*. Other *karma*s are social and moral obligations. Besides this classification, *SMBG* offers another threefold classification as *sātvika*, *rājsika* and *tāmsika* based on the role of three *guṇas*.

Causal body ($\mathcal{C}$): It consists of the EOL, SO alone or $\mathcal{C}$ = {SO}.

Cosmic consciousness field (of which the soul is a part thereof): In analogy with the physical fields, it is the all-pervading subtlest possible field in which not only the cosmic elements (*pañca-mahābhūtas*) in their primordial form but also the cosmic versions of mind, intellect and ego are embedded. The space and time and their mediated four physical fields are the later offshoots of this field. A kind of second quantization process in this cosmic consciousness field gives rise to its discrete version, i.e. the quantum-like soul which, in turn, carries all the features of this most fundamental consciousness field.

Cosmic elements (pañca-mahābhūtas of Vedic Science): In Vedic science, they are believed to be five in number and according to their increasing subtlety they are arranged as earth (E_a), water (W), air (A), fire (F) and ether (E_t). Again, there are concepts of perceived (*pañcīkṛta* according to the *pañcīkaraṇa* rule or the dressed one with consciousness) and the physical or nascent (*apañcīkṛta*) cosmic elements in Vedic science, used heavily in the text.

Definitions of Yoga as per SMBG: According to *SMBG*, the controlling of the flow of consciousness towards worldly objects through mind, body and senses, and reversing the flow towards SO, is called "meditation" – a basis for *yoga*. With reference to other definitions note that relinquishing attachment, and becoming indifferent to success and failure or equanimity is called *yoga*. In fact "skill in action" lies in the practice of this equanimity, which suggests another definition of *yoga*.

Dressing of EOLs with consciousness: The concept of *pañcīkaraṇa* rule for creating the perceived *mahābhūtas* from the nascent (physical) ones was known in Vedic science. The same is now generalized for other EOLs like M, I, E as *tri-karaṇa* rule or for SE and B as *dvi-karaṇa* rule and that too in higher orders (Kaushal 2011). In fact, the infinitely dressed versions of these entities with consciousness become the part of cosmos and embedded in the cosmic consciousness field.

Dressing of objects: The word "dressing", coined by the author in the present context, is basically a discrete method to account for the consciousness. In Vedic science, it appeared only in a "crude" form as *pañcīkaraṇa* rule for *pañca-mahābhūtas* and only in lowest order. But here the author has generalized the concept for other entities and that too in higher orders as well (Kaushal 2011).

Ego (E): Faculty of memory or the self-sense.

Elements of basic goodness (EBGs): Human virtues and qualities that form a basis for framing the norms for an ideal religion and subsequently help in living a peaceful and happy life.

Epi-fields: Cosmic (field) versions of eight components (*aṣṭāṅga prakṛti*) of insentient mode of Nature (cf. *SMBG* VII.4), which are embedded in the cosmic consciousness field Φ_{cc} in their dressed as well as seed-like forms, are termed here as "epi-fields".

Equilibrium and stability: In classical dynamics one defines the equilibrium point corresponding to the zero velocity of the system and it could be stable, unstable and at times semi-stable depending upon its returning to the position of zero velocity as a result of slight perturbation (e.g. the case of a rotating pendulum (Kaushal and Parashar 2008)). Here, however, following Parthasarathy (1992) we talk of three categories of equilibrium in philosophical terms, viz. restless, imperfect and perfect equilibrium depending respectively upon the evolution of the mindset of an always restless person (whose desires are never fulfilled), of a person whose desires crop up (but are mild and temporary mainly due to a change in external agency) and of a person who never desires and always remains undisturbed by any external toppling.

Essences of life (EOLs): Human Being is said to be the perfect creation of God. The entities one needs for his existence in a functional (conscious) form are termed as the "EOL" in this work. In the decreasing order of their fineness and subtlety, they can be listed as: the soul (SO), ego (E), intellect (I), mind (M), senses of knowledge (SEK), motor organs responsible for action (SEA) and the biological body (B). The composite of all of them, i.e. the human Being b works in the field of worldly objects (WO), which basically are the dressed versions of *pañca-mahābhūtas* with consciousness.

Experience-based invariants (EBIs): Like space and time invariants in physics, we do have EBIs, particularly when analysing the sustainability of a religion along with its eternity and universality (cf. *Sanātana Dharma*). In this case, each experiencer undergoes similar experiences during the meditation on a truth or experience. Corresponding to the five existences of a person, these EBIs are classified into five categories (cf. Chapter 13), viz. class I, class II, class III, class IV and class V types of EBIs correspond to $\mathcal{C}$, $\mathcal{M}$, $\mathcal{G}$, $\mathcal{S}$ and $\mathcal{N}$ existences.

Faculty of understanding (FOU): The mind, intellect and ego in the presence of consciousness collectively work in perceiving a physical object with the help of senses of knowledge and action. These inner essences of life working to this effect in a coherent manner constitute the so-called FOU and the development of the same becomes an asset in the process of realization. In some sense it is an elevated version of faculty of memory.

Five existences of human Being: Vedic science clearly emphasizes on the three existences, viz. causal, micro and gross existences of a human Being. In the present work, however, two more, viz. societal and natural existences, of a person are also postulated to define the complete personality of a person. First three existences, in fact, define the vertical component of the personality, whereas the other two define the horizontal component of the personality (cf. Chapter 11).

Forces in nature: Physical theories deal with two types of forces – contact force and action-at-a-distance (AAD) type force. The former comes in existence when the objects are in physical contact, like the railway engine dragging the bogies or the horse dragging the cart. At finer level, there is still a difference between these cases. In the latter case, however, the horse, being a living object, can use his free will in generating necessary self-organizing forces, of course, on the initiative of the cart driver. On the other hand, engine cannot generate self-organizing forces, if at all it can, then it cannot go beyond the defined efficiency for which it is manufactured. AAD type forces come into existence even if the objects are not in contact with each other but are at a distance, like the gravitation force between two masses, Coulomb force between two charges or magnets, etc. In these cases, objects are assumed not to possess memory and this is possible only with inanimate objects. For animate objects, however, not only memory, but emotion and/or decision-making contents are there in the object. As a result, other types of forces like action-at-a-time (AAT) or action-at-a-distance-time (AADT) are bound to come in the dynamics of living object. For this reason the physical laws as such do not work on living objects. If at all they are made to work, then such effects are tactfully avoided at the cost of certain approximations in the theory.

Four categories of persons: On the basis of development of one's FOU, the people in this world can be classified broadly into four categories: common man, scientist, philosopher and *yogī*. The development of FOU in the first case is limited only to day-to-day life, in the second case (extrovert persons) the perception of the outer world is developed more than inner, in the third case (introvert persons) the perception of the inner world is developed more than the outer one and in the case of a *yogī* the perception of both inner and outer worlds is developed to its maximum possible extent. The existence of these categories of persons in a society can be seen at all times and in all cultures. It is only the degree of development of their FOUs that may differ.

Four known fundamental physical forces: They are gravitational forces, working through masses of objects all over the Universe; electromagnetic force working through charges and magnetism of objects all over the Universe; weak and strong forces, work inside the nucleus and also through the phenomenon of radioactivity in some elements. These four interactions differ in strength and range. Gravitational and electromagnetic forces are of infinite range whereas weak and strong forces are of very short finite range. Regarding strength, there are orders of magnitude difference between their strengths; weakest is gravitational, next to it is "weak" force and then electromagnetic and finally the strongest one is the strong force.

God: In addition to several other characteristics, Generator (G), Organizer (O) and Destroyer (D) of five cosmic elements (viz. earth, water, air, fire and ether), which in some sense are essentials for the existence of life in this Universe, is defined as "God". In fact, the Sanskrit word *Bhagavān* for God also carries the spirit of all five cosmic elements when its letters are interpreted as *bha* for *bhūmi* (earth), *ga* for *gagana* (*ākāśa* or ether), *va* for *vāyu* (air), *a* for *anala* or *agni* (fire), and *n* for *nīra* (water). Thus, *Bhagavān* is the controller of the proportion of these five cosmic elements that enables the life in the Universe in general and on the planet earth in particular.

"Golden Rules" in the context of personality: A "golden rule" in the context of personality can be defined as a cluster of human virtues, qualities, characteristics and intents whose systematic and sequential arrangement (in terms of values and place values), if followed in daily life, then it becomes a cause for the upliftment or the downfall of one's personality (cf. Section 5.3.3). Many examples of golden rules can be traced in *SMBG* and other Vedic scriptures.

Gross-body ($\mathcal{G}$): It consists of outer EOLs SE, B and WO, or $\mathcal{G}$ = {B, SE, WO}.

Gross and subtle components of micro body ($\mathcal{M}$): In fact, each of the inner EOL mind, intellect and ego has two components – gross and subtle. The gross components of all the three, combined together, constitute the gross part of $\mathcal{M}$, i.e. $\mathcal{M}_g$, whereas the subtle components of all the three combined together form the subtle part of $\mathcal{M}$, i.e. $\mathcal{M}_s$. It is the gross part that manifests more in the actions of $\mathcal{G}$-domain whereas subtle part plays more active role in the actions of $\mathcal{C}$-domain. In fact, a cut-off in the order of dressing of inner EOLs with consciousness (which varies from person to person) can define such a bifurcation of M, I and E (cf. *fig*. 11.4).

Human Being (b): Life principle or the seed of life (Sanskrit word is *jīva*), the "self" of the "myself".

"Inside out" and "outside out" pictures: For the meaning of these phrases, the attention is drawn to the patomic model of human Being (cf. *fig*. 6.1). The inner contents of the model while control the outward actions, the outer contents of the model however control the inward actions of the Being which again give command for an improved version of outward actions. In atomic model, these are the electrons in the outermost orbits which participate in chemical reactions, i.e. an "outside out" picture, whereas in patomic model, it is B and then SE which are first to participate in interactions with the outer world, i.e. an "inside out" picture.

Intellect (I): Faculty of decision also includes subtle intellect.

Interaction: The resultant effect (normally the force) that comes into existence when two or more than two living or non-living objects come in vicinity or close proximity which otherwise is absent. Here, the word "existence" means it should be detectable or measurable in physical theories, particularly for the inanimate objects and it should be perceptible or realizable in philosophical terms, particularly for living (animate) objects. Similarly, the word "closeness" has different meanings for physical, epi-physical and special epi-physical entities. For physical entities, it should be understood in terms of space–time, whereas for the other two categories of entities, the meditation parameter should also be included in defining it.

Meditation and meditation variable (μ): When a conscious person sits in meditation, the depth or the degree of achieving a focused or directed consciousness is characterized by this variable. In some sense, μ is a collective representation of the parameters responsible for the roles of inner EOLs M, I and E in a decision towards the success of a task. It can never be zero for a living person but can become infinite for a *yogī* sitting in *samādhi*. Note that the same focused attention, when directed towards WO via SE and B, then it is termed as "concentration" (of mind) and when it is directed towards SO via M, I and E, it is called "meditation". For a quantifiable definition of μ, see Section 7.4.1 (iv).

Micro-body ($\mathcal{M}$): It consists of inner EOLs, M, I and E, or $\mathcal{M} = \{M, I, E\}$.

Mind (M): Faculty of emotion also includes subconscious mind.

Mindset function: The state of mind at any stage of meditation is characterized by the so-called "mindset" function $\mathcal{M}$. At a gross level, $\mathcal{M}$ is considered as the function of meditation variable μ and at finer level, however, it is a complicated function of several variables, representing respectively the roles of inner EOLs mind, intellect and ego and that of space, time and circumstances in the dynamics of the system.

Model: As such, it is not possible to express the ultimate reality in Nature through conceptual expression than what to say of verbal expression. A model is a conceptual expression of reality that prevails in a phenomenon. While the ultimate realty remains the matter of realization only, the glimpses of the same one can have through models to a fair degree of accuracy. Note that a model, in fact, is a particular case of analogy (for details, see Kaushal (2003)).

Mind waves: Mind waves, introduced perhaps for the first time in this work, are defined as multifold (eightfold) modulated consciousness carrier waves (CCW) which travel in the space of meditation with infinite (spatio-temporal) or rather undefined velocity and embedded in the all-pervading cosmic consciousness field Φ_{cc}. Eightfold modulation corresponds to the eight components of insentient mode of Nature (cf. *SMBG* VII.4). The corresponding eight cosmic essences that can be loaded on it in accordance with their decreasing subtlety are, first ego, then intellect, mind, ether, fire, air, water and earth. For details, see Section 9.4.

Pañcīkaraṇa rule: In Vedic science, this rule differentiates between the perceived (dressed with consciousness) and unperceived (physical, nascent or not dressed with consciousness) *mahābhūtas*. According to this rule, the perceived *mahābhūta* consists of 50 per cent of its physical version and 12.5 per cent of physical versions of each of the remaining four *mahābhūtas*. For example, the perceived earth consists of 50 per cent of physical earth and 12.5 per cent physical version of each of other four, viz. water, air, fire and ether; and the same is the case with other perceived *mahābhūtas*.

Patomic model: An arrangement of essences of life for a human Being in analogy with the atomic model for the structure of matter, is termed as "patomic" (philosophical atom type) model. The word patomic can also be derived from the word *patois* which means "differing materially from the literary language". Further, an elaborative meaning of the ingredients of patomic model, i.e. essences of life, viz. worldly objects, biological body, senses of knowledge and action mind, intellect, ego and soul including the Being, can be traced in this Glossary.

Physical (P), epi-physical (EP) and special epi-physical (SEP) matter: Physical (P) matter for which the laws of physical or chemical sciences work successfully is basically an object of instrument; otherwise, as and when this matter is watched (or thought of) by a Being, an element of consciousness is added to it. Such a matter is termed as epi-physical (EP) (which has a ground on physical) matter. If the source of consciousness is also contained in the EP-matter (as is the body of a conscious person), then such a matter is termed as special epi-physical (SEP) matter. Sometimes EP and/or SEP-matter is termed as non-physical matter.

Pleasure, peace and joy: The same eternal joy (*ānanda*) – a characteristic of soul comes in three colours at three distinct levels, viz. (sensual) pleasure at the level of $\mathcal{G}$ which one draws by engaging senses in their respective sense-objects; the peace which one draws at the level of $\mathcal{M}$ by employing M, I and E to their maximum efficiency (i.e. to their subtlest capacity) towards the success of an action performed in the outer world. The joy is something which one draws at the level of soul in the causal domain ($\mathcal{C}$) by way of withdrawing the Self from the fruits of all actions performed in the domains of $\mathcal{G}$ and $\mathcal{M}$ and by way of suppressing the subtlest form of ego E. In general, all the three, pleasure, peace and joy, are spatio-temporal. Their eternity however gives a feel for the *ānanda*. Alternatively, a state of satisfaction is achieved by an individual from a successful performance of his actions. If this happens in the domain of $\mathcal{G}$, it defines pleasure; in the domain of $\mathcal{M}$, it defines peace and in the domain of $\mathcal{C}$, it defines joy.

Saṅkalpa: A hardcore decision taken by the subtle intellect (or highly dressed trio of M, I and E at supraconscious or at M_s-level) but with a dominating role of E (cf. *fig.* 5.1) and ready for implementation in the domains of $\mathcal{M}$ and $\mathcal{G}$. Such decisions are normally taken by highly-dressed (with consciousness) versions of EOLs, M, I and E; accordingly, *saṅkalpas* could be emotion-, intelligence- or memory-dominated ones at their very root itself.

Saṅskāraṁ: In some sense, the level of development of one's FOUs defines his *saṁskāras*.

Second quantization: It is purely a mathematical concept of theoretical physics related with the discretization of continuum (continuous medium) having infinite degrees of freedom (the so-called "field").

Sense objects: Corresponding to each of five senses of perception there are five sense objects or stimuli. For example, ears run after nice words, eyes go for a pleasant view, nose goes for pleasant smell, tongue for a tasty food and skin for a pleasant touch.

Senses of knowledge and action (SE): In all there are ten senses – five senses of knowledge (SEK) and five motor organs responsible for action (SEA). Senses of action are hands, feet, power of speech, copulatory organ and anus; and the five senses of knowledge are ear, eye, skin, tongue and nose, whose corresponding sense objects are sound, shape, touch, taste and smell. These five sense objects respectively have an intimate connection with and are sensitive to the five cosmic elements (*pañca-mahābhūtas*) ether, fire, air, water and earth through five *tanmātras* (quanta of interaction).

Sṛṣṭi/Brahman: An all-pervading fundamental cosmic consciousness field.

Soul (SO): The innermost existence, the pure Self characterized by consciousness and bliss and which is beyond the concept of space and time.

Systematic of negative pursuits: The sequence of human characteristics that one is forced to follow towards his downfall when he departs from his higher goal in life. As per *SMBG* such a sequence is attachment to sense objects which brings in desire, from unfulfilled desires comes anger, from anger arises infatuation, from infatuation originates the confusion of memory which in turn leads to loss of reason and there from one suffers from ruination. (Also see, "Golden Rules".)

Systematic of positive pursuits: The sequence of human characteristic that encourages one in achieving his higher goal. This is possible for a self-controlled practitioner who enjoys the sense objects through his senses in an unattached manner (not an easy task but the practice makes a man perfect), which are disciplined and free from likes and dislikes resulting into the placidity of mind. All sorrows come to an end after attaining this placidity of mind and the intellect soon starts withdrawing itself from all sides and becomes established firmly in the higher goal (materialistic or spiritual). (Also see, "Golden Rules".)

Three types of yoga: In Vedic science, we have three major categories of *yoga*, one is *karma-yoga* (*yoga* of action) – connecting $\mathcal{G}$ with the Self in all actions or the performance of actions in a selfless or an unattached manner, is called *karma-yoga*; *bhakti-yoga* (*yoga* of devotion) – connecting $\mathcal{G}$ and emotion-dominated $\mathcal{M}$ with the Self is called *bhakti-yoga*, and finally, connecting the Self with the Self itself through knowledge, called *jñāna-yoga* (*yoga* of knowledge).

Trinity of guṇas: With a view to categorizing each of the human actions, qualities, feelings and experiences, the concept of three *guṇas* (temperaments) is frequently discussed in Vedic science. The concept of trinity of *guṇas,* viz. *tamas* (inactive), *rajas* (active) and *sattva* (trans-active), in the spirit of three adjective degrees (positive, comparative, superlative), i.e. good, better and best, basically, are the three modes of working of non-Self (*Prakṛti*) and the same provide a fine thread in weaving the human dynamics of Vedic science. In fact, *tamas* is the state of inaction, ignorance and inertia; *rajas* is the state of desire-ridden passionate action full of mental agitations and *sattva* is the trans-active state, one of poise and contemplation. The purpose of human existence is to move from *tamas* (state of inertia) to *rajas* (state of activity) and to *sattva* (quality of goodness).

Variables of mindset function: Mindset is a representation of the micro body $\mathcal{M}$ or of its dressed versions as a whole. When it characterizes the mental state undergoing through its three constituents M, I and E (which, in fact, keep on cooking a "pudding" during the process of performing an action of priority), it is quantified through a "mindset function" $\mathcal{M}$ as $\mathcal{M} \equiv \mathcal{M}(\mu, q, t, \sigma) = \mathcal{M}$ (m, i, e, q, t, σ), where m, i, e, q, t, σ are the parameters/variables responsible for the roles of mind, intellect, ego, space, time and circumstances respectively. (Also see, "mindset function".)

Vedic science and Vedic literature: Starting with four Vedas, viz. *Ṛk, Yajur, Atharva* and *Sāma*, the Vedic knowledge later appeared through Brāhmaṇas and *Brahmasūtra*, and then through Upaniṣads. The *Ṛk* deals with the question of eternal truth and processes in the Universe. While the *Yajur* deals with the description of rituals, the *Atharva* is full of the descriptions of technology and Āyurveda. It is the *Sāma* that deals with music and the philosophy of life which later transcended to Upaniṣads and other scriptures. The great epics like the *Rāmāyaṇa* and *Mahābhārata*, written at a later period, are full of this Vedic wisdom in the form of conversations between and among various characters of these epics.

Bibliography

Acharya, Pt Sri Ram Sharma, 1995, *Chetan, Achetan Evam Super Chetan Mana* (Hindi), ed. Brahmavarchas, Mathura: Akhanda Jyoti Seva Sansthan.

Adhia, Hasmukh, 2020, "Why Zero Desire Equals Infinite Happiness", The Speaking Tree Column, *Times of India*, 17 August.

Ādi Śaṅkara, 1962, *Pancikaranam*, Commentary by Swami Kripanand, Calcutta: Ram Krishna Mission.

Ādi Śaṅkara, 1966, *Vivekacūḍāmaṇi* (Hindi), tr. Munilal, Gorakhpur: Geeta Press.

Adler, H., 1960, *Elements of Psychophysics*, New York: Holt, Reinhart & Winston, English translation of the original German book *Elemente der Psychophysik* by G.T. Fechner, Leipzig, 1860. (Fechner rather updated in mathematical terms the original Weber's Law of discrimination and this was a seminal contribution to experimental psychology in which a precise methodology was later developed.)

Angel, A.K., P. Fries and W. Singer, 2001, "Dynamic Predictions: Oscillations and Synchrony in Top-down Processing", *Nature Reviews: Neuroscience*, 2: 704.

Ansfield, M. and D. Wegner, 1996, "The Feeling of Doing", in *The Psychology of Action: Linking Cognition and Motivation to Behavior*, ed. P.M. Gollwitzer and J.A. Bargh, chap. 21, New York: Guilford Publication Press.

Bascompte, J. and R.V. Sole (eds), 1993, *Modeling Spatiotemporal Dynamics in Ecology*, Berlin: Springer-Verlag.

Bascompte, J. and R.V. Sole, 1995, "Rethinking Complexity: Modelling Spatiotemporal Dynamics in Ecology", *TREE*, 10: 361.

Bender, C.M., 2005, *Contemp. Phys*, 46: 277, and the references therein.

Brown, G.E., 1964, *Unified Theory of Nuclear Models*, Amsterdam: North-Holland Publishing Co.

Bruneberg, J., E. Rietveld, T. Parr, L. van Maanen and K.J. Friston, 2018, "Free Energy Minimization in Joint Agent-Environment Systems: A Niche Construction Perspective", *Journ. of Theo. Biology*, 455: 161-78.

Chevreul, E., 1833, "E. Chevreul, Lettre A.M. Ampere", "Surume Classe Particuliere de Mouvemens Muscularies", *Revue des Deus Mondes* 2: 249.

Cosentino, Marc O., 2007, *Case in Point: Complete Case Interview Preparation*, 5th edn, Needham, MA: Burgee Press.

Doyane Farmer, J., Martin Shubik and Erie Smith, 2005, "Is Economics the Next Physical Science?", *Physics Today*, 58: 37.

Ellis, G.F.R., 2005, "Physics and the Real World", *Physics Today*, 58: 49.

Fechner, G.T., 1860, *Elemente der Psychophysik*, Leipzig: Brentkopf and Ha'rtel, and Kessinger Publishing (2010) (see Adler 1960).

Fell, J., G. Fernandez, P. Klaver, C.E. Elger and P. Fries, 2003, "Is Synchronized Neuronal Gamma Activity Relevant for Selective Attention?", *Brain Res. Reviews*, 42: 265.

Fraser, G., 2013, "The Incomprehensibility Principle", *CERN Courier* (*View Point*), 53: 59.

Galam, Serge, 2012, *Sociophysics: A Physicist's Modeling of Psycho-political Phenomena*, Berlin: Springer-Verlag.

Gaur, Shiv Kumar, 1990, *Ayurvedic Śarīra Kriyā Vijñāna* (Hindi), chaps 3-6, Rohtak: Nath Pustak Bhandar. Also see, *Suśruta Samhita*, tr. Atri Dev, (Delhi: Motilal Banarsidass, repr. 1991).

Goldberg, Philip, 2014, "I Am Spiritual But Not Religious", Speaking Tree Column, *Times of India*, 6 February.

Goldstein, H., 1981, *Classical Mechanics*, 2nd edn, Philippines: Addison Wesley Publishing Co.

Goleman, Daniel, 1995, *Emotional Intelligence: Why it can Matter More Than IQ*, USA: Bantam Books.

Gomes, Jenina, 2012, "The Cosmic Christ Reveals by Himself", The Speaking Tree Column, *Times of India*, 12 December.

Goswami, Amit, 2013, *Physics of the Soul: The Quantum Book of Living, Dying, Reincarnation and Immortality*, Charlottesville, VA: Hampton Roads Publishing Company.

Goyandaka, H.K.D., 1994, *Iśādi Nau Upaniṣad* (Hindi) (Compiled), Gorakhpur: Gita Press.

Harari, H., 1983, "The Structure of Quarks and Leptons", *Scientific American,* April Issue, pp. 56-68.

Harrison, David, 1978, "Comment on 'Patrons in Antiquity'", *Am. Journ. Phys.*, 46: 432.

Hilderbrand, F.B., 1965, *Methods of Applied Mathematics*, 2nd edn, chap. 2, New Delhi: Prentice-Hall of India.

Huys, Raoul and Viktor K. Jirsa (eds), 2011, *Nonlinear Dynamics in Human Behaviour*, Studies in Computational Intelligence, vol. 328, Springer-Verlag, Berlin.

Itzykson, C. and J.-Bernard, Zuber, 1986, *Quantum Field Theory*, International Student Edition. McGraw-Hill.

Iśāvāsya Upaniṣad, Gorakhpur: Gita Press.

Jain, M.C., 2007, *Vector Spaces and Matrices in Physics*, 2nd edn, New Delhi: Narosa Publishing House.

Jammer, M., 1974, *Philosophy of Quantum Mechanics*, New York: John Wiley & Sons.

Jordan, D.W. and P. Smith, 1988, *Nonlinear Ordinary Differential Equations*, Oxford: Clarendon Press.

Jung, C.G., 1921, *Psychological Types*, vol. 6 of the Collected Works of C.G. Jung, Princeton/Bollingen edn.

Kaembach, C., E. Schroeger and H. Muller (eds), 2016, *Psychophysics Beyond Sensation: Laws and Invariants of Human Cognition*, Scientific Psychology Series, A Psychology Press Book, New Jersey: Lawrence Erebaum Associate Publishers.

Kahneman, Daniel, 2011, *Thinking, Fast and Slow*, New York: Farrar, Straus and Giroux.

Kaku, Michio, 1993, *Quantum Field Theory: A Modern Introduction*, New York: Oxford University Press.

Kapoor, J.N., 1985, *Mathematical Models in Biology and Medicine*, New Delhi: Affiliated East-West Press.

Kaṭhopaniṣad, Gorakhpur: Gita Press.

Kaushal, R.S., 1990, "Human Beings: From the Point of View of a Philosophical Atom-Type Model", *Journ. of Scientific & Industrial Res.*, 49: 578-82.

———, 1994, *The Philosophy of Vedanta: A Modern Scientific Perspective*, Garib Dass Oriental Series No. 179, Delhi: Indian Book Centre.

———, 1998, *Classical and Quantum Mechanics of Noncentral Potentials: A Survey of Two Dimensional Systems*, New Delhi: Narosa Publishing House and Springer-Verlag, Heidelberg: e-print edn. (2013), Springer-Verlag.

———, 1998a, "Patomic Model of Human Being in the Context of Modern Science", PhD Thesis (unpublished), University of Delhi.

———, 2001, "On the Quantum Mechanics of Complex Hamiltonian Systems in One Dimension", *J. of Phys. A: Math & Gen*, 34: L709.

———, 2002, "Conscious Pendulum: A Physicist's Approach", *Ind. Phil. Quarterly*, 29: 65.

———, 2003, *Structural Analogies in Understanding Nature*, New Delhi: Anamaya Publishers.

———, 2004, "Abstraction and Structural Analogies in Mathematical Sciences", in *History of Mathematical Sciences*, ed. I. Grattan-Guenness and B.S. Yadav, pp. 33-55, New Delhi: Hindustan Book Agency.

———, 2005, "The Pendula in Mathematical Sciences", *Indian Journ. of Pure & Appl. Phys.*, 43: 479-88.

———, 2006, "Structural Analogies, Abstraction and Mathematical Concepts in Vedic Sciences", *Indian Phil. Quarterly*, 33(2): 125-46.

———, 2009, "Classical and Quantum Mechanics of Complex Hamiltonian Systems: An Extended Complex Phase Space Approach", *Pramāṇa - Journ. of Phys.*, 73: 287-97 and references therein.

———, 2011, *The Science of Philosophy: Theory of Fundamental Processes in Human Behaviour and Experiences*, New Delhi: D.K. Printworld.

———, 2011a, "Panca Mahabhutas and Natural Remedies of Diseases", *Light on Ayurveda Journal*, 10(1): 21.

———, 2015, *Psychophysics and Human Interactions: Art and Science of Integrating Body, Mind and Soul,* New Delhi: New Age Books.

———, 2016a, "Revisiting the Personality Traits and Dimensions within the Framework of Vedic Science", *The Int. Journ. Ind. Psycho.,* 3(4): 51-73.

———, 2016b,"The Psychophysics of Chevreul Hand-Held Pendulum", *Journ. of Conscious Studies*, 23(9-10): 134-52.

———, 2017a, "Analysis of Certain Aspects of Nonlinearity in Mental Processes within the Framework of Vedic Science", *The Int. Journ. Ind. Psycho.*, 4(3): 96-106.

———, 2017b, *Psychophysics in New Incarnations: A Unifying Framework to Study Sociophysics and Econophysics*, Lunawada: REDSHINE Publications; Also see, *The Int. Journ. of Ind. Psycho.* 4 (special issue): 1-40.

———, 2018a "All-Pervading Cosmic Consciousness Field of Vedic Science and the Quantum Field Theory of Modern Physics", in *Scientific Aspect of Vedic Knowledge*, ed. Shashi Tiwari, pp. 72-84, Delhi: Pratibha Prakashan.

———, 2018b, *Psychophysics of Personality Development: A Vedic View,* 2nd edn, New Delhi: Vishwa Hindi Sahitya Parishad.

———, 2018c, "Pañci-Karan Rule of Vedic Science: A Possible Generalization and Implications", in *Science and Spirituality in Vedic Traditions*, ed. Shashi Tiwari, WAVES Publication No. VI, pp. 64-73, Delhi: Pratibha Prakashan.

———, 2019, "Psychomechanics and the Trio of Space, Time and Consciousness: The Principle of Minimum effort", *The Int. Journ, Ind. Psycho.*, 7(3): 699-713.

———, 2021, "Some Exotic Phenomena in the Realm of Human Behaviour: Attention Dominated Matter, Waves, Energies and Processes", *Journ. of Psycho. & Psychiatric Res.*, 1(1): 1-18.

———, 2023a, "Tracing a Formal Theory of Subconscious Mind in Vedic Wisdom: A Modern Scientific Perspective", *The Int. Journ. Ind. Psycho.*, 11(1): 780–801.

———, 2023b, "Eternity and Universality of Elements of Basic Goodness in the Context of Vedic Wisdom" *The Int. Journ. Ind. Psycho.*, 11(2): 2814-27.

Kaushal, R.S. and D. Parashar, 2008, *Advanced Methods of Mathematical Physics,* 2nd edn, New Delhi: Narosa Publishing House and Alpha-Science, London.

Kaushal, R.S. and H.J. Korsch, 2000, "Some Remarks on Complex Hamiltonian Systems" *Phys. Lett.*, A276: 47.

Kaushal, R.S. and Parthasarathi, 2002, "Quantum Mechanics of Complex Hamiltonian Systems in One Dimension" *J. of Phys. A: Math & Gen,* 35: 8743.

Kaushal, R.S. and S. Singh, 2001, "Construction of Complex Invariants for Classical Dynamical Systems" *Ann Phys.*, 288: 253.

Kolb, E.W. and H.S., Turner, 1990, *The Early Universe*, Reading: Addison-Wesley Publishing Co.

Mantegna, R.N. and H.E. Stanley, 1999, "Introduction to Econophysics: Correlations and Complexity in Finance", New York: Cambridge University Press.

Misner, C.W. and J.A. Wheeler, 1957, "Classical Physics as Geometry", *Ann. Phys.*, 2: 525 (fn. 9a).

Misner, C.W., K. Thorne, J.A. Wheeler, 1993, *Gravitation*, Francisco: Freeman.

Mitra, A.N., 1962, "Three-Body Problem with Separable Potentials (I): Bound States", *Nucl. Phys.*, 32: 529.

———, 1969, "The Nuclear Three-Body Problem", *Adv. Nucl. Phys.* 3: 1.

Mlodinow, L., 2012, *Subliminal: How Your Unconscious Mind Rules Your Behaviour*, New York: Pantheon Books.

Murray, J.D., 1993, *Mathematical Biology*, New York: Springer-Verlag.

Nowak, A. and R.R. Vallachar, 1998, *Dynamical Social Psychology*, New York/London: The Guilford Press.

Olson, J.A., Ewalina Jeyanesan and Amir Raz, 2017, "Ask the Pendulum: Personality Predictor of Ideomotor Performance", *Neuroscience of Consciousness*, 2017(1); doi: https://obi.org/10.1092/nc/nix014.

Osho, 2020, "Without Meditation all Medicine Is Incomplete", Speaking Tree Column, *Times of India*, 25 June.

Osho: Interactions, 2017, "Humanity and Human Consciousness Are

Different", Speaking Tree Column, *Times of India*, 2 September; Also see, Osho (2012), ibid. Dec. 11.

Parthasarathy, A., 1992, *Vedanta Treatise*, 4th edn, Mumbai: Vedanta Life Institute.

Penrose, Roger, 1994, *Shadows of Mind: A Search for the Missing Concept of Consciousness*, Oxford: Oxford University Press.

Perkins, D.H., 1987, *Introduction to High Energy Physics*, 3rd edn, Chap. 6, New York: Addison-Wesley Publishing Co. Inc.

Pimbley, Joseph, 1997, "Physicists in Finance", *Physics Today*, 50: 42.

Pipes, L.A. and L.R. Harvill, 1970, *Applied Mathematics for Engineers and Physicists*, International Student Edition, New York: McGraw-Hill Book Co.

Popper, K. and J. Eccles, 1981, *The Self and the Brain*, Berlin: Springer-Verlag; as cited in David Hastenes, 1992, "Modeling Games in Newtonian World", *Am. J. Phys.*, 60: 732-48.

Rajoria, Aman K., Govind Kaushal and R.S. Kaushal, 2018, "Searching the Spiritual Content in a Personality Using Vedic Wisdom: Possible Modifications in the Theory of Jung", *The Int. Journ. Ind. Psycho.* 6(4): 21-47.

Rumelhart, D. and L. McClelland (eds), 1986, *Parallel Distributed Processing Explorations in the Microstructure of Cognition*, Cambridge, MA: MIT Press.

Rumer, Y.B. and M.S. Ryvkin, 1980, *Thermodynamics, Statistical Physics and Kinetics*, pp. 234-38, Moscow: Mir Publication.

Saha, M.N. and B.N. Srivastava, 1931, *A Treatise on Heat*, The Indian Press, repr. ed. (1972).

Samuel, P.L., S.P.L. Veissere, A. Constant, J.D. Maxwell and K.J. Friston, 2019, "Thinking through Other Minds: A Variation Approach to Cognition and Culture", *Behav. & Brain Science*: DOI: https//doi.org/10.1017/S0140525X19001213.

Sarasvati, Maharsi Dayanand, 1984, *Satyartha Prakash* (repr.), Delhi: Arya Sahitya Prachar Trust.

Schiff, L.I., 1968, *Quantum Mechanics*, 3rd edn, New York: McGraw-Hill.

Schrodinger, E., 1964, *My View of the World Towards the Development of Quantum Theory*, tr. C. Hastenes, Cambridge: Cambridge University Press.

Schrodinger, E., 1944, *What Is Life?*, Cambridge: Cambridge University Press.

Schwartz, J.M., H.P. Stapp and M. Beauregard, 2005, "Quantum Mechanics in Neuroscience and Psychology: A Neurophysical Model of Mind-Brain Interaction", *Phil. Trans. of the Royal Society*, B360: 1309.

Seager, W., 1995, "Consciousness, Information and Panpsychism", *Journ. Consciousness Studies*, 2(3): 272-88.

Sharma, Mukta, R.S. Kaushal and D. Parashar, 2020, "Psychochemistry: The Science of Human Interactions and Relations", *The Int. Journ. of Ind. Psyco.*, 8(1): 576-600.

Shukla, Pt. Ram Govind, 1992, *Sadānandayati Pranītaḥ Vedāntasāra* (Hindi), 3rd edn, New Delhi: Bharatiya Vidya Prakashan.

Simmons, G.F., 1963, *Introduction to Topology and Modern Analysis*, Tokyo: McGraw-Hill Book Co.

Singh, Jitendra, K., Girishwar Mishra and Boele de Raad, 2013, "Personality Structure in the Trait Laxicon of Hindi: Major Language Spoken in India", *European Journal of Personality*, published online, Wiley Online Library.

Singh, Kavita, 2010, *Organizational Behaviour: Text and Cases*, New Delhi: Pearson Education and Dorling Kindersley (India).

Smith, E. and M. Shubik, 2005, "Strategic Freedom, Constraint and Symmetry in One Period Markets with Cash and Credit Payments", *Economic Theory*, 25: 513.

Smolensky, Paul, 1988, "On the Proper Treatment of Connectionism", *Behavioral and Brain Sciences*, 11: 1.

Spitz, H.H. and Y. Marcuard, 2001, "Chevreul Report on Mysterious Oscillations of the Hand-held Pendulum: A French Chemist's 1833 Open Letter to Ampere" (translated from French), *Skeptical Inquirer*, 25: 35.

Srimad-Bhagavad-Gita (abbreviated as *SMBG* in the text), Gorakhpur: Gita Press. (*Note that English Translation of verses is also borrowed from the same source*).

Stapp, H.P., 2009, *Mind, Matter and Quantum Mechanics,* 3rd edn, New York: Springer-Verlag.

Sulis, W. and A. Combs, 1996, *Nonlinear Dynamics in Human Behaviour*, Studies of Nonlinear Phenomena in Life Sciences, vol. 5, Singapore: World Scientific Publishing.

Śvetāśvataropaniṣad, Gorakhpur: Gita Press.

Vallachar, R.R. and A. Nowak (eds), 1994, *Dynamical Systems in Social Psychology*, San Diego: Academic Press.

Von Neumann, J., 1955, *Mathematical Foundation of Quantum Mechanics*, Princeton, NJ: Princeton University Press.

Vrobel, Susie, 2011, *Fractal Time: Why a Watched Kettle Never Boils?,* Studies of Nonlinear Phenomena in Life Science, vol. 14, Singapore: World Scientific Publishing.

Weisskopf, Victor F., 1977, "Frontiers and Limits of Science", *American Scientist,* 65: 405.

Index